Palgrave Studies in Global Higher Education

Series Editors
Roger King
School of Management
University of Bath
Bath, UK

Jenny Lee
Centre for the Study of Higher Education
University of Arizona
Tucson, AZ, USA

Simon Marginson
University of Oxford
Oxford, UK

Rajani Naidoo
School of Management
University of Bath
Bath, UK

This series aims to explore the globalization of higher education and the impact this has had on education systems around the world including East Asia, Africa, the Middle East, Europe and the US. Analyzing HE systems and policy this series will provide a comprehensive overview of how HE within different nations and/or regions is responding to the new age of universal mass higher education.

More information about this series at
http://www.palgrave.com/gp/series/14624

Tristan McCowan

Higher Education for and beyond the Sustainable Development Goals

palgrave
macmillan

Tristan McCowan
UCL Institute of Education
London, UK

ISSN 2662-4214   ISSN 2662-4222 (electronic)
Palgrave Studies in Global Higher Education
ISBN 978-3-030-19596-0   ISBN 978-3-030-19597-7 (eBook)
https://doi.org/10.1007/978-3-030-19597-7

© The Editor(s) (if applicable) and The Author(s) 2019
This work is subject to copyright. All rights are solely and exclusively licensed by the Publisher, whether the whole or part of the material is concerned, specifically the rights of translation, reprinting, reuse of illustrations, recitation, broadcasting, reproduction on microfilms or in any other physical way, and transmission or information storage and retrieval, electronic adaptation, computer software, or by similar or dissimilar methodology now known or hereafter developed.
The use of general descriptive names, registered names, trademarks, service marks, etc. in this publication does not imply, even in the absence of a specific statement, that such names are exempt from the relevant protective laws and regulations and therefore free for general use.
The publisher, the authors and the editors are safe to assume that the advice and information in this book are believed to be true and accurate at the date of publication. Neither the publisher nor the authors or the editors give a warranty, expressed or implied, with respect to the material contained herein or for any errors or omissions that may have been made. The publisher remains neutral with regard to jurisdictional claims in published maps and institutional affiliations.

This Palgrave Macmillan imprint is published by the registered company Springer Nature Switzerland AG
The registered company address is: Gewerbestrasse 11, 6330 Cham, Switzerland

Acknowledgements

I am indebted to many people, in many different ways, for the completion of this book. I have collaborated with researchers over the years on projects that have fed into the ideas presented here, including Elaine Unterhalter, Ibrahim Oanda, Rebecca Schendel, Moses Oketch, Vincent Carpentier, Cristina Perales, Kelly Teamey, Udi Mandel, Gunther Dietz, Simon Marginson, Elie Ghanem, Caine Rolleston, Christine Adu-Yeboah, Mary Omingo, Richard Tabulawa, Jibo Ibrahim, Stephen Oyebade, Segun Adedeji, Stephanie Allais, Jenni Case, Delia Marshall, Sam Fongwa, Melanie Walker, Cristina Fioreze, Julio Bertolin, Nilda Stecanela and Regina Hostins. My students always give me new inspiration. Many others have contributed through discussions and thoughts shared in seminars, lectures, cafes, pubs and street corners. I am grateful also to the participants in research projects who so generously gave of their time to be interviewed and share their understandings. My thanks go to Rebecca Schendel and Vincent Carpentier for providing insightful comments on chapters. And finally to Vicky, who kept me human, hopeful and laughing.

Some of the chapters in this book draw on previously published articles: Chapter 3 on "Universities and the post-2015 development agenda:

An analytical framework" in *Higher Education* (2016); Chapter 4 on "The university as engine of development" in *Philosophical Inquiry in Education* (2018); Chapter 5 on "Higher education, unbundling and the end of the university as we know it" in the *Oxford Review of Education* (2017); Chapter 6 on "Three dimensions of equity of access in higher education" in *Compare* (2016); Chapter 7 on "Quality of higher education in Kenya: Addressing the conundrum" in the *International Journal of Educational Development* (2018); Chapter 9 on "Five perils of the impact agenda in higher education" in the *London Review of Education* (2018); and Chapter 10 on "Forging radical alternatives in higher education: The case of Brazil" in *Other Education* (2016).

Contents

Part I

1 Introduction — 3

2 The Role of Education in Development — 27

3 The Anatomy of the University — 59

4 The Developmental University — 91

5 Three Global Trends — 115

Part II

6 Access — 149

7 Quality — 175

8 Impact on the SDGs — 211

Part III

9	The Limits of Developmental Impact	251
10	The Post-Development University	277
11	Back from the Brink	305
References		321
Index		355

Acronyms and Abbreviations

AAU	Association of African Universities
AIDS	Acquired Immune Deficiency Syndrome
CUE	Commission for University Education
DESD	Decade of Education for Sustainable Development
DfE	Department for Education
DFID	Department for International Development
EFA	Education for All
GDP	Gross Domestic Product
GER	Gross Enrolment Ratio
GPS	Global Positioning System
HE	Higher Education
HEIs	Higher Education Institutions
HIV	Human Immunodeficiency Virus
ICT	Information and Communications Technology
IIEP	International Institute of Educational Planning
INEP	Instituto Nacional de Estudos e Pesquisas Educacionais Anísio Teixeira (Anísio Teixeira National Institute of Educational Research)
LMICs	Low and Middle-Income Countries
MDGs	Millennium Development Goals
MOOCs	Massive Open Online Courses

Acronyms and Abbreviations

NER	Net Enrolment Ratio
NGOs	Non-Governmental Organisations
OECD	Organisation of Economic Cooperation and Development
PISA	Programme for International Student Assessment
REF	Research Excellence Framework
SDGs	Sustainable Development Goals
STEM	Science, Technology, Engineering and Mathematics
THE	Times Higher Education
TVET	Technical and Vocational Education
UDS	University for Development Studies
UIS	UNESCO Institute for Statistics
UN	United Nations
UNDP	United Nations Development Programme
UNESCO	United Nations Educational, Scientific and Cultural Organisation
UNILA	Universidade Federal da Integração Latino-Americana (University of Latin American Integration)
UVI	Universidad Veracruzana Intercultural (Intercultural University of Veracruz)

List of Figures

Fig. 1.1 Gross enrolment ratios for major world regions (*Source* UIS 2018) — 13
Fig. 7.1 Factors influencing higher education quality (*Source* Author) — 185

List of Tables

Table 3.1	Anatomy of four models of university	81
Table 5.1	Anatomy of three global trends	135
Table 8.1	Breakdown of included studies by development outcome	233

Part I

1

Introduction

On the day that the army of Bakhtiyar Khalji arrived, Nalanda University was by far the largest in the world. Located in what is today Bihar in North-Eastern India, its students came from as far as Turkey in the West and Japan in the East, to study, in addition to the Buddhist scriptures, linguistics, astronomy, logic and medicine. Posing a threat to the occupying force, the university was ransacked and the vast library burnt. It was reported that the books were so numerous that the bonfire stayed alight for three months (Gupta 2018; Sankalia 1934).

The destruction of Nalanda at the end of the twelfth century after seven centuries of existence coincided with the development of the first universities in Europe, with Bologna, Paris and Oxford gathering together their communities of students and professors. These institutions—in the modified forms that would emerge over the subsequent centuries—would come in time to dominate the global stage of higher education, in conjunction with the general cultural, political and economic ascendancy of the West in the second half of the last millennium. With only a few exceptions—for example, the Islamic universities of North Africa, Al-Qarawiyyin in Morocco and Al-Azhar in Egypt—the many other forms of higher learning around the world have faded away, or suffered a more brutal fate as a result of the histories of human conflict and colonisation. While there are some distinctive characteristics in higher education institutions across different countries and regions, for the most part they follow a common epistemic and institutional model.

The global expansion of this modern institution of university has been extraordinary. Few countries in the world do not have their own—and those that do not are often served by cross-national institutions such as the University of the West Indies or University of the South Pacific. Global enrolments in tertiary education (including non-university post-secondary institutions) have increased from 10% of the global cohort in the early 1970s, to 20% at the turn of the millennium, and to 38% in 2017, representing some 220 million students (Marginson 2016; UIS 2018). There are demand and supply drivers for this expansion. On the one hand, growth has been brought about through the pressures of increasing numbers of school leavers aspiring to upgrade their qualifications, and give themselves a better chance of chasing the scarce, high-value jobs. On the other hand, governments have been keen to strengthen their higher education systems as a means to greater economic competitiveness, forming high-level skills in the workforce and developing technological innovation for the industrial sector.

At the same time, in spite of the apparent pre-eminence of higher education in contemporary times, the sector is in the midst of something of a crisis. There are widespread concerns about quality in universities, and a sense of a loss of standards, in many cases as a result of rapid expansion. In particular, critics point to the lack of relevance of universities to the outside world, being out of touch with contemporary society, and as a result not equipping their students with the competences needed, particularly in their employment. Public funding has declined, causing difficulties in keeping pace with massification, and leading to the adoption of income-generation activities that many see as hollowing out the university's soul. The rise of global university rankings has also created anxiety among national higher education systems as they puzzle over how to insert their institutions into the upper echelons of elite research performance. There is, furthermore, an epistemic crisis, with the questioning of knowledge forms from twentieth-century post-modernism coalescing with populist anti-expert and post-truth movements of the twenty-first.

Nevertheless, concerns about the quality and relevance of universities have done little to dent popular demand for university credentials, or governments' desires to have a 'world-class' higher education sector—the latter without increased public investment, thereby passing an ever greater burden onto students and their families, and exacerbating inequalities. In the midst of this contradictory trajectory of expansion and crisis of identity, equity and funding, there has been a renewal of interest in higher education among international development agencies. Following decades of emphasis on primary education, influential organisations such as the World Bank have begun to see universities once again as central to the development project, leading to new waves of activity in higher education in low and middle-income countries (LMICs). This trajectory led to the increasing prominence of the sector in the United Nation's Sustainable Development Goals (SDGs) agreed in 2015, in which access to tertiary education is positioned as a key target, and universities as instrumental in driving all of the goals of development.

Yet the question arises, can the university fulfil this role? Can it reduce poverty, equip people for sustainable livelihoods, develop clean technologies, protect the environment, create prosperity and ensure a healthy population? And if so, what kind of university would that be? All too often, the assumption is made that by simply expanding the higher education system, the benefits will automatically accrue, with little thought for the diverse forms that higher education may take or the nature of the link between higher education and development.

This book addresses these crucial issues of the contemporary age. For those engaged in the pressing task of promoting international higher education, the book poses the question: which higher education for which development? Drawing on empirical evidence from around the world, and theoretical work on the university, it explores the impact that higher education is currently having on society, its barriers and limitations, and ways in which its influence can be enhanced. The book argues that many of the policies currently promoted by national governments and international agencies are in fact undermining the developmental role the same organisations have proposed. If we are serious about achieving the SDGs, then we will need to imagine and create a new university: one committed to universal access, research for the public good and engagement with diverse communities. That university, in turn, has a key role to play in helping us to re-examine and reimagine our fundamental notions of education and development, and to go beyond the sustainable development goals.

The Return of the University

People might be forgiven for thinking that universities are something of a luxury in the poorest countries of the world. Why should some continue their studies to degree level when many are not even going to primary school? Why should a country be investing in libraries and laboratories when it cannot even bring clean water and electricity to all of its population? And why should states be paying the salaries of lecturers when local health workers and police are needed?

These are all valid questions, and—along with economic analyses (e.g. Psacharopoulos et al. 1986; Psacharopoulos 1994) that showed that returns to the lower levels of education were greater—led to a shift of attention towards primary schools on the part of international agencies and national governments from the 1990s (Bloom et al. 2006). Beyond a lack of resources to fund this level, it was considered that public higher education might actually be exacerbating socio-economic inequalities, given the apparently regressive function of giving free university places to the wealthy.

However, the tide began to turn from the start of the new millennium. The publication of the Task Force on Higher Education and Society's (2000) report *Higher Education in Developing Countries: Peril and Promise*, a collaboration between the World Bank and UNESCO, showed a much stronger acknowledgement of the sector's role in economic development (although at the same time questioning the role of the state and recommending private sector expansion). Reports such as that of Bloom et al. (2006) also provided much stronger arguments for HE's economic benefits, in this case in the context of Africa.

Importantly, this role was now seen to be not only one of enhancing economic opportunities for those few lucky enough to go to university (enrolment ratios were still extremely low in this period), but more broadly in society, through the mechanisms of increased tax payments of graduates, creation of employment, innovation, technological catch-up and productivity gains. The large-scale rates of return analyses also started to show that the returns to higher education were increasing in relation to primary and secondary levels—possibly due to saturation of graduates at the lower levels, or to changes in calculations (Oketch et al. 2014).

In many cases, measurements of the impact and cost-effectiveness of higher education are unfair on the sector. The problem lies in the multifaceted nature of the work of the university, involving teaching, but also a range of other functions (a bewildering range in the case of Clark Kerr's [1963] 'multiversity'). The misrepresentation occurs when calculations include all of the costs of these activities, but only some of the benefits. For example, dividing the total expenditure of the university by the number of students being taught often gives the impression of exorbitant expenditure in comparison to schools—but fails to account for the proportion of this expenditure that goes on other publicly beneficial services such as research, health clinics, museums, community engagement and so forth.

Another reason for the rekindling of interest in higher education—one affecting all countries, in fact particularly high-income countries—is the new-found role for the sector within the so-called knowledge economy. The movement from the industrial to the post-industrial age has brought with it an increasing emphasis on the value of 'knowledge' in economic success, taking the form of skills and competence in the workforce (along the lines of human capital theory), but also innovation, knowledge production and technological development across society (OECD 2008; Task Force on Higher Education and Society 2000; World Bank 2002).

Another reason of particular relevance to lower income countries is the need for frontline professionals. The focus on primary education, along with other services such as primary health care, ignored a rather obvious point that the people staffing those services needed professional training, and that the training in question was normally carried out in the tertiary education sector (UN High Level Panel 2013). In many cases, the expansion of education and health systems—and particularly their quality—has been severely hampered by the lack of well-prepared staff. A thriving post-secondary sector has therefore been acknowledged as fundamental to public services (although the question of *how* universities might form professionals to maximise the benefits [Walker and McLean 2013] has not always been addressed).

Furthermore, there are long-standing non-economic arguments for higher education that have been re-invoked in this period. As explored further in Chapter 2, university education has been seen to have a highly positive effect on democracy, political participation, respect for human rights and the rule of law. Universities also have an important role as deliberative spaces, as a critical conscience to society and a source of constructive challenge to governments and other powerful forces.

Finally, from a more counter-hegemonic perspective, maintaining an emphasis on higher education in addition to primary and secondary levels (and clearly it must be addition, not substitution), serves to challenge and reduce dependency within a global capitalist system. Populations without higher education, even if they do receive a high-quality primary education, are unlikely to wrench their countries out of the historical relations as producers of cheap agricultural, mineral and basic industrial goods, while buying back from wealthy countries high-tech value-added goods at a much greater profit margin. Similar dynamics are evident in political and cultural realms as well. Arguments that poorer countries should focus on primary education, while the wealthier ones can develop extensive higher education systems (see Sachs 2008, for example) effectively lock in global inequalities for generations to come.

The *Beyond 2015* campaign was organised by the Association of Commonwealth Universities to explore the role of higher education in this new development agenda. Evidence of the rekindling of interest in higher education could be seen in the UK Department for International Development's (DFID) partnership and innovation scheme SPHEIR,[1] and in the designation of 'Strengthening higher

---

[1] Strategic Partnerships for Higher Education Innovation and Reform.

education and workforce development programs' as one of four priority areas for USAID's education programme (Childs 2015; USAID 2015). In fact, allocation of resources by development agencies to the tertiary level has been reasonably high over recent decades (20% of World Bank funds [MacGregor 2015] and 34% of the total education aid of DAC[2] countries in 2013 [OECD 2015]), but a large proportion has been dedicated to scholarships, particularly in the country of origin of bilateral donors—with 70% of all aid to higher education going on scholarships and imputed student costs according to UNESCO (2016). In contrast, there are signs now of renewed investment in universities and systems *within* LMICs.

The global framework of development goals has reflected this shift of understanding. In 2015, the SDGs replaced the Millennium Development Goals (MDGs) that had oriented international development since the year 2000. The 17 SDGs represent a significant step forward in relation to the previous goals in their more extensive incorporation of environmental elements, confined predominantly to Goal 7 in the previous scheme. Furthermore, there is greater acknowledgement of the synergies between the particular goals, being described as 'integrated and indivisible' (UN 2015: 1), following criticisms of the silo-like nature of the MDGs, with concerns that trying to achieve MDG 7 may actually have negatively impacted the others (Le Blanc 2015). There is a greater emphasis on equality, and therefore of disaggregation between different social groups in the achievement of the goals (UNESCO 2016). Finally, the framework involves all countries in the world, rather than just those considered to be 'developing', and in their requirements for environmental protection and equality, are demanding also for high-income countries. Nevertheless, there have also been critiques of the new framework, for example in relation to the emphasis on measurable targets. King (2017) argues that while there was broad consultation in advance of the adoption of the SDGs, this was not the case with the indicators, which have since become the tail wagging the SDG dog. Furthermore, there are deeper concerns (discussed further in

---

[2]Development assistance committee.

Chapter 10) about the conceptualisation of sustainable development, and its attempt to reconcile the triple bottom line: economic development, environmental sustainability and social inclusion, following the belief that 'With improved technologies and behavioural choices, both development and nature can coexist' (Sachs 2012: 2209).

Higher education was absent from the MDGs which reigned from 2000 to 2015 (except as part of the gender enrolment parity goal that applied to the whole of the education system). The focus of these goals was universal primary education, along with gender equality in education, and while the Education for All goals set in Dakar 2000 were broader, they also left higher education out of the equation. While commitment to the tertiary level was tentative in the discussions around the replacement for the MDGs (King and Palmer 2013; Unterhalter et al. 2013), the new SDGs did make explicit mention of this level, supported by the Incheon Declaration and Framework for Action. There are three ways in which higher education manifests itself in the SDGs: as a target in itself, as part of the education system as a whole, and lastly as a driver for development.

In terms of the first of these, Goal 4.3 states: 'By 2030, ensure equal access for all women and men to affordable and quality technical, vocational and tertiary education, including university'. This explicit mention of tertiary education and university is an important step forward from the lack of mention in the MDGs, and reflects the new acknowledgement of importance of access to this level. However, it is not as demanding a target as first appears. The requirement for 'equal access' is not equivalent to universal or even widespread access: as is the case in international law (McCowan 2012), the emphasis here is on non-discrimination in admissions processes. The requirement is for *accessibility* rather than *availability*, that is to say, states must ensure that all people can fairly access the places that are available, but do not need to provide places for all people, or even a significant proportion of people. States can fulfil the letter of the goal here by ensuring equitable access for only one per cent of school leavers. It is a far cry from the guarantee in 4.1 to 'ensure that *all* girls and boys complete free, equitable and quality primary and secondary education' (emphasis added). The associated indicator of 'Participation rate of youth and adults in formal and non-formal education and training in the previous 12 months, by sex' does show an interest in overall proportions, but does not distinguish between different kinds of education, so tells us little about higher education specifically. As argued by King (2017), the movement from goals to indicators in the SDGs has resulted in a degree of narrowing of the original focus, and in some cases outright omission of certain elements.

The second way in which higher education is involved is as part of the overall education sector. It is one of the factors involved in the aim to 'By 2030, substantially increase the number of youth and adults who have relevant skills, including technical and vocational skills, for employment, decent jobs and entrepreneurship' (4.4), and also:

> By 2030, ensure that all learners acquire the knowledge and skills needed to: promote sustainable development, including, among others, through education for sustainable development and sustainable lifestyles, human rights, gender equality, promotion of a culture of peace and non-violence, global citizenship and appreciation of cultural diversity and of culture's contribution to sustainable development. (4.7)

HE is involved in the broad requirement of Goal 4.5: 'By 2030, eliminate gender disparities in education and ensure equal access to all levels of education and vocational training for the vulnerable, including persons with disabilities, indigenous peoples and children in vulnerable situations'. It is also heavily implicated in Goal 4.B's call to expand the number of scholarships available to developing countries, and 4.C's call to increase the supply of teachers.

Higher education is, therefore, framed as a goal in itself, with value attributed to expanding opportunities for people to access this level. Emphasis is placed on ensuring non-discrimination in access, and promoting participation of disadvantaged groups, facilitated through scholarships. It is also seen as an instrumental force in promoting positive values (such as global citizenship), and ensuring a supply of key professionals such as teachers. However, it has an instrumental role that goes beyond the text of SDG4. In its role in forming professionals and developing high-level skills, in conducting research and producing knowledge, and in engaging directly with communities to solve developmental problems, it can be seen to underpin the achievement of all of the goals, from reducing poverty to ensuring environmental protection. The general interlinkages between education and the other goals are explored extensively in the 2016 Global Education Monitoring Report (UNESCO 2016):

> In each set, at least one target involves learning, training, educating or at the very least raising awareness of core sustainable development issues. Education has long been recognized as a critical factor in addressing environmental and sustainability issues and ensuring human well-being. (p. 9)

Higher education specifically is seen as central to empowering graduates, in providing them with knowledge, skills and attitudes to drive inclusive development, fostering economic growth and technological catch-up, and through its research role, in promoting 'green innovation'. It is this role of the university as a driver of development that will form the main focus of this book.

The Global Landscape of Higher Education

The SDGs represent the stated commitments of the global community until 2030. But where are we at the present time in relation to these goals for higher education? As stated above, there has been a vast expansion in recent years, reaching more than 200 million students and some 20,000 institutions worldwide. Yet, there are dramatic disparities between different world regions in their share of these enrolments (Fig. 1.1).

As can be seen above, all regions with the exception of Central Asia (which started with fairly high enrolments from the Soviet era) have been expanding significantly over the past three decades. The regions with the lowest enrolments are also growing rapidly—Sub-Saharan Africa has doubled its enrolment ratio since 2007, even in the context of rapid increases in youth population, and in South and West Asia this figure has tripled. Yet even if these precipitous rates of growth can be maintained it will still take decades to reach the highest enrolment

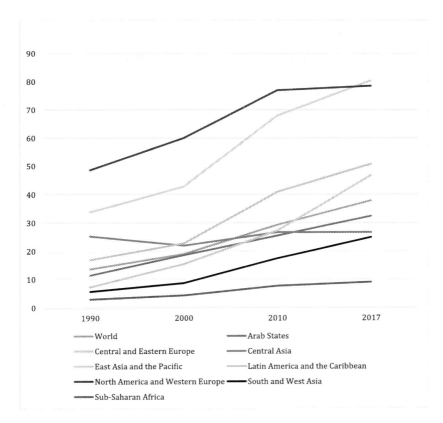

Fig. 1.1 Gross enrolment ratios for major world regions (*Source* UIS 2018)

countries. Worryingly, the gross enrolment ratio (GER) for low-income countries globally did not increase between 2012 and 2017 (staying at 9%[3]), while upper middle-income countries pulled rapidly away, moving from 36 to 52%. Furthermore, even within these world regions, there are significant disparities, with countries varying within Sub-Saharan Africa from Botswana at 23% to Eritrea at only 2%, and in Central Asia, Kazakhstan at 50% and Uzbekistan at 9% (UIS 2018). As stated above, the access goal contained in the SDGs is one of equity in

---

[3]These figures have been rounded to the nearest percentage.

the allocation of places, not availability of places. Yet even taking only the question of non-discrimination, there are still severe injustices. The gap between the richest and poorest is substantial in most countries: in Mongolia, for example, 72% of the top income quintile of 25–29 year olds had completed four years of higher education in 2010, while only 3% of the bottom quintile had (UNESCO/IIEP 2017).

The vast expansion of higher education in recent decades has predominantly benefited the middle classes, with the poorest in society still excluded in most countries, either through prohibitive fees, or due to inability to fulfil entrance requirements or succeed in competitive entrance exams. Depending on the context, factors of region of origin, rurality, religion, ethnicity, language or disability can also present significant barriers to access. Gender is more complex, as the majority of undergraduates globally are female (with the current gender parity index at 1.12), but women continue to suffer disproportionately low levels of access in some countries, with less than half the number of women as men in Burundi, Benin and Togo, for example (UIS 2018). Furthermore, there are continuing inequalities in relation to the learning environment within universities, and in subsequent opportunities as graduates in society. Refugees and the internally displaced also face critical challenges of access, particularly when they fall through the cracks between national systems (the case of Berlin is a hopeful one in respect of concerted efforts to make space for recently arrived refugees [Streitwieser et al. 2017]). Of course, it cannot be forgotten here that initial access is only part of what constitutes inclusion in the higher education system and educational justice, as will be discussed further in Chapter 6.

So much for access, but what about the quality of the systems? Unlike at school level, where there exist (albeit highly contested) tests like PISA[4] and TIMMS,[5] there are few internationally comparable gauges of learning outcomes in higher education. There are some national level gauges (e.g. in Brazil and Colombia), but for the most

---

[4]Programme for International Student Assessment.
[5]Trends in International Mathematics and Science Study.

part quality of institutions is gauged through inputs, procedures or non-learning outputs such as publications. As discussed further in Chapter 7, quality in higher education is something of an ethereal concept, accrued as much through symbolism and historical associations as any concrete feature. To a large extent in the contemporary imagination, quality is indicated by positioning in international rankings: the most prominent being the Shanghai (the Academic Ranking of World Universities), the *Times Higher Education* and QS. These lists rank institutions on the basis of criteria that vary somewhat between them—with Times Higher and QS being wider-ranging—but all focus primarily on research quality. Understandably, given the mismatches in resources available, and the dominance of English language journals to mention just two of the many factors, there are vast disparities between countries in the success of their institutions. A total of 20 countries[6] have institutions in the top 100 of the QS rankings: with the exception of Argentina, all of these are in Europe, North America, East Asia and Australasia. Almost half of these 100 institutions are in just two countries: the USA (31) and UK (18). The grotesque lack of alignment to the reality of the vast majority of universities in the world is shown by the fact that the Shanghai ranking uses as its proxy for teaching quality the number of alumni that have won Nobel prizes!

Metrics based purely on research and publication output show similar disparities. The G20 countries, which have two thirds of the world population, concentrate 87% of the world's researchers, 92% of research expenditure and 94% of academic publications, exceeding even their 85% of world GDP (UNESCO 2015). However, the landscape in this regard is changing, with European and North American proportions slowly diminishing in relation to other regions.

Neither the current international rankings nor high-level publication metrics should be taken as valid gauges of the quality of HE internationally, and there are HEIs across the world which play critical roles for

---

[6]USA, UK, Switzerland, Singapore, China (+Hong Kong), Japan, Australia, Canada, South Korea, France, Netherlands, Germany, Taiwan, Argentina, Denmark, Belgium, New Zealand, Malaysia, Russia, Sweden.

their communities and countries unacknowledged by these assessments. Nevertheless, as explored in Chapter 7, there are substantial disparities of funds, infrastructure and capacity that place significant constraints on their activities. The success story of global higher education, therefore, masks a reality of substantial and enduring inequalities between regions, countries and subnational groups, relating to access, quality and subsequent opportunities. These might be considered by some as inevitable given global inequalities of wealth, and liable to fade away as the tide of expansion of access eventually lifts all boats: yet the *positional* nature of higher education—the relative nature of its benefits—make these disparities highly relevant, intractable, and in many ways determining of the broader global inequalities.

Scope, Methods and Structure

The emphasis in the MDGs on universalising primary education without due regard to quality has been rightly criticised, and in the SDGs, expansion has been made conditional on quality of provision. Attention to quality of HE is without doubt a *sine qua non* of the fulfilment of the ambitious role given to it. Yet 'quality' can be deceptive in its suggestion of a unitary, consensual concept. The challenge goes beyond just achieving quality, to reframing how we understand it, and to interrogating the models of institution underpinning that understanding.

This book has this interrogation as its central aim. Given the inclusion of the SDGs in the title, the reader might assume that its primary focus is higher education's role in relation to the natural environment and the sustainability practices of universities—a topic that has generated a considerable body of literature (on Global North institutions at least), with a journal exclusively dedicated to the topic.[7] Yet this book goes beyond the natural environment to understand holistically the impact of universities on society, including economic, cultural and political dimensions, in addition to the crucial ecological ones.

---

[7] *International Journal of Sustainability in Higher Education.*

Furthermore, the role of higher education in achieving the SDGs is sometimes identified with 'teaching' the framework: raising awareness of the 17 goals among HE students and promoting positive values towards sustainable development. There is also a body of literature focusing on the role of university research in achieving the SDGs (e.g. Clark and Dickson 2003; Waas et al. 2010; Leal Filho et al. 2018; Neubauer and Calame 2017). These activities are laudable for sure, but on their own fall short of the response needed if the world is to come back from the brink of cataclysm. As discussed in Chapter 8, there is no shortage of sustainability initiatives in higher education, promoted by the UN and other agencies, but these interventions are just a first step. Our unsustainable and unequal world has deep foundations, and only a deeper transformation in the university and the higher education system can begin to set it on an alternative course.

The aim of this book is, therefore, to explore the role of higher education in development in its broadest terms. As will be discussed further in the chapters that follow, this is a complex relationship, involving the impact of the university on society (through the work and lives of its graduates, through the production of knowledge and through direct interaction with communities), but also the influence of society on the university, in a cyclical dynamic. The task of understanding this relationship is empirical (making observations about actually existing higher education systems and their host societies), but also conceptual, in creating and applying theoretical tools to aid in our comprehension and analysis of the phenomena.

The work, therefore, involves both theoretical exploration and empirical evidence, as a form of applied philosophy in dialogue with practical realities. In this way, it resonates with many previous attempts to engage in such a dialogue, through ideas of reflective equilibrium (Rawls 1971; Goldmeier 2018), ideal and real (Sen 2009; McCowan 2009), and action and reflection (Freire 1970; Schön 1983). Like much research in the educational field (and international development), it is multidisciplinary, drawing on scholarship and research in sociology, economics, philosophy, law, management and other areas.

The book presents new theoretical categories—for example, the frame of *value*, *function* and *interaction* and the notion of the *generative intrinsic*—to explore the institution of the university. But it also engages with a range of existing approaches such as human capital theory, dependency theory, capabilities, and frames for understanding higher education such as public good, internationalisation, commodification and unbundling. Some of these theories are explanatory, in attempting to analyse and predict empirical phenomena. Yet the book does not shy away from the normative dimension: questions of education and development are intrinsically moral and political, and concern value judgements about what we consider to be justice and the good life. The nature and role of the university are highly contested, and no amount of empirical evidence will adjudicate between, say, a position that asserts that the role of higher education is only to strengthen national industry for greater economic competitiveness with a country's neighbours, and another perspective that holds that the role of higher education is to serve as a space for conscientisation, to form critical, reflective political agents who will challenge and transform capitalist society and create a new form of living. The role of this book is not primarily to adjudicate between different world views (although, of course, as author I hold and express my own positions) but to map the normative terrain, and show the coherence or contradictions of different frames of the university in relation to it.

The book sits at the intersection of large bodies of literature: higher education studies—involving analyses of policy and practice of higher education, dominated by research in high-income countries with well-established higher education systems, particularly the USA; global education policy—involving analyses of supranational policy and governance, as well as policy borrowing and influence, at both basic and higher education levels; and international education and development, focusing on educational interventions in lower income countries, with a strong emphasis on primary education. The intersection of these three areas is, at present, fairly limited in size.

There is a relatively small amount of literature, for example, on higher education and development in the countries in Africa, Asia and Latin America with the lowest GDP levels. A rigorous review of published studies in English (Oketch et al. 2014) found only 100 studies providing empirical evidence of the impact of tertiary education on society in all low and lower middle-income countries, in the time period 1990–2013. In part, this is a result of the imbalances in global academic publishing, with disproportionately few writers from lower income countries able to have their voices heard in major academic journals. But even taking into account the production in local journals, there is an undeniable lack of rigorous research on these issues in particular contexts. There is, however, extensive research in upper middle-income countries, such as South Africa, Brazil and China, and on high-income countries, much of which will be drawn on this book. There is also some noteworthy general work on higher education and international development, such as the literature on the developmental university (Coleman 1986; Court 1980; Yesufu and Association of African Universities 1973), on higher education and the public good in Africa (Singh 2012; Sall et al. 2003; Unterhalter et al. 2017; Walker 2018), and the book *Universities and Global Human Development* by Boni and Walker (2016). Finally, this book builds on general accounts of education and the sustainable development goals (e.g. Bengtsson et al. 2018; King 2017; UNESCO 2016), and works on sustainable development relating to higher education (e.g. Commonwealth Secretariat 2017; Gough and Scott 2007; Leal Filho 2010).

Much of the discussion in this book focuses on low and middle-income countries, those most customarily associated with the task of 'developing'. Despite the huge diversity across these countries, there are two elements that meaningfully tie them together. First, they all experience significant resource constraints in terms of both financial inputs and human resource capacity available in universities. Second, they are disproportionately vulnerable to the decisions of supranational agencies and in many cases dependent on donor assistance; consequently, it matters much more for them what the dominant ideologies at the global level are. Nevertheless, as will be explored further in the chapters that follow, the notion of a 'developing country' is highly problematic, with all countries being on their own trajectories of development. In accordance with the global relevance of the SDGs, while there are some features of this book that are focused on the resource-constrained higher education systems of Africa, Asia and Latin America, the analysis is relevant to all countries. Furthermore, while much of the discussion focuses on the rather specific institution of the 'university', the relevance of this book is for all parts of the higher education system, including non-university institutions (subject-specific colleges, polytechnics and so forth), although with less attention to technical and vocational education (TVET).

This book draws on research, reflection and experiences generated over the last 15 years. From 2003, I was involved in studying the growth of the private higher education sector in Brazil, and its implications for access and quality, which led me to develop a body of theoretical work around equity and fairness. While Latin America has been the region in which I have spent the most time—with experiences in universities particularly in Brazil, but also in Chile, Mexico and elsewhere—since 2012 I have been involved in large-scale research projects in Sub-Saharan Africa. The book draws on studies there on graduate destinations, critical thinking and the public good in higher education in Botswana, Ghana, Kenya, Nigeria and South Africa—with particular reference to Kenya in Chapters 6 and 7. Finally, material is incorporated from a range of small-scale studies I have carried out on alternative or innovative universities in countries including the UK, Mexico and Brazil, and short-term projects on various aspects of higher education for various international agencies. The book also draws inevitably on my experience working in a university in London, with a highly international student and staff body, and all the possibilities and contradictions of a metropolitan and 'global' institution.

As stated above, the analysis of the university presented in this book may serve as a kind of map from which readers from diverse political and epistemological perspectives can chart a course of their choosing. At the same time, it is not free from normativity in this regard, and does put forward some substantive positions as regards the features of higher education systems we should and should not be encouraging. It is important, therefore, that as an author I am open about my core beliefs on these matters from the outset. I am committed to egalitarian values and consider that fairness in the distribution of educational opportunities and the fruits of education is a primary consideration. Social justice needs to express itself not only within nation-states, but also at the global level, at which there are deeply worrying disparities. At the same time, I see most value in the organic emergence of educational practice (often on a small-scale at the local level), and am somewhat distrustful of overly centralised state-planned approaches. While I acknowledge the importance attached to livelihoods and careers by most students and others engaging with universities, I retain a strong commitment to the humanistic, intellectual, civic and emancipatory dimensions of the university, in addition to the vocational ones. Nevertheless, I hope that readers of any persuasion will find value in the book, be able to engage with its arguments and find useful sources of empirical information. Needless to say, I look forward to critical responses to it that will enable me to revise and refine my own positions and further the conversation.

The book is structured in three parts. The first of these provides the backdrop to the study and outlines the conceptual tools that will be employed in the remainder of the book. Following the introduction, there is an analysis of the general relationship between education and development, outlining the complex bidirectional relationship between learning, knowledge production and societal change, and some of the key theories that have influenced the field. Chapter 3 presents the theoretical frame of value, function and interaction, as applied to key historical models of the university: the mediaeval, the Humboldtian the developmental and the entrepreneurial. Following that, Chapter 4 focuses in more closely on the developmental model, which resonates most strongly with the proposed role for the university in the SDGs. Completing this part is an assessment in Chapter 5 of three macro level trends—status competition, commercialisation and unbundling—which are seen to undermine the developmental role of the university.

Part II of the book provides the core analysis of higher education in the contemporary world, taking in turn the questions of access (Chapter 6), quality (Chapter 7), and impact through graduates, research and community engagement (Chapter 8). In each of these there is a general analysis of the current landscape, along with case studies of specific institutions and countries, and proposals for ways forward.

The final part of the book takes a step back to reflect on the significance and implications of the analysis. First, it acknowledges a number of the limitations of the developmental model, in its (often hidden) political assumptions, its crowding out of basic, blue skies research and its emphasis on the short-term. Next there is an exploration of the possible alternatives to the developmental model being nurtured in various parts of the world, particularly among indigenous communities, ones that challenge dominant modernisation-based conceptions of development and Enlightenment epistemologies. Finally, the concluding chapter draws out implications for policy and practice in institutions and higher education systems around the world.

The social and environmental concerns addressed in this book are concrete, urgent and have potentially catastrophic consequences for the survival and well-being of the world's population. This pressing nature of the topic has led to a certain impatience with theory and a rush to practical action. While this action is of course important, it cannot take place in the absence of thought and deliberation—indeed, as argued by Freire (1970), it is perilous without it. This book therefore brings a reflexive dimension to the policies and practices currently underway in global HE, implemented in a rush of desperate adaptation to the challenges of globalisation or threats of financial insolvency. In the words of Žižek (2018):

> The commonplace "enough talking, let's act" is deeply deceiving – now we should say precisely the opposite. Enough of the pressure to do something, let's begin to talk seriously, that is, to think!

The argument put forward in this book is that we need to think of higher education *for* but also *beyond* the SDGs: *for the SDGs* because, despite their limitations, they represent our best chance as human community at the current moment of halting or at least slowing the cataclysmic slide into environmental destruction and conflict; *beyond the SDGs* because they do not provide the final answer, and a more profound transformation in our conception of knowledge, development and university is ultimately needed.

References

Bengtsson, S., Barakat, B., & Muttarak, R. (2018). *The role of education in enabling the sustainable development agenda*. London: Routledge.
Bloom, D., Canning, D., & Chan, K. (2006). *Higher education and economic development in Africa*. Washington, DC: World Bank.

Boni, A., & Walker, M. (2016). *Universities and global human development: Theoretical and empirical insights for social change*. London: Routledge.

Childs, A. (2015). Why does so little foreign aid go to support universities? *The Conversation*. Available at http://theconversation.com/why-does-so-little-foreign-aid-go-to-support-universities-43160. Accessed 13 October 2015.

Clark, W. C., & Dickson, N. M. (2003). Sustainability science: The emerging research program. *Proceedings of the National Academy of Sciences in the United States of America, 100*(14), 8059–8061.

Coleman, J. S. (1986). The idea of the developmental university. *Minerva: A Review of Science, Learning and Policy, 24*(4), 476–494.

Commonwealth Secretariat. (2017). *Curriculum framework for the Sustainable Development Goals*. London: Commonwealth Secretariat.

Court, D. (1980). The development ideal in higher education: The experience of Kenya and Tanzania. *Higher Education, 9,* 657–680.

Freire, P. (1970). *Pedagogy of the oppressed*. London: Penguin Books.

Goldmeier, G. (2018). *Social justice and citizenship education: Reflective equilibrium between ideal theories and the Brazilian context*. PhD thesis submitted at the Institute of Education, University College London.

Gough, S., & Scott, W. (2007). *Higher education and sustainable development: Paradox and possibility*. London: Routledge.

Gupta, V. K. (2018). Burning libraries: A review through the lens of history. *Journal of Indian Library Association, 54*(1), 17–26.

Kerr, C. (1963). *The uses of the university*. New York: Harper Torchbooks.

King, K. (2017). Lost in translation? The challenge of translating the global education goal and targets into global indicators. *Compare: A Journal of Comparative and International Education, 47*(6), 801–817.

King, K., & Palmer, R. (2013). Post-2015 agendas: Northern tsunami, southern ripple? The case of education and skills. *International Journal of Educational Development, 33,* 409–425.

Le Blanc, D. (2015). Towards integration at last: The Sustainable Development Goals as a network of targets. *Sustainable Development, 23,* 176–187.

Leal Filho, W. (Ed.). (2010). *Universities and climate change: Introducing climate change to university programmes*. Berlin: Springer.

Leal Filho, W., Morgan, E., Godoy, E., Azeiteiro, U., Bacelar-Nicolau, P., Veiga Ávila, L., et al. (2018). Implementing climate change research at universities: Barriers, potential and actions. *Journal of Cleaner Production, 170,* 269–277.

MacGregor, K. (2015, April 10). Higher education is key to development—World Bank. *University World News*.

Marginson, S. (2016). The worldwide trend to high participation higher education: Dynamics of social stratification in inclusive systems. *Higher Education, 72,* 413–434.

McCowan, T. (2009). *Rethinking citizenship education: A curriculum for participatory democracy.* London: Continuum.

McCowan, T. (2012). Is there a universal right to higher education? *British Journal of Educational Studies, 60*(2), 111–128.

Neubauer, C., & Calame, M. (2017). Global pressing problems and the Sustainable Development Goals. *Higher education in the world 6—Towards a socially responsible university: Balancing the global with the local.* Global University Network for Innovation.

OECD. (2008). *Tertiary education for the knowledge society.* Paris: OECD.

OECD. (2015). *Development aid at a glance. Statistics by region. 1. Developing countries.* 2015 ed. Available at http://www.oecd.org/dac/stats/documentupload/1%20World%20-%20Development%20Aid%20at%20a%20Glance%202015.pdf. Accessed 13 October 2015.

Oketch, M. O., McCowan, T., & Schendel, R. (2014). *The impact of tertiary education on development: A rigorous literature review.* London: Department for International Development.

Psacharopoulos, G. (1994). Returns to investment in education: A global update. *World Development, 22*(9), 1325–1343.

Psacharopoulos, G., Tan, J.-P., Jimenez, E., & World Bank Education and Training Department. (1986). *Financing education in developing countries: An exploration of policy options.* Washington, DC: World Bank.

Rawls, J. (1971). *A theory of justice.* Cambridge: Harvard University Press.

Sachs, J. D. (2008). *Common wealth: Economics.* New York: Penguin Press.

Sachs, J. D. (2012). From millennium development goals to Sustainable Development Goals. *Lancet, 379,* 2206–2211.

Sall, E., Lebeau, Y., & Kassimir, R. (2003). The public dimensions of the University in Africa. *Journal of Higher Education in Africa, 1*(1), 126–148.

Sankalia, H. (1934). *The University of Nalanda.* Madras: Paul.

Schön, D. (1983). *The reflective practitioner: How professionals think in action.* London: Temple Smith.

Sen, A. (2009). *The idea of justice.* London: Allen Lane Penguin.

Singh, M. (2012). Re-inserting the 'public good' into higher education transformation. In B. Leibowitz (Ed.), *Higher education for the public good—Views from the south* (pp. 1–16). Stoke on Trent, UK: Trentham Books and Stellenbosch: Sun Media.

Streitwieser, B., Brueck, L., Moody, R., & Taylor, M. (2017). The potential and reality of new refugees entering German higher education: The case of Berlin institutions. *European Education, 49*(4), 231–252.

Task Force on Higher Education and Society, World Bank and UNESCO. (2000). *Higher education in developing countries: Peril and promise.* Washington, DC: World Bank.

UNESCO. (2015). *UNESCO science report—Towards 2030.* Paris: UNESCO.

UNESCO. (2016). *Education for people and planet: Creating sustainable futures for all* (Global Education Monitoring Report). Paris: UNESCO.

UNESCO Institute for Statistics (UIS). (2018). *Education: Enrolment by level of education.* Available at http://data.uis.unesco.org/. Accessed 1 September 2018.

UNESCO/IIEP. (2017). *Six ways to ensure higher education leaves no one behind* (Policy Paper 30). Paris: UNESCO.

United Nations (UN). (2015, August 2). *Transforming our world: The 2030 agenda for sustainable development.* New York: United Nations.

United Nations High-Level Panel of Eminent Persons on the Post-2015 Development Agenda. (2013). *A new global partnership: Eradicate poverty and transform economies through sustainable development.* New York: United Nations.

Unterhalter, E., Allais, S., Howell, C., McCowan, T., Morley, L., Oanda, I., & Oketch, M. (2017). *Higher education and the public good: Concepts, challenges and complexities in Africa.* Working paper for the research project, Higher education and the public good in four African countries.

Unterhalter, E., Vaughan, R., & Smail, A. (2013). *Secondary, post secondary and higher education in the Post-2015 discussions.* London: British Council.

USAID. (2015). *Education.* Available at https://www.usaid.gov/education. Accessed 13 October 2015.

Waas, T., Verbruggen, A., & Wright, T. (2010). University research for sustainable development: Definition and characteristics explored. *Journal of Cleaner Production, 18*(7), 629–636.

Walker, M. (2018). Dimensions of higher education and the public good in South Africa. *Higher Education, 76*(3), 555–569.

Walker, M., & McLean, M. (2013). *Professional education, capabilities and the public good: The role of universities in promoting human development.* London: Routledge.

World Bank. (2002). *Constructing knowledge societies: New challenges for tertiary education.* Washington, DC: World Bank.

Yesufu, T. M., & Association of African Universities. (1973). *Creating the African university: Emerging issues in the 1970's*. Ibadan, Nigeria: Oxford University Press for the Association of African Universities.

Žižek, S. (2018). *Like a thief in broad daylight: Power in the era of posthumanity*. London: Penguin.

2

The Role of Education in Development

In the days before GPS, triangulation was a handy tool for finding one's location when out walking on a barren moor. By identifying two features, say a hilltop and a small lake in the distance, using their respective compass points one could trace back two lines with a pencil on the map to find one's own position. With two points of certainty we can accurately calculate a third. With one point of certainty—say only the dark-watered lake—it is no longer possible, but one can narrow down the possibilities and make an educated guess.

In understanding the relationship between education and development, we are in an altogether more precarious position. In this case, we have not two, nor even one, but no points of certainty. Both education and development are open concepts and can be filled in with a range of normative positions, as well as being highly contested as regards the empirical evidence to support them. There is uncertainty as to the nature of education and development separately, and further contestation as to the relationship between them.

This chapter will map this highly complex relationship. After an initial discussion of each of the basic concepts of education and development, there will be an assessment of the metalevel of the forms of

© The Author(s) 2019
T. McCowan, *Higher Education for and beyond the Sustainable Development Goals*, Palgrave Studies in Global Higher Education, https://doi.org/10.1007/978-3-030-19597-7_2

relationships that might exist between them. The chapter first outlines the dominant conception of education as a *driver* for development. This instrumental relationship is primarily economic, as represented by human capital theory, but may relate to other spheres too, including the political. Following that, the analysis addresses the idea of education as *constitutive* of development, involving questions of national status, human rights and human development. The next part of the chapter turns specifically to higher education, to define what is meant by it, and to assess the particularities of this level of education in relation to the general arguments outlined. Finally, implications are drawn out for the role of higher education in the SDGs.

Defining Education and Development

The notions of education and development are highly elusive, and escape precise definitions. In determining what they *are* we often smuggle in our views on what they *should be*; the descriptive becomes colonised by the normative. Furthermore, they are battlegrounds of meaning and values. The notions are contested and uncertain not only in terms of the best strategies to bring them about (say, whether children learn to read best through technical training in phonics or through the real experience of reading children's books), but in the desired end itself (is education about learning to read well or about becoming a good person?).

Nevertheless, it does not follow that there is nothing of use that we can say at the outset about these two concepts. In each case, there is a skeleton that can be identified—even if the flesh and the clothes may be laid on in different ways by different people, by different societies and at different times. This section will serve to outline the essential components of each concept, and identify the areas of legitimate diversity—serving as a basis on which the rest of the book will conduct its inquiry.

Let us start with education. The most basic feature of this concept is that it is an intentional process of bringing about learning. Of course, learning takes place at all times during our lives, even in the act of roughly opening the plastic wrapper of our breakfast cereal only to see the Crunchy Nut Cornflakes spread themselves across the floor. This is undeniably a moment of learning and a potential influence on our future behaviour (in dealing more gingerly with the plastic wrapper), but we would not term it 'education'. Only those activities that have been deliberately designed to bring about learning can be given that name. Most obvious of those activities are those designed within institutions dedicated to that end—in our contemporary times, schools, universities, colleges, nurseries and so forth (what we can conceive as *formal* education). But the notion of education is also valid for organised activities outside of these institutions—for example the structured activities provided for trainee car mechanics in a garage (what we might call *non-formal* education). When we come to higher education, it will be seen that the notion is almost exclusively used in the formal sense—it is rare to speak of non-formal higher education—although as will be seen in Chapter 10, there are new forms of higher learning developing around the world, in indigenous communities, social movements and cooperatives, that challenge our conventional conceptions.

One well-known attempt to dissect the concept in the analytical philosophical tradition is that of R. S. Peters (1966), who proposed a definition of education as distinct from the mere acquisition of facts or skills:

(i) that 'education' implies the transmission of what is worth-while to those who become committed to it;
(ii) that 'education' must involve knowledge and understanding and some kind of cognitive perspective, which are not inert;
(iii) that 'education' at least rules out some procedures of transmission, on the grounds that they lack willingness and voluntariness.

Such unifying definitions of education, however carefully thought out, are fraught with dangers, and Peters's work has over the decades spawned a large number of critiques and alternative accounts (Beckett 2011)—leaving doubts as to whether any definition of education beyond the minimal idea of intentional learning can avoid being culturally specific.

At this point, it is important to distinguish clearly between the *learning* and *certification* functions of formal education. Schools and universities confer benefits on their students of different forms: among these, the most prominent are, on the one hand, the acquisition of knowledge, skills and values, and, on the other, qualifications that testify to that acquisition. We might assume that these two go hand-in-hand. Yet there are many instances in which learning might be acquired without certification, outside formal education institutions or in the context of optional learning within those institutions, and in which certification may be conferred without meaningful learning—whether through ineffective assessment practices, poor quality assurance mechanisms, or corrupt academic practice. Sadly, the primary driver for demand for higher education—the quest for social mobility through employment opportunities (Marginson 2016)—is as much for certification as it is for learning. A degree certificate can confer advantage in the labour market, even when the graduate in question has received poor quality teaching and little learning of value. This phenomenon can create a form of complicity between students and institutions through which students accept poor quality without complaint or withdrawal as long as they will receive their final diploma. This complicity has provided a particular spur to the expansion of for-profit sectors (for example in Brazil—McCowan 2004), but can also be observed in public systems (in relation to higher education in Africa, see McCowan et al. 2015).

The contestation around education occurs firstly in relation to its ends, and secondly its means. What is education for? As Dewey (1966 [1916]: 107) famously stated, 'It is well to remind ourselves that education as such has no aims. Only persons, parents, and teachers, etc., have aims'. Since education is an intentional process to bring about learning, it varies according to the intentions in question. Education is about creating a good person (whether a moral, a religious, a technically competent, or politically aware one) and a good society (whether a co-operative, a bellicose, an innovative or a tradition-bound one), in all the multiple ways they can be conceived.

The second area of significant contestation is about means. Which is the best teaching method for ensuring children understand fractions?

Does competition between schools enhance their quality? Should the curriculum focus on the core subjects of maths and first language, or should there be a broader holistic coverage? Unlike the value-based questions outlined above, these questions should be amenable to answering through empirical evidence: but despite the extensive research on some questions, opinions are still significantly divided, due to the fact that most educational research (even of a quasi-experimental nature) takes place in natural settings, with significant contextual influences.

A final point on these questions is that one of the most pernicious tendencies in educational debates is in fact to focus exclusively on the second type of question (about means) and not on the first (about ends). Debates about educational policies at the macro level, and classroom methods and techniques at the micro level, often take place under the assumption that all parties are agreed on what the ultimate purposes are, and that all that is left is to work out the effective strategies for obtaining them. At best, this shows a lack of awareness of fundamental differences of moral and political view; at worst, this can serve to shut down debates about the direction of society, and so to maintain the status quo and the interests of dominant groups.

We can turn now to the second notion, 'development'. The term has a wide range of different applications, and here is used in the sense of development of a society (as implied in the expressions 'international development' and 'national development') rather than the development of an individual (as used in 'child development' and 'human development' in the psychological sense)—although there are a number of parallels between individual and societal levels. Like 'education' it is a minimalist concept in terms of core content. It refers to a process of change that is usually (although not necessarily) positive; and it is change to an entity that is recognisable throughout the process, rather than replacement of one with another (McCowan 2015). Beyond these very minimal requirements of the concept, the fleshing out of the idea is entirely normative, and is in effect simply an expression of our understandings of 'the good society'.

In a historical sense, we can identify a more specific meaning that developed from the post Second World War period, and in official usage appearing in the inaugural address of President Truman in 1949. This conception of development, one which is absolutely dominant to this day across the globe, sees it as primarily a question of economic growth, along with urbanisation, technological sophistication, extended transport and communications infrastructure, the provision of public services (including health and education), and 'modern' political, economic and social institutions. Despite the dominance of this perspective, there are multiple competing conceptualisations, whether sharply diverging ones of a neo-Marxist leaning, a cultural traditionalist basis, or more subtle modifications such as the capabilities or basic needs approaches. An important part of the evolution of the concept of development has been the progressive emphasis on 'people': moving from a predominantly infrastructural conception—development as roads, bridges, skyscrapers—to a human one—participation, skills and good governance. It is this latter conception that has been most supportive of the notion of education as constitutive of development explored below.

Sustainable development, historically, represents the coming together of the international development and environmental agendas of the post-war period, a supposed win-win between protecting the planet and promoting welfare for all. The Brundtland Report (1987) represented a turning point in global recognition of the environmental crisis, and paved the way for the monumental United Nations Conference on Environment and Development in Rio de Janeiro in 1992. The Rio Declaration which emerged from the summit set the agenda for sustainable development for the years to come, paving the way for the later SDGs. Conceptually, sustainable development simply refers to a form of development that will not extinguish itself, and therefore, like the notion of development as a whole, is open to multiple interpretations and uses. For proponents, it is the perfect reconciliation of all of our global concerns. For detractors, it is simply a way of propping up the current system, satirically referred to as 'growth everlasting', and is really about the 'durability' of the capitalist, Western-led economic model (Rist 2002).

As with education, there is a tendency to focus on the means of development—determining how to catalyse it, speed it up or distribute its benefits more widely—rather than the ends—whether we are focusing on economic growth, democracy, sustainability or some other societal goal. Much development thought and practice has a blind spot over the latter, assuming a consensus over the ends, or (even more worryingly) that there is only one end (economic growth).

Education as a Driver of Development

The most commonly invoked conceptualisation of education and development is that they are in a causal relationship, that the former brings about the latter, and the more we invest in the former, the more of the latter we will get. These arguments are fundamental to national education policy, as well as international movements such as Education for All, and the work of supranational agencies. Three variants of this approach are outlined below.

(a)   Education and economic growth

The most common instrumental rationale for education in contemporary times is that it acts as a motor for economic activity and prosperity, both at individual and national levels. Central to this position is human capital theory, which asserts that investment in education enhances the productivity of workers, and therefore leads to increased economic returns in the form of salary, and greater growth at the macro level. Although its roots stretch back to the ideas of Adam Smith in the eighteenth century, human capital theory became popular in the 1960s through the systematisations of Theodore Schultz (1961) and Gary Becker (1962), and later by Mincer (1981), as a means of explaining differentials in economic growth across countries beyond the traditional factors of (undifferentiated) labour and land, along with investment in physical capital. It has had a central place in the economics of education ever since, although with significant modifications over time—for example the move from years of schooling to quality (gauged through learning outcomes) seen in the work of Hanushek and Woessman (2008; Hanushek 2013).

The theory has also adapted itself in light of the increasing importance of innovation and technology to the economy—with clear relevance for higher education. Endogenous growth theory emerged as an extension of human capital theory by acknowledging to a greater extent the collective advantages of high-level skills formation for generating and sustaining technological innovation (Lucas 1988; Romer 1986). In the context of the so-called knowledge economy, therefore, education has taken on far greater importance than in the industrial age, as a means of training knowledge workers, as well as generating innovation and enterprise.

Human capital theory emerged within economics to explain economic growth, but was gradually adopted as a normative orientation for education (these are distinct as it is quite possible to hold simultaneously that education is key to economic growth, but that schools in practice should not only focus on worker productivity). Governments and supranational agencies such as the World Bank found a new justification for investment in education—both public and private—through the economic returns that can be gained. This justification has brought significant implications for the content of education, in particular the emphasis on basic skills of mathematics, science and language, as well as more specifically vocational learning.

Unsurprisingly, human capital theory has attracted strong criticism. Some of these have been within the field of economics, such as screening hypothesis, which asserts that differentials in productivity are not caused by education, but are just validated by its credentials—those with greater innate ability, according to the theory, being able to endure through the education system and obtain higher qualifications. A further problem in human capital theory is its core assumption that the labour market absorbs and rewards correspondingly those with particular skills (Klees 2016; Marginson 2017; Robertson 2016). It has also been strongly critiqued as an orientation for education policy, given its role in marginalising more humanistic, artistic and critical approaches to the curriculum (McCowan 2013).

(b) Education and basic needs

A second range of arguments are those that focus on the basic needs of the population (Streeten 1977; Stewart 1985). These arguments have been particularly prominent and influential in international development, given the critical levels of poverty and deprivation in many contexts. The distinction from the human capital drivers is that they do not focus solely on enhanced work opportunities and salaries, but on improvement in living standards through direct impact on health, nutrition and other areas of wellbeing. The main rationale here is that literacy and other basic knowledge and skills allow populations access to essential information—for example, on reproductive health, the causes of HIV/AIDs, the value of hand washing for health promotion—and increase their ability to take up public service opportunities, such as use of health clinics and schools. In relation to the SDGs, these broader impacts of education have been amply documented by Bengtsson et al. (2018).

This approach has been particularly prominent in relation to gender. Some of the most persuasive arguments for education among international agencies have been those focusing on the critical role of girls' education in ensuring the health and prosperity of their future children. Although problematic from a feminist perspective due to their instrumentalisation of women, catchphrases such as 'educate a girl and you educate a family', and statistics on the influence of women's educational levels on infant mortality are widespread. These arguments have been influential in linking education to the more powerful health agenda, as well as gender equality, and have been associated with the prominent focus on universal primary education in EFA and the MDGs.

(c) Citizenship, political participation, and conscientization

The third class of reasons may in some instances be compatible with human capital theory, but in many respects challenges its normative underpinnings. Education has been associated with political ends since the training of scribes and state bureaucrats in the earliest civilisations, passing through the founding of the first national education systems in Europe from the eighteenth century—largely for the forging of a national ideology and civil service (Green 1990). Empirical research provides extensive evidence that formal education enhances political understanding and engagement (Almond and Verba 1963; Huntington and Nelson 1976; Milbrath and Goel 1977; Parsons and Bynner 2002). Civic education specifically has long featured in the curricula of liberal and authoritarian states alike, though varying in the extent to which it promotes conformity to existing structures or alternatively empowers citizens to critique, campaign and reconstruct (McCowan 2009).

In recent years, global citizenship education has become increasingly prominent, in part due to the perceived reality of globalisation, and in part to the cosmopolitan commitments of proponents. This wave has been reflected in the SDGs in which global citizenship education features as part of goal 4.7—as well as being one of the three priorities of the UN Secretary General's Global Education First initiative (along with putting every child into school and improving the quality of learning). The above positions rest on the idea that democracy is not only a form of government, but a practice, and one that is learnt. The existence of a genuinely democratic society—and its ability to be inclusive, representative and participatory—is dependent on the prior and ongoing processes of learning that citizens are engaged in.

A more radical version of this approach is that education is key to social transformation through raising the consciousness of learners. The idea that the masses need to be educated to see the injustice of their situation, to develop the capacity for collective organisation and overthrow their oppressors has characterised radical political thought throughout recent centuries, and has led to considerable caution on the part of national governments not to spread education too liberally across the population.

Key to this area of thought is Paulo Freire, the Brazilian educationist whose *Pedagogy of the Oppressed* (1970) has become the seminal work of the left in education since the early 1970s. Freire's basic position is that lasting political change can only occur through a fundamental reorientation of the consciousness of the working class, a change that will allow for an organic transformation of social relations and the possibility of a socialist society (in contrast to the positions that held that this process should occur only after the seizing of power through a military revolution). Education is central to this transformation, but only through a fundamental shift of educational practice—towards horizontal, dialogical relations between teachers and students, and a conscientising, problem-posing rather than a 'banking', or knowledge-transmitting approach.

Development Driving Education

Finally, before ending the treatment of the cause–effect relationship between education and development, it is important to highlight the alternative perspective that the latter drives the former. It could be argued that the expansion of education systems is more a result of greater economic activity than a cause of it, given that increased state funds allow for investment in the system, and increased family wealth for investment in children's tuition fees. Taking a historical perspective, it can been seen that education in the formal sense is a 'fruit' of development, in that it appeared in societies with surplus agricultural production, and bureaucratic needs of emerging statehood (Diamond 1997). There may also be increasing demand for education as an economy industrialises, and reaches post-industrial status, with greater need for knowledge workers. As explored by Marginson (2016), expansion of higher education system has also been brought about by family desires for status and social mobility. Yet while understanding of the interplay between education and development as drivers of each other (and certainly it is a two-way relationship) is highly important, the focus of this book is primarily on education as the causal agent, given its framing as such in the SDGs and the need to develop closer understandings of the complex role of learning in the transformation of society.

Education as Constitutive of Development

The above positions are examples of the most straightforward relationship between education and development: namely, that the former *causes* the latter. However, we may also conceptualise it in another way—that education *is* development, or at least signals development. In some cases this may be because the value attached to education is intrinsic rather than instrumental, or because the existence of educated people or institutions is a symbol of status, or—most interestingly—if development is conceptualised as a state of mind or learning. Three of these forms will be outlined below.

(a) Education as national status

One way in which education may be seen to be constitutive of development is in the simple valuing of educational indicators and institutions as markers of development—regardless of any knock-on impact. In this way, the achieving of the goal of universal primary education or gender parity might be seen to confer 'developed country' status, or at least to raise a county's status within the 'developing' category. As will be discussed further below, the status rationale is strong in higher education, particularly as regards flagship institutions and their positioning on international rankings. In recent years, this kind of status competition has taken on a different flavour through the increasing prominence of international learning outcome tests, most prominently PISA: while there are instrumental rationales for scoring well, there is no doubt that a positive league position is seen to be a good in its own right.

Beyond status posturing at the national level, there is also the intrinsic value of education and learning: in this way, the existence of an educational indicator (mean years of schooling) within the Human Development Index signals that being educated is constitutive of having a dignified and flourishing life, and not only instrumental in achieving other goals. This final point links in with the human development rationale outlined below.

(b) Education as a human right

A second form of the constitutive relationship is the rights-based approach. According to this conception, the most important objectives at the international level are to ensure the full upholding of the rights enshrined in international law—the most important in relation to education being the International Covenant of Economic, Cultural and Social Rights (1966) and the 1989 Convention on the Rights of the Child. While there are some differences between them, the main stipulation is for universal, compulsory and free elementary (primary) education, with rather weaker guarantees at other levels of education (emphasising accessibility rather than availability), and guidance relating to the aims and conduct of education (for example, promoting mutual respect) (McCowan 2013).

According to a rights-based conception, the provision of education is non-conditional—it is not justified by economic returns that might accrue (even though these may be desirable), or by any other kind of societal or individual benefit. It is seen as a fundamental part of a dignified life. Having said that, there is also an instrumental role given to education as a 'multiplier' (Tomaševski 2001): education is seen to underpin the exercising of all other rights, both in terms of possessing the knowledge and skills to participate fully in society (for example, voting, accessing healthcare, obtaining a dignified livelihood), and also in having knowledge of and understanding the significance of human rights themselves. It is this role of education in underpinning all others that has been used as a justification for the (rather unusual) compulsory nature of the right to elementary education.

(c) Human development

The term human development has a range of different usages (being employed in distinct ways in psychology for example), but in international development it is associated with the moves that took place—originally in the United Nations Development Programme (UNDP) through the work of Mahbub Ul Haq and Amartya Sen—to broaden the conception of development from an exclusively economic basis (measured by GDP per capita) to encompass the range of facets of value to human life. The indicator associated with this approach is the Human Development Index (HDI), which includes longevity and education in addition to GDP per capita—not a full expression of human development, but certainly an improvement on GDP alone. Closely associated with human development is the capabilities approach, developed by Amartya Sen (e.g. 1992, 1999a) and further elaborated by Martha Nussbaum (e.g. 2000). Capabilities provide a deeper philosophical rationale for the perspective of human development by providing a frame for evaluating the organisation of society and the lives of individuals. The orienting principle is that all human beings should be free to live the life that they have reason to value: in this way, the approach avoids being based purely on resources available to individuals (being inattentive to heterogeneity of both needs and goals), and entirely subjective, preference-based gauges.

One of the distinctive, and highly valuable, features of human development in relation to other approaches is that it sees human beings' ability to pursue their life goals in all their diversity (their agency freedoms and achievements) as being intrinsically valuable. That is to say, having rich and harmonious social interactions, enjoying artistic pursuits, having mental health or being able to exercise are not only pursued insofar as they support some external goal such as economic growth or nation-building, but are seen as valuable in themselves. Of course, these activities may *also* have instrumental value, acknowledged in ideas such as 'fertile functionings' (Wolff and Shalit 2013), but like human rights they do not stand or fall on this basis.

There are clear implications here for education. Learning is seen to have a dual role within human development frameworks: an instrumental one in developing internal capacities (which together with external circumstances enable full capabilities), and an intrinsic one in which education is valuable in itself. So in this conception, being literate, being able to engage in considered reflection and acquire information and understanding are seen as part of a dignified and flourishing life. As will be drawn out further in the sections and chapters that follow, the implications of this kind of justification for higher education policy, practice and funding are extensive.

As alluded to above, the family of approaches that we could loosely group as human development—including the capabilities approach and the United Nations human development work, but also a range of other people-centred approaches—can be seen as distinct from others in that 'development' is, at least in part, internal to the human being. A society is developed not when it reaches a certain level of economic activity, or can boast high-speed rail and motorway networks, or even efficient institutions, but when its population, individually and collectively, has reached a particular state of being. The specific approaches differ in what they consider to be the nature of that state of being, but they are brought together by the distinctively human nature of it. Into this group, there might also be an argument for bringing the Freirean approaches classified above as having an instrumental role in relation to political participation, insofar as a politically aware individual and population is seen to be a good in itself.

(d) Crafting the concept of development

The approaches associated with education as a 'driver' assume for the most part that development is a fixed notion, and that the task is to assess how and in what ways education can move us towards (or away from) that goal. Yet notions of development are founded on a broad spectrum of moral and political views, and these views are to a large extent constructed and acquired during our lifetimes. Education, therefore, has a pivotal role in influencing what we understand development to be. This is akin to Sen's (1999b) idea of the *constructive* role of democracy (in addition to its intrinsic and instrumental roles) in forming values. Depending on the conception and practice of education, this process could occur in a more transmissive way—as seen in the foundational *raison d'être* of European national education systems in nation-building and promoting national ideology. Or alternatively it could be more participatory, in providing students with the tools they need to think autonomously and construct their conceptions. Higher education, ideally, should be contributing to the latter of these. Universities have the potential to be key players in providing a space for deliberation on conceptions of development, creating new ideas and theories, critiquing flawed conceptions and constituting a hub and clearinghouse for national and global debates. This relationship has been categorised as a constitutive one—but we could easily see it as its own category, since it is not only that an educated population constitutes a developed society, but that education forms the very conception we hold of what development is.

The Other Face of Education

In the urgency to advocate for education in a funding landscape of many competing priorities, there is a tendency to simplify educational practices, and gloss over the more pernicious aspects. But it is undeniable that education (or at least formal education) has or can have negative effects. Perhaps most visible of these are threats to the physical integrity of students, with the urgency of learning having been seen to justify punishment and humiliation for most of history and across many if not most cultures. Corporal punishment is still extremely widespread in schools, and despite the provisions in the Convention on the Rights of the Child that 'States Parties shall take all appropriate measures to ensure that school discipline is administered in a manner consistent with the child's human dignity and in conformity with the present Convention' (Article 28, part 2), there is still no full ban on it in schools in 68 countries (Global Initiative to End all Corporal Punishment of Children 2018). Sexual violence—inflicted by other students or by teachers—is also a considerable risk in many contexts. Unterhalter's (2003) influential article argued that in the context of high levels of rape and HIV/AIDS prevalence in South Africa, schooling for girls may constrain more than facilitate their capabilities. A recent campaign in Kenya—with the Twitter hashtag *tyranny3pc*, referring to the sacrifices necessary to be part of the 3% who make it through the education system—highlights both of these aspects, in light of recent physical and sexual abuse of students, as well as the cruel funnels of success and failure in the system.

A more subtle form of harm inflicted by education systems is through the reproduction of inequalities. In fact, this function is highly contested, with contemporary liberal education systems asserting that they provide a level playing field for all students, and give the promise of social mobility, limited only by talent and effort. Nevertheless, empirical evidence has shown that learning outcomes and exam results are highly correlated with the socio-economic background of the student, starting from the influential Coleman Report (e.g. Coleman et al. 1966). While liberals see this as an unfortunate result of disadvantage in home conditions that must be addressed through social and educational policy, social reproduction theorists interpret it as a deliberate and necessary feature of capitalism. Classic studies such as Bowles and Gintis (1976) in the USA and Willis (1978) in the UK show how the education system channels students from different social classes into their allotted place in the labour market and society. The appearance of a meritocratic education system is even more effective than a forced allocation, since people are more willing to accept their less advantageous place in society on the basis of their supposed inferior abilities or determination.

There are also cultural dimensions to the potential harm that education can cause. While curricula may assume their own universality, knowledge, its organisation and transmission are culturally specific, and in the context of a multicultural society (now the norm rather than the exception), will inevitably lead to the exclusion of some cultural groups. The same occurs in the case of language of instruction, with high proportions of learners in many countries learning in a second or even a third language, leading not only to decreased learning outcomes but to the potential undermining of the languages themselves. These problems are particularly critical for indigenous groups leading lifestyles very different from mainstream society. Even for majority populations, in the context of colonisation and globalisation, cultural traditions may be threatened through the formal education system: postcolonial and dependency theorists (e.g. Mamdani 2018; Mazrui 1975; Prakash and Esteva 2008; Takayama et al. 2015) have shown how education systems inherited from former colonial powers, along with continuing peripheral status in relation to metropole publishing houses and intellectual production, serve to marginalise as well as to remove the possibility of authenticity in thought and expression. In response, some have argued for what Santos (2015) terms 'ecology of knowledges': examples of alternatives in the field of higher education in line with these ideas will be taken up in Chapter 10.

Furthermore, theorists of conflict see these negative dimensions of education—both their distributional and recognitional elements (Fraser 1998)—as a key culprit in the fostering of violence and civil wars, through creating divisions and hatred, as well as resentment through the unfair distribution of opportunities (Bush and Saltarelli 2000; Novelli and Lopez Cardozo 2008; Smith and Vaux 2003). Equally, transforming education can be key to peace building and the promotion of just and harmonious societies.

The Specificities of Higher Education

The points outlined in the above sections are for the most part valid for all of the levels of education. However, there are some specificities of higher education that arise from the distinctive nature of learning at this level, the ways it is organised and funded, and the opportunities it confers in society. The section will start by outlining what is meant by higher education, before assessing areas in which it converges and diverges with basic education in relation to its role as a driver for, constitutive of or a barrier to development. These points will be traced only briefly here—as many of them form the core subject matter of the chapters that follow.

(a) Definitions

Defining any level of education slips easily into tautology. Secondary education is what takes place at secondary schools, and secondary schools are where people go after primary school, where they learn the secondary curriculum and prepare for going on to university, technical college or directly to work. Usually what we are doing is simply reporting on the institutional divisions in our societies, rather than any meaningful underpinning endeavour of an educational nature. So, when defining higher education we can end up making less than useful statements about it providing 'higher learning', or education that takes place in universities and other post-secondary institutions.

While the chapters that follow will go some way towards putting forward a normative conception of the university, this section will stay at the level of a basic descriptive account. One distinctive aspect of higher education is that the institutions delivering it very commonly engage in research or scholarship as well as teaching and learning. Perkin (2007: 159), in this way, defines the university as 'a school of higher learning combining teaching and scholarship and characterized by its corporate autonomy and academic freedom'. This aspect distinguishes it from schools, which engage in the transmission of knowledge, but rarely its production. The research function is most common in the form of institution we call 'university', but can also occur in other forms of HEI—as well as specialist research institutes which are not generally considered part of the higher education system.

The comprehensive university in the contemporary age has become characterised by three pillars: teaching, research and community engagement (the third of these manifesting under many names, as will be explored in Chapter 8). In some countries—particularly in Latin America—the existence of these three pillars is actually definitional of the university: in Brazil there is a constitutional requirement for institutions going by the name of university to carry out these functions. In other contexts, they are less official, but continue to orient the activities of the institution—although usually with considerably less space dedicated to community engagement than the other two, particularly in the context of commercialisation of higher education. When understanding the role of higher education and development, it is essential to acknowledge these diverse roles, as will be explored in the chapters that follow.

Even within the teaching and learning role, there are some specificities in contrast to schools. First is that higher education depends on prior learning: it assumes that learners have extensive grounding in basic skills such as literacy and numeracy, and knowledge of the specific field of study. As will be explored in Chapter 6, this requirement for prior learning justifies the selection procedures to enter higher education institutions (HEIs)—although admissions tests also serve to filter large numbers of candidates for limited places. A second characteristic of learning in higher education is that it is usually highly specialised. This is not always true—particularly in the North American tradition of the liberal arts college—but for the most part higher education involves the selection of a specific area of study, either an academic discipline or a profession, and an in-depth and detailed study of it. With the general trend in science towards ever more specific fields of study, so higher education courses have subdivided, with numerous sub-areas of engineering, biology and so forth appearing as higher education courses. Some of the critiques of so-called Mickey Mouse subjects in contemporary times have also focused on the endless subdivision of professional areas, with courses in 'golf course management' and 'surf science'. A third characteristic is that higher education is generally extended over time: it would be very unusual to describe a taster course or a short term workshop as higher education. Finally, in most cases higher education involves a theoretical element. This is not to say that it does not have practical engagement or purposes—in fact the trends in higher education are exactly towards greater practical application—but that it is conducted with a theoretical underpinning. Winch (2006: 68) outlines this difference helpfully through his distinction between the technical and the technological, the former 'putting in effect a body of theoretical knowledge in a particular context for a particular purpose', and the latter, characteristic of higher education, to become 'innovator[s] in respect of the knowledge which *underlies* the development of new technique' (original emphasis).

There are many types of institution within higher education systems. Most famous is the university, and in many places (including this book) the terms may be used interchangeably. Defining the 'university' in a way that transcends cultural and geographical context, as well as time period, is highly difficult, and institutions using the name are highly diverse, but the term usually refers to the most academic, theoretical and research-based of higher education institutions. Most countries will have official stipulations for university status, and will only allow the designation of university to institutions that fulfil them. Other higher education institutions include polytechnics (more focused on technical and vocational areas), colleges offering short cycle or foundation qualifications, and specialist colleges (relating to teacher education, nursing, business and so forth). Most countries will distinguish between these offerings and post-secondary educational provision usually of a vocational nature that is not considered at HE level, though the distinctions between them again are not always clear or coherent.

Higher education institutions are shifting over time, with some observing processes of homogenisation through 'mission creep' and 'academic drift' (Garrod and Macfarlane 2009), in which more technical institutions become more similar to universities. This process is not universal, however, and in other cases differentiation between institutions may be increasing. One trend that has been very prominent over the past two centuries is the incorporation of new subject areas, particularly of a more applied or vocational nature: professions such as teaching and nursing for which training historically was outside higher education are now predominantly within the university, and new areas continue to enter (for example, sports science, gender studies and media studies), often eliciting scepticism or outright opposition from traditionalists.

(b) Common characteristics

Higher education exemplifies in many ways the general points made above about the relationship between education and development. It is strongly caught up in the beliefs about education's role in economic growth, in terms of government investment and the calculations of individuals and families. This role has become particularly important in the context of the so-called knowledge economy, given the demands for knowledge workers, as well as technological development and innovation to ensure economic competitiveness (Castells 1994; Tilak 2003).

It is also seen as having a significant role in relation to political development: in terms of the formation of political leaders, but also in the strengthening of institutions, and the shaping of positive attitudes towards democracy, tolerance and the rule of law (Bynner et al. 2003; Luescher-Mamashela et al. 2011; McMahon 2009). More radical forms of political development along Freirean lines have been evident particularly in the form of critical pedagogy, popularised in North America through the work of thinkers such as Henry Giroux, Peter McLaren (Giroux and McLaren 1986) and bell hooks (1994).

In terms of its constitutive role, higher education historically has been strongly associated with the designs of the nation-state, and previously the city-state. In the period following the Second World War in which many countries in Africa and Asia gained independence, national universities were established not only to fill the vacuum in human resources left by the departing powers, and to forge cultural and political unity and strength, but also as a marker of nationhood. Many countries to this day have flagship universities that are simply named after the nation: the University of Ghana, University of Botswana, University of Rwanda, University of the Republic (Uruguay), National Autonomous University of Mexico, and so forth. The status marker role of universities has been fuelled by the rise of international rankings in higher education, and countries' obsessions with inserting their institutions into the upper echelons. This fever has led not only to greater investment in 'excellence' and elite institutions, but in some cases (e.g. France) the amalgamation of smaller institutions in order to concentrate outputs.

Constitutive roles in terms of human development are also prominent. The work of researchers such as Alejandra Boni and Melanie Walker (Boni and Walker 2013, 2016; Boni et al. 2016) has shown the centrality of the university experience to the formation and strengthening of capabilities. And there is a longer tradition of liberal education, famously formulated by Cardinal Newman (1947 [1852]) in the nineteenth century, that points to the general cultivation of intellect and character, in the context of ideas that a desirable society is one populated by educated persons.

The neo-Marxist critiques of the role of education are also strongly prominent at the higher education level. It is an essential extension of social reproduction theory in training the elites, instilling them with high-level skills and leadership qualities, and inserting them in the upper echelons of the labour force. As will be explored further in Chapter 6, even within the higher education system there is significant stratification which can be interpreted as an allocative mechanism for scarce positional goods. Furthermore, higher education can be seen to serve the capitalist economy, not only in terms of forging disparate employment opportunities, but also in producing the knowledge required by companies for economic advantage: in the commercialised system companies can commission this kind of research directly, although the diffusion of knowledge is hard to restrict indefinitely.

Higher education also displays the 'other face' through its role in fostering or exacerbating violent conflict—either through its curriculum, or through systematically excluding certain groups from its benefits—and in turn higher education systems and academics are often victims of civil war and other forms of conflict (Milton 2019). At the same time, recent research has shown that inclusive and engaged forms of higher education have a crucial role in peacebuilding (Pherali and Lewis, 2019; Milton and Barakat 2016).

(c) Divergences

Nevertheless, there are some distinctive features of higher education that affect its interrelationship with development. As outlined above, the research and community engagement functions of higher education mean that it impacts on society and development not only through the inculcation of learning in students but also directly through the production of knowledge and interaction with other citizens. The university's role in science, technology and innovation has been widely recognised as central to the challenge of sustainable development (Sachs 2008; Stiglitz 2007; World Bank 1999). Furthermore, the advanced level of studies conducted and the degree of specialisation mean a weaker role in the promotion of basic needs, which is a strong justification for basic education.

One fundamental difference in teaching function between higher and basic education (here used in the sense of primary and secondary education, which are compulsory or widely available in most countries), is the non-obligatory nature of the former. The optional character of higher education leads to some specific considerations. First, states assume less of a requirement to make higher education available and accessible to citizens. There are few countries that provide universal free-of-charge higher education, and it is becoming increasingly prevalent even for public universities to charge fees, with state funding focusing on the most disadvantaged or in backing loan schemes. The ambiguity of an entitlement to higher education is reflected in international law in which there is a guarantee of 'equal access' (meaning non-discrimination in selection) but not availability (these points will be explored further in Chapter 6). As a result of the non-compulsory and non-universal nature of higher education, its curriculum is less often used as a vehicle for state purposes, in terms of features like mandatory citizenship education, health, nutrition and hygiene, sexual and relationship education and so forth. There is also a strong assumption that learners should be free to choose what they want to study, and in some cases decide on the pace and sequence of those studies—features that are only occasionally present in basic education.

The specificities have particular implications in relation to fairness and social justice, making the question of who should go to university (and who should pay for it) more complex than that of who should go to school. It also raises interesting questions about the extent to which university should be an instrument for the promotion of positive values in society, such as citizenship or sustainable development (as explored, for example, in Martin 2018).

Implications of the Higher Education-Development Link

What are the implications of these conceptual considerations for the central question of this book, namely the role of higher education in the SDGs? Supporting the instrumental conception—of education as a driver of development—the evidence that is available shows resoundingly that universities do have a significantly positive impact on society, even in the world's poorest countries (e.g. Oketch et al. 2014). So the natural conclusion would be simply to go about the business of strengthening and extending our university systems, campaigning for funding and working to ensure effective implementation. But is it really that simple? The affirmation above assumes that both 'development' and 'higher education' are singular phenomena, ones that we can easily define and all agree on. But development of course is a 'shell' concept: it provides only an outline of meaning, while most of the way we understand it is simply a reflection of our political and moral values. Education (and consequently higher education) too is minimalist in its core meaning—a purposeful process of bringing about learning—with the questions of what kind of learning and how it should be brought about left down to the designs and customs of particular individuals and groups. The conventional conceptualisation of the relationship between education and development also makes a problematic assumption of a straightforward linear relationship, moving from the former to the latter. The reasoning goes that we have particular aims as a society—economic growth, social cohesion, democracy and so forth—and we deploy education to achieve these ends.

This linear, instrumental rationale for education is without doubt dominant at the international level, and in the policies of national governments. As argued by McGrath (2010, 2014), the relative absence of academic educationists from the debates on the role of education in the post-2015 agenda has left the important job of promoting education to advocates from NGOs and other development agencies, and led to a loss of nuance and understanding of the complexity of these processes. So, the debates have been dominated by eye-catching statistics that a single extra year of schooling brings a 10% increase in lifetime income, or one additional year of maternal education decreases child deaths from pneumonia by 14%.

The problems with the above are not only that they focus exclusively on the direct instrumental benefits of education, but also that in some cases they assume that these impacts occur automatically as a result of increasing the length of time or investments in the education system. However, it is now commonplace in educational circles to acknowledge that it is learning outcomes and not time in school that bring positive influences—and that we cannot assume that these two necessarily correspond. Despite caricatures to the contrary (pointing to early studies based on years of schooling), even mainstream economists working with human capital theory have overwhelmingly moved towards this position. As a result, widespread efforts have been made to determine what the learning outcomes of students are—and this emphasis has been reflected in the targets of SDG4. In high-income countries, these initiatives have burst into the non-specialist imaginary through the PISA tests, which have gained widespread recognition in public debates and policymaker attention, leading at times to situations of panic and despair among countries performing poorly in relation to their self-conception. In low and middle-income countries there have been a variety of initiatives, such as OECD's PISA for Development (linked with the SDG4 target on minimum learning proficiency for those at the end of lower secondary education), and at the regional level, SAQMEC (Southern and Eastern Africa Consortium for Monitoring Educational Quality). As will be explored further in Chapter 7, these efforts have been much less visible at the level of higher education, and despite some proposals, there is as yet no internationally comparable test of learning outcomes from universities.

However, the linear rationale fails to acknowledge the ways in which the education system itself is conditioned by those external factors—the most obvious being the amount of funding that is available for it—in a complex circular relationship. One way in which this relationship has manifested itself has been in the intractable 'chicken and egg' problem of which comes first, economic growth or expansion of university enrolments. But there is also a sense in which education is *constitutive* of development: that developing as a society is about learning, that the development is not outside of the human beings that comprise a society, and instead resides in their level of knowledge, understanding and skill. Furthermore, education can be seen not only as instrumental in bringing about a particular kind of society, but as an arena of society in its own right, thus involving questions, for example, not only of how it might produce democratic citizens, but also how it might express democracy in its own workings.

So we are dealing with two concepts in movement—as a result making understanding the relationship between them highly challenging. Clearly, posing the question 'does higher education have an impact on development' is entirely inadequate, even if we qualify it with 'under which conditions', or show sensitivity to contextual differences. Instead, the question is really that of which forms of higher education lead to which forms of development, and conversely how do forms of development condition higher education systems and institutions.

The question 'Which higher education for which development?' is not merely one of philosophical interest. Higher education has historically been restricted to the elites in all countries, and their near monopoly on access has allowed them in turn to dominate elite professions, government roles and economic opportunities. As discussed further in Chapter 6, the accessibility of the higher education system, along with the ways it distributes the knowledge it produces, influence the levels of socio-economic inequality in society. The selection of degree courses available and curricula of those courses will have a significant impact on the forms of work undertaken by graduates, and the ways in which they carry out that work, and therefore have a significant impact on the development trajectories of their countries. Educational forms in the West are strongly implicated in the cultural norms that have fuelled the acquisitive, consumerist habits that are largely responsible for the current environmental crisis: even if curricula may not have actively promoted these attitudes, they are at the very least at fault for not having combated them.

It is therefore completely inadequate to simply promote *more* higher education across the world. It matters what kind of higher education is developed and how it is distributed. And yet there is a remarkable lack of attention to and imagination about forms of the university. For the most part, it is assumed that if an institution can attract students and ensure completion of their degrees then it has succeeded. Consequently, *affordability* has become the buzzword of development agencies in their approach to higher education development: getting as many students as possible through at the least possible cost. Despite the apparent social justice appeal of this approach, not to mention its desirability in addressing the significant funding shortfalls, it is dangerous as it fails to acknowledge the disparities in quality of provision, and the possibilities that many forms of higher education are providing little in the way of meaningful learning for their students.

While welcoming the renewed support for higher education among international development agencies, therefore, this book presents a critique of their dominant policies. As will be explored further in the chapters that follow, there is an apparent contradiction between the proposed role of higher education in fostering inclusive development, protecting the environment and reducing poverty, and the forms of higher education supported—ones which frequently foster stratification of systems leading to lower quality provision for the least advantaged, as well as promoting irresponsible capitalist development leading to exploitation of workers and destruction of the natural environment. While the emphasis of international agencies on innovation is again very welcome, this notion is too often identified exclusively with the use of technology in delivery of higher education services. Technological developments in higher education as in other sectors are exciting and promising in many ways, but they are one of a range of forms of needed innovation, and cannot provide a solution to all challenges.

But perhaps the most important, and elusive, relationship between education and development is the fact that the former determines the very nature of our conversations and understandings of the latter. Universities influence development not as an ox pulls a cart, but as a potter turns a pot, seeing it gradually taking shape between her hands. It is important, therefore, that we foster the deliberative space that exists in HEIs, and deepen the enquiry that takes place so as to make reflexive and democratic our conception and expression of development. But ultimately these processes interact in a cyclical manner, with education and development constantly conditioning and forging each other. Our task is to make the cycle enriching and generative, rather than reproductive and destructive.

References

Almond, G., & Verba, S. (1963). *The civic culture: Political attitudes and democracy five nations*. London: Sage.
Becker, G. S. (1962, October). Investment in human capital: A theoretical analysis. *Journal of Political Economy, 70*(Suppl.), 9–49.
Beckett, K. (2011). R. S. Peters and the concept of education. *Educational Theory, 61*(3), 239–255.
Bengtsson, S., Barakat, B., & Muttarak, R. (2018). *The role of education in enabling the sustainable development agenda*. London: Routledge.
Boni, A., Lopez-Fogues, A., & Walker, M. (2016). Higher education and the post 2015 agenda: A contribution from the human development approach. *Journal of Global Ethics, 12*(1), 17–28.
Boni, A., & Walker, M. (2013). *Human development and capabilities: Re-imagining the university of the twenty-first century*. London: Routledge.
Boni, A., & Walker, M. (2016). *Universities and global human development: Theoretical and empirical insights for social change*. London: Routledge.
Bowles, S., & Gintis, H. (1976). *Schooling in capitalist America: Educational reform and the contradictions of economic life*. New York: Basic Books.
Bush, K., & Saltarelli, D. (2000). *The two faces of education in ethnic conflict*. Paris: UNICEF Innocenti Research Centre.
Brundtland Commission. (1987). *Our common future* (Report of the World Commission on Environment and Development). Oxford: Oxford University Press.

Bynner, J., Dolton, P., Feinstein, L., Makepiece, G., Malmberg, L., & Woods, L. (2003). *Revisiting the benefits of higher education: A report by the Bedford Group for Lifecourse and Statistical Studies, Institute of Education*. Bristol: Higher Education Funding Council for England.

Castells, M. (1994). The university system: Engine of development in the new world economy. In J. Salmi & A. Verspoor (Eds.), *Revitalizing higher education* (pp. 14–40). Oxford: Pergamon.

Coleman, J. S., Campbell, E. Q., Hobson, C. F., McPartland, J., Mood, A. M., Weinfeld, F. D., et al. (1966). *Equality of educational opportunity*. Washington, DC: U. S. Office of Education.

Dewey, J. (1966 [1916]). *Democracy and education*. New York: MacMillan.

Diamond, J. M. (1997). *Guns germs and steel: The fate of human societies*. New York: W. W. Norton.

Fraser, N. (1998). From redistribution to recognition? Dilemmas of justice in a 'post-socialist' age. In A. Philipps (Ed.), *Feminism and politics*. New York: Oxford University Press.

Freire, P. (1970). *Pedagogy of the oppressed*. London: Penguin Books.

Garrod, N., & Macfarlane, B. (2009). *Challenging boundaries: Managing the integration of post-secondary education*. Abingdon: Routledge.

Giroux, H., & McLaren, P. (1986). Teacher education and the politics of engagement: The case for democratic schooling. *Harvard Educational Review, 56*(3), 213–240.

Green, A. (1990). *Education and state formation: the rise of education systems in England, France and the USA*. London: Macmillan.

Hanushek, E. (2013). Economic growth in developing countries: The role of human capital. *Economics of Education Review, 73*, 204–212.

Hanushek, E., & Woessmann, L. (2008). The role of cognitive skills in economic development. *Journal of Economic Literature, 46*(3), 607–668.

hooks, b. (1994). *Teaching to transgress: Education as the practice of freedom*. London: Routledge.

Huntington, S., & Nelson, J. (1976). *No easy choice: Political participation in developing countries*. Cambridge, MA: Harvard University Press.

Klees, S. J. (2016). Human capital and rates of return: Brilliant ideas or ideological dead ends? *Comparative Education Review, 60*(4), 644–672.

Lucas, R. E. (1988). On the mechanics of development. *Journal of Monetary Economics, 22*(1), 3–42.

Luescher-Mamashela, T. M., Kiiru, S., Mattes, R., Mwollo-ntallima, A., Ng'ethe, N., & Romo, M. (2011). *The university in Africa and democratic citizenship: Hothouse or training ground?* Wynberg: Centre for Higher Education Transformation.

Mamdani, M. (2018). The African university. *London Review of Books, 40*(14), 29–32.

Marginson, S. (2016). The worldwide trend to high participation higher education: Dynamics of social stratification in inclusive systems. *Higher Education, 72,* 413–434.

Marginson, S. (2017). Limitations of human capital theory. *Studies in Higher Education, 44*(2), 287–301.

Martin, C. (2018). Political authority, personal autonomy and higher education. *Philosophical Inquiry in Education, 25*(2), 154–170.

Mazrui, A. A. (1975). The African university as a multinational corporation: Problems of penetration and dependency. *Harvard Educational Review, 45,* 198.

McCowan, T. (2004). The growth of private higher education in Brazil: Implications for equity and quality. *Journal of Education Policy, 19*(4), 453–472.

McCowan, T. (2009). *Rethinking citizenship education: A curriculum for participatory democracy.* London: Continuum.

McCowan, T. (2013). *Education as a human right: Principles for a universal entitlement to learning.* London: Bloomsbury.

McCowan, T. (2015). Theories of development. In T. McCowan & E. Unterhalter (Eds.), *Education and international development: An introduction.* London: Bloomsbury.

McCowan, T., Ananga, E., Oanda, I., Sifuna, D., Ongwenyi, Z., Adedeji, S., et al. (2015). *Students in the driving seat: Young people's views on higher education in Africa* (Research Report). Manchester: British Council.

McGrath, S. (2010). The role of education in development: An educationalist's response to some recent work in development economics. *Comparative Education, 46,* 237–253.

McGrath, S. (2014). The post-2015 debate and the place of education in development thinking. *International Journal of Educational Development, 39,* 4–11.

McMahon, W. W. (2009). *Higher learning, greater good.* Baltimore: John Hopkins Press.

Milbrath, L., & Goel, M. (1977). *Political participation: How and why do people get involved in politics?* (2nd ed.). Chicago: Rand McNally College.

Milton, S. (2019). Syrian higher education during conflict: Survival, protection, and regime security. *International Journal of Educational Development, 64,* 38–47.

Milton, S., & Barakat, S. (2016). Higher education as the catalyst of recovery in conflict-affected societies. *Globalisation, Societies and Education, 14*(3), 403–421.

Mincer, J. (1981). Human capital and economic growth (Working Paper 80). Cambridge, MA: National Bureau of Economic Research. http://www.nber.org/papers/w0803.pdf.

Newman, J. H. (1947 [1852]). *The idea of the university: Defined and illustrated*. London: Longmans, Green.

Novelli, M., & Lopez Cardozo, M. (2008). Conflict, education and the global south: New critical directions. *International Journal of Educational Development, 28*(4), 473–488.

Nussbaum, M. (2000). *Women and human development: The capabilities approach*. Cambridge, MA: Cambridge University Press.

Oketch, M. O., McCowan, T., & Schendel, R. (2014). *The impact of tertiary education on development: A rigorous literature review*. London: Department for International Development.

Parsons, S., & Bynner, J. (2002). *Basic skills and political and community participation: Findings from a study of adults born in 1958 and 1970*. London: Basic Skills Agency.

Perkin, H. (2007). History of universities. In J. J. F. Forest & P. G. Altbach (Eds.), *International handbook of higher education* (pp. 159–206). Dordrecht: Springer.

Peters, R. S. (1966). *Ethics and education*. London: George Allen and Unwin.

Pherali, T., & Lewis, A. (2019). Developing global partnerships in higher education for peacebuilding: A strategy for pathways to impact. *Higher Education*. https://doi.org/10.1007/s10734-019-00367-7.

Prakash, M. S., & Esteva, G. (2008). *Escaping education: Living as learning in grassroots cultures* (2nd ed.). New York: Peter Lang.

Rist, G. (2002). *The history of development: From western origins to global faith*. London: Zed Books.

Robertson, S. (2016). Piketty, capital and education: A solution to, or problem in, rising social inequalities? *British Journal of Sociology of Education, 37*(6), 823–835.

Romer, P. M. (1986). Increasing returns and long-run growth. *The Journal of Political Economy, 94*(5), 1002–1037.

Sachs, J. D. (2008). *Common wealth: Economics*. New York: Penguin Press.

Santos, B. de S. (2015). *Epistemologies of the south: Justice against epistemicide*. New York: Routledge.

Schultz, T. W. (1961). Investment in human capital. *American Economic Review, 51,* 1–17.
Sen, A. (1992). *Inequality re-examined.* Oxford: Clarendon Press.
Sen, A. (1999a). *Development as freedom.* New York: Oxford University Press.
Sen, A. (1999b). Democracy as a universal value. *Journal of Democracy, 10*(3), 3–17.
Smith, A., & Vaux, T. (2003). *Education, conflict and international development.* London: DFID.
Stewart, F. (1985). *Planning to meet basic needs.* London: Macmillan.
Stiglitz, J. E. (2007). *Making globalization work.* London: Allen Lane.
Streeten, P. (1977). The basic features of a basic needs approach to development. *International Development Review, 3,* 8–16.
Takayama, K., Sriprakash, A., & Connell, R. (2015). Rethinking Knowledge production and circulation in comparative and international education: Southern theory, postcolonial perspectives, and alternative epistemologies. *Comparative Education Review, 59*(1), v–viii.
Tilak, J. B. G. (2003). Higher education and development in Asia. *Journal of Educational Planning and Administration, 17*(2), 151–173.
Tomaševski, K. (2001). *Human rights obligations: Making education available, accessible, acceptable and adaptable.* Right to Education Primers No. 3. Gothenburg: Novum Grafiska.
Unterhalter, E. (2003). The capabilities approach and gendered education: An examination of South African complexities. *Theory and Research in Education, 1*(1), 7–22.
Willis, P. (1978). *Learning to Labour: How working class kids get working class jobs.* Aldershot Gower: Saxon House/Teakfield.
Winch, C. (2006). Graduate attributes and changing conceptions of learning. In P. Hager & S. Holland (Eds.), *Graduate attributes, learning and employability* (pp. 67–89). Dordrecht: Springer.
Wolff, J., & de-Shalit, A. (2013). On fertile functionings: A response to Martha Nussbaum. *Journal of Human Development and Capabilities,* 14(1), 161–165.
World Bank. (1999). *Knowledge for development.* World Development Report. New York: Oxford University Press.

3

The Anatomy of the University

If we peel away the layers of the university—and there are many—is there a kernel at the centre? Is there something we can point to that is the essence of university-ness? Or can we determine the essential features of the outer appearance of the institution and assess other entities in accordance with them? And if we cannot do these things, how indeed can we determine what the quality of a university is, or indeed if something is a university at all?

Defining the university, similarly to defining education, is a descriptive and normative venture. In part, it involves observations of actually occurring universities through history, and across space, and deriving from them a set of essential properties. As with all areas of human experience, this process involves significant challenges of determining whether everything that goes by the name of the university is in fact a university, and if not, what coherent boundaries we might place on the notion. Yet it is also a normative task, as by defining what we mean by university, we are very often asserting what we would like the university to be. We might argue, for example, following Newman (1947 [1852]), that the university should be understood as a site for the deep cultivation of the intellect and the transformation of the person, but we would have to recognise that not all universities in practice may achieve this aim.

Writings and debates on higher education frequently merge the descriptive and normative dimensions. Frequently we hear assertions that we are living in the age of, say, the post-industrial or networked or information age university: it is not always clear whether this is a claim that universities in practice have divested themselves of the industrial and preindustrial age, or alternatively a demand or a hope for them to do so. One of the tasks of this book in fact is to disentangle the normative from the descriptive and shine light on both—not because we need to disinfect our decisions from ideology (as argued by the 'what works' movement), but because we need a full and open debate about what we want to achieve, as well as gathering evidence on how it is achieved in practice.

The task of determining what the university is and should be has been made even more challenging by the increasing complexity of the institution since the early twentieth century. Most famously represented in Clark Kerr's (1963) 'multiversity', the institution is no longer just a space in which a community of students receives instruction from a community of scholars, but a vast enterprise involving formal courses at many levels, online and face-to-face provision, research, consultancy, student services, accommodation, sports, hospitals, spin-off businesses, community services and much more. 'But where is the university?' asked a visitor, after being shown the University of Oxford's numerous colleges, libraries, laboratories, playing fields and museums, in the well-known anecdote related by Gilbert Ryle (1949)—and that was before the emergence of many of the contemporary university's services.

While this book does not provide a detailed history of the university (comprehensive accounts can be found in Anderson 2004; Carpentier 2019; Perkin 2007; Rüeg 1992, etc.), engagement with historical manifestations of the institution can illuminate analysis of contemporary ones. The chapter discusses four models of the university: the mediaeval, the Humboldtian, the developmental and the entrepreneurial. These are engaged with in the full awareness that they are to some extent historical fictions, and never existed in a pure form: they are constructed from actual practices of the times together with ideal depictions.

Nevertheless, while we cannot point to a 'pure' Humboldtian university, for example, as an ideal type the idea is useful in illuminating the various influences moving the institution in different directions through history. While we live primarily in the era of the entrepreneurial university, it will be argued that all of these models continue to live on within our contemporary institutions, though with different types of 'mix' depending on the country and institution in question—leading in some cases to a 'schizophrenic' identity, in the view of Shore (2010).

As discussed further below, the four models chosen for the purposes of this article are not the only possible categorisation, but highlight the dimensions most relevant to the debates in this book. The developmental model corresponds most closely to the ideal vision of higher education outlined in the SDGs and in the development plans of supranational and national agencies. It will, therefore, have a more prolonged treatment than the other models in the chapter that follows. However, all of these models have some relevance to the trajectories of development of their societies—whether constructive or destructive, through engagement or disengagement—and all have influenced contemporary institutions. The key elements of these models (drawing on the accounts of Barnett 1990; Carpentier 2019; Clark 1998; Kerr 1963; Perkin 2007; Wissema 2009) are outlined in the section that follows.

A further clarification on scope is required. The discussion here focuses on the tradition in higher learning associated with the term 'university', originating in Europe. As discussed in the previous chapters, it is important to remember that the university (now the dominant form) is just one of many traditions of higher education around the world, from Buddhist monasteries in India, to the mosques in North Africa, and the training of scribes in Mayan Mesoamerica and in Mesopotamia. Furthermore, within all systems there is institutional differentiation, and many non-university institutions—specialised colleges, polytechnics, etc.—will not have all of the characteristics discussed here.

From the discussion of the models, this chapter derives an analytical tool for understanding the university, comprised of three elements: value, function and interaction. These three dimensions are the crucial determinants of the role that higher education plays in development, in describing the institution's purpose and principles, its action and practices, and finally its relationship with the society outside. This tool serves to identify significant differences between institutions and models of institution, as well as areas in which interventions might be made—and in particular, in identifying the characteristics of a university that might effectively serve to achieve the SDGs.

What is presented in this chapter is a structural account, one that abstracts from the realities of our lived institutions to construct a theoretical framing which can be applied to the diversity of actual instances. As such, it suffers from the defects of all human derivations from the touch and feel of the material world. Nevertheless, it is not proposed as a universal explanatory scheme, but as a portrayal of anatomy, a sketch of the inner workings of the institution that can aid in our understanding of its functioning and impact. To fully understand the organism, it is necessary to observe the unique experience of institutions in practice, in interaction with their diverse contexts.

Models of the University

Mediaeval

The first universities in Europe were essentially *communities* of scholars: in the case of Bologna, a community of students, and in the case of Paris, a community of teachers—the latter model with time becoming dominant. The scholars organised themselves into guilds largely for their own protection and guarded their autonomy jealously from their host cities and states, with which they were sometimes in conflict These were highly international institutions, with scholars from many countries circulating around the different centres of learning.

The task of the university was primarily to transmit to students the bodies of knowledge inherited from the classical world and the Christian theological tradition, combining a broad-based education in the *trivium* (grammar, rhetoric and dialectic) and the *quadrivium* (music, arithmetic, geometry and astronomy) with specialisations in areas of law, theology or medicine. While there was a strong religious influence, and they could trace their origins to monastic schools, relations between universities and the Church varied, with the critical examination of biblical texts, and engagement with classical texts via Arabic scholars, a potential danger to orthodoxy.

Barnett (1990: 19) identifies the characteristics of the mediaeval university as:

> a participative approach to learning and enquiry, a collaborative form of internal government, institutional autonomy, institutions open to all-comers, and a belief in the value of study in itself tempered by a critical discourse.

The conception of knowledge dominating the institution—and indeed the age—was one of the primacy of authoritative texts: while there was vigorous debate and argumentation, the task was to interpret, understand and elaborate on respected theorists, rather than create new knowledge. The mediaeval university then had a primary function of conservation, transmission and interpretation of knowledge, although it also served an important purpose of training professionals in specific areas.

Humboldtian

The early form of university proved remarkably successful for a number of centuries, but began to lose relevance in the eighteenth century with the radically changing ideas of the Enlightenment and the emergence of scholarly societies in which much scientific enquiry took place. However, a new chapter in the history of universities was initiated with the creation of the University of Berlin in 1810 by Wilhelm von Humboldt. The new model of university—which would subsequently go on to provide the blueprint for research universities worldwide—placed academics now in the role of creators or discoverers of knowledge, rather than simply custodians.

While there were stronger links between universities and the nation-state in this period, principles of academic freedom were introduced, allowing scholars to develop new lines of enquiry in accordance with the pursuit of truth. New disciplines and degrees were introduced in the course of the nineteenth century—including engineering and accountancy—reflecting the gathering pace of the industrial revolution as well as changes in scientific enquiry, and the need for new forms of professional. While historians such as Nybom (2003, 2007) argue that in reality the Humboldtian university was short-lived and inadequately implemented, Humboldt's ideas have had a profound influence on the institution, and laid the basis for the later US research university.

Developmental

These initial openings of the university to the more practical world of work and economic production were hard to reverse. In nineteenth-century USA a number of 'land-grant' universities were created with a distinct remit for contributing to local development, through fostering technical skills for agriculture and industry. These institutions were seen as forerunners of the later 'developmental university', a term emerging in the twentieth century to describe the new emphasis in institutions in the developing world, particularly Africa, and endorsed by the Association of African Universities (Coleman 1986; Yesufu and AAU 1973). The primary characteristic of the developmental model is that universities are explicitly oriented towards those activities that will enable the development of the economy and society, particularly in what might be considered 'underdeveloped' regions.

A parallel current had also been seen in Latin America from the reforms at the University of Córdoba in 1918 that went on to influence public universities across the region, and to place the third pillar of 'extension' or public service on a par with teaching and research (Bernasconi 2007). Through the twentieth century, service has become a key mission of the university, and there has been an increasing pressure on institutions to engage with non-academic communities and bring concrete benefits to society.

Entrepreneurial

More recently, in the context of expanding enrolments and declining proportions of public funding, institutions have had to become more financially savvy and self-sufficient, leading to the emergence of the entrepreneurial or 'enterprise' university (Marginson and Considine 2000). This shift has involved changes in the curriculum, funding, the nature of knowledge production and academic work—leading to what Slaughter and Leslie (1997) have termed academic capitalism. While the term 'entrepreneurial university' is used by some proponents (e.g. Shattock 2009) to emphasise the innovative and risk-taking nature of certain contemporary institutions, in this study the term is used to designate the reorientation of the institution towards income generation, in the context of the loss of non-market revenue streams.

Moves towards the entrepreneurial model have both pragmatic and ideological roots: the former due to increasing constraints on public funding, particularly in the context of the costs of rising enrolments; and the latter due to the rise of neoliberal ideas from the 1980s. Universities in this conception need to be enterprising within the market: instead of conserving or pursuing truth or serving society, they need to identify and provide products that can be sold in the marketplace so as to ensure their financial viability. Fees are introduced for taught courses, with universities competing for students and creating new courses in response to market demand; research is tailored increasingly towards the demands of industry and at least in part funded by the private sector; public service now becomes third stream income-generation activities of consultancy and other services. As expressed in Wissema's (2009) 'third generation' university, the entrepreneurial university may aim to become a technology hub, as seen in Silicon Valley or Cambridge at the heart of a web of high-tech companies with constant cross-fertilisation and mutual financial benefit. These characteristics undoubtedly form the dominant model in contemporary times, although the entrepreneurial university has not completely superseded the previous forms, and many ideas and practices from mediaeval, Humboldtian and other models are still present in our contemporary institutions.

Other Models

This chapter has not attempted to provide a comprehensive history of the university or a typology of all models of institution. Instead, it has highlighted four primary models—mediaeval, Humboldtian, developmental and entrepreneurial—which have an analytical purpose in outlining key characteristics of the institution, and assist in building the theoretical frame of value, function and interaction. To a large extent, they are reflections of dominant political and intellectual currents of their day—scholasticism, liberalism, pragmatism, neoliberalism and others. As outlined above, it must be borne in mind that these are something of an artifice: they neither represent historical periods neatly succeeding one another, nor are they isolated or identifiable singularly within an actual university. They are a construction of ideas—derived in part from observing the movements of universities through the ages, and in part from the normative writings of theorists, critics and reformers. In spite of that, they are useful in allowing us to identify competing visions of the institution, ones which can still be seen to jostle for space in our contemporary universities.

There are other models that could be considered. The Napoleonic university in nineteenth-century France is often included in categorisations of institutional types, given its distinctive characteristics in terms of focus on new technical areas of learning, emphasis on professional education, the separation between faculties, separate elite institutions (*grandes écoles*) at the top of the pyramid, centralised and coordinated management and the conducting of teaching and research in distinct institutions (Anderson 2004). In many ways it does represent a shift from the mediaeval university, in its forms of organisation for example: at the same time, it is not as dramatic a move as the Humboldtian model, as it continues essentially the same emphasis on transmission of bodies of knowledge within specified professional areas, rather than production of new knowledge. So it has not been considered as a separate model here—although its strong influence on the systems of many countries is acknowledged, not only in France, but also Spain, Portugal and Italy, and across most of Latin America, and other former colonies of those countries.

The 'multiversity' discussed above could also be considered a distinct model, as could the English tradition of character-building undergraduate education in the Oxbridge mould. More recently there have been discussions of the welfare university (Molebatsi 2018), the postmodern university (Smith and Webster 1997), the university of excellence (Readings 1996), and the digital university (Goodfellow and Lea 2013). We might even think of the 'world-class university' (for all its elusiveness) as a type. Furthermore, there has been diversification of institutional forms in distinct geographical and cultural contexts, such as the Nordic university (Välimaa 2018), the Latin American university (Bernasconi 2007) and the post-Confucian university (Marginson 2014).

Or we could look at entirely different forms of categorisation. Wissema (2009) makes a distinction between first, second and third generation universities: the first corresponding to the mediaeval institution, the second for the most part to the Humboldtian and the third to the university as technology hub, incorporating elements of the entrepreneurial model. Etzkowitz et al. (2000), in a similar vein, distinguish three phases, with a 'first academic revolution' moving the institution from transmission to production of knowledge, and the second, 'the assumption of a role in economic development through extensions of both their research and teaching missions' to become the entrepreneurial university.

Furthermore, there are also models of institution proposed with an entirely normative orientation—without claiming to have a basis in current empirical or historical reality. So, most famously we have Newman's (1947 [1852]) idea of the university in the nineteenth century, Karl Jaspers's (1960) and Michael Oakeshott's (1989) in the twentieth, and more recently there is Barnett's (2017) ecological model and Selingo's (2017) networked university. Zgaga (2009) adds a 'Deweyan' model with the goal 'to prepare citizens for active life in a democratic society' (p. 180) to the Napoleonic, Humboldtian and Newmanian in his set of four 'archetypal models'. As discussed above, while categorisations may pertain to be either describing historical reality or putting forward an ideal scheme, in some cases they are merging the two: quite often this is the case with the final step in the progression—for example Wissema's third generation—in which it is presented as an inevitability, but actually presents a value-laden (and highly contested) vision.

So there is a degree of arbitrariness in the choice of the four models covered in this chapter. Nevertheless, it is held that they cover distinctive and significant emphases of the university, and so are generative for our understanding of the institution. Yet what is it in these four models of university that distinguishes them meaningfully from each other—beyond the obvious links to the prevailing epistemological and political currents of their time?

Value, Function and Interaction

This book adopts an analytical framework of three components—value, function and interaction—in order to identify salient characteristics of the institution. First, there are differences in the fundamental justification for the existence of the university—the *why* of higher education. This can be termed the *value* dimension. Second, there are differences in what the university actually does, the range of activities and roles that it fulfils, which can be termed the *function* dimension. Third, there are differences in the way the university relates to the outside society, and the movement of peoples and ideas inwards and outwards—the *interaction* dimension.

Value

The value attached to the university revolves largely around the axis of intrinsic versus instrumental worth. On the one hand, the knowledge stored, generated and transmitted by the university might be seen to be intrinsically valuable, being worthwhile in itself without any further justification. Alternatively, the knowledge in question might serve an instrumental purpose, in contributing to individual and societal goals, and interests of an economic, political or cultural nature. Instrumental or extrinsic is here taken to mean that the value of an activity resides outside itself, whereas intrinsic indicates that it has reached its 'resting place' and as a source of value in itself.

The best-known expression of the intrinsic value of university education is Cardinal Newman's *The Idea of a University Defined and Illustrated* (1947 [1852]). In this work, in which he defends a model of liberal education in the establishment of a new Catholic university in Dublin, he asserts that:

> I am asked what is the end of University Education, and of the Liberal or Philosophical Knowledge which I conceive it to impart: I answer, that what I have already said has been sufficient to show that it has a very tangible, real, and sufficient end, though the end cannot be divided from that knowledge itself. Knowledge is capable of being its own end. Such is the constitution of the human mind, that any kind of knowledge, if it be really such, is its own reward. (p. 128)

Newman is here referring to knowledge acquired through teaching and learning, although we could apply the same idea to research and scholarship. There may of course be some combination of these, with intrinsic and instrumental value not being mutually exclusive categories. (So, we might hold that there is intrinsic worth in furthering human understanding of the deep structures of language, while also valuing its contribution to developing computer programming.)

The dimension of value concerns not only the extent to which knowledge is instrumental rather than intrinsic, but also the purpose of the instrumental activity. So, the knowledge produced by the university could be instrumental in strengthening the military capacity of a nation in order to conquer its rivals, or alternatively it could function to produce globally available cures for diseases. In relation to graduate outcomes, we can distinguish between economic ends—associated with human capital theory—and broader conceptions of outcome in terms of developing freedoms to pursue one's life goals, such as those associated with the capabilities approach (Boni and Walker 2013, 2016).

The value dimension, therefore, leads us to a consideration of the private or public benefit of the goods produced by higher education, and the locus of benefit at local, national and global levels (Marginson 2014; Bloom et al. 2006; Tilak 2008). This topic has had significant attention in the field of higher education in recent years, spawning a wealth of literature, mainly critical of the processes of commodification and privatisation of the sector which are seen as crowding out the possibilities providing public benefit (e.g. Calhoun 2006; Locatelli 2017; Marginson 2007, 2011, 2016, 2018; Nixon 2011; Singh 2012).

Marginson's (2011) well-known account provides a distinction between countable conceptions of public goods common in economics, characterised by their non-rivalrous and non-excludable nature, the singular public good with a more normative and collective orientation, and the public sphere, as a space for interaction and deliberation. All three of these relationships can be observed clearly in higher education. Through research, teaching and community engagement functions, universities produce a range of goods—as will be outlined more fully in Chapter 8. Knowledge in many ways is a quintessential public good, since it is hard to confine to certain individuals and groups (even though it may initially be acquired only by certain individuals, or restricted to a corporation by intellectual property rights). Stiglitz's (1999) exploration of the public nature of knowledge shows furthermore how it ultimately constitutes a *global* public good, moving beyond even national boundaries. The singular collective public good is also promoted by universities, through the impacts outlined above, but also in shaping narratives around society, community and nation, and around the nature of the good. Finally, the university functions as an important space for deliberation and communication—a public sphere in the Habermasian sense—in which ideas are formed and scrutinised. The role of the university as a critical friend to the state (sometimes more friendly, sometimes more critical) is an important one, though these kinds of direct entries into the political sphere also create challenges for the institution.

Finally, there is the associated notion of 'common good': while this expression is used by some as being synonymous with public good, it carries with it more of the processual dimension, relating to the coming together of diverse individuals and groups into a common practice. As Deneulin and Townsend (2007: 25) state:

> [T]he common good is not the outcome of a collective action which makes everybody better off than if they acted individually, but is the good of that shared enterprise itself. It is the good of the community which comes into being in and through that enterprise.

While most of the literature has been generated in relation to Europe and North America, recent research projects have explored public good in the context of Africa (Unterhalter et al. 2017) and East Asia (Tian and

Liu 2018, 2019; Yang 2017) and Global South conceptualisations of the notion are discussed in Walker (2018).

While knowledge is ultimately hard to restrict, there are benefits of higher education that can be private: for example, access to places in elite institutions—in this case, the good in question is not only knowledge, but also the diploma, which carries exchange value that goes beyond the knowledge acquired. The private returns resulting from direct access to higher education courses include increased employment opportunities and higher salaries, but also a range of other non-market benefits. Private returns can also be obtained for companies or other groups commissioning research or consultancy, though as discussed above, it is hard to retain the private nature of this benefit indefinitely.

In contrast to public good, private good appears altogether more straightforward, relating to individuals or groups obtaining and confining the good to themselves, possible only in the cases of excludable or rivalrous goods. However, there are challenges to the notion of 'private' as well: South African writers (e.g. Masehela 2018; Mathebula and Calitz 2018) have alluded to the fact that the so-called private returns to graduates from traditional communities are often shared with the extended family (known colloquially as the 'black tax'), in the context of partial absence of the welfare state, thereby questioning a firm barrier between public and private.

While we would expect a correspondence between the public or private nature of an institution and the benefits it brings, public institutions can generate private goods (e.g. highly remunerated jobs for business executives), and private institutions can generate public goods (e.g. medical research carried out by Ivy League universities). Universities inevitably have both private and public goods—as argued by Marginson (2007)—and the mixture depends on their practices and choices. The extent of private and public benefit generated has obvious implications for the funding of higher education, and of whether it is legitimate to charge fees to students—as discussed further in the chapters that follow.

The value dimension of the university also relates to equality, involving both *import* and *export* roles of the university in Brennan and Naidoo's (2008) terms, referring to equality of opportunity for students entering the university, and subsequent impact on equality in the outside society. There has been extensive policy and research attention on the former, relating to equitable admissions procedures (e.g. Meyer et al. 2013; Mountford-Zimdars and Sabbagh 2013), but less so on the latter, relating to the impact of teaching, research and other activities on equality, as seen in Walker et al.'s (2009) study of pro-poor professionals.

A subspecies of instrumental value is *positional* value—a person's opportunities and benefits relative to others, in areas of scarcity in which there is a zero-sum game, for example, high-value employment opportunities (Unterhalter and Brighouse 2007). Positional advantage may be obtained through screening or signalling functions of education, even when there is no tangible instrumental benefit gained through learning (McCowan 2015). Higher education is particularly influential in relation to positional goods, and historically has acted as a key mechanism for maintenance and sometimes intensification of elite privilege in relation to wealth and political power.

There is an ambiguity when we speak of value, however, as regards whether we are referring to intentions and principles, or alternatively outcomes. There is a chronological dimension to this, in the sense of the value intended at the start of the process as opposed to the value achieved at the end of it. But more significantly, there is a difference between 'value' understood, on the one hand, as something subjective and inherently internal to the human being in her interaction with the world (as in the use of 'values', 'moral values' and 'aesthetic values', etc.); and, on the other, value understood as something objective, or at least intersubjective, something actually occurring or existing in the world (for example, 'what's the value of that vase', or 'what value did that bring to our negotiations?').

Both of these are evident in relation to higher education. On the one hand we have the things that people find of value: the view that university education should be an opportunity to achieve emancipation from the shackles of ignorance of self and universe, or alternatively an initiation into a professional practice that will provide a secure livelihood for oneself and one's family. And on the other hand, we can observe the extent to which this value is actually provided: what kind of learning do graduates come out with, and what are the employment rates and salary dividends achieved? One important instance of the difference between these two perspectives is positional value. While universities certainly assist graduates in gaining advantage over others without aggregate benefit to society, these positional benefits are rarely proposed as explicit goals of universities (although entrepreneurial universities frequently advertise the benefits of their degrees in the labour market).

For the most part, in this book the notion of value will be used in the former sense—to indicate the principles (of an epistemic, moral and political nature) that orient the university's behaviour. The actual outcomes will instead be referred to by other terms such as 'impact', as explored in Chapter 8.

There is a further question of the extent to which value, as used here, relates to the *aims* of a university. There are certainly differences between these two concepts, but in the case of education—which necessarily involves purposeful action aligned with the achieving of an intention—they are closely associated. The only exception here being that in the case of intrinsic value, it may not be possible to distinguish the means or process, from the ends or aims.

Another important question (in relation to the subjective notion of value) is that of who holds the university's value. Is it the community of scholars, which formed the backbone of early institutions such as the University of Paris, or perhaps the community of students as in Bologna? Or in our current managerial times, is it university leaders, vice chancellors and their administrative directors? Or perhaps it is contained somewhere within the mission of the university, independently of any specific individual or group? And are we only talking about the value held by those directly involved in the university, or the broader society? For sure, it is also possible to trace the changing perceptions of and values attached to the university among the general population in each successive age, and across contexts. The truth is that in real institutions, these different groups are rarely aligned (see Shields and Watermeyer 2018), and all can make a claim in some way to 'be' the university. Bacevic (2019: 3) goes further in putting forward the idea of the university as assemblage—'Rather than as a stable or bounded entity, an agent can thus be thought of as a network or "bundle" of objects, persons, and relations, which change over time'. So all of our attributions of values to the institution must bear in mind their contested nature, and that what we are determining is tendencies or leanings, and not precise attributes.

Function

Function relates to the concrete activities undertaken by the institution. There are different ways of categorising these activities. Most commonly, the triad of teaching, research and community engagement or public service is used as a frame for understanding the functions of the university—sometimes in an official or constitutional form, as in Brazil, or in a de facto sense. Within these three, there are a range of possibilities. Teaching can be focused on particular disciplinary areas, or can categorise disciplinary areas in different ways. There are also differences in relation to the balance between undergraduate and graduate study, in providing for a more professional or more academic formation and so forth. 'Research' so to speak only becomes a function of the university with the advent of the Humboldtian model, but is now a core activity of many institutions—and in elite universities, the most valued of all activities. Nevertheless, the majority of higher education expansion across the world is taking place in teaching only institutions (Altbach et al. 2009)—at least in the sense of not engaging in coordinated and funded research projects (although some would argue that all university staff do or at least should engage in research in the broader sense of scholarly enquiry and exploration).

Finally, there is community engagement (alternatively known as service, public service, public engagement or extension). This is the least clearly defined of the three pillars, and the most uneven in terms of coverage. In Latin American countries, it has an explicitly social justice character, sharing the fruits of the (public) university with the general population—viewed as an obligation on account of the university's public nature. In Anglo-Saxon countries, community engagement has largely morphed into 'third stream' activities, understood as commercial opportunities. More progressive approaches have re-conceptualised 'knowledge transfer' as 'knowledge exchange', allowing for the community's ideas to enter the university as well.

However, these broad categories do not exhaust the specific activities undertaken, nor the ways in which we might understand those activities. The World Declaration on Higher Education of 1998 (UNESCO 1998) provides a more extensive outline of the missions of higher education in Article 1 (providing a kind of melding between 'value' and 'function'):

(a) educate highly qualified professionals
(b) provide opportunities for lifelong learning and citizenship
(c) advance and disseminate knowledge through research
(d) promote and disseminate culture
(e) protect and enhance societal values
(f) contribute to improvement of education at all levels

We might possibly map (a) and (b) onto teaching, (c) onto research, and the remainder onto community engagement—although the fit is not exact (b for example could also come under the latter category). These functions, importantly, relate to the direct 'users' of universities (a, b and c), but also to broader contributions to society (d, e and f).

Moving away from conventional conceptions of the university's activities, we might, alternatively, highlight four primary functions of the university in relation to knowledge:

1. Archiving
2. Production
3. Communication
4. Validation

Universities function as sites for archiving of knowledge, for the maintenance, interpretation, sorting and selection of intellectual traditions and texts. The archiving function was critical for society in the early centuries of the university, and in pre-European universities—as shown by the tragic loss of stores of knowledge caused by the fires at Nalanda University in the late twelfth century. With the advent of the printing press, this role of the university became less critical, and in the digital age has receded even further.

'Production' corresponds to the research function, as outlined above, and the creation or discovery of new knowledge (depending on one's epistemological position). 'Communication' of knowledge mainly corresponds to the teaching function, of imparting it to students, but also relates to community engagement, for example in public dissemination of science, or provision of evening courses for adults. Finally, an important role less discussed is validation, through which the university acts as an arbiter between valid and invalid knowledge. This validation occurs on an individual level through the conferring of diplomas, to certify that a graduate has reached the required level of knowledge in a particular area (and in more applied fields, to practice as a professional); at a more general level, the university validates scientific knowledge through academic journals, by means of the peer review process. Umberto Eco (2013) in his lecture to mark the 25th anniversary of the signing of the Magna Charta Universitatum at the University of Bologna, made reference to this validation role through his idea that the primary purpose of the university in fact is not to remember but to forget: faced with the prodigious quantities of information available in today's world, to decide what is worth keeping and what is not. As will be seen later in the discussion of unbundling, the validation role is rapidly being undermined, particularly in relation to the individual level of the graduate.

There are of course a range of other functions that universities provide outside of these core activities: services such as medical treatment, venues for community and corporate meetings, sporting facilities and events. For students in campus universities, they also find in the university their residence, and spaces for social interaction, recreation and cultural enrichment. The extent of these non-core activities varies dramatically between institutions today, but there has been a general trend towards diversification of function—captured in Clark Kerr's (1963) idea of the *multiversity*. In this idea, the university starts to take on a bewildering array of functions, involving some aspects of the developmental model through its emphasis on service, but defined by its great size, varied functions and units—including, in addition to traditional faculties, hospitals, laboratories, extension centres and a multiplicity of roles in relation to society.

It will be noticed that the term 'function' is here being used in the sense of activity or practice, rather than in the stronger sense of 'role' (since this latter idea encompasses all three aspects of value, function and interaction in the present scheme). This broader sense of role, however, is evident in the categorisation made by Castells (2001), who highlights four functions that 'represent the main tasks performed by universities, with different emphases on one or another according to countries, historical periods and specific institutions'. These are:

1. Generation and transmission of ideology
2. Selection and formation of elites
3. Production and application of new knowledge
4. Training of bureaucracy/skilled labour force

According to his historical analysis, the first two of these functions have always been present in universities—and relate to the longer tradition in sociology referred to by Brennan and Naidoo (2008) of seeing socialisation and selection as the primary roles of higher education. The third, however, emerged with the Humboldtian model, and the fourth—while in some ways always present—has intensified in the contemporary age. There is a further implicit function of surplus labour absorption, given the university's role in delaying young people's entry into the job market. Castells's categories are very much a view of the macro-level—concerning what universities do for society as a whole, and as such are quite different from how an individual student may approach university, or how a lecturer may approach it. (There is also a difference with the position put forward in this book, in that higher education here is seen to have a potentially transformatory and not only a reproductive role.) Furthermore, we need here to distinguish between underlying (or hidden) functions, and explicit ones. Universities would rarely characterise themselves explicitly, or consciously intend to, act as institutional apparatuses or mechanisms for selecting the elites, though they may end up serving this function. This feature, therefore, links back to the discussions in the previous section about positional advantage and the values of the university.

The discussion thus far has focused on which functions the university has (a feature we can term *spread*), but it is also necessary to assess the *weighting* between those functions. Universities may differ significantly in the relative emphasis they place on each, with some, say, being predominantly knowledge production institutions with a little teaching (of graduate students), and others primarily teaching institutions with sporadic research. The influences of these activities on each other are also significant: in many cases taught courses may determine what research is undertaken (if staff are employed to cover the former), in others research agendas may spur new areas teaching. Similar points could be made about the multiplicity of functions of the university outside of teaching and research. In assessing these relationships, we can observe the level of *unity*, that is the extent to which the functions are coherent, or alternatively disparate and unconnected; and second, its *binding*, the ways in which those activities interrelate and condition one another.

Interaction

The university is a distinct institutional entity, and in many cases a physical place with physical boundaries. Yet universities vary considerably in the extent to which they are porous to the outside world, in terms of the human actors able to participate in their activities, and in terms of the flow of ideas. This porosity may express itself in a general sense, or it may be that an institution is porous in some areas, and impermeable in others. We can distinguish here between *inbound* and *outbound* porosity, the ease of flow from society into the university and vice versa.[1] So, in some cases universities are porous in relation to knowledge from other sectors—for example, technological developments from industry—or conversely, are active in translating and communicating the knowledge produced within them to partners outside, say

---

[1] A similar idea to porosity is expressed by the term 'connectivity', as used in the U21 Ranking of National Higher Education Systems, although the latter is often restricted to a technological meaning.

new research on water sterilisation for the local council. Or alternatively they can be more resistant to flow in both of these directions. Academic publishing can be more or less accessible to the public, depending on subscriber-only or alternatively open access formats, as well as the extent to which writing style is opaque, esoteric and jargon-filled. (Clearly, these considerations assume a meaningful boundary between university and society in the first place, an assumption that has been questioned by theorists such as Bacevic [2019], who propose instead understanding these changes in terms of *deterritorialization* and *reterritorialization*.)

The flow relates not only to ideas, but also to actors. We can view access for students as a form of porosity—the extent to which universities are open to a broad range of students or alternatively restrict entry. Also included here is the extent to which universities are permeable to incorporation of professionals from outside in the teaching staff, and open their doors to community members to participate in courses and activities. The idea of 'citizen science', and the involvement of the public in research can also be included here. All of these dimensions of porosity can be seen at different scales: in relation to local communities, the national and the global, thereby linking it into debates over internationalisation.

Within this discussion of interaction, we can also include the question of control and autonomy. Relationships with the society inside involve not only exchange, but also influence, with the history of the university characterised by oscillating levels of independence from various external powers: whether the Church, private patrons, the state or the market. The university has relied on these external authorities for funding, protection and recognition, but at the same time has fought for its autonomy from them, so as to protect its integrity, independence of thought or academic freedom.

Applying the Three Dimensions

When applied to the four models of university outlined above, we can see some marked differences and evolution in the three dimensions. In terms of value, the mediaeval university is known for its conception of intrinsic value of knowledge, though it also had an instrumental role in training professionals. The Humboldtian university continued with a strong sense of the intrinsic value of knowledge, but with an additional instrumental role, contributing to society through research and scientific discoveries and an emerging political role in relation to the nation-state. The developmental university moves away from the intrinsic value of knowledge and has a predominantly instrumental one, closely linked to the interests of society, especially for segments of the population not previously enjoying the fruits of higher education. For the entrepreneurial university, the value of knowledge is primarily in the demand that there might be and the price that can be obtained for it—along with its impact on driving economic growth in the broader society.

There are similarly notable changes in terms of function. The university moves from a role of archiving, scholarship and transmission of bodies of knowledge, to one of original research and discovery, to the application of knowledge to society's problems and finally to its commercialisation. In terms of the third of the dimensions, interaction, we see a progressive movement of opening, from the low porosity mediaeval and Humboldtian models with limited flow of people and ideas, towards a much greater interaction in the developmental university, with the trajectory continuing in the entrepreneurial model.

Table 3.1 summarises the key characteristics for each of the three dimensions. The designations are necessarily reductive—particularly for 'function'—but serve to give an overall characterisation.

We can therefore identify three major trends, one for each of the three dimensions. First, *instrumentalisation*, a movement from valuing knowledge for its intrinsic worth towards its instrumental worth; second, *application* of knowledge, of employing theoretical ideas increasingly for practical ends; and third, *opening*, as universities become more porous with the outside world. The implications of these trends for development will be drawn out in greater detail in the chapters that follow.

Table 3.1 Anatomy of four models of university

	Value	Function	Interaction
Mediaeval	Intrinsic (+instrumental)	Stewardship and transmission	Low porosity
Humboldtian	Intrinsic (+instrumental)	Discovery	Low porosity
Developmental	Instrumental (service)	Application	Medium porosity
Entrepreneurial	Instrumental (economic)	Commercialisation	High porosity

Relationships Between the Three Dimensions

Thus far we have discussed these three dimensions in isolation. But what relationship exists between them? Some interlinkages are evident: it would be impossible for an instrumental conception of the university not to have any porosity with the outside world; some functions—such as the existence of a university hospital and adult education courses for the local community—would also necessarily involve interaction. Likewise, a strong intrinsic value attached to knowledge would encourage the functions of archiving and maintenance of that knowledge, while the authoritative value given to historical texts in the mediaeval university would encourage low porosity.

It is also important to observe the relative influence of the three. The most logical approach would be for the values underpinning an institution to determine its functions and interactions. So, a university may take as its starting point the bolstering of a nation-state that has recently gained independence: its values would be those of national unity, social cohesion, strengthening of national culture and language, and furthering state interests. Its functions would therefore include taught courses in national language, literature and history, as well as professional courses for strengthening national bureaucracy, with research oriented towards national development priorities and a close bidirectional relationship with the state.

Yet this is far from being the only kind of relationship that can exist between value, function and interaction. In many cases, convention dictates what the functions of the university are. So subjects may be taught because they have always been taught, and lines of enquiry may be pursued in order to continue the traditions of academic mentors and lineages. Values and forms of interaction thereby emerge from the practices themselves. We can call this the 'traditional' mode of relationship, in contrast to the 'mission-led' mode outlined above.

Finally, the process may be led by forms of interaction, according to what we may call the 'responsive' mode. In this case, opening to the ideas of the broader society and influence of decision-making of external stakeholders can determine what the university does and how it values its activities. So, for example, growth of popular interest in virtual reality can lead to increasing activities of teaching and research in these areas, as well as towards application of basic science to technological innovation. The response made may be democratic the sense of attending equally to all external communities—but a subspecies of the responsive mode is market-based, in which the interaction-centred influences are mediated by transactional relationships. As will be discussed further below, in the contemporary world institutions are dominated by the market mode, although with evidence of non-market democratic, traditional and occasionally mission-led modes as well.

The three modes, therefore, are as follows:

- *Mission-led mode*: value determines function and interaction
- *Traditional mode*: function determines value and interaction
- *Responsive mode*: interaction determines value and function

We can associate these modes with the models of institution outlined above.

- Mediaeval—Traditional
- Humboldtian—Mission-led
- Developmental—Responsive (state/democratic)
- Entrepreneurial—Responsive (market)

The mediaeval university has function as its leading dimension, as it is oriented around a set of practices of teaching and debate. In contrast, it is the values of disciplinary exploration that orient the Humboldtian model, with activities and interactions emerging from them. Function and value are determined by the priorities of the state and outside society in the case of the developmental model, with a similar orientation for the entrepreneurial model, except that led by the market.

The practical importance of this frame resides in the simple point that changing the university depends on an understanding of how its practice is formed—whether through aligning of activities with a mission, with custom and convention or with external demands, or some combination of these. Equally, proposals for reform of the sector—for example, led in the mission mode through the values presented in the SDGs, or alternatively becoming more responsive to local communities—need to acknowledge the ways in which the institution's actions may also be determined by the other modes.

The 'traditional' mode in which function leads the other dimensions of value and interaction is problematic as it may involve a blind adherence to tradition and custom, or a laziness or complacency in terms of change. In this mode, universities merely continue to do what they have been doing, independent of their underpinning principles or stated aims, and regardless of the desires and needs of society. For much of history, universities have operated in this mode, and much of what is still done in universities (for example forms of teaching, grouping of students, assessment) is in this mode.

The prevalent assumption in contemporary societies is that universities should be working in the responsive mode, in the sense that their activities should be determined by the will and needs of society, and not by any internal principle of academic value. This mode, in which the value and function of universities are determined by interaction, is commendable in terms of its democratic engagement, although is at risk of capture by particular interests, if democracy is not functioning adequately—as is the case in our current society. There is the question of whose will and whose need is actually represented: what we have currently is a market form of responsive mode in which those who can pay more have greater influence on the institution. Furthermore, the challenges that universities have in responding to those diverse desires and needs will be addressed in Chapter 10 in relation to the question of impact.

The mission-led mode is the most coherent, in that it bases its activities and forms of relationship on its underpinning aims and principles. Nevertheless, it faces a similar problem to the responsive mode. Which values or whose values should be taken to characterise the institution? Our problems are solved if we take there to be a unitary academic value—such as the Western scientific project of attaining objective truth through the accumulation of empirical observations—or endorse the set of values of a specific national or cultural community. Yet in practice, institutions very rarely have, or can be justified in having, this kind of unified view, and the mission-led mode can lay itself open to capture by specific interest groups, corporate control or heavy-handed state interference (as occurred in some instances of the developmental university in Africa).

It is not possible to state definitively which of these three modes should be in the ascendance. Although the traditional mode appears the least desirable at first sight, yet even here there may be positive aspects to a commitment to practice, and to processes with intrinsic value, such as enquiry and Socratic dialogue. Ultimately, we need to hold these three modes in balance, and in clear sight.

There is, of course, no consensus as to which forms of value, function and interaction the university should have. The following chapter will argue that the type of university that can fulfil the SDGs has particular characteristics in relation to all three. Yet ultimately, there will always be some contestation around the orientations of the university, and this contestation can be seen as positive, and in keeping with the spirit of enquiry and debate. What is important is that we retain a sense of the principles that are disputed, the axes on which contestation can occur, and the terrain on which differences play out—and it is this role that is proposed for the theoretical frame outlined in this chapter.

References

Altbach, P. G., Reisberg, L., & Rumbley, L. E. (2009). *Trends in global higher education: Tracking an academic revolution*. A Report Prepared for the UNESCO 2009 World Conference on Higher Education. UNESCO, Paris.

Anderson, R. D. (2004). *European universities from the enlightenment to 1914*. Oxford: Oxford University Press.

Bacevic, J. (2019). With or without U? Assemblage theory and (de)territorialising the university. *Globalisation, Societies and Education, 17*(1), 78–91.

Barnett, R. (1990). *The idea of higher education*. Buckingham: Society for Research into Higher Education and Open University Press.

Barnett, R. (2017). *The ecological university: A feasible utopia*. Abingdon: Routledge.

Bernasconi, A. (2007). Is there a Latin American model of the university? *Comparative Education Review, 52*(1), 27–52.

Bloom, D., Canning, D., & Chan, K. (2006). *Higher education and economic development in Africa*. Washington, DC: World Bank.

Boni, A., & Walker, M. (2013). *Human development and capabilities: Re-imagining the university of the twenty-first century*. London: Routledge.

Boni, A., & Walker, M. (2016). *Universities and global human development: Theoretical and empirical insights for social change*. London: Routledge.

Brennan, J., & Naidoo, R. (2008). Higher education and the achievement (and/or prevention) of equity and social justice. *Higher Education, 56*(3), 287–302.

Calhoun, C. (2006). The university and the public good. *Thesis Eleven, 84*(1), 7–43.

Carpentier, V. (2019). The historical expansion of higher education in Europe: Spaces, shapes and rationales. In J. L. Rury & E. H. Tamura (Eds.), *The Oxford handbook of the history of education*. Oxford: Oxford University Press.

Castells, M. (2001). Universities as dynamic systems of contradictory functions. In J. Muller, N. Cloete, & S. Badat (Eds.), *Challenges of globalisation: South African debates with Manuel Castells*. Pinelands: Maskew Miller Longman.

Clark, B. R. (1998). *Creating entrepreneurial universities: Organisational pathways of transformation*. New York: Elsevier.

Coleman, J. S. (1986). The idea of the developmental university. *Minerva: A Review of Science, Learning and Policy, 24*(4), 476–494.

Deneulin, S., & Townsend, N. (2007). Public goods, global public goods and the common good. *International Journal of Social Economics, 34*(1/2), 19–36.

Eco, U. (2013). *Perché le università?* Universitas 131. Available at http://disf.org/files/eco-perche-universita.pdf. Accessed 1 December 2018.

Etzkowitz, H., Webster, A., Gebhardt, C., & Cantisano Terra, B. R. (2000). The future of the university and the university of the future: Evolution of ivory tower to entrepreneurial paradigm. *Research Policy, 29*, 313–330.

Goodfellow, R., & Lea, M. (Eds.). (2013). *Literacy in the digital university: Critical perspectives on learning, scholarship and technology (research into higher education)*. London and New York: Routledge and Taylor & Francis.

Jaspers, K. (1960). *The idea of the university*. London: Peter Owen.

Kerr, C. (1963). *The uses of the university*. New York: Harper Torchbooks.

Locatelli, R. (2017). *Education as a public and common good: Revisiting the role of the state in a context of growing marketization* (Unpublished PhD thesis). University of Bergamo.

Marginson, S. (2007). The public/private divide in higher education: A global revision. *Higher Education, 53*(3), 307–333.

Marginson, S. (2011). Higher education and public good. *Higher Education Quarterly, 65*(4), 411–433.

Marginson, S. (2014). Emerging higher education in the post-confucian heritage zone. In D. Araya & P. Marber (Eds.), *Higher education in the global age* (pp. 89–112). New York: Routledge.

Marginson, S. (2016). *Higher education and the common good*. Melbourne: Melbourne University Press.

Marginson, S. (2018). Public/private in higher education: A synthesis of economic and political approaches. *Studies in Higher Education, 43*(2), 322–337.

Marginson, S., & Considine, M. (2000). *The enterprise university: Power, governance, and reinvention in Australia*. Cambridge, UK: Cambridge University Press.

Masehela, L. (2018). The rising challenge of university access for students from low-income families. In P. Ashwin & J. Case (Eds.), *Higher education pathways: South African undergraduate education and the public good*. Cape Town: African Minds.

Mathebula, M., & Calitz, T. (2018). #FeesMustFall: A media analysis of students' voices on access to universities in South Africa. In P. Ashwin & J.

Case (Eds.), *Higher education pathways: South African undergraduate education and the public good*. Cape Town: African Minds.

McCowan, T. (2015). Should universities promote employability? *Theory and Research in Education, 13*(3), 267–285.

Meyer, H.-D., St. John, E. P., Chankseliani, M., & Uribe, L. (Eds.). (2013). *Fairness in access to higher education in a global perspective: Reconciling excellence, efficiency, and justice*. Rotterdam: Sense Publishers.

Molebatsi, P. (2018, June 19). *How can the notion of the 'public good' contribute to conceptions of the 'developmental university'?* Paper presented at the CEID Annual Conference 2018—Higher Education and International Development, University College London.

Mountford-Zimdars, A., & Sabbagh, D. (2013). Fair access to higher education: A comparative perspective. *Comparative Education Review, 57*(3), 359–368.

Newman, J. H. (1947 [1852]). *The idea of the university: Defined and illustrated*. London: Longmans, Green.

Nixon, J. (2011). *Higher education and the public good: Imagining the university*. New York and London: Continuum.

Nybom, T. (2003). The humboldt legacy: Reflections on the past, present, and future of the European university. *Higher Education Policy, 16*, 141–159.

Nybom, T. (2007). A rule-governed community of scholars: The humboldt-vision in the history of the European university. In P. Maassen & J. P. Olsen (Eds.), *University dynamics and European integration* (pp. 55–79). Dordrecht: Spinger.

Oakeshott, M. (1989). The idea of a university. In T. Fuller (Ed.), *The voice of liberal learning: Michael Oakeshott on education* (pp. 95–104). New Haven and London: Yale University Press.

Perkin, H. (2007). History of universities. In J. J. F. Forest & P. G. Altbach (Eds.), *International handbook of higher education* (pp. 159–206). Dordrecht: Springer.

Readings, B. (1996). *The university in ruins*. Cambridge, MA: Harvard University Press.

Rüeg, W. (Ed.). (1992). *A history of the university in Europe*. Cambridge: Cambridge University Press.

Ryle, G. (1949). *The concept of mind*. London: Penguin Books.

Selingo, J. J. (2017). *The networked university: Building alliances for innovation in higher education*. London: Pearson.

Shattock, M. (2009). *Entrepreneurialism in universities and the knowledge economy: Diversification and organisational change in European higher education.* Bletchley, UK: Open University Press.

Shields, R., & Watermeyer, R. (2018). Competing institutional logics in universities in the United Kingdom: Schism in the church of reason. *Studies in Higher Education.* https://doi.org/10.1080/03075079.2018.1504910.

Shore, C. (2010). Beyond the multiversity: Neoliberalism and the rise of the schizophrenic university. *Social Anthropology/Anthropologie Sociale, 18*(1), 15–29.

Singh, M. (2012). Re-inserting the 'public good' into higher education transformation. In B. Leibowitz (Ed.), *Higher education for the public good—Views from the south* (pp. 1–16). Stoke on Trent, UK: Trentham Books and Stellenbosch: Sun Media.

Slaughter, S., & Leslie, L. L. (1997). *Academic capitalism: Politics, policies, and the entrepreneurial university.* Baltimore, MD: Johns Hopkins Press.

Smith, A., & Webster, F. (Eds.). (1997). *The postmodern university? Contested visions of higher education in society.* Buckingham, UK: Open University Press.

Stiglitz, J. E. (1999). Knowledge as a global public good. *Global Public Goods, 1*(9), 308–326.

Tian, L., & Liu, N. C. (2018). *Local and global public good contributions of higher education in China* (Working Paper No. 37). Centre for Global Higher Education. Available at https://www.researchcghe.org/perch/resources/publications/wp37.pdf. Accessed 1 December 2018.

Tian, L., & Liu, N. C. (2019). Rethinking higher education in China as a common good. *Higher Education, 77*(4), 623–640.

Tilak, J. B. G. (2008). Higher education: A public good or a commodity for trade? Commitment to higher education or commitment of higher education to trade. *Prospects, 38,* 449–466.

UNESCO (United Nations Educational, Scientific and Cultural Organization). (1998, October). *World declaration on higher education for the twenty-first century: Vision and Action.* Adopted at the World Conference on Higher Education, Paris.

Unterhalter, E., & Brighouse, H. (2007). Distribution of what for social justice in education? The case of education for all by 2015. In M. Walker & E. Unterhalter (Eds.), *Amartya Sen's capability approach and social justice in education.* New York: Palgrave Macmillan.

Unterhalter, E., Allais, S., Howell, C., McCowan, T., Morley, L., Oanda, I., & Oketch, M. (2017). *Higher education and the public good: Concepts, challenges and complexities in Africa*. Working paper for the research project, Higher education and the public good in four African countries.

Välimaa, J. (2018). The Nordic idea of university. In R. Barnett & M. Peters (Eds.), *The idea of the university: Contemporary perspectives*. New York: Peter Lang.

Walker, M. (2018). Dimensions of higher education and the public good in South Africa. *Higher Education, 76*(3), 555–569.

Walker, M., McLean, M., Dison, A., & Peppin-Vaughan, R. (2009). South African universities and human development: Towards a theorisation and operationalisation of professional capabilities for poverty reduction. *International Journal of Educational Development, 29*(6), 565–572.

Wissema, J. G. (2009). *Towards the third generation university: Managing the university in transition*. Cheltenham: Edward Elgar.

Yang, L. (2017). *The public role of higher learning in Imperial China* (Working Paper No. 28). Centre for Global Higher Education. Available at https://www.researchcghe.org/perch/resources/publications/wp28.pdf. Accessed 1 December 2018.

Yesufu, T. M., & Association of African Universities. (1973). *Creating the African university: Emerging issues in the 1970's*. Ibadan, Nigeria: Oxford University Press for the Association of African Universities.

Zgaga, P. (2009). Higher education and citizenship: 'The full range of purposes'. *European Educational Research Journal, 8*(2), 175–188.

4

The Developmental University

Introduction

The shiny, escalator-adorned library at Kenyatta University (known as the 'Postmodern' Library) heralds a new era in African higher education: built through partnerships with the Chinese government, it is fruit of the new entrepreneurial spirit, in which the university looks to society as a source of business opportunity, rather than as the beneficiary of the knowledge it generates. In contrast to the overcrowded lecture halls and demoralised academic staff prevalent in the institution, it stands as a striking symbol of excellence understood as enterprise, modernity and alliance with industry. Yet this university, and many others in East Africa, were in fact established on very different foundations, being seen as of the people and for the people, labouring to build the nation and ensure prosperity for all. The lofty aspirations for the institution in the post-independence period as the cornerstone of development for the benefit of the disenfranchised majority seem but a distant memory.

In the 1970s, there were widespread calls in African countries to do away with the fossilised colonial model of institution, and in its place establish a university that could support the newly independent governments in creating inclusive societies (Ajayi et al. 1996; Yesufu and AAU 1973). Indeed, this was the only kind of institution that could be justified, given the scarce state resources, and significant competing demands, including low levels of enrolment even at primary level. But despite the good intentions, and the support of charismatic leaders like Julius Nyerere, few institutions in this mould were in fact created, and in the context of dwindling state funds and political instability in succeeding decades, the idea fell by the wayside.

It might have been tempting to consign the developmental university to the annals of history, had it not been for the establishment of the Sustainable Development Goals (SDGs). The new landscape created post-2015, along with the renewed interest in higher education for international development since the turn of the millennium, has given the model of the developmental university a new lease of life. As discussed in Chapter 1, In addition to an (albeit partial) goal for access to tertiary education, it places universities crucially in the role of drivers of development, facilitating the changes in society necessary to achieve the full set of goals—economic, social and environmental. This role bears a striking resemblance to that put forward in the developmental university half a century before.

The developmental model is important not only for the low and middle-income countries of Africa, Asia and Latin America which are grappling with extreme problems of poverty, social exclusion, environmental catastrophes and violent conflict, but also for high-income countries in which these issues may be less visible. The SDGs are demanding on all countries, given the requirements for protection of the natural environment and reduction of socio-economic inequalities. Furthermore, there are increasing signs in high-income countries that universities are being placed in the developmental role: as motors for local economies, fostering innovation and solutions to societal problems, at the hub of a thriving network of companies and government agencies.

The roots of the developmental university in fact go back to the US land grant institutions in the nineteenth century, and the notion of *service* solidified during the twentieth century to form a key part of the university's remit. Given constraints on public funding for higher education in all countries, service for society—particularly in boosting the economy—has come to be seen as essential payback for the now reluctant taxpayer contribution. Analysing the developmental model is, therefore, essential to understanding the modern university in all contexts. A number of highly relevant contemporary experiences use different terminology, and there are strong parallels between the ideas of the developmental university and those of the 'engaged university' (Benneworth 2013), the 'civic university' (Goddard et al. 2016), the 'service university' (Cummings 1998; Tjeldvoll 1998), 'anchor institutions' (Birch et al. 2013) and the 'utilitarian university' (Cowen 1971; Lauglo 1982), as well as with the extensive literature on higher education and public good (Calhoun 2006; Marginson 2011; Nixon 2011 etc.). The relevance of the model is to all of these forms of institution that focus on service to external communities.

This chapter will first provide some historical background on the emergence of the developmental model and, assess its trajectory in the USA, Latin America and Africa. It then highlights the distinctive characteristics of the developmental model in its commitment to public service, its focus on the most marginalised in society, and its emphasis on application of knowledge and impact on non-academic communities. Finally, there is discussion of two recent examples of development universities: the University for Development Studies in Ghana, and the 'thematic' federal universities in Brazil. These cases illustrate the important innovations but also the challenges of implementation of the model.

Historical Trajectory of the Developmental University

The eighteenth and nineteenth centuries brought a number of challenges to the university. With the Industrial Revolution, new forms of livelihood and profession emerged, ones that were not represented in the offer available in the existing university curriculum (Perkin 2007; Carpentier 2019). Experimental scientific research gathered momentum rapidly, and although often located outside universities in scholarly societies, began to be incorporated in the emerging model of the German research university. When Cardinal Newman wrote his seminal work *The Idea of a University: Defined and Illustrated* (1947 [1852]), the form of broad liberal education advocated for, unsullied by the practical concerns of the world, was already becoming a thing of the past, as universities creaked into the new age and little by little absorbed its influences.

However, it was in the New World that the next major innovation in higher education would emerge in the form of the land grant universities (McDowell 2003). While the ideas of Wilhelm von Humboldt had transformed many of the aspects of the mediaeval institution, universities still had restricted relationships with the society outside. In 1862, the Morrill Act in the USA granted federal land to the states for the establishment of new universities, with the aim not just to expand access to new populations, but to form a new orientation and role for the institution. Instead of focusing on the conventional subject areas, they were intended to support farming and heavy industry, to develop an altogether more porous relationship with the communities around them.[1] In many ways this institutional form was in keeping with broader trends in the US society, of community involvement in education and practical technology, but the precedent set in these institutions was to have a significant impact globally in subsequent years. In particular, the notion of service to society emerged and became one of the cornerstones in due course of US higher education generally speaking—as part of the diversity of functions in the 'multiversity' (Kerr 1963).

In Latin America, a different kind of transformation was taking place that would also provide some of the building blocks of the developmental model. Following a student uprising at the University of Córdoba, Argentina in 1918, demanding autonomy of the university from state interference, democratic governance and modernisation of the curriculum, a series of reforms was undertaken in the institution and across

---

[1]Orr (1994) argues, however, that the land grant institutions did not fully succeed in their goal of revitalising rural communities.

the country. The influence of these reforms would reverberate through the whole region, and form the model that would characterise Latin American public institutions for the next century (Arocena and Sutz 2005; Bernasconi 2007). The new commitment of the public universities was to expand access beyond the traditional elites, but also to incorporate democratic governance (following the idea of *co-gobierno* or co-governance [Arocena and Sutz 2005]). To this day, Latin American universities often have direct elections for senior management, with participation of students and staff.

Bernasconi (2007) derives from this regional movement a Latin American model of the university, involving seven principles:

1. Democratic governance, or cogovernance by students, professors, and alumni, whose representatives were to be elected to Faculty-level and university-wide decision-making councils
2. Orientation of the mission of the university toward the solution of the social, economic, and political problems of the country
3. Institution of an extension function of the university, alongside those of research and teaching, the purpose of which was to bring the university to the working masses
4. Democratization of access through tuition-free education and expansion of enrollments
5. Autonomy from state intervention and academic freedom
6. Selection of faculty through competitive and public contests based on academic merit
7. Original research by full-time professors committed to the university

As can be seen, some aspects of these reforms were related to the Humboldtian model, for example, academic freedom and research focused professors. There are others that brought an altogether more political dimension. One element of these reforms that was closer to the land grant model was the introduction of *extensión* (community engagement or public service) alongside teaching and research as the third fundamental pillar of the university. In Brazil, for example, universities are constitutionally required to consider activities of teaching, research and public service as inseparable. As will be discussed further in Chapter 8, while community engagement is often the 'poor sister' to the other two pillars, it does provide a precious opportunity for universities to involve themselves in the social justice and natural environment dimensions of the SDGs.

The next key moment in this trajectory is the emergence of the developmental university itself in Africa in the post-war era. Institutions established in the metropolitan image were in this period soon seen to be objectionable in principle and in practice. As Court (1980: 658) stated:

> Adherence to the colonial model from which they sprang was seen to be inhibiting their ability to respond to the needs of their own society and leaving them as islands of unbecoming detachment in a sea of poverty.

Given the urgent and concrete needs of the populations in many countries in terms of food and healthcare, not to mention the basic infrastructure of the state, universities were tasked with converting the idealism of national independence into practical help for the outside society. The outcome document of the Association of African Universities workshop in 1972 stated:

> The emphasis here must be on the pursuit and inculcation of practical knowledge, not esoteric knowledge or knowledge for its own sake. It must be immediately useful for the generality of people, and, therefore, locally oriented and motivated. (Yesufu and AAU 1973: 42)

Taking the lead from the higher education system in the Soviet Union, 'manpower' planning was to be a central role of these universities, with an aim to form middle-level as well as high-level professionals (Yesufu and AAU 1973). It was not only national governments that were dissatisfied with the traditional institutions. Development agencies by the 1970s were already disillusioned with the ability of universities to fulfil the high expectations that had been laid on them at independence, and were starting to pull funds in favour of primary and vocational education, so in the context of scarce public resources the university needed to justify its significant costs (Coleman 1986).

However, the model was short-lived in Africa, and only practised sporadically. Some universities such as Nairobi and Dar es Salaam that were intended to be developmental (Court 1980) soon reverted to being traditional flagship institutions catering to the elites and with uncertain connections to the well-being of society more broadly. In more recent times, the elite higher education system in Africa, as elsewhere in the world, has largely given way to a massified one in which the public sector has expanded through cost-sharing, with a new commercialised private sector growing around it to absorb excess demand (Oanda et al. 2008; Sawyerr 2004). Nevertheless, there are some contemporary examples of developmental universities in the region and elsewhere, as will be outlined later in the chapter.

Although this brief historical review has shown that 'pure' instances of developmental universities are rare, there are influences of the model in many contemporary institutions in all regions, and governments and international agencies often expect higher education systems to fulfil this role. While what is being addressed here is the *model* of the developmental university—in the sense of an ideal type which may not correspond directly to an actually existing historical instance—it is generative in terms of understanding different approaches to the institution of university present in all HE systems. The characteristics of this model will be analysed in the section that follows.

Principal Characteristics of the Developmental Model

The triad of teaching, research and community engagement manifest themselves in distinct ways in the developmental model. Taught courses are offered not on the basis of disciplinary tradition, but on the needs for forming professionals with skills relevant to local and national development: there may, therefore, be courses in ecotourism, renewable energy or community development, in addition to more traditional academic courses. They will also be taught in a way that connects students more closely to the realities in which they will be working—including contexts of hardship. Research will be guided as much by national and local priorities as by the interests and curiosities of the researchers themselves. It will be predominantly of an applied nature, and oriented towards providing solutions to development challenges. Finally, the third pillar of community engagement gains much greater prominence in comparison with other models. Not only are there extensive community outreach projects, but lecturers are encouraged to work widely as consultants and advisers to local and national government. Other services provided include legal clinics, lab schools, health clinics and continuing education for adults.

We can derive four main features that characterise the developmental model of university. First, it is an institution oriented towards serving society; it appeals to no other purpose than that of attempting to address the needs and promote the benefits of its surrounding communities. The second is that it does so in an egalitarian way, not confining its fruits to the elites, but aiming to support in particular the least advantaged populations. Third, it aims to bring *non-academic* benefit to the population—i.e. of an economic, social and political nature. Finally, it aims to fulfil this role through the application of knowledge, the turning of the theoretical and abstract towards practical and immediate ends.

To take the first of these, the role of the developmental university is to serve society—not to serve the interests of the community of scholars, or even the community of students, nor to serve the quest for truth, knowledge and understanding, nor indeed simply to serve a monarch, wealthy patron or religious body. This characteristic to aid in solving societies' problems stands in marked contrast to the earliest European universities in mediaeval times which were based around the collective study of bodies of knowledge considered to be intrinsically valid, and to the Humboldtian institution with its research professors protected by academic freedom, pursuing ever greater depth in their disciplinary areas. But equally it contrasts with the later entrepreneurial university (Clark 1998), which purports to serve society, but only as a means of generating income—income that it needs to survive (the entrepreneurial university has no moral compass as it were, it follows whichever paymaster happens to be present).

At this point, it is important to disambiguate this use of the term 'service' from that employed in Tjeldvoll (1998) in his 'service university'—which in its emphasis on 'develop[ing] products that are competitive in a knowledge market' is more akin to the entrepreneurial university than the developmental university outlined here.[2] Thus, the usage here is of a public service that is provided on the basis of the commitment to society, rather than financial gain.

If we assess the four diverse models of the university discussed in the previous chapter, it can be seen that they differ markedly in the provenance of their objects of study. For the mediaeval European university, scholarship was oriented around the bodies of work inherited from classical times and produced by contemporary scholars—it was internal to the academy so to speak. In the Humboldtian university, with its emphasis on academic freedom and the professor's quest for truth, the focus of research came from the curiosities of the individual and scholarly community, and the organic movements of enquiry. In the developmental university and the entrepreneurial university, on the other hand, the focus comes from outside, but in different ways. For the former it is the needs of society, the problems that need to be addressed, and aspirations for positive change; for the latter it is the demand of consumers, whether students purchasing courses, or external bodies commissioning research and consultancy.

There are also differences in the audiences or destinations of that research and scholarship. With the mediaeval and Humboldtian universities, it was predominantly an internal affair, and the consumers of the work were for the most part the academic community itself. That is not to say that there were no external audiences, or external impact—the institutions had patrons, and of course students went to work outside, taking the influences and ideas with them, while professors also disseminated their ideas in their lives outside the institution. Nevertheless, universities were not obliged to communicate their research findings publicly in the same way as the later models of institution. In contrast,

---

[2] The term 'service university' in Cummings (1998) is, however, used in a sense consonant with that in this article.

with the developmental and entrepreneurial models, the primary audiences are outside the institution. With the developmental university, the state is the primary recipient of the knowledge produced: the different levels of government utilise the applied research findings, and university lecturers will themselves have extensive roles as consultants on government projects. In the case of the entrepreneurial institution, there will be a range of different consumers of research, including government but also commercial sponsors.

While the role of serving society is a feature of both developmental and commercialised institutions, the determination of the service in question is distinct in each case. The former is characterised by a strong supply-side control, rather than the kinds of demand-led trends dominant in today's entrepreneurial universities. Taught courses in the developmental model are established on the basis of need, and not on the ability to recruit students; research is planned on the basis of social benefit rather than commercial demand.

Another important element that distinguishes the developmental model from commodified higher education is its egalitarian, and even pro-poor nature. Instead of attending to and benefiting the intellectually gifted, the socially privileged or the economically advantaged, its duty is to distribute its benefits equally, and furthermore to gradually equalise society through disproportionately benefiting the worst off. It does this in part through expanding the range of people able to access the institution. But equally significantly, it challenges the dominance of private goods from higher education—the personal benefits in terms of enhanced employment prospects, increased income etc.—to focus on public goods emanating from teaching and research. In addition to the reorientation of courses and academic activities, this aim has been realised through national service programmes, through which graduates can give back to society through dedicating their newfound skills and knowledge to disadvantaged populations, often in remote rural areas. Examples are the obligatory service year in Nigeria and Ghana for all students after completing undergraduate degrees, and for medical students in South Africa.

The third characteristic is its focus on non-academic impact. The benefit that the developmental university is intended to bring is not that of

Newman's education of the intellect, nor the Kantian (1979 [1878]) exercise of reason—or indeed of any academic goal. Even though they may emanate from academic pursuits, the benefits are realised outside: they include equipping individuals for gainful employment, enhancing macro-economic growth, fostering social cohesion and strengthening political institutions. In the context of the SDGs, a central role of universities in this vein is the development of clean technologies to replace forms of production and consumption that threaten the natural environment.

The fostering of non-academic benefits involves the fourth characteristic—the application of knowledge. In terms of Boyer's (1990) characterisation, therefore, the developmental university embodies a scholarship of *application* rather than of *discovery,* of *integration;* or of *teaching*. It still conceives of itself as a knowledge-based institution, but of the 'Mode 2' applied knowledge rather than the 'Mode 1' blue skies variety (Gibbons et al. 1994).[3] It values the theoretical and abstract only in so far as it can be useful in real-world situations. Related to this is the idea that multidisciplinary approaches are needed to solve real-life problems (Court 1980), with attempts to break down rigid disciplinary barriers, to collaborate across areas in research and create new cross-disciplinary areas in teaching. Another way in which the knowledge production function of universities can manifest itself is in generating evidence to support the development of policy and practice (Grobbelaar and de Wet 2016).

Contemporary theorists of developmental higher education emphasise particularly its role in *innovation*. Cloete et al. (2011) distinguish between more restricted instrumental roles of the university (human capital formation and political socialisation), from becoming what they call an 'engine for development', involving the production of new knowledge. Importantly, this new knowledge is not the traditional abstract, theoretical, disciplinary type, but *applied* to the specific problems, challenges and visions of the locality. The role of the

---

[3]Carayannis and Campbell (2012) have more recently put forward the notion of Mode 3 knowledge, involving civil society as well as government, academia and industry, in a more collaborative and networked set of relations.

developmental university specifically is not just to be the engine for the knowledge economy, but to act as a vehicle for the *democratisation* of knowledge (Arocena et al. 2015).

These four characteristics are *necessary* conditions of the development university. Displaying some but not others would have significant implications: an institution oriented towards service, application of knowledge and non-academic benefit but lacking the egalitarian dimension is likely to be more along the lines of the training institutions set up by large corporations (take for example McDonald's Hamburger University)—aiming for practical impact, but confined to a select few, or generating private rather than public goods. An institution serving society with egalitarian principles, but shunning application of knowledge for non-academic benefit would have a very different character, and be more akin to historical efforts to extend theoretical knowledge and the intellectual pursuits of the university to populations previously excluded from them. Whether these four conditions are *sufficient* is less certain—some may argue that there are additional requirements, such as being legally public, or being in receipt of substantial state funding: while there are possible examples of developmental universities in the private sector (see, for example, the community universities in the South of Brazil outlined below), in most cases resource constraints limit the model to institutions with state funding.

Developmental Universities in Practice

In terms of the materialisation of these abstract characteristics in real developmental institutions, we can identify two broad types: the *developmental flagship*, and the *experimental university*. The former type—of which historical examples have been Universities of Dar es Salaam, Mauritius and Nairobi—are prominent, national universities, usually located in capital cities, highly sought after by students and with a close relationship to government. Very often there have been struggles over the direction of these institutions, moving between more universalist, colonial and globalised orientations, or alternatively more nationalist, decolonised and locally engaged ones (for a discussion of these historical dynamics in Makerere and Dar es Salaam, see Mamdani 2018). In periods more broadly characterised by a developmental state, governments have sought to engage these flagship universities for development ends, with reforms made to curricula, departmental structures and research priorities, and by engaging academic staff for public roles.

The second type is the experimental university. In contrast to the developmental flagships, these are more peripheral institutions often located in impoverished regions of their countries, and aiming to accommodate new and previously underserved populations. On account of their less prominent national position, and their having been founded explicitly for this purpose, the scope for experimentation is much greater than in the flagships, and these institutions have shown evidence of more innovative practice and in some cases significant outcomes. The downside is the relative ease with which they can be sidelined, and the greater difficulty in influencing mainstream policy and institutional norms. While flagship developmental institutions were more common in the post-war period, nowadays most examples are experimental, two of which are outlined below.

The University for Development Studies (Ghana)

One clear and explicit case of a contemporary developmental university is the University for Development Studies (UDS), created in Ghana in 1992. In contrast to the majority of institutions located in the more affluent and better educated south of the country, this institution was founded in the arid and impoverished north, as a conscious attempt to develop the region. In order to penetrate even deeper into unserved areas, it established campuses in Wa (Upper West Region), Navrongo (Upper East Region) and Nyankpala (Northern Region) in addition to its main campus in Tamale (Northern Region). Courses were established to foster agricultural development and environmental management, as well as train local professionals to staff education and health services. Its faculties also include Planning and Land management, Integrated Development, Applied Sciences and Horticulture. Its motto, 'knowledge for service' illustrates well its alignment with the principles of the developmental model outlined above.

An innovative aspect of UDS's work—and one that illustrates well its developmental role—is the adoption of a trimester rather than semester system, in order to make possible the Third Trimester Field Placement Programme. In this programme, all students are required to undertake an eight-week placement in each of their first three years in a local community, carrying out developmental diagnostics and supporting the community in implementing projects. This experience serves not only to provide support to the impoverished communities of the region, but also to foster social cohesion through intercultural dialogue: for the most part, the students of the university are different from the host communities in their regions of origin and language groups (Abukari 2010).

The *Thematic* Federal Universities

In a situation of less extreme poverty than Ghana, though nevertheless severe inequality and deprivation, a small number of innovative universities were established in the government of Lula da Silva in Brazil, at the end of the decade of the 2000s. Sometimes referred to as the *thematic* universities, they in part served the function of extending access to higher education and productive skills to underserved regions of the country, as with UDS, but added to that a specific remit or mission linked in with various social movements active in the country.

The best known of these new institutions is the University of Latin American Integration (UNILA[4]). Founded in 2010 in the symbolic location of the triple border of Brazil with Paraguay and Argentina near the Iguaçu Falls, the institution aims to provide a space for teaching, research and community service linked not to the national context but to pan-Latin American concerns (Comissão de Implantação da UNILA 2009a, b; Trindade 2009). While funded entirely by the Brazilian government, it is a bilingual institution (Portuguese and Spanish, with some engagement with indigenous languages) and with the intention to have an even balance in the student and staff body between Brazil and

---

[4]Universidade Federal da Integração Latino-Americana.

other countries in Latin America (although with a majority of the former in practice). The curriculum offered is distinct from conventional universities, through the emphasis on interdisciplinarity, the 'common cycle' of Latin American studies that all students undergo in their first year, and the pan-Latin American focus of the degree courses, including Latin American Cultural Diversity, Rural Development and Food Security, and Engineering for Sustainable Energy.

The university also has a social justice agenda, aiming to serve the local population which would not normally have access to a federal institution (many of the inhabitants of Foz de Iguaçu are descendants of the migrant workers who built the Itaipú dam), as well as maintaining a range of community engagement activities. Motter and Gandin (2016) highlight the distinctiveness of the institution in reverting the dominant forms of internationalisation in higher education globally, promoting South–South cooperation and engaging with neighbouring and more distant countries in a spirit of solidarity rather than income generation or competition.

Created at a similar time to UNILA was another thematic university, this time with a focus on Africa. The University of Lusophone Afro-Brazilian International Integration (UNILAB[5]) is aimed at articulation with the Portuguese speaking countries of Africa, primarily: Angola, Mozambique, São Tomé and Príncipe, Guinea-Bissau and Cape Verde, but with links to other Portuguese speaking countries, such as East Timor. The location[6] of the university is again symbolic, in this case in Redenção, Ceará, in the impoverished north-east of Brazil, the first city in the country to abolish slavery in 1883. Like UNILA, it aims to have half of its students from Brazil and half from overseas, funded by the Brazilian government. Aware of the dangers of brain drain, provisions are in place to ensure the relocation of the overseas students back to their countries of origin, and their insertion in areas of work beneficial to local development. Not only does the university aim to strengthen links between Brazil and Africa, but also to provide a focal point for

---

[5]Universidade da Integração Internacional da Lusofonia Afro-Brasileira.
[6]An additional campus has been established in São Francisco do Conde, Bahia.

engagement with African cultures and history within Brazil. Courses and research again are focused on themes of relevance to inclusive development in all of the countries: research groups include Agro-Ecology and Organic Produce; Popular Education, Micro-Finance and Solidary Economy, and African Thought and Philosophy. Unusually for Brazil, students undertake a third term each year engaging in interdisciplinary academic, cultural and community development activities.

Other examples of thematic federal universities include the Federal University of the Southern Frontier (UFFS[7]), a multi-campus institution focusing on the agricultural worker population of southern Brazil; the Federal University of Western Pará (UFOPA,[8] originally intended as the University of Amazonian Integration) aiming for transnational cooperation between the countries of the Amazon rainforest; and the Federal University of Southern Bahia, focusing on community engagement, digital inclusion and broad personal and civic formation in the disadvantaged inland areas of the north-east (Almeida and Coutinho 2018; Santos and Almeida 2008; Tavares and Romão 2015).

Other Forms of Developmental Institution

Not all developmental institutions follow the model of the experimental examples given above. A contemporary example of a developmental flagship is the University of the Republic in Uruguay, discussed in Arocena et al. (2014, 2015). Representing a new brand of developmental university for the age of the knowledge economy, the university through its research council has fostered applied developmental research in a range of areas, leading to new projects in areas such as health communication for disadvantaged teenagers, development of artificial skin and nutritional impact of school food.

While the majority of examples of developmental universities have been public, state-funded institutions, there are some in the private

---

[7]Universidade Federal da Fronteira Sul. UFFS has a total of over 8000 students. It goes beyond the legal requirement (of 50%) and reserves 90% of its places for students from public schools.

[8]Universidade Federal do Oeste do Pará.

sector. In Latin America, influenced by liberation theology as well as their adoption of some of the principles of the Córdoba reform, many of the traditional Catholic universities have adopted substantial programmes of community engagement and research in the public benefit. These commitments are in marked contrast to the new generation of entrepreneurial private universities, whose for-profit status, more precarious finances and lack of a social conscience preclude any substantial work in this area.

A very distinctive profile, and one that escapes categorisation with either the traditional religious or entrepreneurial institutions, are the community universities in the south of Brazil (Fioreze and McCowan 2018). These institutions were established by local communities—mainly of German and Italian origin—in smaller cities in the interior of the southern states of Rio Grande do Sul and Santa Catarina, ones that were not lucky enough to have a federal institution. They are legally private, but do not have an owner, and are considered to be the property of the community, with the estate returning to public ownership in the case of closure. In some ways they are conventional institutions, and are fully recognised within the mainstream accreditation system, with a large range of undergraduate and some postgraduate courses. Yet they have some specific characteristics that mark them as being in the developmental mould. First is their close connection to local communities, in partnering with local businesses and industry, training the workforce for locally relevant employment, developing research and innovation related to developmental needs, as well as providing facilities and cultural events enjoyed by community members. Perhaps the most distinctive characteristic, however, is their democratic governance, with representatives from various walks of life in the surrounding areas on key decision-making boards. These universities are widely acknowledged to have contributed to the relatively high levels of prosperity in the region, with the three southern states (along with the Federal District and São Paulo) enjoying the highest human development indicators in the country.

However, their role in relation to widening participation is limited by the need to charge fees, and their lack of an endowment makes it hard to provide extensive scholarships or other affirmative action policies for lower income students. Furthermore, the community universities now face a severe threat to their very survival from the for-profit institutions, which are pulling away students through their lower fees and aggressive advertising, while providing minimal public benefit for the local communities. A landmark law in 2013 has meant that the community universities are now able to receive some public funds, but they still need to raise the majority of their resources from private sources, thus limiting their capacity for action. Nevertheless, they do still represent a noteworthy case of what might be understood as non-state public higher education, and a rare example of an organic link to local communities.

Barriers to Implementation

The earliest discussions of the developmental university in the 1970s and 1980s already highlighted a number of problematic aspects of the model. Some of the critiques raised by Coleman (1986), Court (1980) and others were of a practical nature: funding and support for the universities were precarious in the context of changes in government; capacity among staff members for implementing the developmental vision was limited, given the fledgling nature of the higher education systems and institutions; many had been trained in traditional (colonial) institutions and so struggled to change their mindset; and traditional university functions of teaching and research were seen to suffer through excessive engagement of staff members with government and development agency work. This final point is seen strongly to this day, with the consultancy culture among some academics in low-income countries being a significant distraction from teaching and research responsibilities. This issue has become more critical with the increasing commercialisation of institution, and in the context of low academic staff salaries. Another barrier is the tenuous relationship between public engagement activities and career progression—though some universities have started to include it in their recruitment and promotion criteria.

All of the contemporary examples of developmental universities given above face significant challenges in practice. Those located within the mainstream system of public universities are constrained by the regulatory logic of that system. In the case of the thematic universities in Brazil, the job security, prestige and relatively generous remuneration makes working in a federal university highly attractive to early career academics, but there is no guarantee that those applying for the posts will genuinely buy into the vision of pan-Latin American solidarity, for example, or have the appropriate knowledge and experience. Conversely, the relatively remote location of the universities in relation to the population centres of Brazil has in some cases made it hard to attract the experienced staff required. Finally, there are significant cost implications in funding the non-Brazilian students, particularly in terms of maintaining the support package of accommodation and other services.

The thematic universities' interdisciplinary curriculum is also strongly challenged within the federal system. Furthermore, being publicly funded and endorsed, they rely on the continuing support of the government and are vulnerable to changes: this is a particular problem in Brazil, where the federal institutions in question are associated with the left-leaning Workers' Party that has now lost power. With the election of the far-right president Bolsonaro at the end of 2018, there is likely to be intense pressure on these progressive institutions. In 2017, there had already been an attempt to change the name of UNILA to the Federal University of West Paraná and thereby divest it of its distinctive mission.

In the case of UDS in Ghana, massification of the system has created problems, as there are insufficient resources to support all of the students in their community placements. There have consequently been issues of inadequate accommodation, and security and health risks for the students, lack of pedagogical support and feedback, as well as overloading on the communities themselves. More generally, the institution has suffered from serious resource constraints, with lack of laboratory equipment, basic infrastructure and very high student–staff ratio. The university has also shown evidence of the mission creep that is so common in institutions of this type, struggling to maintain its distinctive mission among a student and staff body that may in part at least be seeking any opportunity for public higher education.

Developmental universities, therefore, face two primary challenges: centripetal forces and reliance on paymasters. The first is the encroaching pressures of the conventional university, the pulls that come from being part of the mainstream higher education system, and isomorphism with institutional norms. This dynamic occurs through a combination of factors: the beliefs and practices of staff (seen in the case of UNILA in lecturers who may not buy into the vision), the existence of formal standardisation requirements and qualifications frameworks, demand from students for particular courses and practices, as well as more subtle pressures to revert from the original radical to more conventional ways of working. Second is reliance on funding sources, leading to a lack of autonomy, recalling the saying 'he who pays the piper calls the tune'. This can be problematic in the case of conflict of perspectives between the university and the government, conflicts within the government, or a change of government, as has been seen in Brazil (the broader issues of institutional autonomy will be taken up again in Chapter 9).

However, there is a more fundamental threat that is not only impeding the effective functioning of these institutions, but is threatening their very existence—and it applies not only to full developmental universities, but also to the public service component of all universities. The reductions in public funding of higher education throughout the world, partly through ever-present budgetary pressures but also contestation over whether this kind of investment is publicly justifiable, has significantly decreased the possibilities of the developmental work of universities. Marketised systems are characterised by underinvestment in public goods, as individual and corporate entities acting independently will allocate their resources so as to maximise their own, rather than collective, benefit. The public service function of universities requires either state funding or philanthropic funding, neither of which are available plentifully in the new commercialised setup. Yet if the international community is serious about the SDGs, then this funding is a *sine qua non*.

The hopeful vision presented by development agencies of the potential role of universities in poverty reduction and development in LMICs is to a large extent dependent on particular orientations for the characteristics of *value*, *function* and *interaction* outlined above. A university engaged in achieving the SDGs would largely follow the developmental model of institution. It would be characterised by instrumentally valuable knowledge, yet by a form of instrumentality with strongly egalitarian orientations, requiring that the fruits of the institution be distributed in the interests of all in society. It would require a range of teaching, research and community engagement functions in the public interest. As regards interaction, there would be significant levels of porosity as regards both agents and ideas. In terms of inbound porosity, access for students would need to be open and equitable for those from all social backgrounds, and participation would need to be widened considerably. Universities would also need to be porous to the entry of ideas from outside, particularly the priorities of development: agendas for research and teaching would be set by the needs of society. Outbound porosity would also be high: university staff would be expected to engage actively with external bodies, disseminating research findings and providing advice. Ideas generated within the university would be shared externally, seeking tangible application in different spheres of society.

Yet as will be explored further in the chapter that follows, broader global trends such as commercialisation and unbundling have challenged this development role of universities, and the lack of acknowledgement of developmental impact (particularly at the local level) in international university rankings acts as a further disincentive. Development agencies at the supranational and national levels have either turned a blind eye to these trends or in some cases actively promoted them, a posture that presents a stark contradiction to their stated aims in relation to the SDGs. There may be some positive externalities of commercial investments and of individuals pursuing their own private benefit within a marketised higher education system, but these are fragile and fall far short of the role that universities can play when dedicated to public service. Beyond funding, there also needs to be a change of mindset—to acknowledge the potential and importance of the university for the public good, in order to escape from the self-fulfilling logic of private returns.

References

Abukari, A. (2010). The dynamics of service of higher education: A comparative study. *Compare, 40*(1), 43–57.

Ajayi, J. F. A., Goma, L. K. H., Johnson, G. A., & Association of African Universities. (1996). *The African experience with higher education*. Accra: Association of African Universities in association with James Currey and Ohio University Press.

Almeida Filho, N., & Coutinho, D. (2018). Counter hegemonic higher education in a remote coastal region of Brazil: The Federal University of Southern Bahia as a case-study. In R. Aman & T. Ireland (Eds.), *Educational alternatives in Latin America: New modes of counter hegemonic learning*. London: Palgrave Macmillan.

Arocena, R., Göransson, B., & Sutz, J. (2014). Universities and higher education in development. In B. Currie-Alder, S. M. R. Kanbur, D. Malone, & R. Medhora (Eds.), *International development: Ideas, experience, and prospects*. Oxford: Oxford University Press.

Arocena, R., Goransson, B., & Sutz, J. (2015). Knowledge policies and universities in developing countries: Inclusive development and the "developmental university". *Technology in Society, 41*, 10–20.

Arocena, R., & Sutz, J. (2005). Latin American universities: From an original revolution to an uncertain transition. *Higher Education, 50*(4), 573–592.

Benneworth, P. (Ed.). (2013). *University engagement with socially excluded communities*. Berlin: Springer.

Bernasconi, A. (2007). Is there a Latin American model of the university? *Comparative Education Review, 52*(1), 27–52.

Birch, E., Perry, D. C., & Taylor, H. L., Jr. (2013). Universities as anchor institutions. *Journal of Higher Education Outreach and Engagement, 17*(3), 7–16.

Boyer, E. L. (1990). *Scholarship reconsidered: Priorities of the professoriate*. Princeton, NJ: The Carnegie Foundation for the Advancement of Teaching.

Calhoun, C. (2006). The university and the public good. *Thesis Eleven, 84*(1), 7–43.

Carayannis, E. G., & Campbell, D. F. J. (2012). *Mode 3 knowledge production in quadruple helix innovation systems: 21st-century democracy, innovation, and entrepreneurship for development*. New York and London: Springer.

Carpentier, V. (2019). The historical expansion of higher education in Europe: Spaces, shapes and rationales. In J. L. Rury & E. H. Tamura (Eds.), *The Oxford handbook of the history of education*. Oxford: Oxford University Press.

Clark, B. R. (1998). *Creating entrepreneurial universities: Organisational pathways of transformation*. New York: Elsevier.
Cloete, N., Bailey, T., Pillay, P., Bunting, I., & Maassen, P. (2011). *Universities and economic development in Africa*. Cape Town: Centre for Higher Education Transformation.
Coleman, J. S. (1986). The idea of the developmental university. *Minerva: A Review of Science, Learning and Policy, 24*(4), 476–494.
Comissão de Implantação da UNILA. (2009a). *A UNILA em construção: Um projeto universitário para a América Latina*. Foz do Iguaçu: IMEA.
Comissão de Implantação da UNILA. (2009b). *UNILA: Consulta internacional. Contribuições à concepção, organização e proposta político-pedagógica da Unila*. Foz do Iguaçu: IMEA.
Court, D. (1980). The development ideal in higher education: The experience of Kenya and Tanzania. *Higher Education, 9*, 657–680.
Cowen, R. (1971). The utilitarian university. In B. Scanlon (Ed.), *The world yearbook of education 1971/72: Higher education in a changing world*. London: Evans Brothers Limited.
Cummings, W. (1998). The service university in comparative perspective. *Higher Education, 35*(1), 69–90.
Fioreze, C., & McCowan, T. (2018). Community universities in the South of Brazil: Prospects and challenges of a model of non-state public higher education. *Comparative Education, 54*(3), 370–389.
Gibbons, M., Limoges, C., Nowotny, H., Schwartzman, S., Scott, P., & Trow, M. (1994). *The new production of knowledge: The dynamics of science and research in contemporary societies*. London: Sage.
Goddard, J., Hazelkorn, E., Kempton, L., & Vallance, P. (Eds.). (2016). *The civic university: The policy and leadership challenges*. Cheltenham: Edward Elgar.
Grobbelaar, S., & de Wet, G. (2016). Exploring pathways towards an integrated development role: The University of Fort Hare. *South African Journal of Higher Education, 30*(1), 162–187.
Kant, I. (1979). *The conflict of the faculties*. Lincoln: University of Nebraska Press.
Kerr, C. (1963). *The uses of the university*. New York: Harper Torchbooks.
Lauglo, J. (1982). *The 'utilitarian university', the 'centre of academic learning' and developing countries* (EDC Occasional Papers No. 2).
Mamdani, M. (2018). The African university. *London Review of Books, 40*(14), 29–32.

Marginson, S. (2011). Higher education and public good. *Higher Education Quarterly,* 65(4), 411–433.

McDowell, G. (2003). Engaged universities: Lessons from the Land-Grant universities and extension. *Annals of the American Academy of Political and Social Science,* 585 (Higher Education in the Twenty-First Century), 31–50.

Motter, P., & Gandin, L. A. (2016). Higher education and new regionalism in Latin America: The UNILA project. In S. Robertson, K. Olds, R. Dale, & Q. A. Dang (Eds.), *Global regionalisms and higher education: Projects, processes, politics.* Cheltenham: Edward Elgar.

Newman, J. H. (1947 [1852]). *The idea of the university: Defined and illustrated.* London: Longmans, Green.

Nixon, J. (2011). *Higher education and the public good: Imagining the university.* London and New York: Continuum.

Oanda, I. O., Chege, F., & Wesonga, D. (2008). *Privatisation and private higher education in Kenya: Implications for access, equity and knowledge production.* Dakar: CODESRIA.

Orr, D. (1994). *Earth in mind.* Washington, DC: Island Press.

Perkin, H. (2007). History of universities. In J. J. F. Forest & P. G. Altbach (Eds.), *International handbook of higher education* (pp. 159–206). Dordrecht: Springer.

Santos, B. de S., & Almeida Filho, N. (2008). *A universidade no século XXI: Para uma universidade nova.* Coimbra: Almedina.

Sawyerr, A. (2004). Challenges facing African universities: Selected issues. *African Studies Review,* 47(1), 1–59.

Tavares, M., & Romão, T. (2015). Emerging counterhegemonic models in higher education: The Federal University of Southern Bahia (UFSB) and its contribution to a renewed geopolitics of knowledge (interview with Naomar de Almeida Filho). *Encounters in Theory and History of Education,* 16, 101–110.

Tjeldvoll, A. (1998). The idea of the service university. *International Higher Education,* 13(Fall), 9–10.

Trindade, H. H. C. (2009). UNILA: Universidade para a integração Latino-Americana. *Educación Superior y Sociedad,* 14(1), 147–153.

Yesufu, T. M., & Association of African Universities. (1973). *Creating the African university: Emerging issues in the 1970's.* Ibadan, Nigeria: Oxford University Press for the Association of African Universities.

5

Three Global Trends

Basil Bernstein famously stated that 'education cannot compensate for society' (in fact it was the title of his 1970 article in *New Society*). Educationists over the past century half century have sparred over this issue, debating whether education merely reproduces and reinforces inequalities and other characteristics of the outside society (as argued by many sociologists of education), or whether (following Freire and other critical pedagogues) it can have a transformative effect. While the agency-structure debate is far from over, positions near each of the poles are hard to sustain, with education and society clearly having some impact on each other, and conditioning in some way the other's possibilities. 'Education can compensate for society – a bit' in the words of Stephen Gorard (2010).

The account of the models outlined in the previous two chapters might appear to give the impression that higher education institutions are operating in something of a vacuum from societal influence, and are able to act freely to influence the societies in which they are located. Clearly this is not the case, and this chapter will provide some assessment of the external conditions influencing the operation of universities. In doing this, it will not focus on the deepest levels of structure, ones which have been amply covered in other general works. Universities, and the societies in which they are located, are imbued with and influenced by the fundamental ontological, epistemological and political assumptions and principles of the age and context, as well as their material conditions. Prominent among these are capitalism, and the rise of cumulative, empirically generated knowledge as the most authoritative guide to societal organisation, replacing religion and charismatic leadership. Instead, this chapter will focus on three trends more specific to the field of higher education—status competition, commodification and unbundling—dynamics which nevertheless manifest aspects of these deeper structures.

The first two of these dynamics were highlighted in Marginson's (2011) account of the public good in education, with market competition and status hierarchy being identified as features that would potentially constrain the realisation of institutions' public good contribution. To these I have added a third, *unbundling*, a more incipient and less well-known process, but one that could prove deeply challenging for the university in the years to come. All three of these trends undermine the developmental model characterising the role proposed for higher education in the SDGs.

Status competition refers to the processes through which higher education institutions compete with each other for prestige and standing. In the contemporary world, this competition takes place primarily through international rankings, which give credit principally to elite research and publications. The trend is most relevant to high-income and upper middle-income countries, and within those the elite institutions, but nevertheless exerts a strong influence over the values of the entire global sector.

Commodification refers to the process of conversion of the functions of the university into products and services for sale, while unbundling refers to the separating out of those functions from packages into individual units. Both may be present in institutions influenced by the 'entrepreneurial' model outlined above. Commodification is widely practised by contemporary institutions, though usually in combination with non-profit-making activities and state-funded activities. What characterises the contemporary entrepreneurial university is not the complete abandonment of teaching and research of intrinsic value or in the public good, but the continuance of some of these activities alongside the revenue generating ones. The coexistence of these missions (either complimentary or contradictory, depending on one's point of view) is what distinguishes the model from the trend towards total commodification, outlined below.

Unbundling is also a logical result of the emergence of entrepreneurial activities in institutions, as it seeks to drive down costs and maximise profits through separation of activities. The two processes are linked, since unbundling often occurs as a means to maximise commercial profits. However, they are not identical, since it is possible to have a commercialised comprehensive university, and to provide unbundled higher education on a non-profit or public basis. The following sections outline the basic characteristics of the three trends and assess their implications for the three dimensions of value, function and interaction.

Status Competition

As long as there has been higher education, there has been competition for status. Universities have always vied with each other for the renown of their scholars, the vibrancy of their intellectual community, the excellence of their courses and the influence of their academic production. Given the internationalised nature of universities since their earliest days, and the possibility of mobility, competition between them for lecturers and students has also been intense. So the new era of competition in the context of the international rankings is not completely new—it has simply taken on a new form, one that is much more explicit (in having purportedly objective gauges of quality) and with stakes that are high both for institutions, their prestige and financial health, and for nations, which see top ranking institutions as a source of national pride, like a prize fighter carrying the honour of a town.

The purpose of this section is not to provide a comprehensive account of rankings, or even a full critique, but to draw out the implications for achieving the sustainable development goals, implications that are almost entirely negative. The origin of ranking of higher education institutions is usually attributed to the U.S. News & World Report list of universities in the USA that developed from the 1980s, followed by others in the UK, Germany, Canada and Mexico (Hazelkorn 2015). While these national rankings now exist in many countries—particularly in those in which there exists a market or quasi-market for students, where they serve as a mechanism of consumer information—the most prominent are the international rankings. These function not so much as a practical guide to student choice (except perhaps for the global super-elite) but as a measure of prowess, and of the success of nation-states in projecting their intellectual glory internationally. The first of these rankings to gain international renown was the Shanghai Jiao Tong *Academic Ranking of World Universities* (ARWU) established in 2003, but it was joined the following year by the *Times Higher Education* (THE), and later by QS, which was originally partnering with THE, but from 2010 went solo. These three are the most prominent comprehensive rankings, but there are also a range of more specific ones, for example: the Webometrics Ranking of World Universities, gauging the presence of universities on the internet, and the CWTS Leiden Ranking which focuses solely on bibliometric data from academic publications. The major players have also produced more focused lists: QS provides subject-specific rankings and also one on graduate employability; regional specific rankings are also provided, for example the THE Emerging Economies and Latin America rankings. Other companies are also entering the fray: the lawnmower producer Flymo[1] in 2018 created a UK university ranking based on the amount of green space on campus!

University rankings have achieved extraordinary exposure globally, becoming in a few years followed and debated throughout the world, with university leaders and higher education policymakers on tenterhooks observing their year on year progress. Yet they have also attracted a good deal of criticism, being met by many working inside universities with scepticism and disdain. These reservations take a range of different forms. The mildest endorse the idea of rankings, but question

---

[1] https://wonkhe.com/blogs/super-grasses-exciting-new-green-uni-ranking-flies-in/.

the specific methodology used. In this way, there are vigorous debates about the calculations adopted and weightings between the different elements. Beyond these mathematical discussions, there are deeper questions about which aspects of university activity are being measured. The focus in the rankings is predominantly on research and publications: the Shanghai ranking[2] devotes 40% of its weighting to research, but the 40% it allocates to faculty quality is entirely research and publication-based, and the 10% to teaching uses as its proxy the number of alumni who are Nobel prizewinners—hardly a meaningful gauge of the quality of general teaching in a regular HEI! The proxies used by QS and THE for teaching quality are largely focused on reputation and staff–student ratio, which say as much about research as teaching. There is almost no attention paid to community engagement: the only component that might be categorised in this way is the 2.5% given to knowledge transfer in the THE, and this focuses only on one element—income from industry.

Doubt is also cast on the objectivity of these rankings by the fact that reputation is a key part, with 40% of the weighting in the QS ranking allocated to surveys of academics about which they feel is the best university, and 10% to employers of which university produces the best recruits. This point links in with a broader problem of the engrained nature of our preconceptions of university quality. It is joked (though it is not far from the truth) that whenever a new methodology is tested, if Harvard does not come out in the top five it is discarded as being obviously faulty. There are compelling reasons for believing that rankings ultimately shore up our pre-existing notions of which universities are the best, rather than providing us with any new objective evidence about quality.

And that is not all. There are also concerns that the rankings system is a money-making venture, with vested interests on the part of the ranking agencies: QS, in addition to deciding where institutions are ranked, conveniently provides paid consultancy services for institutions to improve their positioning. There are also questions of the impact of

---

[2]http://www.shanghairanking.com/ARWU-Methodology-2018.html.

rankings on the behaviour of institutions—linking in with broader critiques of performativity in education in the context of neoliberal target setting (Ball 2012). Finally, there are objections to rankings per se, that any form of ordering, regardless of the indicators used, is negative because it fosters competition rather than collaboration.

In partial response to some of these critiques, there have been some alternative gauges produced. There is the U-rank created by the European Commission which allows users to weight the different criteria according to their own preferences and values, and thereby get around what are seen to be skewed value judgments in the dominant rankings (although it has cynically been considered simply a way to improve the rather disappointing results of continental European institutions on the other rankings).

The U21 ranking—produced by the Universitas 21 association of research-intensive universities—is innovative in providing not a ranking of institutions but of systems. It gauges four areas—resources (20%), environment (20%), connectivity (20%) and output (40%). While the USA did top the list, followed by Switzerland and the UK, the other countries in the top five (Sweden and Denmark) do not fare so well on the institutional rankings, so it does appear to be employing a different set of criteria. This experiment is important as it draws attention to what a system comprised of multiple institutions might be able to do when they are working in a coordinated way to address the diverse needs of the society. QS now also has a 'system strength' ranking.

There have been some attempts to provide more radically alternative forms of ranking. David Orr (1994), for example, put forward a proposal for a ranking of environmental sustainability, with the following five principles:

1. Consumption and waste per student
2. Management policies on sustainability
3. Curriculum for ecological literacy
4. Support for local economy
5. Environmental impact of graduates

These alternative forms of ranking, not unexpectedly, have gained little purchase in the public domain. Nevertheless, in 2018 *Times Higher Education* announced that it is developing a new ranking of universities based on the SDGs, evaluating performance on 11 of the goals, including metrics such as proportion of graduates in health professions, proportion of female professors and employment security practices (Bothwell 2018). It remains to be seen whether this welcome development will be taken seriously in the higher education community, and will avoid overly reductive proxies for the different goals.

What influence does status competition have on the dimensions of value, function and interaction? Rankings and other forms of status competition clearly privilege a particular conception of academic quality: in the terms of the Harvey and Green (1993) typology, it is 'quality as exceptional', in that by definition it can only pertain to some universities. It is also characterised by status in relation to conventional indicators and awards, showing high esteem in the (predominantly English-speaking) academic community and mainstream academic journals. The overriding value, therefore, is that of academic excellence, rather than service to society, nation building or economic growth—in different ways, therefore, it challenges both the developmental and entrepreneurial models, and provides a reinforcement of an elite form of the Humboldtian one.

In terms of function, there is a clear privileging of research over other activities of the institution. As seen above, proxies in the rankings used for teaching and community engagement are wholly inadequate, and compared to research excellence have a very minor weighting. Within research, there is an emphasis on externally funded, large-scale, high-profile work, and publication in Web of Science listed journals. The trend is ambiguous in relation to interaction. On the one hand its elitism and exclusivity in relation to student intake indicates low porosity, although internationalisation (in terms of staff and student body and collaborations) is rewarded in some of the lists. Outward-bound interaction is valued in terms of disseminating knowledge (and increasing citations), but much less in terms of inward-bound interaction and absorbing ideas and priorities from other communities.

The rankings are not only important in the imaginary of universities in the population, but have also led to concrete policy changes. In an eagerness bordering in some cases on panic, countries have sought to improve their institutions' positionings on the rankings through a variety of measures. These have included increasing resources for elite institutions (for example, the Excellence Initiative in Germany), and amalgamating institutions so as to improve their metrics, as in France and a number of other European countries. These policies are inevitably leading to an even greater concentration of funds for research in a few elite institutions.

For the post-2015 development agenda and the achievement of the SDGs, rankings present a very real threat. First, they value exclusivity rather than inclusivity, and act against the agendas of widening participation so urgently needed in most parts of the world. Second, there is almost no acknowledgement or valuing of community engagement, reinforcing the sense of this pillar being the poor sister of teaching and research, unless it is generating income for the institution. Finally, even teaching is hardly visible, with few incentives for universities to create a rich learning environment for their students.

For many countries, the goal is to insert one institution into the top 200. Even among the powerful BRICS countries this is a challenge—in the Shanghai ranking, China have 12 in the top 200 (its top ranked institution is Tsinghua University at 45th), but Russia and Brazil have just one apiece (Moscow State University in 86th and the University of São Paulo in the 151–200 bracket), while South Africa's top-ranked institution (University of the Witwatersrand) is in the 201–300 bracket and India's (Indian Institute of Science) is in the 401–500 range. The Shanghai list stretches to 1000 institutions, with the THE slightly larger at 1258. Yet even these are a mere fraction of the more than 20,000 HEIs in the world. Rankings then are in practical terms irrelevant for the majority of countries and the vast majority of institutions within them. Nevertheless, the discursive impact on the creation of norms and ideals, and concrete impact through distribution of resources, are significant and in many ways work against the developmental model outlined in the previous chapter.

Commodification

Commodification refers to the process of conversion of services or products not initially for sale into ones oriented towards profit-making. This term is close in meaning to 'commercialisation', although the latter has a rather broader application. In higher education, commercialisation has affected all of the diverse forms of function. As explored in Bok (2003), US universities were early examples of commercialisation of their campuses, starting with those activities at the periphery of the university experience, such as catering, sports and institutional merchandise. In more recent years, that commercialisation has crept towards the core, affecting teaching—with the raising or introduction of fees, and competition between institutions for prospective students; research—with significant amounts of funding provided by corporate entities, often with intellectual property restrictions; and community engagement—replacing freely given public service with income-generating consultancy and other services. These processes of commercialisation manifest themselves in the emergence of purely private institutions, and a rapidly growing for-profit sector, but also affect previously public institutions. The very life of the faculty member through this process becomes one of 'academic capitalism' (Slaughter and Leslie 1997). While forms of commercialisation are present in all higher education systems, there are significant differences, with public universities in Continental Europe and Latin America being much more resistant than those in Anglophone countries, for example.

While many aspects of the university can be commercialised—including conventional commodities such as branded clothing, rental of space, etc.—the term commodification as employed in this section will refer specifically to the sale of knowledge. It refers to the process through which knowledge that could be freely imparted and acquired—whether through activities relating to teaching, research or community engagement—is organised and made available for the purpose of generating income, and potentially profit.

The most obvious manifestation of commodification in higher education is the growth of the private sector, and specifically for-profit institutions. Private higher education has always been significant, and in many ways, state-run higher education, which had its heyday in the twentieth century with the rise of the welfare state, has been the exception. However, private institutions have traditionally been religious (for example the Catholic universities in Latin America), or philanthropic, non-profit foundations, such as the Ivy League colleges in the USA (Geiger 1986; Levy 1986; Kinser et al. 2010). The new generation of universities presents a very different profile. It sees higher education primarily as a business investment, has for-profit status, and in order to turn a profit has developed some distinctive characteristics—for example standardisation of curricula, teaching materials and teaching methods, tailoring courses to working adults, focusing on courses with low costs in terms of infrastructure, laboratories and so forth.

For-profit higher education is not legal in all countries, and has blossomed only in those places in which the high cost or exclusivity of existing institutions has created demand for them. The USA and Brazil are global leaders in the for-profit higher education business. The University of Phoenix was a pioneer in the US context, creating a network of campuses delivering standardised courses for working adults: while the courses are more expensive than community colleges, they provide convenient offering for those in work and are seen to be closely attuned to the labour market. There has been significant controversy over the aggressive marketing adopted by the for-profit universities, particularly in preying on prospective students who are entitled to federal (Pell) grants.

In Brazil, the expansion of this sector has been even more striking. As much as ¾ of all enrolments are now in the private sector, which is dominated by for-profit institutions (INEP 2017). The sector has grown exponentially since the late 1990s, through the opening of lower cost evening courses: in 2017, students could pay R$621 (£125) a month (average cost for a course in pedagogy), rather than the R$6203 (£1250) a month (average cost for medicine) needed for higher prestige courses (Globo 2017), but must be content with 'high school' style instruction in classroom hubs dotted around cities in high street locations and even shopping centres, with little in the way of library resources and autonomous study (McCowan 2004). In recent years there has been a significant consolidation of the sector, with the 'mom and pop' institutions being progressively absorbed by larger groups. Just one of these groups, Kroton-Anhanguera, has 16.5% of all students, and 45% of distance learners (Carvalho 2017). Five of these groups are now listed on the stock market, and are developing significant holdings that will ensure their involvement in higher education will only increase—in all probability expanding to enter other countries as well.

But commodification does not occur only in the private sector. Forms of privatisation have been introduced in public institutions around the world as part of the wave of neoliberal reforms in all sectors since the 1980s. These changes have been promoted on the basis of the lack of state funds available for an ever-expanding student body, the efficiency benefits accrued by the introduction of new forms of management, the positive impact on quality from competition between institutions, and on academic work through market incentives.

Markets, however, do not function in higher education in the same way as other tangible products. First, it is hard for the consumer to assess the quality of the product. Prospective students may use official indicators or rankings, or more ethereal notions of prestige, but it is almost impossible to choose on the basis of personal experience—unless they were to do a trial term at each of the institutions they were interested in. Second, it is hard for the consumer to swap or exit the product. Costs of all types (financial, time, emotional) of dropping out of a degree before the end are considerable, and in some instances it may not be possible to restart elsewhere. Third, there are geographical barriers to choice, with lower income students particularly constrained in their ability to move to institutions beyond their local one.

From the supply side, 'successful' institutions might be expected to increase their offer in the context of healthy demand for their services: yet in many cases they will not do so on account of the need to protect the exclusivity of the product (if everybody had a degree from Yale it would lose its value), or to protect the pedagogical environment, ensuring the intimate dialogical learning that takes place in a liberal arts college, for example.

The promise of markets in higher education has been that competition will enhance quality. For sure, there is an influence of competition on quality, and in some cases the former may enhance the latter, but it is absolutely not enhanced in all cases, and in many cases will lead to a reduction in quality. In this sense, competition in higher education is like other products: a 'free' market for shoes ensures not that all of them are of higher quality, but that there is diversity of quality, including some that are long-lasting or beautiful or exclusive, and only within the reach of the wealthy, and others that will fall apart swiftly, are simple-looking or undesirable, and are financially within the reach of all. Marketisation of higher education, therefore, inevitably reinforces inequities on the basis of the prospective students' socioeconomic status.

In terms of the notion of *value* outlined in Chapter 3, a commodified system will encourage instrumental benefit: if the production and transmission of knowledge are dependent on an external client, then normally the client will expect to receive benefit deriving from that knowledge, and direct their purchases towards the sources of greatest benefit. At first sight, the market would appear to be attuning the activities of the university to the needs of society. However, as with all markets, supply follows not need but demand, and the latter is dependent in turn on purchasing power. We move, therefore, from a notion of *service* value to one of *exchange* value. Knowledge in this conception is valued not for the benefits that it can bring directly, but for value it can obtain on the market, and which can be used to purchase other desired goods. The university in turn is incentivised to create and disseminate not the kinds of knowledge that will bring the greatest benefit to society, but those which will bring the greatest revenue in relation to cost.

The commodified university may well have a multiplicity of *functions*, as in the 'multiversity', but the nature of those functions will be determined by considerations of financial viability. Teaching activities will for this reason migrate gradually towards courses that have high marginal profit: i.e. those for which there is high demand but in which the costs are lower. In consequence, for-profit universities tend to have a high proportion of students in applied social science courses, such as business studies, education and law; with low provision of more costly courses, such as medicine or engineering, or lower demand courses such as philosophy, even if there are significant societal needs in these areas.

In terms of *interaction*, the commodified university is characterised by a high level of porosity. As regards flow of people, the market has no interest in restricting access to the few, as in the traditional elite university. However, in order to cater to high-income and low-income students a diversity of products is made available, with a range of prices, leading to a stratified system. Some consumers will be unable to purchase even the cheapest products, or may decide it is not worth their while. In terms of outbound movement of people, there is also a high degree of porosity, with academics engaging closely with industry, as well as potentially starting up their own spin-off businesses. There is also extensive flow of ideas—deriving the 'subject matter' of research and teaching from the economic interests of external consumers, and in return providing a range of products for the external market.

Unbundling

In contrast to the other two trends, we are only seeing the initial signs of unbundling in higher education. As a concept, it has its origins in business, referring to the movement from a set of products sold together as a bundle—for example, the traditional music 'album', or the Microsoft Office package—to one in which the consumer instead is able to purchase the individual components—so the preference for downloading or streaming 'singles', or purchasing only Excel if one does not need the other programmes. While in markets for some products it may be essential to purchase all products together ('interrelated bundles'), and there may be considerable advantages in bundles—for example, the package holiday—providing savings of money as well as time for consumers ('convenience bundles'), in other cases they simply lock consumers into paying for products they do not want ('tie-in bundles').

In higher education, the bundle in question is that of packaging tuition along with a range of other services: including libraries and information technology; broader learning opportunities such as overseas exchanges and language classes; sporting, recreational and cultural activities; not to mention the research and scholarship undertaken by academic staff. Challenges to this package have been particularly prominent in the US campus-based institution, in which fees have been escalating in recent years as universities try to outdo each other in the facilities available for students (Selingo 2013; Bowen 2013). Unbundling, therefore, refers to the process of selling to consumers only those parts of the university experience that they want or can afford: in particular, providing just the basic tuition, without the extras (Barber et al. 2013; Macfarlane 2011). While the process is present in public institutions, it has been fuelled primarily by the growth of the for-profit sector (Robertson and Komljenovic 2016a, b). In addition, although not always involving technology, unbundling is closely linked to technological developments in higher education, including the rise of e-learning, big data and learning analytics (Williamson 2018).

However, we are not here faced with a simple mono-directional trajectory from bundled to unbundled. As shown by Gehrke and Kezar (2015), unbundling is not a new phenomenon, and there have been moves towards and away from different forms of bundle throughout the history of higher education. Indeed, the bundling of teaching and research only took place in the nineteenth century, and there have been significant fluctuations in the roles pertaining to academic staff, with the pastoral role, for example, periodically emerging and receding from view. Furthermore, there has not always been a coexistence of instruction and assessment (Anderson 2006): new universities created in England in the nineteenth and early twentieth centuries commonly had their courses validated by existing institutions, and the University of London awarded degrees for overseas colleges such as Nairobi, Dar es Salaam and Makerere in their early stages. Nevertheless, the current trends in unbundling are far more radical than the previous ones, and pose a greater challenge to our assumptions about the higher education institution.

An obvious manifestation of unbundling—and one that has been in evidence for some time—is outsourcing of services within universities such as catering, cleaning, information and communications technology (ICT), library services and accommodation. It is important to highlight that this trend is not exclusive to private universities, and in many countries is now the norm in public institutions. While this outsourcing is often to external companies, in some cases universities have established their own firms, as is the case of FX Plus, created by Falmouth University and the University of Exeter in the UK to provide support staff, including academic support (Grove 2013). Another aspect is location, with challenges to the idea of the university as 'place', with the emergence of multiple campuses, or hubs replacing campuses, or with students studying at a distance in any part of the world. Following from the early success of the Open University in the UK, there has been a huge expansion of distance providers, with institutions such as the Indira Gandhi National Open University in India and the Allama Iqbal Open University in Pakistan boasting student numbers in the millions.

An integral part of the process is the unbundling of taught courses and academic work. In the case of the former, the design, delivery and assessment of the course may be conducted by different institutions. A case in point here is the emergence of alternative providers of validation of knowledge, and the likelihood of companies such as Pearson in taking up an increasingly significant role in the assessment of competencies in particular areas (with learners awarded a series of discrete badges or micro-credentials, rather than a single coordinated degree). In the area of online courses, there is a common separation between course design and delivery. Unbundling, therefore, signals the end of the programme of study, in which academics curate learning through a process of selection and sequencing of knowledge content. Massive open online courses (MOOCs) are the most radical manifestation of this form of unbundling, given the common dislocation between curriculum content, pedagogical orientation and assessment.

These changes inevitably lead to shifts in the role of academic staff. As explored by Macfarlane (2011), the 'all-round' academic is being progressively replaced by 'para-academics' such as 'skills advisers, educational developers, learning technologists and research management staff' (p. 59), with a deskilling of the former and an upskilling of the latter. These shifts—evident in public as well as private institutions— have been linked to the growth in the proportion of non-tenured faculty, most prominently in the USA. Developments in ICT have facilitated relatively easy broadcasting of lectures and other communications, enabling students in multiple locations to have contact with the ideas of well-known academics (Paulson 2002). These 'stars'

(Barber et al. 2013) are not, of course, able to have actual interactions with students, thus opening the door to a supplementary group of tutors who service the students' pedagogical needs. This trend would inevitably signal the end of the university professor, in the role most famously promoted by Wilhelm von Humboldt, as one who engages in the pursuit of knowledge and simultaneously supervises students in their own pursuit. Commentators have also linked these changes in academic faculty to the decline of collegiality and democratic governance in universities (Macfarlane 2011).

Another manifestation of unbundling is the 'no-frills' model of higher education. In order to combat the escalating costs outlined above, for-profit providers have emerged in many countries, as discussed in the previous section, offering degrees at a low cost, but with limited pedagogical interaction and access to resources, and without the broader enrichment activities characteristic of the campus university experience. The University of Phoenix is a prime example in terms of the unbundling of the faculty role, standardisation of the curriculum and use of blended mode (Kinser 2002), although many of these for-profit institutions directed at working adults actually charge more than public institutions. Coventry University in the UK has established 'CU Coventry', where students pay only half the cost of a regular degree, but are barred from accessing some university facilities such as libraries and sports centres (Vasagar 2011). Beyond these forms, there is a further stage of unbundling displayed in cases in which an online platform is provided to coordinate students' learning, but without itself providing the content. Western Governors University, for example, which advertises itself as 'half the cost of other online universities', does not provide instruction at all, but acts as a broker for courses provided by other institutions, offering assessments to certify competency (Paulson 2002). UniversityNow (2017), with a mission to 'make a quality college education available and affordable to people everywhere', offers competency-based courses through its child institutions Patten and New Charter.

Universities have been described as the oldest European institution with the exception of the Catholic Church (de Ridder-Symoens 1996), and their ability to survive through the dramatic political, economic, social and scientific changes of the past eight centuries is testament to both the importance of their core role in society and their ability to adapt to changing circumstances. So why are there signs now of the unravelling of the institution? There are two broad drivers for contemporary processes of unbundling: financial and pedagogical. As will be seen below, these are not entirely discrete—for example, some of the pedagogical changes are intended to bring long-term economic benefits—but do represent distinct modes of justification.

Given the origins of unbundling in business, and the strong links to the for-profit sector in HE, the financial motivations are the most evident. These may relate either to the provider or the consumer, or both. For providers, efficiency savings can be made through unbundling, for example through changes in processes of course design, by centralising and standardising, and freeing up more academic staff time for delivery. Focusing on a specific piece of the puzzle can also create economies of scale for institutions. In some cases, savings are made through the extraction of superfluous elements (i.e. the no-frills model) and possibly through a simple reduction in the quality of the product. These changes can drive up profits for education companies, and provide greater incentives for new providers to enter the market. While there is no consensus that innovations such as online provision always represent a reduction in costs, there is certainly the potential for them to do so (Bowen 2013). Costs can be reduced through simplification of the provision, and thereby bring in new students who would have been excluded from the market in the context of conventional institutions. Some manifestations of unbundling—most prominently MOOCs—are currently offered on a free of charge basis. Nevertheless, commercial MOOCs are starting to predominate (Dianati 2016; McKenzie 2018), and even for the non-profit courses, there is still a significant financial motivation for universities in terms of enhancing the visibility of their brand, while small private online courses (SPOCs) have also emerged in their wake.

There are also a range of arguments based on the desirability of unbundling for enhancing teaching and learning. According to this view, the conventional university is deficient in the preparation it provides for students, through lack of adaptation to the specific needs of contemporary society. There are two main pedagogical arguments put forward. First of these is personalization—that learners need to have a higher degree of control over their own learning, in terms of the content, process and timing. Second, that learning needs to be more attuned to the needs of the workplace and the demands of employers, particularly in the context of a rapidly changing labour market.

The primary vehicle for achieving both of these ends is through the movement from structured degrees and courses to competencies. Craig (2015) and others write disparagingly of the reliance of traditional universities on 'seat time', credits based at least in part on compulsory course attendance. Instead, students should piece together a range of different competencies, areas of knowledge and skill aligned with employer requirements, ideally organised via a competency management platform. Students should be able to acquire these competencies from a range of sources of learning, and have them assessed when they feel ready, allowing for the different rhythms of learning and other commitments of students. In addition to 'adaptive learning', unbundling is seen to facilitate *gamification*, the introduction of techniques from videogames to make learning more entertaining, to increase engagement and reduce dropout (Craig 2015). These changes, according to advocates, serve to make learning more relevant and engaging for the individual learner (personalization) and more attuned to the needs of the economy (employability).

These benefits are sometimes presented as a social justice justification for unbundling. The incentives for new providers to enter the market and the lowering of costs together lead to the conditions for expansion of access to higher education, while personalization and employability are seen to make HE more beneficial to disadvantaged students. MOOCs are seen by some as a potentially radical disruption to elitism in higher education, opening the door to academic knowledge that had previously been confined to the privileged (DeMillo 2015; Laurillard and Kennedy 2017). Nevertheless, unbundling is also entirely consistent with increasing stratification of the system, and intensification of a 'law of the jungle' in which those already advantaged are better equipped to seek valuable opportunities in the fragmented array of offering.

Unbundling has no necessary position on the question of *value*. It leads to a significant increase in individual choice over what is learned, and a corresponding decrease in lecturer and institutional stipulation of what is of value and why. This involves a personalization of learning—as discussed above—but also a deeper process of removal of the collective orientation of the institution in terms of vision and role.

The clearest implication of this process is that it leads to a fragmentation or multiplicity of values. While unbundling is largely associated with commercialization, the door is therefore left open to intrinsic as well as instrumental rationales for learning: for example, the MOOC phenomenon has involved people signing up for courses which provide no concrete benefit other than the acquisition of the knowledge in question. On the one hand, this implies a certain democratisation in that the university becomes more responsive to the particular needs and goals of students—indeed, this democratisation is heralded by unbundling's advocates (e.g. DeMillo 2015). On the other hand, it leads to an undermining of collective values, and also of the possibility that there exist people who are more experienced and knowledgeable, and who might provide guidance for those less so—as occurred in the traditional course structured and sequenced by lecturers. (There may be some echoes here of the 2016 leitmotif 'post-truth', and the reaction against experts in recent popular votes.) Furthermore, at both system and institutional levels, it undermines the ability to promote the public good and affirmative action in accordance with social justice.

The key point in relation to function, and indeed the central characteristic of unbundling, is that it separates functions from each other. It therefore represents the contrary tendency to the multiversity. While the previous diverse functions of the university may still continue, the higher education provider itself becomes more exclusively focused on teaching, and within teaching, on the packaging and delivery of knowledge, and possibly tutoring support. The research function of the university is then moved over to specialised research institutes, laboratories and think tanks, or research wings of private corporations. Taken to its ultimate length, unbundling results in the disintegration of these elements to the extent that we cannot meaningfully speak of a university at all.

In response to the claimed pedagogical benefits of unbundling—personalization and employability—a range of limitations can be identified. A primary factor is that unbundled forms of teaching may not provide sufficient learner support. There is substantial research evidence of the negative impact of the fragmentation of the learning environment, particularly for non-traditional students, and conversely of the positive impact of interactions with academic staff outside the classroom, for example through participation in research projects, or through seeking general advice and guidance (see Gehrke and Kezar 2015). Furthermore, the portrayal of learning associated with unbundling is predominantly transmission-based, involving the acquisition of knowledge and skills through mono-directional absorption in isolated individuals. Unbundled pedagogy undermines the relational dimension of teaching and learning. The benefits of learning in a collective, of dialogue and of Illich's (1973) more demanding conception of 'conviviality', are no longer available in this model. While the campus university may have some apparently unnecessary luxuries, the existence of extra-curricular activities including artistic and sporting pursuits, political and social activities, is central to a holistic conception of learning—particularly if we envisage higher education as a space for civic and personal, as well as vocational development. There are also questions relating to the curriculum, and the advantages of exposure to the whole of a canon within a disciplinary area, rather than a fragmented selection based on students' current interests. Finally, while it is not essential for universities to be the validators of knowledge, and other institutions may carry out this role effectively—there are advantages in integration of teaching and assessment, in opening possibilities for constructive alignment (Biggs 1999).

Of the three dimensions, interaction is the most clear-cut in its implications. The tendency of unbundling is unequivocally towards porosity, with an increasing weakening of the boundary between university and society. Unbundling leads to the highest degree of porosity, to what we might describe as *hyper-porosity*. First, it represents an almost complete destruction of the idea of university as a place. Through multipolar and distance provision, learners can access knowledge and instruction from anywhere, and are interacting with students and instructors in other locations. The instructors themselves are unlikely to be full-time staff members and may have most of their lives outside of

Table 5.1 Anatomy of three global trends

	Value	Function	Interaction
Status competition	Academic excellence	Elite research and publication	Medium porosity
Commodification	Exchange	Determined by demand	High porosity
Unbundling	Any	Knowledge delivery	Hyper-porosity

the higher education space. In relation to ideas, there is also an extreme degree of porosity, with learners developing a portfolio of knowledge and skills partly from higher education providers and partly from other knowledge sources, and having them validated by a third party. While most would agree that increasing porosity is a positive trend, there are some risks presented by these extreme forms, as will be discussed further in Chapter 9.

The overall emphases of the three trends in relation to value, function and interaction are displayed on Table 5.1.

Implications for International Development

What then are the prospects of these three trends for international development and the SDGs? As intimated above, status competition is antithetical to the developmental role of universities due to its encouragement of elite rather than locally relevant research, its lack of emphasis on teaching and community engagement, exclusivity in relation to access and concentration of funding in a few institutions. Elite traditional higher education is not in all aspects antithetical to development, as much research produced by these universities brings significant public benefit, even to the poorest in society, in the areas of health, engineering, arts and many other areas. Yet in a direct sense these institutions are largely impermeable to the majority of the global population, and even to many within high-income countries. Furthermore, the idealisation of the 'world-class university' is encouraging practices and policies that act against the inclusive, democratic and public-oriented work necessary to fulfil the SDGs.

In relation to the other two trends, commodification and unbundling, the implications are contested. The movements towards porosity are undoubtedly positive for development. While the 'ivory tower' conception of university may bring (sometimes unexpected) benefits of a concrete nature to society in the long-term, the increased openness to society's demands and needs is without doubt important in the short term, particularly for lower income countries. Development of distance education and new providers have the potential to bring higher education to a greater proportion of the population. With streamlined forms of provision and greater efficiency, they also have the potential to increase availability through lower costs to the state and greater affordability to consumers.

However, the implications of the move towards exchange value and private benefit are of great concern in terms of sustainable development. As discussed in Chapter 5, a university for development would need to have primarily instrumental benefit. The value of its activities would be judged by its effectiveness in solving critical problems facing society, enhancing economic growth, ensuring poverty reduction and promoting sustainability. The kinds of benefits provided would need to be available for all of the population, and in a relatively short time frame (given the pressing nature of many of the challenges). It would avoid becoming merely a positional good—for example in the case of diploma bestowal becoming a means for elites in society maintaining advantage over others, without an aggregate benefit. Yet in this move towards instrumentalism, it is important to avoid the emphasis on exchange value brought by commodification: the worth of the goods provided by the university should reside in the tangible benefits brought to society, not in the success of their sale (which depends as much on the availability of a buyer as on the worth of the product).

In addition to problematic implications raised by commodification and unbundling in relation to *value*, there may also be issues in relation to *function*. Commodification, as outlined above, assigns its functions in relation to demand. As with all markets, this mechanism has apparently positive points in its responsiveness to individuals and groups in society, but has downsides in relation to its dependence on purchasing power. There are further distortions that occur through advertising, in convincing consumers to have particular 'wants' that may not be in their interests.

Most examples of the operation of marketisation in higher education are of the quasi-market type, with significant state involvement in funding—either directly to students or to institutions—and regulation of fee levels and student numbers. Brazil is an example of a country with something closer to a free market within the private sector. In this case, the benefits and dangers of commodification are clearly seen. On the one hand, private sector expansion has enabled a rapid increase in enrolments, giving access to populations previously unable to find a place. On the other, it has led to a worryingly low level of quality in many institutions, a narrowing of the disciplinary range of course offerings, a movement away from community engagement and research activities, and increasing inequities through stratification of opportunity (McCowan 2004; Sampaio 2011).

In Kenya—and a number of other African countries—on the other hand, marketisation has occurred to a large extent through the public sector. In addition to government-sponsored places allocated on the basis of academic merit, public institutions have in recent years been allowed to admit fee-paying students on parallel programmes. Here too, there has been a negative impact on quality. Incentives for revenue maximisation have led to an uncontrolled influx of these parallel stream students, without corresponding recruitment of faculty, leading to a significant worsening of the conditions for learning (Oanda and Jowi 2012; Wangenge-Ouma 2007).

Equally, commodification of the products of research and community engagement place constraints on the possibilities for development, particularly if the aim is for 'inclusive development', one in which the fruits are equitably distributed across the population, with a focus on maximising of the prospects of the least well-off. Commercially funded research may at times have knock-on public benefit, but it will be filtered first through the profit requirements of the corporation; in some cases it may even have a negative impact. The growth of the so-called consultancy culture among lecturers in lower income countries—through which academic staff supplement their meagre incomes by renting out their services—has also had a prejudicial effect on their institutions, reducing their available time for core activities.

In relation to unbundling specifically, it is important to state from the outset that there is nothing inherently wrong with the process, or anything inherently valuable in the packaged university. It is necessary to assess the implications of the alternative scenarios for the role of the institution and benefits emerging. Furthermore, as argued by Bacevic (2018), the discourse of crisis around changes to the contemporary university is predicated on a mythical construction of the Humboldtian institution, so should not be perceived as threatening a previously unsullied and coherent whole.

One difficult question is whether unity of teaching, research and service is necessarily needed, or whether these functions can be performed equally well by different institutions. In the Magna Charta Universitatum signed by the rectors of European universities on the 900th anniversary of the University of Bologna, the inseparability of teaching and research is strongly emphasised. In fact, empirical evidence is conflicting on the link between research and teaching activities (de Jonghe 2005; Gehrke and Kezar 2015), with a prominent meta-review of 58 studies showing no significant link between excellence in the two areas (Hattie and Marsh 1996). Nevertheless, this finding may be an indication of problems in the coordination of the two forms of activity within institutions (and within the workloads of individual academics), rather than of the lack of synergies between the two. There are strong reasons to believe that there are cross-fertilisation benefits to the coexistence of teaching and research: for instance, with teaching enhanced by lecturers' engagement in research, and potential for student learning through their participation in research projects. Interaction between research and service can also lead to positive synergies. The movement of research out of universities towards specialised (often private) units has been argued for on the basis of greater efficiency and attunement to industrial needs, but it has deeper implications in terms of the shift from basic towards applied research, with a movement from mode 1 (blue skies, academic, disciplinary-based) knowledge towards mode 2 (interdisciplinary, applied) knowledge (as discussed in relation to Botswana in Tabulawa et al. 2013): this shift has apparent short-term benefits, but the longer term ramifications are a source of concern. Furthermore, unbundling also prevents cross-subsidisation, through which institutions can use more lucrative activities to support those pursuits with less potential for profit generation but with other forms of value.

In addition to cross-fertilisation and cross-subsidisation, there is also the question of equality of opportunity. A coordinated higher education sector, or even a comprehensive institution, can allow for mechanisms that ensure equitable chances for all students, including affirmative action programmes and extra support for disadvantaged students. This political and financial leverage is weakened through unbundling. Furthermore, extreme forms of unbundling such as MOOCs, while touted as the solution for impoverished countries with low higher education coverage, have mostly been accessed by learners from higher income countries (Watters 2013; Wildavsky 2014), and present particular difficulties for disadvantaged students. In resource-constrained countries in which there are problems of quality at primary and secondary levels, students are unlikely to have the learner autonomy necessary to navigate and learn effectively from a MOOC. The well-known initiative Kepler in Rwanda has in fact introduced a form of 'rebundling' in response to these challenges, combining US-accredited MOOCs with face-to-face tuition and student accommodation, so as to make the course content more relevant to the local context and to provide learning support for students, thereby improving retention.

It is understandable that commodification and unbundling appear attractive options to those looking to expand opportunities for higher education in the poorest parts of the globe. Some nation-states lack the funds to support anything beyond a 5% higher education enrolment rate, and the introduction of private providers and streamlined, affordable courses seems like the only solution to the conundrum. In addition, there is the perception that because MOOCs are new and use cutting-edge technology, then they are the best preparation for young people entering the contemporary technology-driven world.

However, there are a number of problems presented by these trends. As seen above, they show positive points in relation to *interaction*, but raise a number of concerns in relation to *value* and *function*. In particular, there are issues relating to inequities of access and the undermining of the public good function of universities. Above all, it is problematic to consider that trends whose worth in high-income countries has been shown to be uncertain (to say the very least) should be exported to the 'developing world' as the preferred options.

Equity of access is intrinsically important, for those who hold to the value of fairness. But it also has an instrumental value in allowing for talented individuals with an interest in higher study to pursue their interests, produce new knowledge, develop technology and become competent professionals. An inequitable higher education system, therefore, is also an inefficient one in relation to the interests of society. The marketisation of higher education—whether through private providers or quasi-markets within public sectors—has generally exacerbated inequities of access. While free-of-charge public higher education systems in the elite phase were far from equitable—with the privilege of access conferred through apparently meritocratic admissions, but in practice out of the reach of most of the population—private systems make those inequalities even more entrenched and impede attempts at affirmative action. Unbundling also weakens levers to ensure equality of opportunity. It also presents greater barriers to those with less learner autonomy, meaning that epistemic access is not possible for those from disadvantaged backgrounds. As discussed above, for access to be meaningful it also needs to be linked to a consistently high quality of provision, involving opportunities to learn and to convert that learning into subsequent opportunities.

The combination of the profit incentive and disassociation of the diverse functions of the university also undermines its ability to provide teaching, research and community engagement in the public interest. The underpinning value of the university moves towards exchange rather than intrinsic and (net gain) instrumental benefit, and its functions become fragmented and unable to reinforce one another.

Nevertheless, some forms of unbundling are genuinely democratising and transformative. As explored by Mason (2015) and others, while capitalism is constantly adapting to new forms of technology, there are ways in which the networking potential provided by digital technologies is opening up new forms of non-commodified interaction (Wikipedia being a case in point). These ideas link into new movements for open science, open access publishing and what have been termed 'open knowledge institutions' (Montgomery and Neylon 2018). It is possible, then, that the democratising promise of MOOCs may bear fruit, at least in some instances—when free from the strictures of profit-making, and when presented in ways that are inclusive of diverse communities—and lead us to new and more democratic forms of higher education (as explored in Chapter 10)—fostering Marginson's (2011) 'networked', rather than market or status ranking imaginary. These more progressive forms of unbundling can be termed 'de-institutionalisation', as opposed to the 'disaggregation' (market-making separation of functions) and 'no frills' versions.

* * *

There appears to be a fundamental contradiction in the policies of many development agencies, which are, on the one hand, endorsing the role of higher education in international development proposed in the SDGs, and on the other, promoting or turning a blind eye to the trends in international higher education working against that role. Policies such as supporting the development of the for-profit private sector, of 'no frills' higher education (under the aegis of 'affordability'), of concentration of research in a few elite institutions, and a narrowing of the curriculum towards work skills all run in this vein.

Of course, external support to higher education through development aid—while in some cases enjoying substantial funding—is small compared to the mainstream flows of national higher education funding. More significant than donor preferences for the trajectory of higher education in low- and middle-income countries will be the global trends in the sector affecting national systems, spread through a combination of desire for emulation of 'successful' systems (especially through national and international rankings), student and staff mobility, the preferences of transnational employers, the direct operations of transnational higher education providers and the agenda setting of influential international organisations such as the World Bank and OECD. It is these trends that need to be borne in mind when assessing the likely trajectory of higher education and its ability to attend to development goals.

Status competition, commodification and unbundling—in their different ways—are all exerting an influence on this trajectory. Elite institutions are more influenced by status competition, while commodification is more central to the demand-absorbing institutions, and unbundling for the 'new kids on the block'. Yet all institutions are subject to the discursive influence, and construct their own identities and practices in relation to them. The next three chapters will assess core aspects of the higher education institution—access, quality and impact through research and community engagement—aiming to understand them through the interplay of these external influences and the models and purposes of the university.

References

Anderson, R. D. (2006). *British universities past and present*. London: Continuum.
Bacevic, J. (2018). With or without U? Assemblage theory and (de)territorialising the university. *Globalisation, Societies and Education*. https://doi.org/10.1080/14767724.2018.1498323.
Ball, S. J. (2012). Performativity, commodification and commitment: An I-spy guide to the neoliberal university. *British Journal of Educational Studies, 60*(1), 17–28.
Barber, M., Donnelly, K., & Rizvi, S. (2013*). An avalanche is coming*. London, UK: Institute for Public Policy Research. Available at http://www.ippr.org/files/images/media/files/publication/2013/04/avalanche-is-coming_Mar2013_10432.pdf?noredirect=1. Accessed 9 February 2017.
Biggs, J. (1999). What the student does: Teaching for enhanced learning. *Higher Education Research & Development, 18*(1), 57–75.
Bok, D. (2003). *Universities in the marketplace: The commercialization of higher education*. Princeton: Princeton University Press.
Bothwell, E. (2018, September 6). THE developing ranking based on Sustainable Development Goals. *Times Higher Education*.
Bowen, W. G. (2013). *Higher education in the digital age*. Princeton: Princeton University Press.
Craig, R. (2015). *College disrupted: The great unbundling of higher education*. New York, NY: Palgrave Macmillan.

de Carvalho, C. H. (2017). Capital concentration and financialization in Brazilian private higher education. *Academia*. Available at http://academia.lis.upatras.gr/index.php/academia/article/view/2835 Accessed 9 November 18.

de Jonghe, A. (2005). Reorganising the teaching-research tension. *Higher Education Management and Policy, 17*(2), 61–76.

DeMillo, R. A. (2015). *Revolution in higher education: How a small band of innovators will make college accessible and affordable.* Cambridge: MIT Press.

de Ridder-Symoens, H. (Ed.). (1996). *A history of the university in Europe: Volume 2, Universities in early modern Europe (1500–1800).* Cambridge: Cambridge University Press.

Dianati, S. (2016). *What do Massive Open Online Courses (MOOCs) have to do with 'good' education? An ideology critique of MOOCs* (Unpublished PhD thesis). Flinders University.

Gehrke, S., & Kezar, A. (2015). Unbundling the faculty role in higher education: Utilizing historical, theoretical, and empirical frameworks to inform future research. In *Higher education: Handbook of theory and research* (pp. 93–150). Cham: Springer International Publishing.

Geiger, R. (1986). *Private sectors in higher education: Structure, function and change in eight countries.* Ann Arbor: University of Michigan.

Globo. (2017, August 28). *Estudo mostra que mensalidade média de medicina é 10 vezes maior que a de pedagogia no Brasil.* Available at https://g1.globo.com/educacao/noticia/estudo-mostra-que-mensalidade-media-de-medicina-e-10-vezes-maior-que-a-de-pedagogia-no-brasil.ghtml. Accessed 1 June 2018.

Gorard, S. (2010). Education can compensate for society—A bit. *British Journal of Educational Studies, 58*(1), 47–65.

Grove, J. (2013, January 3). Troubling FX as Falmouth forces staff to go private. *Times Higher Education*.

Harvey, L., & Green, D. (1993). Defining quality. *Assessment and Evaluation in Higher Education, 18,* 8–35.

Hattie, J., & Marsh, H. W. (1996). The relationship between research and teaching—A meta-analysis. *Review of Educational Research, 66,* 507–542.

Hazelkorn, E. (2015). *Rankings and the reshaping of higher education: The battle for world class excellence* (2nd ed.). Basingstoke, UK: Palgrave Macmillan.

Illich, I. (1973). *Tools for conviviality.* New York: Harper & Row.

INEP. (2017). *Censo da Educação Superior. Notas Estatísticas 2017.* Brasília: INEP.

Kinser, K. (2002). Working at for-profit universities: The University of Phoenix as a new model. *International Higher Education, 28,* 13–14.

Kinser, K., Levy, D., Casillas, J. C. S., Bernasconi, A., Slantcheva Durst, S., Otieno, W., et al. (2010). *The global growth of private higher education*. ASHE Higher Education Report Series. Wiley: San Francisco.

Laurillard, D., & Kennedy, E. (2017). *The potential of MOOCs for learning at scale in the Global South* (Working Paper No. 31). London: Centre for Global Higher Education.

Levy, D. C. (1986). *Higher education and the state in Latin America: Private challenges to public dominance*. Chicago: University of Chicago Press.

Macfarlane, B. (2011). The morphing of academic practice: Unbundling and the rise of the para-academic. *Higher Education Quarterly, 65*(1), 59–73.

Marginson, S. (2011). Higher education and public good. *Higher Education Quarterly, 65*(4), 411–433.

Mason, P. (2015). *Post-capitalism: A guide to our future*. London: Penguin.

McCowan, T. (2004). The growth of private higher education in Brazil: Implications for equity and quality. *Journal of Education Policy, 19*(4), 453–472.

McKenzie, L. (2018, December 18). EdX's struggle for sustainability. *Inside Higher Education*. Available at https://www.insidehighered.com/digital-learning/article/2018/12/18/quest-long-term-sustainability-edx-tries-monetize-moocs#.XBjaIfy8UTo.twitter. Accessed 20 December 18.

Montgomery, L., & Neylon, C. (2018). *In a globalised and networked world, what is the unique value a university can bring?* Introducing Open Knowledge Institutions. Available at http://blogs.lse.ac.uk/impactofsocialsciences/2018/09/17/in-a-globalised-and-networked-world-what-is-the-unique-value-a-university-can-bring-introducing-open-knowledge-institutions/. Accessed 5 October 2018.

Oanda, I. O., & Jowi, J. (2012). University expansion and the challenges to social development in Kenya: Dilemmas and pitfalls. *Journal of Higher Education in Africa, 10*(1): 49–71.

Orr, D. (1994). *Earth in mind*. Washington, DC: Island Press.

Paulson, K. (2002). Reconfiguring faculty roles for virtual settings. *Journal of Higher Education, 73*(1), 123–140.

Robertson, S. L., & Komljenovic, J. (2016a). Non-state actors, and the advance of frontier higher education markets in the global south. *Oxford Review of Education, 42*(5), 594–611.

Robertson, S. L., & Komljenovic, J. (2016b). Unbundling the university and making higher education markets. In A. Verger, C. Lubienski, & G. Steiner-Kamsi (Eds.), *World yearbook in education: The global education industry*. London: Routledge.

Sampaio, Helena. (2011, Outubro). O setor privado de ensino superior no Brasil: continuidades e transformações. *Revista de Ensino Superior da UNICAMP* (Edição nº 4). https://www.revistaensinosuperior.gr.unicamp.br/edicoes/ed04_outubro2011/05_ARTIGO_PRINCIPAL.pdf.

Selingo, J. J. (2013). *College unbound: The future of higher education and what it means for students*. Boston: New Harvest.

Slaughter, S., & Leslie, L. L. (1997). *Academic capitalism: Politics, policies, and the entrepreneurial university*. Baltimore, MD: Johns Hopkins Press.

Tabulawa, R., Polelo, M., & Silas, O. (2013). The state, markets and higher education reform in Botswana. *Globalisation, Societies and Education, 11*(1), 108–135.

UniversityNow. (2017). *Why we're different: Making higher education affordable*. Available at http://unow.com/making-education-affordable/. Accessed 9 February 2017.

Vasagar, J. (2011, October 11). No frills university college offers half price degrees. *The Guardian*. Available at https://www.theguardian.com/education/2011/oct/17/coventry-university-college-half-price-degree. Accessed 9 February 2017.

Wangenge-Ouma, G. (2007). Higher education marketisation and its discontents: The case of quality in Kenya. *Higher Education, 56*(4), 457–471.

Watters, A. (2013, April). MOOC Mania: Debunking the Hype around Massive Open Online Courses. *School Library Journal*. Available at http://www.thedigitalshift.com/2013/04/featured/got-mooc-massive-open-online-courses-are-poised-to-change-the-face-of-education/. Accessed 12 September 2018.

Wildavsky, B. (2014, May/June). Evolving toward significance or MOOC ado about nothing. *International Educator*, 74–79.

Williamson, B. (2018). The hidden architecture of higher education: Building a big data infrastructure for the 'smarter university'. *International Journal of Educational Technology in Higher Education, 15*(1), 1–26.

Part II

6

Access

Who should go to university? Should it be all who meet a given standard or only the highest performing students of each age group? Or should everybody go to university? And if a society decides that it cannot afford for everybody to go, to whom should priority be given: those with the greatest academic potential, those with the greatest need, or those studying subjects considered to make a particular contribution to society?

These are highly complex questions that have been debated extensively in the literature over recent decades, as well as in policy-making circles, and among decision-makers at the institutional level (Brennan and Naidoo 2008; Clancy and Goastellec 2007; Duru-Bellat 2012; Meyer et al. 2013). Access is certainly not the only question of importance in relation to social justice in higher education—the university provides benefits (and potentially harm) to others in society indirectly through its graduates, and through research and community engagement, so the fairness of distribution of these aspects also needs attention. Nevertheless, student admissions are the most prominent element, and constitute one of the key mechanisms for distributing opportunity in contemporary societies.

This chapter will argue, however, that the terms on which this debate has normally been carried out have significantly restricted our imagination about possible responses. They have for the most part rested on the idea that there are limited places available, and have traced out ingenious schemes for allocating priority. This chapter will take a different approach: that we should start with assessing who is able and willing to attend higher education and construct the higher education system (and its numbers of places) around them.

Questions of access are relevant to this book in the first place because the SDGs contain an explicit goal for coverage at the tertiary level ("By 2030, ensure equal access for all women and men to affordable and quality technical, vocational and tertiary education, including university"). Yet they are also important as they influence the composition of the student body, the nature of the university, its values and functions, and the kinds of impact it will have on society.

As discussed in Chapter 1, there are startling disparities of access between regions, between nations and within nations. The gross enrolment ratio for Sub-Saharan Africa is still under 10% while Central and Eastern Europe has a rate of over 80% (UIS 2018). Higher education systems are expanding rapidly but without becoming substantially fairer in many cases. In the UK, for example, where there has been a range of 'widening participation' policies, while the percentage of students on free school meals (a proxy for low socio-economic level) going on to university has risen from 15 to 26% between 2006/2007 and 2016/2017, the rate for other students has risen from 34 to 43%, representing only a slow reduction in the gap (DfE 2018). The disparities are more extreme in many other countries (UNESCO/IIEP 2017).

These disparities are a concern in the first place because they constitute unfairness in themselves, given that higher education is a valued good. But beyond the intrinsic value of fairness, disparities in access also bring knock-on problems for societies: in countries in which almost all people are excluded from higher education, there are significant disadvantages to the whole of society in remaining bereft of this source of generation of knowledge, understanding and skill; in those countries in which only certain social groups are excluded, there is the loss of the substantial talent of those particular populations. In one sense, therefore, it is in the benefit of all that access to higher education is fair and open; although it must be recognised that—on account of the *positional* benefits of higher education—an unfair system is certainly of benefit to elites in situations in which it can protect their privileges in the employment market.

Before embarking on the analysis, it is important to lay on the table some prior assumptions—particularly since these may not be held by all contributors to the debate. First, this book is based on a view that higher education should not be rationed on the basis of the number of jobs available in society. While it is often lamented that there is an 'oversupply' of graduates, a 'mismatch' with the job market or that people might be 'overeducated', professional development is just one of a range of important outcomes of studying at university. Even if there is no so-called 'graduate job' waiting at the end, it is still worth going to university—both for the individual and society. Second, all people can benefit from higher education. This is not to say that anyone can go to university at any point in their life: as will be outlined further below, it is important that people have the requisite academic level to take advantage of it. But this level of study is not confined to the few due to inherent deficiencies of the many. At the same time, it should not be an obligation to go to university, and society should provide a range of different post-school educational options.

A qualification regarding scope is also needed at this point. This chapter will focus primarily on the question of admissions to higher education: that is to say, the gaining of a place to study in a higher education institution. Clearly, this is not the only factor of relevance to equity of access: it also matters what students learn in the course of their studies, how they experience their institutions, and whether they are able to convert that learning and the resulting qualifications into meaningful opportunities afterwards (issues explored in Morley and Lugg 2009, for example). Furthermore, access requires a range of financial considerations, including maintenance throughout the course of a student's time at university, without which dropout or delayed completion are common.

The chapter will start with a discussion of conceptual issues pertinent to the question: primarily the concept of equity itself, as well as the broader approaches to justice underpinning it (egalitarianism, sufficientarianism and prioritarianism). These ideas are then explored in the context of three cases: England, Brazil and Kenya. These three locations have been chosen as they represent different types: a high-income country with a long-standing higher education system and something approaching 'universal' access in Trow's (1974) typology; a middle-income country with a rapidly expanding system entering the massification phase; and a low-income country with an expanding system but still restricted to a very small proportion of the age cohort. These three contexts, while grappling with the challenge of providing an equitable expansion, have also adopted diverse policy responses that highlight important aspects of the theoretical questions at stake. Finally, implications are drawn out from the partial success but significant limitations of these three systems, leading to the formulation of principles of equity of access and discussion of ramifications for policy. The chapter argues that we should view equity of access in terms of three dimensions—availability, accessibility and horizontality—all of which must be present in order to consider a higher education system to be fair.

Approaches to Fair Access in Higher Education

Clancy and Goastellec (2007) argue that approaches to higher education access have passed through three historical phases: initially, universities were only available for those from particular backgrounds, whether relating to gender, religion or racial origin—termed by the authors 'inherited merit'. In the twentieth century this state of affairs gave way to 'equality of rights', through which no explicit discrimination was permitted, though practice showed that, despite the lack of formal barriers, access was still extremely difficult for marginalised groups. As a consequence, 'equity' or 'equality of opportunity' approaches have been adopted to address the more subtle mechanisms that prevent students from disadvantaged backgrounds obtaining places in higher education, and particularly in the most elite institutions.

The last of these phases has been characterised by a range of affirmative action or positive discrimination policies and practices. Affirmative action challenges the supposedly meritocratic basis of admissions procedures—particularly those of elite institutions—giving preferential access to students with particular characteristics. In the USA, where debates over affirmative action have been most vigorous for the last half century (e.g. Bowen and Bok 1998; Gurin et al. 2002), the key dimension has been race, but affirmative action based on other characteristics has been seen elsewhere: for example, by gender (e.g. Sweden), by caste (e.g. India) or by district of origin (e.g. Sri Lanka). It also takes a range of forms: in some cases specific quotas of places, and in others a bonus on admissions scores, scholarships or outreach programmes.

Affirmative action has been justified on a range of grounds. The distinction is sometimes made (e.g. Rhoads et al. 2005) between 'backward looking' and 'forward-looking' justifications: the former relating to the need for redress for historical discrimination against particular groups, and the latter aiming to achieve a goal for the future, i.e. the composition of a more just society through enabling people from disadvantaged groups to take up positions of influence, thereby setting in motion a process of social transformation. There is also a more individualised form of affirmative action that relates to the increasing recognition of 'potential' as legitimate grounds for selecting candidates for entry. In this instance, the difficulties that some students face in their earlier lives and the poor quality of their previous schooling are taken into account when evaluating their admissions scores—on the basis that even with a lower score they may have more potential than another candidate. (In fact, this hypothesis has been borne out in empirical research: at the University of Bristol, for example, students from impoverished neighbourhoods entering on a widening participation programme outperformed students entering with higher grades by the end of their courses [Hoare and Johnston 2011].)

Affirmative action, therefore, puts in tension conceptions of procedural justice and social justice (the latter sometimes referred to as 'background justice', e.g. Jacobs 2013): that is to say, considerations of what is fair in terms of the process of admissions and impartiality of the treatment of candidates, as opposed to what is fair in terms of the broader society, and the existence of historical and ongoing discrimination of and structural barriers for certain groups. To these two, Jacobs (2013) has added a third form—*stakes justice*—to refer to the outcomes of the process, and the extent to which the distribution of benefits to 'winners' and 'losers' is fair. These tensions have led to a series of high profile court cases in the USA, such as *Regents of the University of California v. Bakke*, in which an unsuccessful candidate sued the Medical School of the University of California—Davis for being unfairly barred, in violation of the 14th Amendment. In this case, the court ruled unconstitutional the use of racial 'quotas', but upheld the 'diversity' position: asserting that affirmative action is justified in enhancing the educational climate through the development of a diverse student body, given the benefit for all students (and not just those from disadvantaged groups). This 'compromise' position is distinct from the earlier demands for affirmative action on the basis of historical redress emerging from the civil rights movement, and also from the conservative position of rejecting positive discrimination in any circumstances (Rhoads et al. 2005).

A further debate has emerged in recent years concerning what has been referred to as 'epistemic', or 'epistemological' access (Clegg 2011; Morrow 2009; Stevenson et al. 2014; Wheelahan 2007). Following sociological work spanning a number of decades, these positions acknowledge that access to formal educational institutions for disadvantaged groups does not necessarily translate into meaningful access to the curriculum, or to conversion of education into opportunities in the broader society. Curricula and institutional cultures are seen to favour dominant social groups and can serve to marginalise others and lead to their 'failure' within the system. This premise has led to two contrasting responses in higher education: first, calls for transformation of curricula to include non-dominant forms of knowledge; and second, work associated with the ideas of Michael Young (2008) and others around 'powerful knowledge', which argues that disadvantaged groups must be given access to the forms of thought that confer advantage in society, in particular traditional disciplinary areas. As an example of the latter position, Clegg (2011) and Wheelahan (2007) have problematised the confinement of lower income students to vocational courses in the UK and Australia, without access to context-independent knowledge and the structuring principles of disciplines. Questions of curriculum and knowledge will not be fully covered in this chapter (they will be taken up again in Chapter 10), but differentiated provision between institutions within a system is central to the concept of horizontality outlined below.

In understanding positions on access it is useful to bear in mind the distinction between egalitarian, sufficientarian and prioritarian approaches to social justice made by Brighouse and Swift (2006). Egalitarian approaches sensu stricto assert the necessity of an 'equal' distribution of given resources or opportunities—if not identical in every way, at least in certain significant ways. A sufficientarian approach, on the other hand, asserts that there is a minimal level to which all people should be raised, but that inequality beyond that point is acceptable. In particular, this is to guard against 'levelling down', restricting (in the interests of equality) the achievements of those with the most talent or who put in the most effort, but with potentially negative results for the individuals in question and society as a whole. Prioritarian approaches, on the other hand, drawing on Rawls's difference principle, require the primary emphasis to be on improving the lot of the worst off; inequalities are justified only in so far as they serve to make the position of the worst off higher than they would have been with an equal distribution.

Sufficientarian approaches would certainly seem justifiable in some cases. We might consider it just that all people have access to clean and safe drinking water: if some people want sparkling mineral water from the Italian Alps, and are willing to expend their own resources on it, we might not consider it a real challenge to justice. But is a sufficientarian approach to higher education access adequate? Is it acceptable, as happens in many national systems in practice, for access to *some* form of higher education to be widely available, but for significant inequality to be allowed in relation to its quality? To answer this question we need to look more closely at the kind of benefits that higher education provides, recalling the distinction made in Chapter 3 between intrinsic, instrumental and positional value. The existence of positional benefits from higher education makes the sufficientarian position outlined above highly problematic. If higher education only had intrinsic value then it would be more acceptable for everyone to have access to a minimum, and be allowed to pursue further opportunities in accordance with their particular interests and values. However, in the context of positional benefits, the overall distribution of higher education is highly significant. Expanding access to higher education in a stratified way (in providing higher quality provision to students of a higher socio-economic status) may increase the overall intrinsic benefits of higher education to the population, but will not provide any more positional benefits to the previously disadvantaged population, and ultimately will not lessen inequalities.

So justice may require an egalitarian approach to access. But does that mean that all people, regardless of their abilities, interests and circumstances, should have exactly the same form of higher education? There may be a range of objections to this position. Limitations of resources in a given country are often cited as an insurmountable barrier, although it is important to consider first the principles of fairness: the task of reforming systems and economies to make them possible in practice comes later and should not limit deliberations on justice. However, there are further objections relating to the differing interests and abilities of prospective students. As argued in McCowan (2012), higher education should not be compulsory in either a *de jure* or a de facto manner, the latter occurring in cases in which university level study becomes essential in order to secure employment. Access is only required, therefore, for those people who actually desire to study in higher education.

Another objection to universalisation of access relates to ability to study at the higher education level. Clearly, there is little point in a person enrolling in university studies if they are not able to engage fully with them. Fairness does not, therefore, require all selection criteria to be abandoned. All students need a certain level of preparation in order to engage meaningfully with the content, so universities are justified in gauging preparation and admitting only those who fulfil the minimum requirements. Access to higher education institutions then should be based on criteria, not competitive allocation of a fixed (and small) number of places.

International rights instruments defend equitable procedures for selecting students to higher education, but say nothing about the total number of places available (McCowan 2012). The same is true of goal 4.3 of the SDGs. The principle of *accessibility* is, therefore, present, but not that of *availability*. It is clearly inadequate for a system to have an equitable procedure for selecting students but only places for a small proportion of the age cohort. Attention is needed, therefore, to both fair selection and availability of places. These two, along with horizontality—addressing the injustices of stratified systems—are the principles proposed in this chapter.

Access to Higher Education in National Contexts

Entry to higher education institutions is regulated by two primary mechanisms: academic performance and tuition fees. There is considerable diversity between countries in relation to these mechanisms, and even within countries, particularly between public and private sectors. In relation to the first, there is a continuum from open access systems requiring only a secondary leaving certificate (e.g. Argentina, Italy, France), to academic entrance examinations with intense competition for places (e.g. national universities in Japan and public universities in Brazil). The existence and level of fees also varies significantly between countries, and between sectors, as do the schemes in place to support those without sufficient financial resources to pay for them. In some cases the barrier is either competitive entrance exams or fees, but in others (such as the traditional universities in Chile) these are combined to present what often ends up as an insurmountable barrier for the poor.

Higher education policy in practice has not fulfilled even the partial view of accessibility put forward in international law. While few systems exclude explicitly on the basis of background characteristics of the individual, most rely on a fairly high level of material wealth—either directly in order to pay fees, or indirectly in order to obtain the required level of previous educational achievement. De Gayardon (2018) identifies 81 countries in which some kind of free higher education is available, although not always for a high proportion of students. While there are some countries such as Chile which are partially reintroducing free places in response to student mobilisation, global tendencies have been strongly towards cost-sharing even in public sectors.

Supranational agencies have for the most part encouraged moves away from free higher education. World Bank (e.g. 1994) policy has advocated expansion of higher education through new private providers, or through cost-sharing in public institutions, aiming for a diversity of institutions across the sector. There has been substantial global convergence around this model of higher education development. While UNESCO has had a somewhat different approach to access and curriculum (with a more humanistic and citizenship-based, and less narrowly economistic vision), it has been more marginal in terms of its influence. One document presenting a more robust view of educational justice is the Declaration from the 1998 World Conference on Higher Education. The declaration states in relation to equity:

> [A]dmission to higher education should be based on the merit, capacity, efforts, perseverance and devotion, showed by those seeking access to it, and can take place in a lifelong scheme, at any time, with due recognition of previously acquired skills. As a consequence, no discrimination can be accepted in granting access to higher education on grounds of race, gender, language or religion, or economic, cultural or social distinctions, or physical disabilities. (UNESCO 1998)

This passage from Article 3 provides a broad expression of equity of access, and is supplemented by three further sections of the Article, emphasising, respectively, the importance of links with lower levels of the education system, the merit-based admissions system and affirmative action for specific groups such as indigenous peoples. This document provides an admirable defence of equality of opportunity, reconciling requirements of both procedural justice and social justice. However, it remains an aspirational document, not binding on countries, and for the most part playing second fiddle to visions of higher education based on what are considered to be the more pressing demands of economic competitiveness and efficiency.

In spite of global policy convergence, there are nevertheless discernible national characteristics, and countries have adopted different strategies to address the common problem of ensuring equitable expansion of the system in the context of budgetary constraints. The following sections will assess the distinct approaches taken by England, Brazil and Kenya, and the resulting landscape of access.

In the space available, it will not be possible to provide adequate coverage of the relevant contextual factors in each case: the accounts should therefore be treated in the spirit of vignettes, in order to highlight the key characteristics of interest. As stated above, the three territories have high (England), upper middle (Brazil) and lower middle (Kenya) income, in terms of the World Bank's income classification, and have gross enrolment ratios of 59, 34[1] and 12%, respectively (INEP 2017; UIS 2018). They also have different forms of inequality presenting barriers to particular groups in society. Yet in all three cases, the governments are essentially engaging with the same task: that of expanding access to higher education as broadly as possible within the constraints of public finances, while attempting to maximise the impact of the system on society and the economy.

England

Higher education in England[2] has a long history, with Oxford and Cambridge dating from the twelfth and thirteenth centuries, but with major expansion only taking place in the twentieth century. With the exception of a few purely private providers, most universities in the country have a hybrid nature, being private foundations with a public mission and significant amounts of public funding. In recent years, the proportion of this public funding has been reduced considerably (Carpentier 2012): fees were introduced in 1998, and steadily increased to the level of £9250 in 2018 for most institutions. There

---

[1] The figure from the national agency rather than UIS has been used in the case of Brazil, due to disparities of calculation.

[2] On account of the significant differences between the higher education systems in England, Wales, Scotland and Northern Ireland, this discussion will relate only to England, rather than the whole of the UK.

are nevertheless full loans available for all students studying their first undergraduate degree, thereby ensuring the possibility of continuing uptake of higher education places. Overall enrolment rates for the age cohort have expanded from 39% in 1999/2000 to 50% in 2016/2017 (DfE 2018).

The model adopted by England for equitable higher education expansion has therefore been that of cost-sharing and government-backed loans. This strategy has enabled the continuing expansion of the system without immediate state investment (although ultimately the costs of the loans to the state will be high, with most graduates not repaying the debt in full [de Gayardon et al. 2018]). An accompanying policy emerging in recent reforms has been the entry of for-profit providers: while potentially a highly significant development, it is not one that is yet having a significant impact on access.

There are some positive points to the English higher education landscape. In the first place, there is substantial availability at one of more than a hundred universities for those students who have completed upper secondary education. Second, loans are universally available to cover the fees. These loans only have to be repaid once the graduate is earning above a particular salary level, and function in practice as a mark-up on tax rates. Third, entry requirements are flexible for 'mature' students, allowing for re-entry into the system at a later stage for those who missed out first time around and do not have the necessary academic qualifications. There has also been a range of 'widening participation' policies in place, and outreach work in schools to raise aspirations of prospective students from non-traditional backgrounds (Hoare and Johnston 2011).

Nevertheless, there are significant inequities. As stated above, the gap between the higher and lower socio-economic groups has not changed dramatically even in the context of rapid expansion. Social class (intersecting with other dimensions of inequality such as gender and race/ethnicity) is the key barrier to higher education access in England. While loans are universally available, there are various factors that may act as subtle barriers for low-income or working-class students, including debt aversion, high opportunity costs and a perception of 'not belonging' in the university (Reay et al. 2001), not to mention the problems of debt in graduates' subsequent lives (de Gayardon et al. 2018). There are further factors compounding opportunity barriers for refugees and migrants (Stevenson and Willott 2007). Furthermore, it is a highly stratified system. At the top of the heap are the selective and research-intensive Russell Group universities, followed by a range of middle-level institutions, the more vocationally oriented former polytechnics (granted university status in 1992) and new institutions which—while often providing high-quality teaching—suffer from lower prestige. Students from lower socio-economic backgrounds are disproportionately represented in the newer and lower prestige universities (Universities UK 2013). England, therefore, scores fairly well on availability and accessibility, but poorly in relation to stratification. Furthermore, the strategies in place to ensure access are precarious to say the least, with the sustainability of the generous loan system in question.

Brazil

In contrast to England, Brazil has highly differentiated public and private sectors. Public universities still have a strong link to the state (either the federal government or one of the state governments), and are completely free of charge to students. Private universities, on the other hand, have significant autonomy, and little public funding, generating necessary revenue mainly through direct fees to students (McCowan 2004). With the exception of the long-standing Catholic universities, most of the prestigious institutions are in the public sector. The system expanded rapidly from the 1990s in the context of neoliberal policies of privatisation in many social sectors. A very rapid growth in the number of private higher education institutions allowed for an increase in student numbers from 1.5 million in 1992 to 5.3 million in 2007 and to 8.3 million in 2017, with a current enrolment rate of 18% (net) and 34% (gross) (INEP 2013, 2017; OPNE 2018).

Access to higher education is severely limited for lower socio-economic groups in Brazil (Pedrosa et al. 2014). While public universities are free, entrance is dependent on passing competitive examinations, with more than 50 candidates per place for popular courses (INEP 2013). Chances of passing these exams are strongly linked to prior attendance at high quality primary and secondary schooling and fee-paying preparatory courses, all of which are out of reach of most lower income students. Even though many middle-class Brazilians are able to self-fund their degrees by working full time while studying in the evening, even the low fees available at some private institutions act as a barrier to most lower income students.

While there was some increase in the number of places available in federal universities during the Workers' Party government from 2002 to 2016, the primary model of expansion has been through the private sector. Access has to some degree been facilitated by loans, but unlike in England, these are not universal and lack the same preferential repayment safeguards; while they did expand significantly during the administration of Dilma Rousseff, the public investment has proved hard to sustain, with reductions in numbers from 2016, leading the private groups to develop their own finance schemes (Chaves and Amaral 2016; Chaves et al. 2018). The most significant programme for widening participation has been *Prouni (Programa Universidade Para Todos)*, which grants tax breaks to private institutions in exchange for allocating free-of-charge places to low-income students (Neves 2009; Carvalho 2006). This scheme has been highly successful in quantitative terms, with over 2 million students gaining access to higher education through the scholarships in the decade from 2005 (MEC 2018). However, once again this is a stratified model of access, with these low-income students entering for the most part the lower prestige institutions, conferring less subsequent value on the employment market (Leher 2010; Norões and McCowan 2015).

Perhaps the most visible policy on higher education access has been the quotas in public institutions (Childs and Stromquist 2015; Noroes and Costa 2012). Following the actions of various universities, the federal government passed a law in 2012 guaranteeing the allocation of 50% of places to students from government schools, with the same proportion of those places being allocated to those of African or indigenous descent as in the general population of the state in question. African Brazilians are significantly underrepresented in Brazilian universities:

the participation rate for these students has been estimated as being as low as 9%, compared to 23% for the white population, though this is a significant improvement since the year 2000 when the rate for black students was only 2% compared to 9% for white students (CTB 2018). The quota policy is having a significant impact on the composition of students in the high prestige public universities, although in the context of limited expansion of the overall number of free-of-charge places. In addition to quotas, there are also some further affirmative action policies in public universities such as a score bonus on entrance exam results for lower income students.

Brazil has made significant strides in terms of availability of places, although it still has lower overall enrolments than many other middle-income countries, including those in the Latin American region. Accessibility for lower income and disadvantaged groups has been facilitated by targeted policies including *Prouni* and quotas. Nevertheless, it is still a highly stratified system with access to institutions of quality or prestige for the most part restricted to the upper income groups.

Kenya

Higher education in Kenya began with the University of Nairobi, which gained independence in 1970 from its previous affiliations to the University of London and the University of East Africa. Expansion of the system was slow until 2000, but since then many new public and private institutions have been created. There are now 74 universities (37 public and 37 private, with 15% of students in private institutions), and a number of campuses have been established in smaller towns across the country (CUE 2016; Kenya Bureau of Statistics 2018). Access is still very restricted, with the most recent statistics from UIS showing a GER of only 11.6% (UIS 2018); there is also low female enrolment (only 72 women enter for every 100 men) and low rates of representation from geographically marginalised regions of the country (Oanda and Jowi 2012; UIS 2018). As with Brazil, competitive exams for public universities and fees for private universities ensure that lower income students have access to neither; there is also a minimum score (C+) in the secondary leaving examination KCSE for entering university, which in 2018 was only achieved by 15% of school leavers (Mokua 2018).

Perhaps the most significant and distinctive development, however, is the emergence of the parallel stream within public universities (Oketch 2003; Turner Johnson and Hirt 2014; Wangenge-Ouma 2007). Students not passing the competitive entrance exams can nevertheless be admitted to the prestigious public universities (e.g. Nairobi, Kenyatta) by paying a substantial fee. Given that these students ultimately obtain a diploma that is indistinguishable from those of the competitive entrance stream, there are obvious implications for equity, with the elites able through their financial resources to insert their children into prestigious universities that will then ensure their future financial security. There are also issues of quality, with the additional students (since 2013 the majority of the students in public universities have been in the parallel stream) presenting an intolerable burden on human and physical resources (Oanda 2013). Numbers in the parallel stream have tailed off significantly from 2018 on account of insufficient students available with the required university entrance scores, and increased competition from the private sector, which since 2016 had been able to enrol publicly sponsored students (Oanda 2018; Opembe 2018). Nevertheless, universities remain substantially overcrowded.

Kenya's model of expansion, therefore, has been one of maintaining a highly restricted number of free-of-charge places allocated on the basis of competitive exams, while addressing rising demand from the upper middle classes by allowing the expansion of private institutions and private streams within public institutions. Neither of these strategies is adequately enabling an equitable expansion.

Three Dimensions of Equity

From these vignettes we can see that all three countries have attempted to increase *availability* of places over recent years—and all have succeeded in it, although Brazil and particularly Kenya have started from a low base. However, this expansion has not in all cases been accompanied by the facilitation of *accessibility*, with the major barriers being competitive exams for free-of-charge places, and tuition fees in the private institutions. There have been two partially successful forms of policy to address these barriers. The first and most prominent is the allocation of loans and scholarships to facilitate entry to fee-charging institutions—particularly the universal loan system in England, and also the *Prouni* initiative and partial loans in Brazil. The second is affirmative action policies in relation to selection of students to high prestige institutions, for example the racial quotas in Brazil.

However, even these more progressive policies do not represent an entirely adequate solution. Quota policies address the unfair disadvantage groups may have on account of discrimination in society or poor quality of previous schooling, but ultimately they are working within the constraints of availability. They provide a fairer allocation of those places that are available, but do not ensure sufficient places. Loan systems go some way towards addressing accessibility, although as discussed above there may still be more subtle barriers for lower income students. However, even if disadvantaged students can in fact gain access to the system via loans and the kinds of scholarship made available by *Prouni*, there is still the problem of stratification. In Brazil and England, 'non-traditional' students are predominantly filling the low prestige institutions: in the case of Brazil the new demand-absorbing private institutions, and in England the former polytechnics and newly established, more vocational, universities.

The two choices on the table then appear to be allocating an insufficient number of places more equitably, or expanding the system inequitably—in other words, either cutting the same cake in a different way, or increasing the size of the cake but still distributing it unfairly. What we need instead is an approach to higher education access that simultaneously ensures sufficient places (availability), conditions to support all to access those places (accessibility) and consistently high quality and recognition (a principle that we might term 'horizontality', drawing on the idea of horizontal, as opposed to vertical, differentiation [Brennan and Naidoo 2008; Teichler 2008]).

In assessing whether policies on access to higher education are equitable or not, attention is therefore needed to three dimensions: availability, accessibility and 'horizontality'. *Availability* relates to the overall number of places available, as well as the existence of adequate facilities, teaching staff and so forth. The term is employed in international law, and appears as one of the '4As' in Tomaševski's (2006) scheme for understanding the right to education, although unlike accessibility, its applicability is restricted to the primary and secondary levels. If applied to higher education, this principle would require systems to expand in almost all cases, though not necessarily to provide vacancies for 100% of each age cohort: as discussed above, places are only required for those people who are interested in studying at this level and who have the minimum level of preparation. Furthermore, availability would not necessarily require the expansion of individual institutions, as long as there was sufficient capacity across the whole of the system.

However, the existence of places does not mean that they will be accessible, or at least not to all individuals or groups. Barriers exist such as tuition fees, competitive exams that disadvantage those with poor quality previous schooling, geographical location of institutions, the opportunity costs of spending years out of employment, as well as a range of other constraints relating to language, culture and identity. *Accessibility* requires the removal of these barriers, along with policies and interventions to provide information, raise aspirations and ensure adequate preparation. Challenges to accessibility and the mechanisms employed to address them will necessarily vary by context.

Yet even in a context in which strategies are in place to ensure access of all students to the system, there is still the problem of stratification: a hierarchy of prestige and quality among universities, with disadvantaged students generally confined to the lower ranked institutions. *Horizontality*, therefore, is the characteristic of even prestige and quality across the system: this is not to say identical institutions, and there may well be value in diversity in relation to ethos, specialisation, size of institution, distribution of taught courses, research focus and so forth (Huisman 2000). Nevertheless, this diversity should exist in the context of consistently high quality and recognition of all diplomas in the broader society. As discussed above, an egalitarian rather than sufficientarian basis for distribution of higher education is necessary, given the positional nature of the good.

But what about arguments that unevenness across a system in fact creates benefits? That horizontality is undesirable because only with the existence of a differentiated system with some elite and exclusive institutions, and other lower level demand-absorbing institutions, can we achieve a prosperous society? Meyer et al. (2013) assert that there are three considerations in deciding how to allocate the scarce commodity of higher education—need, talent/merit and ability to contribute. On the basis of the third of these, we might consider that unequal opportunities were in fact justified, if, for example, such a system would allow the emergence of a high-level cadre of surgeons, architects and judges, needed by all in society. As discussed above, this position can be seen to relate to the prioritarian critique of egalitarianism. Two points are of relevance in response to this argument. First, a *horizontal* system does not preclude differentiation in study type or outcome, and can allow for highly specialised forms of training and subsequent work: the point is that it does not restrict these opportunities to those with prior socio-economic privilege. Differentiation is justified in so far as it maximises *instrumental* benefits (allowing for people to contribute to society in highly specialised ways), but not in so far as it enables capture of *positional* goods. A second point is that societal considerations should not entirely subsume individual ones in our reasoning about opportunities in higher education—at least not from the Kantian perspective of seeing human beings as ends rather than means. From this perspective, it is illegitimate to restrict valuable opportunities to the few on the basis of a perceived need in society for only a small proportion of high-level workers. While there are many benefits to society as a whole accruing from higher education (ones which may justify collective funding through taxation), having access to higher education is important primarily because of the enhancement of the lives of those engaging with it—and if it is indeed an intrinsically and instrumentally valuable experience, then it should be made available to as wide a proportion of the population as possible.

As stated above, the 1998 Declaration of the World Conference on Higher Education provides a firm basis for a conception of equity of access with its emphasis on protecting against discrimination on the basis of background characteristics, entry to university at any point in life and affirmative action for specific groups. Nevertheless, there are some further areas needing attention. First, as in international law, the question of availability is not fully addressed—the existence of sufficient places is a primary characteristic of an equitable system. Second, the focus on merit is problematic as it suggests selection of 'the best' rather than of all who are capable of higher education study. Instead, as stated above, what is required is criterion-based rather than norm-based admission. Third, attention is needed to stratification between institutions—occurring primarily through fee levels and entrance exams—and to guarding against the relegation of disadvantaged students to lower quality/prestige institutions. These problems are exacerbated in a situation of variable fees, with wealthier students able to purchase diplomas of a higher value. This phenomenon is seen particularly in the private sector in Brazil, in which the average fee for the most expensive course (medicine) is 10 times that of the average fee for the least expensive course (pedagogy) (Globo 2017).

The affirmative action policies adopted in a number of countries are primarily mechanisms for enabling *accessibility*: they address the barriers to entry for disadvantaged groups—in particular, highly competitive entrance exams that require extensive preparation not available to all social groups. However, they can also address *horizontality*, by allowing access for disadvantaged groups to the most elite institutions. The one area they do not address is *availability*. Debates on affirmative action are for the most part predicated on the existence of limited space in higher education systems and institutions: they assume that there will be more candidates than there are places, and deliberate on the highly complex question of the fairest way of allocating those places. With sufficient capacity, these trade-offs between procedural and social justice would no longer be necessary, since there would be places for both disadvantaged students and higher performing students from advantaged backgrounds. (There would, nevertheless, still be room for affirmative action policies to raise aspirations and to ensure that all reach the required level of academic preparation.)

The one selection criterion admissible according to these principles is minimum academic preparation. It is not possible within this chapter to fully address the issue of how this preparation should be conceptualised within criterion-based admission: the question depends on context and on the specific subject to be studied, and a degree of variation is legitimate. Care must be taken, however, not to allow the minimum preparation criterion to be abused and become another mechanism for exclusion. There are significant implications here for primary and secondary schools, and it is important to look at issues of access to higher education in relation to the whole of the education system. If some students are inadequately prepared by their previous experiences of schooling, then further free-of-charge preparatory provision should be made available. In addition, for those people deciding not to study at university aged 18, there need to be easy re-entry points at later stages in life. These points bring into play the debates on epistemic access discussed above, making necessary not only horizontality across higher education situations, but also attention to the forms of support and institutional transformation needed for non-traditional students to meaningfully access the curriculum.

The global landscape is not encouraging in relation to the upholding of the three principles of equity outlined here. As discussed in the previous chapter, systems for the most part are on a trajectory of increasing marketisation of access, economisation of curriculum and stratification of institutional type, with inequalities exacerbated even in the context of expansion. National and institutional initiatives to facilitate access for marginalised groups have received some support from international agencies, while at the same time being undermined by the deeper global trends that the same agencies are supporting. This scenario calls for a radical revisioning of the higher education system, one that will be outlined in the course of the chapters that follow.

References

Bowen, W. G., & Bok, D. (1998). *The shape of the river: Long-term consequences of considering race in college and university admissions.* Princeton, NJ: Princeton University Press.

Brennan, J., & Naidoo, R. (2008). Higher education and the achievement (and/or prevention) of equity and social justice. *Higher Education, 56*(3), 287–302.

Brighouse, H., & Swift, A. (2006). Equality, priority, and positional goods. *Ethics, 116*, 471–497.

Carpentier, V. (2012). Public-private substitution in higher education: Has cost-sharing gone too far? *Higher Education Quarterly, 66,* 363–390.

Carvalho, C. A. (2006). O PROUNI no governo Lula e o jogo político em torno do acesso ao ensino superior. *Educação & Sociedade, 27*(96), 979–1000.

Chaves, V. L. J., & Amaral, N. C. (2016). Política de expansão da educação superior no Brasil – o Prouni e o Fies como financiadores do setor privado. *Educação em Revista, 32*(4), 49–72.

Chaves, V. L. J., Reis, L. F., & Guimarães, A. R. (2018). Dívida pública e financiamento da educação superior no Brasil. *Acta Scientiarum. Education, 40*(1). https://doi.org/10.4025/actascieduc.v40i1.37668.

Childs, P., & Stromquist, N. (2015). Academic and diversity consequences of affirmative action in Brazil. *Compare, 45*(5), 792–813.

Clancy, P., & Goastellec, G. (2007). Exploring access and equity in higher education: Policy and performance in a comparative perspective. *Higher Education Quarterly, 61*(2), 136–154.

Clegg, S. (2011). Cultural capital and agency: Connecting critique and curriculum in higher education. *British Journal of Sociology of Education, 32*(1), 93–108.

Commission for University Education. (2016). *State of university education in Kenya*. Nairobi: Commission for University Education.

CTB. (2018). *Mesmo com mais estudantes negros na educação superior o racismo avança*. Available at http://portalctb.org.br/site/secretarias-da-ctb-nacional/igualdade-racial/mesmo-com-mais-estudantes-negros-na-educacao-superior-o-racismo-avanca. Accessed 1 October 2018.

de Gayardon, A. (2018). There is no such thing as free higher education: A global perspective on the (many) realities of free systems. *Higher Education Policy*. https://doi.org/10.1057/s41307-018-0095-7.

de Gayardon, A., Callender, C., Deane, K. C., & DesJardins, S. (2018). *Graduate indebtedness: Its perceived effects on behaviour and life choices—A literature review* (Centre for Global Higher Education Working Paper no. 38). Available at https://www.researchcghe.org/perch/resources/publications/wp38.pdf. Accessed 5 September 18.

Department for Education (DfE). (2018). *Widening participation in higher education, England, 2016/17 age cohort—Official Statistics*. Available at https://www.gov.uk/government/statistics/widening-participation-in-higher-education-2018. Accessed 28 November 2018.

Duru-Bellat, M. (2012). Access to higher education: What counts as fairness in both an individual and systemic perspective? (Methodological Discussion Paper No. 1).

Globo. (2017, August 28). *Estudo mostra que mensalidade média de medicina é 10 vezes maior que a de pedagogia no Brasil*. Available at https://g1.globo.com/educacao/noticia/estudo-mostra-que-mensalidade-media-de-medicina-e-10-vezes-maior-que-a-de-pedagogia-no-brasil.ghtml. Accessed 1 June 2018.

Gurin, P., Dey, E. L., Hurtado, S., & Gurin, G. (2002). Diversity and higher education: Theory and impact on educational outcomes. *Harvard Educational Review, 71*(3), 332–366.

Hoare, A., & Johnston, R. (2011). Widening participation through admissions policy—A British case study of school and university performance. *Studies in Higher Education, 36*(1), 21–41.

Huisman, J. (2000). Higher education institutions: As different as chalk and cheese? *Higher Education Policy, 13,* 41–53.

INEP (Instituto Nacional de Estudos e Pesquisas Educacionais Anísio Teixeira). (2013). *Censo da Educação Superior 2013*. Brasília: INEP.

INEP. (2017). *Censo da Educação Superior. Notas Estatísticas 2017*. Brasília: INEP.

Jacobs, L. (2013). A vision of equal opportunity in postsecondary education. In H.-D. Meyer, E. P. St. John, M. Chankseliani, & L. Uribe (Eds.), *Fairness in access to higher education in a global perspective: Reconciling excellence, efficiency, and justice*. Rotterdam: Sense Publishers.

Kenya National Bureau of Statistics. (2018). *University enrolments*. Available at https://www.knbs.or.ke/download/university-enrolment/. Accessed 15 September 2018.

Leher, R. (2010). Educação no governo de Lula da Silva: a ruptura que não aconteceu. In J. P. de A. Magalhães (Ed.), *Os anos Lula: contribuições para um balanço crítico 2003–2010* (pp. 369–412). Rio de Janeiro: Garamond.

McCowan, T. (2004). The growth of private higher education in Brazil: Implications for equity and quality. *Journal of Education Policy, 19*(4), 453–472.

McCowan, T. (2012). Is there a universal right to higher education? *British Journal of Educational Studies, 60*(2), 111–128.

MEC. (2018). *Prouni – Programa Universidade para Todos*. Available at http://prouniportal.mec.gov.br/dados-e-estatisticas/10-representacoes-graficas. Accessed 15 October 2018.

Meyer, H.-D., St. John, E. P., Chankseliani, M., & Uribe, L. (Eds.). (2013). *Fairness in access to higher education in a global perspective: Reconciling excellence, efficiency, and justice*. Rotterdam: Sense Publishers.

Mokua, E. (2018, December). Massive student failure in 2018 KCSE exam signals system crisis. *Daily Nation*.

Morley, L., & Lugg, R. (2009). Mapping meritocracy: Intersecting gender, poverty and higher educational opportunity structures. *Higher Education Policy, 22*(1), 37–60.

Morrow, W. (2009). *Bounds of democracy: Epistemological access in higher education*. Pretoria: HSRC Press.

Neves, C. E. B. (2009). Using social inclusion policies to enhance access and equity in Brazil's higher education. In J. Knight (Ed.), *Financing access and equity in higher education*. Rotterdam: Sense Publishers.

Norões, K., & Costa, B. (2012). Affirmative policies in Brazil: Black movements and public higher education. *Educational Thought, 9*(1), 24–31.

Norões, K., & McCowan, T. (2015). The challenge of widening participation to higher education in Brazil: Injustices, innovations and outcomes. In M. Shah, A. Bennett, & E. Southgate (Eds.), *Widening higher education participation: A Global perspective*. Amsterdam: Elsevier.

Oanda, I. (2013). Implications of alternative higher education financing policies on equity and quality: The Kenyan experience. In D. Teferra (Ed.), *Funding higher education in Sub-Saharan Africa*. Basingstoke: Palgrave Macmillan.

Oanda, I. (2018). Admission policies and practices and the reshaping of access patterns to higher education in Africa. In M. E. Oliveri, C. Wendler, & R. Lawles (Eds.), *Higher education admissions and placement practices: An international perspective*. Cambridge: Cambridge University Press.

Oanda, I. O., & Jowi, J. (2012). University expansion and the challenges to social development in Kenya: Dilemmas and pitfalls. *Journal of Higher Education in Africa, 10*(1), 49–71.

Oketch, M. O. (2003). Market model for financing higher education in Sub-Saharan Africa: Examples from Kenya. *Higher Education, 16*(3), 313–332.

Opembe, N. (2018, January 28). State-sponsored students in the private universities got raw deal. *Daily Nation*.

OPNE. (2018). *12—Educação Superior*. Available at http://www.observatoriodopne.org.br/indicadores/metas/12-ensino-superior/indicadores. Accessed 1 August 2018.

Pedrosa, R., Simões, T., Carneiro, A., Andrade, C., Sampaio, H., & Knobel, M. (2014). Access to higher education in Brazil. *Widening Participation and Lifelong Learning, 16*(1), 5–33.

Reay, D., Ball, S. J., David, M., & Davies, J. (2001). Choices of degree or degrees of choice? Social class, race and the higher education choice process. *Sociology, 35*(4), 855–874.

Rhoads, R. A., Saenz, V., & Carducci, R. (2005). Higher education reform as a social movement: The case of affirmative action. *The Review of Higher Education, 28*(2), 191–220.

Stevenson, J., & Willott, J. (2007). The aspiration and access to higher education of teenage refugees in the UK. *Compare, 37*(5), 671–687.

Stevenson, J., Burke, P.-J., & Whelan, P. (2014). *Pedagogic stratification and the shifting landscape of higher education*. York: HEA.

Teichler, U. (2008). Diversification? Trends and explanations of the shape and size of higher education. *Higher Education, 56*(3), 349–379.

Tomaševski, K. (2006). *Human rights obligations in education: The 4-A scheme*. Nijmegen: Wolf Legal Publishers.

Trow, M. (1974). Problems in the transition from elite to mass higher education. In OECD (Ed.), *Policies for higher education* (pp. 51–101). Paris: OECD.

Turner Johnson, A., & Hirt, J. (2014). Universities, dependency and the market: Innovative lessons from Kenya. *Compare, 44*(2), 230–251.

UNESCO (United Nations Educational, Scientific and Cultural Organization). (1998, October). *World declaration on higher education for the twenty-first century: Vision and Action*. Adopted at the World Conference on Higher Education, Paris.

UNESCO Institute for Statistics (UIS). (2018). *Education: Enrolment by level of education*. Available at http://data.uis.unesco.org/. Accessed 1 September 2018.

UNESCO/IIEP. (2017). *Six ways to ensure higher education leaves no one behind* (Policy Paper 30). Paris: UNESCO.

Universities UK. (2013). *Patterns and trends in UK higher education 2013: Section B—Patterns of institutional diversity*. London: Universities UK.

Wangenge-Ouma, G. (2007). Higher education marketisation and its discontents: The case of quality in Kenya. *Higher Education, 56*(4), 457–471.

Wheelahan, L. (2007). How competency-based training locks the working class out of powerful knowledge: A modified Bernsteinian analysis. *British Journal of Sociology of Education, 28*(5), 637–651.

Young, M. F. D. (2008). *Bringing knowledge back in: From social constructivism to social realism in the sociology of education*. London: Routledge.

7

Quality

'Well it is a very good university', says a mother to her daughter as they ponder the different options for her impending transition from school. Similar discussions are played out in living rooms around the world each year. But what do is meant by 'good' here? Questions of quality are treacherous in any area of human experience, and more so in an area like education which is so value-bound and contested. And universities are more complex even than schools in this regard, given their multiplicity of functions, involving non-educational as well as educational activities. The mother may mean a whole range of different things in this statement, but in the majority of cases it will be something like, 'This is a university with substantial public recognition, staffed by renowned scholars, where you will be interacting with other bright and talented students, be intellectually stimulated and at the end of the day receive a certificate that will open up possibilities of employment and other high level opportunities in society'.

According to this dominant conception, not all universities can be good, by definition. Attracting the 'best' students and professors, receiving the highest places in the rankings and capturing scarce opportunities for one's graduates are relative pursuits, zero-sum games, and as some institutions get better, others will get worse. Both within countries and internationally the odds are stacked in favour of a few institutions in achieving what we might call *positional* quality: first, because the availability of resources breeds further resources—the ability to provide top-notch facilities makes it possible for universities to attract high paying students, while the existence of highly paid researchers and research infrastructure enables the university to obtain large research grants—and second, because prestige is gained over a substantial time period and has a long half-life. If Harvard were to pass through a series of corrupt administrations which pulled money from teaching and research quality, it would still take many decades before prospective students felt it was not worth going there. David Graeber (2018) quips that such is the pointlessness of a marketing department for a university like Oxford, that even if it set out to undermine and destroy the university's reputation, it would be unlikely to succeed.

The vast majority of universities in the world are not 'good' in this elite sense—and not only in low- and middle-income countries, but also in high-income countries. Yet by virtue of its inherently relative nature, because it can only be held by a few institutions, and in many ways does not actually produce marginal benefit (only capturing the existing positional benefits—rather like a rentier in the economy) it is an unhelpful notion. Instead, this book will work from a notion of quality that can, at least in theory, be held by all institutions. Universities around the world do not all need to play the game of positional capture, and moreover they may well be harming themselves and their societies if they do.

Naturally, it is extremely challenging to establish a unitary conception of quality of higher education that all can subscribe to—even when discounting the above positional notions. What we think of as quality is dependent on what we consider to be the nature and purpose of the entity in question, and in the case of the university it is clear that this matter is far from consensual. Given the overall focus of the book, this chapter will base its conception of quality on the form of developmental university needed for achieving the SDGs: promoting among students personal, civic and professional development, with a strong ethical and social justice orientation. It is closest to the 'transformation' conception of quality, in Harvey and Green's (1993) terms. (The chapter will focus primarily on the teaching and learning dimension of quality, since research and public service are dealt with in the following chapter.) As in previous chapters, it takes as foundational the purpose of the university to promote human understanding through open-ended inquiry. At its heart, therefore, quality involves the existence of an environment in which open-ended inquiry for human understanding can be pursued.

Sadly, much of what goes by way of attention to quality is little more than an empty process of box-ticking, a hall of mirrors in which quality is determined through the existence of procedures to determine whether there is quality. Or alternatively it resides in a faith that market competition will automatically raise quality across the board—an assumption that was critiqued in Chapter 5. Very often, the notion of quality is taken as given, as self-evident, its submersion thereby precluding closer analysis and debate. Instead, this chapter aims to unpick the concept of quality, to show its relativity to particular conceptions, and explore how it can be more effectively pursued.

Goal 4.3 of the SDGs specifies that 'tertiary education, including university' must be of 'quality', and its positive impact on development is predicated on this feature. Unfortunately, at present those conditions do not pertain in many if not most institutions—partly on account of lack of available resources, but also a range of other issues relating to governance and pedagogical culture. Attention to quality is essential if universities are going to achieve the impact that they are capable of in society. The chapter will first explore the concept of quality and outline some of the ways in which it has been categorised in higher education. There will then be an extended case study presented on higher education in Kenya and the changes needed to address the quality challenges there. Finally, implications are drawn out for our understanding of quality in the context of the achievement of the SDGs.

What Is Quality in Higher Education?

There is considerable debate and disagreement as to what constitutes quality in higher education (Cheng and Tam 1997; Harvey and Green 1993; Tam 2001). These are not semantic niceties, but touch on fundamental divides of educational vision: as Harvey and Green (1993: 10) state: 'This is not a different perspective on the same thing but different perspectives on different things with the same label'.

We can cut quality in different ways. In the first place, there are different aspects of the entity in question whose quality we can gauge. Quality in higher education can refer to any of the diverse functions of the university, including teaching, research or community engagement activities: although in practice the latter is rarely included in any serious way. The learning environment in the university can be seen to comprise not only formally taught courses, but also extracurricular learning activities on campus and beyond, as well as the resources available in institutions for autonomous study, including libraries and information and communications technology (ICT).

Alternatively, we can assess quality according to the different stages of flow. Following the conventional systems model, it can be divided into elements of inputs, processes and outcomes. This kind of model has been commonly used in education, in some cases rather simplistically, although in others such as UNICEF (2000) and UNESCO (2004) showing sensitivity to broader factors of influence. When applied to higher education, inputs include the investments made, the staff employed (number and qualification levels) and the students admitted, processes relate to the experiences of actors in the university and their interactions, and outputs to the learning that graduates take into society, research impact and publications.

Finally, a deeper set of distinctions can be made in relation to what is actually meant by 'quality'. Harvey and Green's (1993) influential account provides a useful taxonomy in this respect. They distinguish between five versions: *exception*—an instinctive notion exclusive to traditional, elite institutions; *perfection*—conforming to product specification, associated with business models; *fitness for purpose*—fulfilling the aims and objectives set by the institution; *value for money*—efficiency, gauging performance in relation to cost; and finally, *transformative*—the empowerment of learners. These vastly differing takes on what quality in HE refers to are all in common usage in policy, institutional strategy and everyday speech. In these, we see tensions between absolute and relative criteria of quality. The *perfection* and *fitness for purpose* forms display ideas of quality that are unique to the institution in question, precluding cross-institutional comparison. As Harvey and Green (1993: 16) state in relation to the 'perfection' conception:

> [T]here are no absolutes against which the output can be assessed, no universal benchmarks. In this sense, for example, a quality Volkswagen car is one that on delivery from the manufacturer exhibits no defects at all. This approach does not provide a basis for comparison with the specification of a Ford or a Honda.

On the other hand, the exceptional version requires a hierarchy between institutions, with not all universities able to be good at the same time. This hierarchy may be based on objective or purportedly objective criteria, or it may be instinctive, apodictic or self-evident.

Barnett (1992) in this way provides a distinction between objectivist and relativist positions on quality. These differences imply *hierarchical* or *parallel* conceptions, having a necessary ordering in the case of the former, with only some obtaining the 'gold standard', but in the latter the possibility of multiple valid forms. But he also adds a third, 'developmental', relating to ongoing enhancement of quality through self-assessment—corresponding to 'quality improvement' rather than 'quality assurance'.

As is often the case in educational matters, it is hard to disentangle questions of *quality* from those of *equality*. The question arises of quality *for whom*: as seen in the previous chapter, most contemporary education systems display markedly stratified opportunities, with high-quality learning experiences to a large extent restricted to the more privileged. Even within particular institutions, gender, social class, regional background and other factors play a part in diminishing the quality of students' experiences (as shown in detail in Morley and Lugg's [2009] research on higher education in Tanzania and Ghana).

How does quality relate to the frame of value, function and interaction outlined in Chapter 3? What we think of as quality is relational to the particular value held by an institution. Gauges of quality are normally applied to the effectiveness of functions, and sometimes interactions. But what qualifies as a valid function, and indeed effectiveness, is determined by value. So, for example, for an institution holding to the intrinsic value of knowledge production through advances in basic science and scholarly writing, it will be coherent to gauge its quality through its publications in high-level journals. If the fundamental value of the university is its instrumental contribution to reducing poverty in surrounding communities, then these gauges will be largely irrelevant, and instead it will need to look to evaluate its community engagement programmes, applied research and so forth.

For the developmental university, one that is aligned to the achievement of the SDGs, quality would in this way reside in the effectiveness of the institution in fulfilling its instrumental aims: promoting inclusive growth, addressing developmental challenges, strengthening public services such as education and health, and building robust and democratic institutions. The ultimate gauges of quality, therefore, are those of impact. It may then appear rather artificial to distinguish quality from impact (discussed in the following chapter): in an entirely instrumental institution they are inextricably linked. Bearing in mind the ultimately porous boundary between them, this chapter will focus more on the internal workings of quality—the functioning of the institution—while the next chapter will focus on external impact—the imprint of the institution on the outside society.

To what extent does quality in the developmental model corresponds to a *hierarchical* or a *parallel* conception (Barnett 1992)? While the developmental university in no way adheres to the *exception* conception of quality, it does retain an absolutist notion through its prioritising of institutions' impact on national development. The creators of the SDGs were at pains to establish objective gauges for each, so an absolute conception of quality can be applied to the effectiveness of institutions in contributing to the achievement of those objectives. As the underpinning notions of 'development' come to be questioned and critiqued, with greater diversity of understanding of the good society, then we start to move towards a parallel conception—an idea that will be discussed further in relation to post-development in Chapter 10. Ultimately, the divide between absolutist and relativist positions on quality is based on whether we see the university as unitary, with only one valid form for the institution, or whether there are multiple possible realisations.

Quality, therefore, is a battleground in two ways: first, in terms of the underpinning idea of university to which the conception of quality is relative, and second, in the task of ensuring that a university, or perhaps all universities, achieve quality in practice. While much of this book is concerned with the first, the following sections will focus primarily on the second, through a case study of Kenya—unique like all contexts, but illustrating many of the challenges of lower income countries around the world.

Enhancing Quality: The Case of Kenya

Kenya is a critical case in relation to the challenge of ensuring quality of higher education. As outlined in the previous chapter, participation in higher education in Kenya is relatively low (with a gross enrolment ratio of 11%, well below the global average of 38% [UIS 2018]), though the system has grown significantly. The number of institutions has more than doubled since 2012, and overall enrolments doubled in just three years: from 218,628 in 2011–2012 to 443,783 in 2014–2015, and increasing again to 564,507 in 2016–2017 (Republic of Kenya 2015, 2017). However, this expansion has come in the context of a squeeze on public investment: HE funding as a percentage of GDP fell from 0.94 to 0.74% between the periods 1996–2000 and 2001–2005 (Wangenge-Ouma 2007), and recurrent expenditure on universities decreased by 18% between 2012–2013 and 2015–2016, in spite of the rapid increase in student numbers—although it did recover substantially in 2016–2017 (Republic of Kenya 2017).

After the independence of the University of Nairobi in 1970 from previous links to the University of East Africa and University of London, it was not until 1984 that a second institution, Moi University, was created. There has been a gradual expansion in the number of public institutions since that date, with considerable acceleration in recent years due to the conversion of a large number of middle-level technical colleges to university status. There were 14 new public universities created in 2013 alone. Further expansion was encouraged by the 2014 amendment to the Universities Act requiring the provision of university education in each of the newly designated counties. However, the majority of the growth in student numbers in the public sector can be attributed to the 'parallel stream', a policy common to East African countries and emerging originally from Makerere University in Uganda

(Court 1999). Historically, entrance to public institutions had been controlled by highly competitive admission exams, selecting the highest performing secondary leavers and providing them with generous scholarships including accommodation. Liberalisation of the sector in the 1990s allowed universities to diversify their funding streams, and the major institutions took advantage of the opportunity to admit fee-paying students. Alongside the quota of government-funded students, these universities now admit a large proportion of 'parallel programme' or Module II students, who are often in full-time employment and study in evening or weekend courses. These fee-paying students constitute a significant majority of the total enrolment in the largest and best established public universities (Odhiambo 2011).

While in the end it has been the public sector in which the rapid increase has taken place, initially it was the private sector that was touted as the key location for growth (Oanda et al. 2008). The first private institution—the United States International University—dates from as early as 1970, but the major expansion of the sector took place from the 1990s, after which a number of mainly faith-based institutions were established. Most of these institutions are small in size, and cater primarily to students from higher socio-economic groups who are unable to obtain the grades to enter the elite public institutions. While comprising approximately 15% of total enrolments (CUE 2016), the private sector has not acted as a major demand-absorbing segment, on account of the restricted proportion of the population able to pay the fees, as well as the aforementioned emergence of the 'parallel stream' in public institutions.

The introduction of the dual track in public institutions has significant implications for equity, as discussed in the previous chapter. Those students who can afford the fees bypass a highly competitive selection procedure, as students can be admitted to parallel programmes with a grade of C+ in the Kenya Certificate of Secondary Education (Odhiambo 2011). Although deterioration of quality did not begin with the introduction of the parallel stream, researchers (e.g. Wangenge-Ouma 2007; Boit and Kipkoech 2014) have highlighted the strongly negative impact of this development in public institutions. The strain on the public institutions has been exacerbated by the 'double intake' of government-sponsored students in 2011–2012 (Gudo et al. 2011).

There have also been significant quality challenges raised by the 'upgrading' of middle-level colleges to university status referred to above, and the setting up of small campuses of established universities in interior towns, often with precarious infrastructure. A potentially significant change in the state of play came in 2016 with the enabling of private universities to admit publicly sponsored students (Oanda 2018). Since this change, and also as a result of rapid increases in the number of institutions, public universities have struggled to keep up the very high numbers of parallel stream students—worrying for their budgets, though possibly a relief on the straining infrastructure.

The negative impact of the rapid expansion on quality is recognised by all stakeholders and supported by existing research (e.g. Chege 2015; Oketch 2003; Owuor 2012; Sifuna 1998, 2010). A study by the Inter-University Council of East Africa (2014) asserted that 49% of graduates are inadequately prepared for work in their areas of study. These issues affect public and private sectors in different ways. While public universities—particularly the flagship institutions in Nairobi—have the greatest concentration of highly qualified academic staff and research activity, they suffer from significant overcrowding, insufficient numbers of lecturers and degraded facilities. Private universities have lower student-to-staff ratios, but also have severe challenges, with staff characterised by part-timers with lower qualifications working in multiple institutions. As stated above, while there is far from consensus as to what constitutes quality of higher education, there is a compelling array of evidence in Kenya pointing to quality challenges that would satisfy most conceptualisations, in the three key areas of inputs, experiences and outcomes. In terms of the diverse stakeholders, government, university staff, students, researchers and graduate employers concur that a significant transformation in the system is needed.

There are a range of policies underway to support quality of higher education in Kenya. The country is placing significant emphasis on the role of higher education in national development, as evidenced by the Vision 2030 document, which places technological innovation and high-level skills centre stage (Chege 2015; Republic of Kenya 2007). Oversight of the sector is with the Commission for University Education (CUE) (created in 2012 to replace the previous Commission for Higher Education), whose main responsibility is for accreditation of institutions, recognition of qualifications and quality assurance. While historically the Commission has used its regulatory function mainly in relation to private institutions, its actions are increasingly relevant for the public sector (Otieno 2010). Ever since reforms in 2003—before which date the President of the Republic was Chancellor of every university—public universities have had autonomy from the state, but with the Universities Act in 2012 they are required to adhere to the regulations of the CUE. Current actions taken by CUE to enhance quality of higher education include requirements for institutional quality assurance, rolling out of course evaluation procedures and changes to promotion criteria. The Inter-University Council for East Africa also has an important role in quality assurance and has run a capacity building programme (with the German agencies DAAD and HRK) to develop institution level practice. The East African Quality Assurance Network (EAQAN) also has a range of activities in this area (Brewis and McCowan 2016).

However, as will be discussed in greater detail below, while these initiatives have brought some important changes, they have not as yet ensured the enhancement of quality across the system. The question then arises: given the consensus of all stakeholders, why is the quality of higher education in Kenya not being maintained and enhanced? What are the barriers to upholding quality? The following sections focus on understanding the root causes of the problems of teaching and learning quality in Kenyan higher education.

Barriers to Quality

The following account draws on research undertaken between 2013 and 2015 in a range of public and private universities in Kenya.[1] Analysis of respondents' views, documentary sources and secondary literature

---

[1] The research in question was part of a three-year project commissioned by the British Council focusing on higher education, employability and development in four countries in Sub-Saharan Africa. This part of the study provides a qualitative analysis, drawing on 16 key informant interviews with policymakers, directors of quality assurance, representatives of teaching and learning units and lecturers, as well as field visits, observations of classes and publicly available documentary and statistical sources.

points to a large range of barriers to achieving quality in Kenyan universities. These barriers can be grouped into three categories: those relating to resource constraints and lack of investment in universities; those relating to how the system and the individual institutions are run, the deployment of academic staff and their career incentives; and lastly dominant approaches to teaching and learning, forms of assessment and the relations and interactions between lecturers and students. All of these, in turn, are underpinned by deeper cultural, political and economic forces in society, as indicated by Fig. 7.1.

This analysis will focus primarily on the intermediary ring, that of the immediate factors affecting quality, as this is the level at which

Fig. 7.1 Factors influencing higher education quality (*Source* Author)

interventions in the short term can most meaningfully be made. Nevertheless, while this is the explicit focus of this chapter, it must be recalled, as with all questions of policy and practice in the social sphere, that many of these issues are rooted in deeper historical and contemporary questions such as colonialism, neo-colonialism, dominant economic and political structures, epistemologies and cultural norms.

Resources

The financial allocation made to universities is essential so as to ensure sufficient staffing and physical resources. Considerations of resources include the total amount available nationally for higher education, as well as effective allocation and equitable distribution between and within institutions. Perception of lack of resources may be common to all universities across the world, and desire for additional funds may indeed be limitless. However, in Kenya resource levels have not reached even a minimum acceptable level. As outlined in the previous section, problems have been caused first and foremost by the rapid increase in enrolments without corresponding investment, leading to a drop in the level of resource per student. The rapid expansion of the parallel stream, as well as the double intake, have exacerbated these problems in public universities. Resourcing issues for the most part are less acute in private institutions, though many of these also suffer from inadequate physical infrastructure and equipment.

Staffing

The most evident manifestation of poor quality higher education in Kenya is large class sizes. For many students in Kenya, large-scale lectures represent the only form of teaching, with few opportunities for tutorials or breakout seminar groups. Very high student lecturer ratios are evident across public institutions in Kenya, with an average of one lecturer for 70 students (Chege 2015). In fact, these figures may even underestimate the ratio, given that public universities are believed to under-report student numbers on account of confidentiality of the exact size of their private student cohort. One respondent spoke of class sizes of 1200 at his institution. Another lecturer reported that his institution had attempted to continue with 'tutorials', in addition to lectures, but that these groups customarily had as many as 200 students.

In part the lack of academic staff is caused by a lack of investment in universities. However, there is also a lack of capacity, with insufficient qualified candidates to fill places (Wangenge-Ouma 2007). Given the low turnover of new Ph.D.s in the country, and the loss of many highly qualified staff through brain drain, it is hard for universities to find adequately qualified applicants when they are looking to recruit (Odhiambo 2013). In addition to unfilled places, this lack of capacity has led to inadequate qualifications of academic staff in some cases, or of staff taking on responsibilities beyond their level of seniority or outside their area of specialisation, taking on extra teaching load for more pay, or assigning teaching assistants to full teaching responsibilities—all of which have a potential negative impact on quality (Gudo et al. 2011; Wangenge-Ouma 2007). Difficulties of recruiting full-time staff—as well as the corresponding expense—have also led a number of institutions to take on high proportions of part-time staff. In one of the prestigious private institutions, 80% of credit hours are taught by part-time staff. Lecturers moving between a number of institutions are seen to have less time and commitment to ensuring the broader development of their students.

The difficulties described here relate mainly to undergraduate teaching, but there are also staff shortages at the postgraduate level: while class sizes are generally much smaller for Masters students, allowing for a greater amount of discussion and debate, there is a critical lack of supervisors in many cases, as well as downgrading of dissertation requirements (Wangenge-Ouma 2007). Strains on administration are also brought about by the lack of non-academic staff in universities.

A further resource issue is the relatively low level of salary paid to staff. As is the case with teachers at the school level, low salary has a number of negative effects on quality of education. First, it reduces the attractiveness of the profession, thereby making it harder to recruit high performing graduates. Second, it has a negative effect on lecturers' sense of recognition from their institutions and society, leading to a decrease in motivation. Third, it increases likelihood of lecturers seeking additional sources of income. This final point was highlighted by a number of respondents: 'moonlighting' of lecturers in other institutions is seen to be very common, leading to absenteeism, cancelled classes, burnout of lecturers and lack of time to devote to students. As an academic developer in a private institution stated:

> [I]f you ask me, that interferes with the quality of teaching that you engage in because I can't be in Nairobi today, Mombasa tomorrow, Nakuru…when do I have time to sit and reflect and think through my teaching?

Physical Resources

Quality of higher education is also dependent on an adequate physical environment and specific teaching resources. Universities report minimal facilities available in classrooms, and lack the specialised equipment needed for particular fields of study: laboratories for science subjects, fisheries for aquaculture and so forth. Library and ICT resources are also inadequate for students to partake in individual study outside class time. The combination of lack of human resources and teaching resources has a magnifying effect, as effective teaching of large classes to a large extent depends on audio-visual and other equipment in classrooms, and other forms of virtual learning and library facilities to ensure individual and group learning outside of formal classes (Allais 2014). Only a handful of elite private universities in the capital city are seen to have adequate facilities and equipment, with projectors in each classroom, broadband access for students and classrooms with an adequate layout to allow for interaction and discussion.

In some cases, greater financial autonomy has allowed institutions to enhance their infrastructure: a prominent example here is Kenyatta University, in which international collaborations have enabled the construction of a number of new university buildings, most notably the Campanile and the Post-Modern Library. Nevertheless, respondents were sceptical about whether these eye-catching displays of institutional development had actually lead to any improvements in the infrastructure for learning.

Governance

Resources, however, can only act to boost quality if they are allocated effectively and efficiently. Conversely, even in the context of resource constraints, respondents considered that the higher education system could be managed in ways that enhanced quality to a greater extent. These points relate in part to national-level governance, as well as the management of individual institutions, and broader questions of the participation of key stakeholders.

Marketisation

The broader backdrop of marketisation and commercialisation cannot be ignored in relation to the question of quality. While liberalisation of the private sector and autonomy of public institutions to generate income has rapidly increased the number of places, they have not ensured maintenance of an adequate quality of provision. Crudely put, competition between providers has not 'weeded out' poor quality products, as a HE degree still has considerable attractions (and in many cases real value), even if the diploma has been gained with little meaningful learning.

A further point is that instead of having a well thought out national plan for student numbers and distribution across disciplinary areas, unbridled commercialisation has led to institutions rushing to offer courses in any area in which there is a perceived market for students, regardless of the capacity of the institution to provide a quality offering in that area, or of the employment opportunities for students subsequently. 'Duplication' of courses has therefore become a key concern for many commentators. The financial incentives to recruit ever greater numbers of students is also encouraging institutions to admit students without the requisite level of preparation (Oanda 2018). As one lecturer in a private university stated: 'The cut-off point is a C with a C+ in Maths and English but some universities flout the rule as they need students'. As discussed above in relation to physical resources, marketisation of admissions and entrepreneurial activities of universities have allowed for the entry of new funds, although not always leading to improvements in research and teaching quality.

Quality Assurance and Quality Enhancement

As outlined above, there have been a range of measures put in place to ensure quality in the Kenyan higher education system, and relevant bodies have been established at institutional, national and regional levels. However, action to date has been largely in the realm of 'quality assurance' as opposed to 'quality enhancement' (Brewis and McCowan 2016; Odhiambo 2014), focusing on course validation, accreditation and audit procedures rather than in supporting lecturers in developing their teaching practice and students in enhancing their learning.

Universities are required by CUE to have a director of quality assurance and procedures in relation to programme delivery and evaluation, yet the Commission was seen by respondents to lack expertise on issues of teaching and learning, and also to place a strong emphasis on traditional exams, resisting the alternative forms of assessment proposed by some universities. One academic developer at a private university interpreted this tendency towards inertia as being a result of the fact that those in power had succeeded in the system:

> And the people who are running, you know, the ministry of education, the people who are running CUE, these are the people that excelled in that system. They were the *crème de la crème*, they were the best of the best in that system. And it's really hard for them to look back on it and say, "You know, that system needs to change," because it worked for them. You know, they got the big titles and the big offices and the big leather desk and so forth. So it's hard for them to see that there's a real problem with it.

Furthermore, respondents pointed to a mismatch between the official requirements and the reality in institutions. CUE (2014), for example, has guidelines on the maximum student–lecturer ratio (ranging between 1:7 for medical sciences and 1:18 for social sciences), but according to the respondents, no public university in Kenya is complying with them.

Nevertheless, a number of universities have recently set up teaching and learning support units or Centres for Excellence in Teaching and Learning, for example Kenyatta University, University of Nairobi, Moi

University and Daystar University. These units provide professional development workshops for staff, advice on pedagogy and assessment, peer observations and sometimes other functions such as coordinating student course evaluations. Furthermore, a number of universities are developing formal qualifications in higher education teaching and learning: for example, Strathmore has a new certificate for education in academic practice, and Daystar is developing a postgraduate diploma. These are promising developments, and have allowed for innovative teaching practices to blossom at the local level. Nevertheless, across the system there is still a severe lack of teaching and learning support. With the exception of those universities that have dedicated teaching and learning centres, most institutions offer little more than an initial induction day.

Corruption

An investigative report (Okari 2015) published in the *Daily Nation* in February 2015 showed the widespread corruption in the higher education sector and the selling of degrees in certain institutions, most notably the Nairobi Aviation College. According to the exposé, 'A lecturer at the college told us that he had helped thousands of students to acquire certificates without their setting foot in class'. While pointing the finger at corruption can sometimes serve to deflect attention from the deeper roots of political and economic problems, it is important to acknowledge its relevance for the issue of quality of higher education in Kenya. CUE has become more active in this regard in recent years, for example shutting down 'Barack Obama University' in 2015, which was attempting to sell its courses despite not having been registered.

Two forms of corruption were pointed to as challenges by the respondents: first, the existence of diploma mills and bogus degrees of the type outlined above; and second, and most commonly, malpractice in relation to assessments. In some cases, there was a lack of confidence in assessment procedures, or outright manipulation of grades.

Engaging Academic Staff

Next, there are a range of factors related to the status, working conditions, management and support of academic staff. To a large extent, lecturers have little encouragement, incentives or time availability for developing their teaching practice. First, promotion requirements are primarily oriented around research, with little recognition of teaching (for example one of the participating universities attributed 20% of the evaluation to this dimension); Kenya is certainly not unusual in this globally, in giving research funding and publications the greatest weight in promotions. The establishment of new qualifications for teaching and learning are going some way to addressing this issue, as is the increasing attention given to course evaluations, but stronger links with enhancing teaching quality are needed.

Workload is therefore a significant issue, exacerbated by the question of low salaries and moonlighting discussed above, as well as increasing enrolments (Calvert and Muchira-Tirima 2013; Wangenge-Ouma 2007). Consequently, there is little time available for academic staff to attend professional development activities. Arasa and Calvert (2013) in their study found that lecturers did in fact value teaching highly, but were prevented from dedicating sufficient time to it not by the competing demands of research, but by extra paid teaching work and non-university commitments. Engagement is seen to be undermined by all of these factors:

> [H]ow do you feel about yourself when you've got two *matatus*[2] into work because you're saving on petrol because you feel you're under-rewarded and you're not being paid enough. You may well be moonlighting or you may be doing extra courses instead of doing some of your research study... So it's...the actual lives of the lecturers I don't see being terribly enjoyable. And a lot of them have got their own farms or they've got their building projects or they've got their businesses.... They're earning money in other ways to make do. So, if you take all of those together, and it's a wonder that some of them go in as bright-eyed and bushy-tailed as they do. (International partner)

---

[2]Minibuses commonly used in Kenya for public transport.

A further issue is around the lack of meaningful engagement of 'rank and file' academics in decision-making, leading to a lack of ownership. The feeling of powerlessness, combined with the sense of not being valued, leads to a reluctance to engage in professional development activities unless made obligatory, and adherence to the minimum acceptable in terms of teaching responsibilities.

Empowering Students

One of the major blockages for improving quality, therefore, is responsiveness of institutions to their stakeholders. In addition to lecturers, another key constituency in this regard is the students themselves. As shown in previous research (McCowan et al. 2015), students are reluctant to complain publicly about their institutions, even when they have a range of serious concerns. Despite the formal representation on university boards and committees, they lack channels to express their views and have them listen to seriously—a fact which at times has led to dissatisfaction 'boiling over' into violent unrest (Amutabi 2002).

Course evaluations are in fact used by a majority of institutions. These provide an opportunity for students to comment on their experience in a particular module, and provide feedback on the quality of teaching and curriculum, although have limited impact in practice. An associated, and perhaps more serious point, relates to the potential disjuncture between actual learning and the awarding of the degree. If students are confident that they will leave the university with the required qualification—and the receiving of that qualification is more important even than learning anything of use—then they have little incentive to complain about lecturer absenteeism, overcrowded classrooms and lack of learning resources. There is even less likelihood of them speaking out about these problems given the direct threats of withholding the awarding of the degree made to some student activists across the continent.

Pedagogical culture

The third of the dimensions relates to the practices of teaching and learning themselves, the curricular offering, and importantly the set of collective beliefs and relationships that support those practices. As argued by Schendel (2016), it is not enough for academic departments to adopt progressive pedagogical forms, without a deeper process of transformation of lecturers' understandings and cultures of practice.

Curricular Offering

A full analysis of the curriculum in Kenyan universities is not possible here, but some brief points will be made. There are widespread concerns in the national media about problems of employability and 'half-baked graduates' (Republic of Kenya 2013; IUCEA 2014), and to some extent at least these problems are attributed to the irrelevance of curricula, to the courses being out of touch with advances in industry and changes in the employment market, as well as dislocation of theoretical knowledge from application in real-life situations. In some cases, professional bodies have refused to recognise degrees (Wanzala 2015). In relation to the integration with the workplace and application of knowledge, differences were observed between disciplinary areas. Health-related courses have been active in introducing problem-based learning (e.g. in Moi University), and business studies makes extensive use of cases. However, even some highly applied courses—such as project management or agriculture—can lack a practical element, in many cases exacerbated by lack of resources.

Two specific trends in relation to distribution of courses were identified by respondents. First, there is what has been called 'programmatic isomorphism' (Wangenge-Ouma 2007), related to the globally identified trend of 'mission creep'. On account of desire for prestige and emulation—and in some cases market benefit—the new entrants to the higher education sector end up duplicating the kinds of courses available at the better established institutions. This dynamic prevents positive forms of diversification of the sector, resulting particularly in technical institutions starting to resemble academic ones. Furthermore, the new courses offered have for the most part been in the applied social sciences, leading to a shortfall in the areas of natural science and engineering, which are more demanding in terms of infrastructure (Oanda and Jowi 2012).

A second—and apparently contradictory—tendency is that of 'course splintering'. In this case, in order to gain commercial benefit, universities will divide a single area into a number of more specific courses, thereby making them too narrow for use in later employment, or at least providing little added value. One public institution provides separate undergraduate degrees in 'Hospitality Management', 'Tourism Management', 'Leisure and Recreation Management' and 'Philosophy in Hospitality and Tourism Management', with further new courses planned in 'Catering and Institutions Management', 'Restaurant Management', 'Food and Beverage Management' and 'Meetings and Events Management'.

A final point relating to the curriculum concerns the lack of a broader campus (or beyond campus) experience of learning. With the exception of the elite Nairobi-based universities, there is a lack of extra-curricular provision—in the form of sports, artistic and creative pursuits—as well as support services such as careers and counselling. Given the centrality of these activities in enhancing students' employability, and broader civic development, this is a worrying state of affairs, and is particularly critical for those lower income students who will often not have access to these activities outside of the university.

Teaching Methods and Pedagogical Relations

Without doubt, it is dangerous to peddle stereotypes about pedagogy in African universities, and many lecturers use progressive methods to ensure a rich and engaging learning environment for students. Findings from another research study showed evidence of effective use of problem-based learning, flipped classrooms, collaborative group work and community placements.[3] Nevertheless, in many institutions transmission pedagogy does dominate, and the 'yellow notes' phenomenon—of

---

[3] *Pedagogies for Critical Thinking: Innovation and Outcomes in African Higher Education* (2015–2019), funded by the UK Economic and Social Research Council and the Department for International Development.

lecturers delivering lectures for years (if not decades) based on the same outdated content—is a reality in many cases. As has been seen, the causes for adherence to transmission pedagogy are complex, and relate to issues of a macro-political nature, involving allocation of resources and governance, as much as they do to micro-level social and cultural interactions. As stated by the head of the teaching and learning support unit at a public university:

> Because if ever I ask a question, the student is sitting very far. They don't have a microphone. I can't even write on the white board. So you just go in and you are just talking.... Sometimes maybe the rooms are not available, lecture rooms… if you have three hundred students in a room of one-fifty, some of them will be standing at the windows also.

An international partner confirmed this view:

> [W]hen the students are crammed in…it makes it very, very hard. And, of course, the simple way of doing things is transmission-mode teaching: the definition of which is the most economical way of getting the lecturers' notes into the students' notes without passing through the brain of either party.

Large classes are seen to make building personal relationships impossible. However, resources are not the only determinant of pedagogy. Teaching practices are also dependent on the availability and type of training and staff development (discussed above) and dominant pedagogical and cultural views and trends. As seen in relation to school teachers (e.g. Brinkmann 2015; Schendel 2016), adoption of learner-centred pedagogies is highly difficult when teachers hold deeper beliefs that run contrary to the underlying principles.

One cultural feature reported as a barrier in transforming pedagogy is deference to authority. The hierarchical nature of Kenyan society—particularly in relation to age, but also to rank seniority—can serve to silence those in more junior positions, and acts against the kind of open dialogical space conducive to development of critical learners. Beyond the classroom, it can also serve to silence committed staff attempting to introduce innovations in teaching and learning. Fears of speaking out relate not only to hierarchies, but also operate horizontally with peers:

> And it's possible that you ask questions in class and you end up answering them yourself, because…because of that distance. And even with the students, amongst the students themselves, they tend to have a fear of, you know, looking bad in front of their colleagues and so they won't speak. (Lecturer, private university)

Perhaps surprisingly, a number of respondents pointed to resistance from students as a key barrier. For those lecturers who had implemented changes and were encouraging a more participatory dialogical space in their classrooms, students sometimes complained, calling for a return to the comfort of the familiar:

> [M]y students were getting shocked by my approach…at first they were very resistant….. [T]hey think she's making us do everything, you know? They didn't like it… [T]hey just sit back and they just…they want the notes so that they can cram for the exam. (Lecturer, private university)

However, the same respondent highlighted that after a few weeks they became increasingly comfortable with the approach. The indications are that after a short period of resistance, students appreciate a more dialogical and active approach to learning, even if it may require more effort. Overall, resistance among faculty was seen to be more of a problem than resistance among students.

Exam Culture

A key barrier to development of more effective pedagogy highlighted by many of the respondents was the culture of examinations. While exams rarely count for all of the student assessment in university courses—commonly there will be 70% awarded for exam, and 30% for continuous assessment—nevertheless, it continues to be the 'gold standard' for validating students' knowledge. Attachment to the exam is seen to go right from the top at the level of CUE, down to the faculty and departmental level. This relates to a deeper question of the relation to knowledge:

> [T]here's an interesting phenomenon, especially when you're done with primary school and you're moving on to high school, there's a tendency for people to burn their books. You literally just set them on fire because then, you know, that's the end. When you're just about to go to the university you do the same thing.... [I]t really waters down what learning is all about, so it stops being lifelong and it begins to become exam-long. As soon as the exam is over, then that's it. (Lecturer, private university)

Respondents pointed not only to the existence of exams, but also to negative practices within exams, in particular marking focused on regurgitation of a number of key points. Assessment, as ever, has a 'backwash' affect, influencing prior teaching and learning. Dominance of exams as a system of assessment leads to emphasis on memorisation and on faithful reproduction rather than critical reflection and creative engagement.

> [H]ow many of us have heard horror stories, I know it happens in the government universities here, where professor shows up on day one of the class, four hundred/five hundred students in the class, tells them, you know, "Here's the list of books to read, I'll see you at the exam." And that's it! Never another class. And the students go and cram and cram and read and then they take the exam and they pass the course. (Academic developer, private university)

A range of factors relating to pedagogical culture are therefore seen to be influential in facilitating and strengthening quality enhancement. The following section will distil the key elements from these findings and draw out implications for responses on the part of the government and institutions.

Implications for Policy

In categorising the factors of resources, governance and pedagogical culture, it is important to emphasise the significant interaction between the three elements. Insufficient resources make it hard to practice pedagogy conducive to deep forms of learning—as has been seen in the literature on the challenges of implementing learner-centred pedagogy in schools in low-income countries with very large class sizes (Schweisfurth 2013; Tabulawa 2013). Poor governance and low remuneration lead to a lack of trust and motivation on the part of academic staff, which in turn undermines efforts to ensure ongoing professional development and high standards of practice. In some cases, poor quality of provision and ineffective governance may make it harder for universities to attract both public and private funds. Or in a more positive way we can say that these three areas—resources, governance and pedagogical culture—are mutually reinforcing: as one starts to be enhanced it will facilitate improvement of the others.

We, therefore, need a three-pronged approach to address these areas simultaneously. It is not uncommon to hear proposed solutions that focus exclusively on one side of the problem—professional development, say, or recruitment of new lecturers. These will only work if corresponding changes are made in other areas. Resource constraints cannot be ignored, as ultimately the system can only fully improve with greater investment. The financial challenge of funding higher education is one that must be faced head-on by Kenyan state and society—in conjunction with (and not as a trade-off against) funding for primary and secondary education. Yet resources are a necessary but not a sufficient condition for improvement. There are also a range of other changes that must be made. Furthermore, these are changes that can take place at relatively low cost, and in the short term—whereas increased investments may require significant change of political will, or improvement of the national economic situation. For example, a small-scale partnership between Strathmore University and York St John's University in the UK, involving a professional development course for a small number of staff committed to teaching and learning enhancement in institutions in Nairobi, led to observable transformation of practices, as knock-on staff development programmes and enhanced teaching and learning support were rolled out through a 'ripple effect' in the subsequent months and years.

In terms of governance, it is clear that a substantial amount of caution is needed with marketisation of the system. Resource constraints had instigated the policies of privatisation from the 1990s, leading both to the emergence of a number of private providers and the development of the dual track in public institutions. However, while these responses have ensured the continuing expansion of the system, they have done so at the expense of quality. As discussed above, the disjuncture between degree diplomas and quality learning experiences means that market mechanisms are not enough to ensure consistently high quality across the system. Low-quality courses will still attract fee-paying students if the latter are confident they will obtain a qualification of value in the job market. Nevertheless, net gains for society are only obtained through the maintenance of a high-quality learning environment, leading to increases in workplace productivity in graduates and other positive contributions to society. State intervention in the system is therefore necessary in order to ensure quality across the system, involving a combination of investment of public resources—so as to fund areas in which there is market failure, and ensure equity; of regulation—including mechanisms conventionally associated with quality assurance, as well as addressing issues such as lack of incentives for individual lecturers to focus on teaching excellence; and of information for prospective students. Furthermore, the student voice needs to be engaged with to a far greater extent, allowing involvement of students in decision-making relating to their learning and ensuring greater accountability of institutions to their interests.

Finally, efforts are needed at the grassroots level to enhance pedagogical culture. Studies such as that of Schendel (2016) in Rwanda show the significant impact that conducive departmental culture can have transforming the rhetoric of learner-centred education into pedagogies that can enhance student learning. Academic staff development is an important part of this process, and there are a number of promising new initiatives in this area. The development of credit-bearing qualifications in teaching and learning in higher education provide a potential solution, by ensuring that incentives are in place and time ring-fenced for lecturers to engage in these activities wholeheartedly. Mentoring and peer observation schemes, as well as changes in promotion criteria, are also important interventions. As with many debates in higher education, it is impossible to divorce them completely from dynamics at the primary and secondary levels. So, habits and expectations among students and lecturers about teaching methods, assessment and interpersonal relations are entrenched by earlier experiences of learning. Addressing these challenges at the higher education level—as is the case with questions of equity of access—involves simultaneous interventions at the lower levels of the system. Furthermore, as emphasised above, a number of the challenges in pedagogy are rooted in deeper cultural questions of social hierarchies and relationships to knowledge, and as such will require a long time frame for change to take place.

As seen above, there are a range of innovations and progressive movements in pedagogy already in place, emerging from particular champions within institutions, as well as coordinated institutional efforts. Effective academic staff development programmes (some involving blended learning) have been set up in a range of institutions—including Strathmore, Daystar and Aga Khan, with its Network of Teaching and Learning. Approaches such as problem-based learning and constructive alignment, use of student learning mentors and alternative forms of assessment such as portfolios, have also been incorporated in courses across the country. Nevertheless, even those institutions at the forefront of progressive practice struggle to universalise these reforms. In order to address this challenge, the Association for Faculty Enrichment of Learning and Teaching (AFELT) has been established: this grassroots networking organisation of institutional leads in academic development and quality assurance was founded in 2014 with the mission of advocating teaching and learning enhancement initiatives in the country. It has the potential to bring lasting change in the system through capacity building, ensuring buy-in of academic staff, providing a forum for sharing innovations and bringing tangible changes to teaching and learning practice. These initiatives and innovations need to be nurtured and supported if system-wide changes are to take place and achieve lasting effect.

Global Challenges of Quality

Challenges of quality are the norm, rather than the exception, in higher education institutions around the world. First, the generally high level of economic inequality means that resources for all forms of human activity are highly skewed in favour of a few countries and certain social groups within them, and universities are no exception. Second, the extremely rapid expansion of higher education—fuelled by credentialism in many cases—has placed intolerable strains on most systems. Third, in many countries, the model of the Western university has been transplanted without strong rooting in local intellectual and educational traditions. Add to those factors the reproductive nature of national and global systems of higher education outlined above, through which it is hard for institutions to break the cycle of low prestige and low funding.

These disparities of quality are undermining the developmental potential of universities. Starting with expenditure, there are significant differences: even within Organisation of Economic Cooperation and Development (OECD) countries, the expenditure (PPP) per student per year on tertiary education varies from US$30,000 in the USA to less than US$10,000 in Turkey, Hungary, Poland, Mexico and Chile, and only US$4000 in Greece (OECD 2018). In many countries, expenditure is less than US$1000 and in some cases less than US$500 (e.g. Armenia, El Salvador, Kyrgyzstan, Madagascar, Mongolia, Myanmar and Nepal [UIS 2019]). Levels of spending per student in many cases have been decreasing on account of rapid expansion and prioritising of other levels of education. Annual expenditure per higher education student in Africa dropped from US$2900 per year in 1990 to US$2000 in 2006 (World Bank 2010).

While debates rage and will continue to rage about whether class size is a determinant of teaching and learning quality, the ratio of academic staff to students is still an important indicator. For sure, high-quality teaching is still possible with a large group, particularly if lecturers have developed appropriate strategies, are assisted by teaching aids, and can utilise diverse forms of technology. Unfortunately, these factors rarely pertain in resource-constrained contexts, and very large classes (often of many hundreds) usually mean very little learning (Foley and Masingila 2014; Allais 2014). Furthermore, there are a range of benefits that a low student–staff ratio can bring to an institution: including more frequent contact between students and lecturers outside of class, and more time available to lecturers for research, service and community engagement.

There are also significant challenges of infrastructure in universities in LMICs, with poorly equipped laboratories, classrooms without visual aids, lack of computers on campus, and inadequate sporting and recreational facilities. My personal experience visiting numerous universities in Latin America and Africa has taken me to a wide variety of different kinds of university: including some very well equipped as well as dilapidated campuses. Yet, as seen in the above research on Kenya, among them were an alarming number in which the very basic physical infrastructure of an educational institution was absent, making it hard for students to learn, and for academics to teach and research.

There are also questions regarding the university as a safe, inclusive and respectful environment. Research such as that of Morley and Lugg (2009) has documented the discrimination and barriers that women can face within university, even once they have overcome the odds to be admitted. There have been a large number of cases of sexual harassment, sex for grades and other abuses of power. Examination malpractice, involving cheating on the part of students and acceptance of bribes on the part of lecturers is prevalent, with India recently rocked by these kinds of scandals. Plagiarism and essay mills are now common throughout the world, including high-income countries, with one study estimating that one in seven students globally had used these services (Newton 2018).

Finally, there is the perennial issue of academic freedom. The kinds of open-ended enquiry that characterise the university are predicated on a degree of autonomy for the institution to appoint and reward appropriate staff, to pursue teaching and research in accordance with scholarly values, and to pursue critical agendas, even when they go against the government. In all parts of the world these kinds of freedoms are vulnerable, and at specific points of history have been severely curtailed

(Odhiambo 2011; Sifuna 1998). The rise of the far right in recent years has threatened even countries with traditions of freedom of expression, with severe crackdowns on academics in Turkey under Erdogan, and at time of writing in 2018 the first signs of repression of academics in Brazil under President-elect Bolsonaro.

One of the most prominent discourses globally in higher education is that of the crisis of employability. Images of unemployed graduates lining highways with placards proclaiming their job-seeking credentials adorn the newspapers of African countries. Rates of graduate unemployment are indeed high in some countries, with figures of 24% in Rwanda, 21% in Bangladesh and 20% in Greece (World Bank 2018[4]), although reliable figures are frequently unavailable. Furthermore, even those graduates who do have employment are very often working in non-graduate jobs, or jobs outside their specialist areas. Beyond unemployment rates, there are serious concerns about the extent to which graduates are actually prepared for the workplace, contributing to unemployment and underemployment, as well as poor performance. Employers and other stakeholders across the world routinely bemoan the lack of skills and preparedness in a range of areas, including critical thinking, problem-solving and IT skills, as well as attributes such as responsibility and punctuality (Dabalen et al. 2000; IUCEA/EABC 2014; Oketch 2016; Pitan and Adedeji 2012; McCowan et al. 2016). Commonly, there is seen to be a negative shift over time, with today's graduates less well-prepared than those of previous decades.

In fact, the evidence base to support the above claims is extremely thin (McCowan 2014). Most research on graduate preparedness for the workplace in LMICs is based on employer surveys, which are highly impressionistic. Even objective gauges such as employment rates have ambiguous implications, since it is uncertain to what extent they reveal structural problems in the economy (i.e. there simply are not enough jobs) or skills mismatches and gaps.

Gauges of actual learning, on the other hand, are extremely rare. In educational research and policy, there has been a marked shift towards

---

[4]Includes graduates of short cycle tertiary education.

learning outcomes as a gauge of quality in recent years, popularised by the Programme for International Student Assessment (PISA) assessments. Yet comparable tests do not exist for higher education. The OECD developed the cross-national Assessment of Higher Education Learning Outcomes (AHELO) programme for this end, although it was suspended following opposition (Altbach and Hazelkorn 2018). The European Union is currently experimenting through the CALOHEE initiative, involving cross-national assessments in five subject areas. There are also some national level tests, such as the ENADE in Brazil and Saber Pro in Colombia, but these initiatives struggle to gauge the value-added of university study. They are also hampered by the discipline-specific nature of higher education (in contrast to schools) and contestation over what generic learning outcomes there might be. While there are rich qualitative studies on the impact of higher education on graduates' lives (e.g. Case et al. 2018; Walker and Fongwa 2017), most of the large scale data held on graduates concerns their levels of employment and income. While it is often assumed that poor quality university education leads to graduate unemployment (and human capital theory assumes that higher graduate earnings are due to increased productivity through learning) there is insufficient evidence to show direct connections.

Nevertheless, for all of the reasons outlined above—lack of resources, large class sizes, poorly qualified staff and so forth—the learning outcomes for students in many institutions of the world are likely to be suboptimal not only as regards work skills, but also in terms of the transformational conception of quality, equipping students—in Amartya Sen's terms—with capabilities, and the possibility to lead the lives that they have reason to value.

In the context of a bewildering multiplicity of conceptions of quality, this chapter has oriented its discussions around the form of university necessary to achieve the SDGs. This version contrasts noticeably with dominant conceptions of quality as elite research status—crystallised in the international rankings—and quality as market efficiency and profitability, neither of which are equipped for this developmental purpose. There are of course problematic aspects even of the developmental conception, ones which will be discussed further in Chapters 9 and 10, but at the very least they provide the possibility of reducing poverty, providing public services and generating knowledge in the public interest.

The challenges of quality discussed in this chapter should not be read as a characterisation of the worthlessness of higher education systems around the world. Higher education is still a transformatory process for large numbers of people in all regions, even in highly difficult conditions and with constraints on resources. The interaction of students and lecturers committed to deep exploration of the world is the primary ingredient of transformatory higher education, and that can occur even in a bombed-out classroom, an ill-equipped lab or an institution oppressed by an authoritarian government.

Nevertheless, it is important to recognise the significant challenges that are there, so they can be rectified and universities allowed to function in the optimum conditions. Most of these are not the fault of the universities and their immediate actors at all, but are caused by the neglect of governments, the damaging influences of international trends and organisations, historical processes of colonisation and engrained social norms. The potential of universities for bringing positive impact on society is much greater than is currently perceived because the quality constraints outlined above are holding them back.

References

Allais, S. (2014). A critical perspective on large class teaching: The political economy of massification and the sociology of knowledge. *Higher Education, 67*(6), 721–734.

Altbach, P. G., & Hazelkorn, E. (2018, August 14). Can we measure education quality in global rankings? *University World News*. Available at https://www.universityworldnews.com/post.php?story=20180814184535721. Accessed 5 September 2018.

Amutabi, M. N. (2002). Crisis and student protest in universities in Kenya: Examining the role of students in national leadership and the democratisation process. *African Studies Review, 45*(2), 157–178.

Arasa, J., & Calvert, M. (2013). Negotiating professional identities in higher education in Kenya: Dilemmas and priorities of faculty. *Journal of Post-Compulsory Education, 18*(4), 402–414.

Barnett, R. (1992). *Improving higher education: Total quality care.* Bristol: SRHE and Open University Press.

Boit, J. M., & Kipkoech, L. C. (2014). Effects of democratizations of university education on quality of higher education in Kenya: A case of Moi University. *International Journal of Educational Administration and Policy Studies, 6*(1), 5–8.

Brewis, E., & McCowan, T. (2016). *Enhancing teaching in African higher education: Perspectives of quality assurance and academic development practitioners in Ghana, Nigeria, Kenya and South Africa.* British Council.

Brinkmann, S. (2015). Learner-centred education reforms in India: The missing piece of teachers' beliefs. *Policy Futures in Education, 13,* 342–359.

Calvert, M., & Muchira-Tirima, K. (2013). Making sense of professionalism and being a professional in a Kenyan higher education context. *Journal of Education for Teaching, 39*(4), 370–382.

Case, J. M., McKenna, S., Marshall, D., & Mogashana, D. (2018). *Going to university: The influence of higher education on the lives of young South Africans.* Cape Town: African Minds.

Chege, M. (2015). Re-inventing Kenya's university: From a "Graduate-mill" to a development-oriented paradigm. *International Journal of Educational Development, 44,* 21–27.

Cheng, Y. C., & Tam, W. M. (1997). Multi-models of quality in education. *Quality Assurance in Education, 5*(1), 22–31.

Commission for University Education. (2014). *Universities standards and guidelines, 2014.* Available at http://www.cue.or.ke/images/phocadownload/UNIVERSITIES_STANDARDS_AND_GUIDELINES_June_2014.pdf. Accessed 24 May 2016.

Commission for University Education. (2016). *State of university education in Kenya.* Nairobi: Commission for University Education.

Court, D. (1999). *Financing higher education in Africa, Makerere: The quiet revolution.* New York and Washington: Rockefeller Foundation and The World Bank.

Dabalen, A., Oni, B., & Adekola, O. A. (2000). *Labour market prospects for university graduates in Nigeria.* The Nigeria University System Innovation Project Study.

Foley, A. R., & Masingila, J. O. (2014). Building capacity: Challenges and opportunities in large class pedagogy (LCP) in Sub-Saharan Africa. *Higher Education, 67*(6), 797–808.

Graeber, D. (2018). *Bullshit jobs: a theory.* London: Penguin.

Gudo, C. O., Olel, M. A., & Oanda, I. O. (2011). University expansion in Kenya and issues of quality education: Challenges and opportunities. *International Journal of Business & Social Science, 2*(20), 203–214.

Harvey, L., & Green, D. (1993). Defining quality. *Assessment and Evaluation in Higher Education, 18,* 8–35.

Inter-University Council for East Africa, IUCEA. (2014). *Regional higher education qualifications gaps* (Vol. II).

McCowan, T. (2014). *Can higher education solve Africa's job crisis? Understanding graduate employability in Sub-Saharan Africa* (Policy Brief). Manchester: British Council.

McCowan, T., Ananga, E., Oanda, I., Sifuna, D., Ongwenyi, Z., Adedeji, S., et al. (2015). *Students in the driving seat: Young people's views on higher education in Africa* (Research Report). Manchester: British Council.

McCowan, T., Walker, M., Fongwa, S., Oanda, I., Sifuna, D., Adedeji, S., et al. (2016). *Universities, employability and inclusive development: Repositioning higher education in Ghana, Kenya, Nigeria and South Africa* (Final Research Report). British Council.

Morley, L., & Lugg, R. (2009). Mapping meritocracy: Intersecting gender, poverty and higher educational opportunity structures. *Higher Education Policy, 22*(1), 37–60.

Newton, P. M. (2018). How common is commercial contract cheating in higher education and is it increasing? A systematic review. *Frontiers in Education, 3,* 67.

Oanda, I. (2018). Admission policies and practices and the reshaping of access patterns to higher education in Africa. In M. E. Oliveri, C. Wendler, & R. Lawles (Eds.), *Higher education admissions and placement practices: An international perspective.* Cambridge: Cambridge University Press.

Oanda, I. O., Chege, F., & Wesonga, D. (2008). *Privatisation and private higher education in Kenya: Implications for access, equity and knowledge production.* Dakar: CODESRIA.

Oanda, I. O., & Jowi, J. (2012). University expansion and the challenges to social development in Kenya: Dilemmas and pitfalls. *Journal of Higher Education in Africa, 10*(1), 49–71.

Odhiambo, G. O. (2011). Higher education quality in Kenya: A critical reflection on key challenges. *Quality in Higher Education, 17,* 299–315.

Odhiambo, G. O. (2013). Academic brain drain: Impact and implications for public higher education quality in Kenya. *Research in Comparative and International Education, 8,* 510–523.

Odhiambo, G. O. (2014). Quality assurance for public higher education: Context, strategies and challenges in Kenya. *Higher Education Research & Development, 33*(5), 978–991.

OECD. (2018). *Education at a glance 2018.* Paris: OECD.

Okari, D. (2015, February 1). How universities and colleges sell diplomas and clean up degrees. *Daily Nation.*

Oketch, M. (2016). Financing higher education in Sub-Saharan Africa: Some reflections and implications for sustainable development. *Higher Education, 72*(4), 525–539.

Oketch, M. O. (2003). Market model for financing higher education in Sub-Saharan Africa: Examples from Kenya. *Higher Education, 16*(3), 313–332.

Otieno, W. (2010). Growth in Kenyan private higher education In K. Kinser, D. Levy, J. C. S. Casillas, A. Bernasconi, S. Slantcheva Durst, W. Otieno, et al. (Eds.), *The global growth of private higher education* (pp. 51–62). ASHE Higher Education Report Series. San Francisco: Wiley.

Owuor, N. A. (2012). Higher education in Kenya: The rising tension between quantity and quality in the post-massification period. *Higher Education Studies, 2*(4), 126–136.

Pitan, O. S., & Adedeji, S. O. (2012). Skills mismatch among university graduates in the Nigerian labour market. *Journal of US-China Education Review, 2,* 90–98.

Republic of Kenya. (2007). *Kenya Vision 2030—A globally competitive and prosperous Kenya.* Nairobi: Office of the Prime Minister, Ministry of State for Planning, National Development and Vision 2030.

Republic of Kenya. (2013). *National manpower survey basic report.* Nairobi: Ministry of Labour.

Republic of Kenya. (2015). *Economic survey.* Nairobi: Kenya National Bureau of Statistics.

Republic of Kenya. (2017). *Economic survey.* Nairobi: Kenya National Bureau of Statistics.

Schendel, R. (2016). Constructing departmental culture to support student development: Evidence from a case study in Rwanda. *Higher Education, 72*(4), 487–504.

Schweisfurth, M. (2013). *Learner-centred education in international perspective: Whose pedagogy for whose development?* Oxford: Routledge.

Sifuna, D. N. (1998). The governance of Kenyan public universities. *Research in Post-Compulsory Education, 3*(2), 175–212.

Sifuna, D. N. (2010). Some reflections on the expansion and quality of higher education in public universities in Kenya. *Research in Post-Compulsory Education, 15*(4), 415–425.

Tabulawa, R. T. (2013). *Teaching and learning in context: Why pedagogical reforms fail in Sub-Saharan Africa*. Dakar, Senegal: Council for the Development of Social Science Research in Africa.

Tam, M. (2001). Measuring quality and performance in higher education. *Quality in Higher Education, 7*(1), 47–54.

UNESCO. (2004). *Education for all: The quality imperative* (EFA Global Monitoring Report 2005). Paris: UNESCO.

UNESCO Institute for Statistics (UIS). (2018). *Education: Enrolment by level of education*. Available at http://data.uis.unesco.org/. Accessed 1 September 2018.

UNESCO Institute for Statistics (UIS). (2019). *Initial government funding per student, US$*. Available at http://data.uis.unesco.org/. Accessed 9 January 19.

UNICEF. (2000). *Defining quality in education*. New York: UNICEF. Available at http://www.unicef.org/education/files/QualityEducation.PDF. Accessed 25 May 2016.

Walker, M., & Fongwa, S. (2017). *Universities, employability and human development*. New York: Springer.

Wangenge-Ouma, G. (2007). Higher education marketisation and its discontents: The case of quality in Kenya. *Higher Education, 56*(4), 457–471.

Wanzala, O. (2015, October 3). Suspension of courses puts varsity regulator on the spot. *Daily Nation*.

World Bank. (2010). *Financing higher education in Africa*. Washington, DC: World Bank.

World Bank. (2018). *Data. Unemployment with advanced education (% of total labor force with advanced education)*. Available at https://data.worldbank.org/indicator/SL.UEM.ADVN.ZS. Accessed 5 November 2019.

8

Impact on the SDGs

Introduction

The community of Tequila in central Mexico (not in fact the birthplace of the famous drink) nestles in the green mountains of Veracruz and is home to scattered villages of Nahuatl-speaking peoples. Like many indigenous communities in Mexico, these have disproportionately high levels of poverty and food insecurity, low levels of educational access and suffer from sustained undermining of their distinctive culture and language. For those young people tenacious enough to make it through the poorly equipped primary and secondary schools, the options await of either returning to a precarious livelihood on the land, leaving to seek another way of life in the nearby town of Orizaba, or making the treacherous journey north towards the US border.[1]

Some rays of hope for the community have come, however, with the founding of the Intercultural University of Veracruz (UVI) in 2005, one

---

[1] This section draws on research carried out as part of the 'Innovative universities and their impact on local development: the case of the intercultural institutions in Mexico' research project, funded by University College London Institute of Education seed fund, 2017.

© The Author(s) 2019
T. McCowan, *Higher Education for and beyond the Sustainable Development Goals*, Palgrave Studies in Global Higher Education, https://doi.org/10.1007/978-3-030-19597-7_8

of 17 created around the country. These institutions were established to address one of the demands of the 1994 Zapatista uprising, namely the creation of educational institutions not only to provide access for indigenous peoples (significantly underrepresented in existing higher education institutions) but also as a space for expression of their linguistic, intellectual and cultural traditions and a means of capacitating a locally relevant workforce (Mateos Cortés and Dietz 2016; Schmelkes 2008, 2009).

The Tequila campus is one of four located in different regions of the state. UVI has very distinctive ways of working in comparison to conventional HEIs. Its students are enrolled in an Intercultural Management for Development degree with five different orientations—communication, sustainability, languages, rights and health—equipping them to stay in the region and support the development of their communities. It maintains very close links with the surrounding community, with local representatives on its governing body, opening its doors to those in need of treatment at its health clinic (combining traditional and mainstream medicine) and running a range of projects relating to food security, environment, languages and other areas. Unusually, all undergraduate students carry out research and development projects together with community members.

Through its innovative work, the university has made a range of contributions to achieving the SDGs. It has contributed to Goal 4 by expanding access to higher education for a significantly marginalised group. In particular, the presence of a local institution has enabled women to attend university, given the greater barriers placed on them to relocate from their family homes. The intercultural university also has promoted gender equality through its curriculum and the spaces that have been opened for discussion of the issue. There are a range of positive impacts on health, agriculture, livelihoods and environmental protection, through its community engagement work, participatory research and campus activities.

Yet perhaps its most significant contribution is in changing conceptions of what the university is, and of the status and role of graduates. The following dialogue with two students is telling:

Student 1: In my house my dad says "well, why do you go to that university? I made a mistake in letting you go there", because he says "I thought you would come back and you would not clean the fields anymore, you would not do this anymore; why do you talk to the people that speak Náhuatl? You have to talk to educated people". So that is the debate with the community, because once you come to university people think that you are going to—how do you say?— go up socially or something like that. And that is a debate, because to come to uni is to be socially above.

Researcher: And you don't think that going to uni gives you a different status?

Student 1: Well, in part, because it opens more opportunities, but here the difference is that we consider the communities, we do not only think about ourselves, it's like we don't have that ego that only thinks about ourselves.

Student 2: Maybe when we had just started uni, it's like you want to move up, but then you realise it's not like that, things are not like that. You change that way of thinking, and here we learn to be the same as the rest of the people, not above, and not below. We don't lose what we have learned, but we have to mediate, we have to respect this person and others.

UVI has challenged the idea that university necessarily extracts young people from their cultural context, and having denigrated it, inserts them into a more desirable *milieu*, from which there is little chance of return. Instead, the graduates of UVI can be educated, informed and critical young people even when returning to their rural, indigenous lives.

* * *

Clearly, universities cannot achieve the Sustainable Development Goals on their own. The task of moving the course of the global ocean liner away from social injustice and environmental destruction is such that it requires the action of all in society, its institutions and individuals. Nevertheless, universities like UVI, and conventional ones, do have a crucial role to play. Bringing change is not only about will, it is also about knowledge, understanding or even wisdom (Maxwell 1984), and it is in this latter area that they can make a particular contribution.

This chapter aims to develop understanding of how universities might contribute to this change. Development agencies, donors and national governments do now, on the whole, acknowledge the crucial role of education in achieving the full range of development outcomes, yet very often assume that doing so is straightforward and automatic. Anyone who teaches a class of real children, or manages a real institution, knows that this is not the case. The complexities are particularly great in the case of universities which, as explored in previous chapters, are far more complex even than schools.

The previous two chapters explored, in turn, the questions of access and quality. These are the two essential building blocks for a fair and effective higher education system: ensuring that the university is open to all and can provide the conditions for meaningful learning so as to enable personal and societal transformation. The impacts on the SDGs analysed in this chapter are predicated on these building blocks. The disheartening lack of evidence regarding the positive impact of universities on society in many countries is primarily caused by the absence of either one or both of them—though there may be ways in which universities can enhance their impact even given the lack of optimal circumstances.

The chapter will pose two primary questions. First, what are the means through which HE can impact the SDGs? And second, what evidence do we have about the impact of higher education currently, and which areas need to be strengthened? To address the former, the chapter will outline the diverse range of goals and connect these with the potential contributions of universities, putting forward a typology of five modalities. An assessment is subsequently made of existing research, the grounds for optimism, and also areas of significant need. The focus in this chapter is primarily on universities in lower income countries, since they face the most critical challenges in enhancing their impact. While 'impact' strictly speaking requires causal attribution through assessing counterfactuals, it is not always possible to disentangle the diverse influences on individuals and society in educational research, and hence the term is at times used in a more general sense of a positive influence.

In looking for impact from the university, we are already positioning ourselves in relation to the models of the university discussed in chapter three. The mediaeval university does not seek impact in this way, and even the Humboldtian institution does so only in a much longer term sense. The quest for impact on the SDGs places us firmly within the developmental model, with a prioritisation of instrumental value, concrete and relatively short-term influences, particularly on the most disadvantaged segments of society.

The notion of impact in higher education has quite rightly received a good deal of scrutiny in recent years, in particular through its associations with competitive and elitist publishing practices ('journal impact factor') and instrumentalisation of research. These more critical perspectives on the concept will be considered at length in the chapter that follow. For the purposes of this chapter, the idea will be used in a positive sense, within the confines of the desirability of the SDG framework.

Impacting the SDGs

The SDGs as agreed by the United Nations in 2015 are as follows:

Goal 1	End poverty in all its forms everywhere
Goal 2	End hunger, achieve food security and improved nutrition and promote sustainable agriculture
Goal 3	Ensure healthy lives and promote well-being for all at all ages
Goal 4	Ensure inclusive and equitable quality education and promote lifelong learning opportunities for all
Goal 5	Achieve gender equality and empower all women and girls
Goal 6	Ensure availability and sustainable management of water and sanitation for all
Goal 7	Ensure access to affordable, reliable, sustainable and modern energy for all
Goal 8	Promote sustained, inclusive and sustainable economic growth, full and productive employment and decent work for all
Goal 9	Build resilient infrastructure, promote inclusive and sustainable industrialization and foster innovation
Goal 10	Reduce inequality within and among countries
Goal 11	Make cities and human settlements inclusive, safe, resilient and sustainable

Goal 12	Ensure sustainable consumption and production patterns
Goal 13	Take urgent action to combat climate change and its impacts
Goal 14	Conserve and sustainably use the oceans, seas and marine resources for sustainable development
Goal 15	Protect, restore and promote sustainable use of terrestrial ecosystems, sustainably manage forests, combat desertification, and halt and reverse land degradation and halt biodiversity loss
Goal 16	Promote peaceful and inclusive societies for sustainable development, provide access to justice for all and build effective, accountable and inclusive institutions at all levels
Goal 17	Strengthen the means of implementation and revitalize the global partnership for sustainable development

The goals therefore cover a wide range of desirable ends for humankind, involving survival and material well-being of all human beings, equality and justice, and protection of the ecosystem. Much can be said, and already has been said, about the blind-spots and contradictions of this list—and Chapter 10 will address some of these points—but this chapter will take them at face value in order to focus in on the role the universities might play.

The broader concept of sustainable development represents a coming together of the international development agenda from the Second World War onwards, with environmental concerns later in the century, with a view to understanding their interlinkages and the need to address both of these critical spheres without one having a detrimental effect on the other. There are various ways of understanding the concept. It is often understood as having three dimensions: economic, social and environmental. A sustainable form of development is seen to require attention to economic prosperity and distribution of wealth, social well-being and environmental protection (although there are counter-arguments that it is dangerous and fallacious to separate out the social and economic realms). The SDGs specifically have been understood in relation to the 5 Ps, as listed in the UN (2015) resolution itself:

People
We are determined to end poverty and hunger, in all their forms and dimensions, and to ensure that all human beings can fulfil their potential in dignity and equality and in a healthy environment.

Planet
We are determined to protect the planet from degradation, including through sustainable consumption and production, sustainably managing its natural resources and taking urgent action on climate change, so that it can support the needs of the present and future generations.

Prosperity
We are determined to ensure that all human beings can enjoy prosperous and fulfilling lives and that economic, social and technological progress occurs in harmony with nature.

Peace
We are determined to foster peaceful, just and inclusive societies which are free from fear and violence. There can be no sustainable development without peace and no peace without sustainable development.

Partnership
We are determined to mobilize the means required to implement this Agenda through a revitalized Global Partnership for Sustainable Development, based on a spirit of strengthened global solidarity, focused in particular on the needs of the poorest and most vulnerable and with the participation of all countries, all stakeholders and all people.

The environmental dimension of sustainable development is present in the second of these (planet), while the human dimension is divided into people, prosperity and peace (justice is often added to the last of these). Partnership, as in the 17th SDG, is a means of achieving them, but might also be seen as an end in itself.

Understanding the nature of sustainable development, and of the goals, is important for determining the role of universities in relation to them. The goals differ in the extent to which they require changes in human consciousness or in the material world, or both. Some are rooted more in thought and values (e.g. gender equality) while others are more material (e.g. building infrastructure), but most involve both. If the former, they differ in the extent to which they require widespread or more focused intervention. For example, preventing the spread of HIV requires all people to be aware of and change their behaviour. Identifying a cure for HIV/AIDS on the other hand may depend on only a few biochemists and pharmacologists (although ensuring it reaches people will depend on a much larger network). Some of the goals require refraining from doing something (e.g. polluting the waters) and therefore depend on awareness-raising and regulation, while others require active provision (e.g. universal primary schooling).

An associated distinction is made by Gough and Scott (2007) in their Type I and Type II interventions. Type I are 'those in which it is assumed that environmental problems have environmental causes' and therefore require 'solutions through natural-scientific enquiry': the research findings must then be communicated to the public, leading to behaviour change. In contrast, Type II interventions 'work from the premise that the core problem of environmental sustainability is not environmental at all but social' (p. 162). They further outline the responses required:

> This model essentially entails two rounds of learning. In the first, people's eyes are opened to social and environmental truths. In the second, they learn (with others) how to live sustainably, typically through collective action. (p. 162)

This diversity of the goals makes distinct demands on universities: whether to train specialist professionals for specific roles, or to provide broader changes in public consciousness; whether to engage purely at the level of ideas, or to carry out practical work. Also relevant is the fact that the goals are strongly interrelated. Ending poverty depends on education, reducing inequalities and peace; ensuring quality education for all in turn depends on addressing gender inequality, ending hunger and ensuring peaceful and inclusive societies. Equally, the various kinds of impact universities can make—most commonly through teaching and research—are also strongly interrelated and can reinforce one another.

The Five Modalities of the University in Sustainable Development

What kind of higher education institution can play the roles outlined above and contribute to the SDGs? This book has taken as its foundation stone that not any higher education will do: it is perfectly possible for institutions and systems to act against the achievement of the goals—providing opportunities for the few, fostering corrupt governance and environmental destruction—even while conforming to many of the normal criteria of quality. The university for the SDGs would need to adhere to certain characteristics in relation to value, function and interaction, as outlined in Chapter 4 through the discussion of the model of the developmental university. This chapter takes the discussion to a greater level of specificity, assessing the kinds of practices that would support the varied roles identified above.

Part of the contribution that universities can make to the SDGs is through explicit teaching of the framework. In fact, there is a wealth of literature (e.g. Fensham 1978; Huckle and Sterling 1996; McKeown and Hopkins 2003; Mogensen and Schnack 2010; Sauvé 1996; Vare and Scott 2007) on the promotion of knowledge, skills and values for sustainable development, stemming from the older traditions of environmental education and development education, through the Earth Summit and the more recent ideas of education for sustainable development and global citizenship education. Much of this literature is directed at schools, but can also be applied to universities, and some are explicitly related to this level (e.g. Arbuthnott 2009; Barth et al. 2007; Barth 2015).

Yet teaching is only part of the contribution. Most obvious of the other roles that the university can play is conducting research (added to the teaching function of universities largely through the Humboldtian revolution, as discussed in Chapter 3). One immediate contribution the university can make is in researching changes in climate, the impacts arising from it and possible mitigating factors. Yet there are further highly significant roles. Universities play an important part in promoting public debate, contributing to deliberation in society, in providing a space for that deliberation to take place, and raising public awareness of critical issues. These activities can take place through community engagement work, public communication of research or hosting debates and discussions. The university also has a role in service provision, i.e. direct delivery of services such as education, health and environmental monitoring. In some cases this service provision could be made by another agency without any loss (universities may only be fulfilling this function due to the failings of other agencies); in other cases there are important synergies with the core functions of the institution, for example in the case of 'lab schools' (experimental primary or secondary schools in which educational innovations and training takes place) or teaching hospitals.

Finally, it is important to remember the university's existence as a sphere of society in its own right. It is not only fostering positive change in the society outside, but is constituting and representing a part of society itself. In this way, it is important that universities practice, say, gender equality within their own processes and structures, and environmental sustainability in relation to their own use of resources, carbon footprint and local emissions. We can call this final role 'embodiment'.

We can therefore identify five modalities for the university:

1. Education
2. Knowledge production
3. Public debate
4. Service provision
5. Embodiment

How do these roles relate to the 17 SDGs? In most cases achieving the SDGs relies on all of these roles being in operation. Ending poverty (Goal 1), for example involves *education*—through equipping young people with the knowledge and skills to ensure decent livelihoods; *knowledge production*—in developing technologies for ensuring food security for subsistence farmers; *public debate*—in raising awareness of the negative impact of punitive debt repayments on the poorest countries; *service delivery*—in providing a free-of-charge internet facility for local communities; and *embodiment*—in paying its own cleaning staff a living wage.

Some of the SDGs show a particular link with some of the modalities. Affordable and clean energy (Goal 7), for example, depends strongly on knowledge production, to generate new forms of technology and adaptation to different contexts. Gender equality depends significantly on public debate in challenging social norms. Nevertheless, all of the goals, at least partially, depend on all five modalities.

1. Education

The teaching function of universities in relation to the SDGs involves both the specific courses offered, and the general education acquired while at university. It requires the availability of subject areas that correspond to the different goals (marine conservation, sustainable energy, peace studies, etc.), but also a broader environment conducive to the transformation of the learner. Postgraduate as well as undergraduate education is central to this task, with the doctoral component linking into the second role of knowledge production. University education should have personal, professional and civic dimensions: learning to be in the world and live with others, to engage in rewarding work and to participate politically. In these economised times, universities and often the students themselves place most emphasis on the professional dimension, but the other two are essential to the collective interests of society as well as individuals' lives. Benefits are provided by a broad range of disciplines, from natural sciences, engineering and technology to social sciences, arts and humanities, as well as interdisciplinary study. Yet governments appear to give almost exclusive value to STEM (science, technology, engineering and mathematics) subjects, seeing them as the key to economic development: Ghana, for example, influenced by global assumptions about the importance of science and technology, has introduced a 60:40 policy for the ratio of STEM to other students, despite the fact that STEM students in OECD countries comprise only 27% of all students on average (Gardner 2017).

Within the formal taught curriculum, there is significant scope for incorporation of material relating to sustainable development—in developing students' knowledge, skills and values. The Commonwealth Secretariat's (2017) Curriculum Framework for the Sustainable Development Goals focuses on the kinds of learning (in schools and non-formal education as well as universities) that graduates need in order to support the SDGs, highlighting five core competencies: envisioning, critical thinking and reflection, systemic thinking, building partnerships and participation in decision-making. UNESCO (2017) puts forward a similar list of competencies, incorporating systems thinking, anticipatory, normative, strategic, collaborative, critical thinking, self-awareness and integrated problem-solving. While the notion of competency is contested in educational debates, these qualities are without doubt important ones for graduates in their working lives, and significantly (and in contrast to many competency frameworks) they do contain ethical elements.

All students, in this way, should develop sustainability literacy, with the UN supported 'Sulitest',[2] for example, developed to gauge these competencies. Indications are, however, that university curricula in practice are far from fulfilling this goal. In an international survey reported in Leal Filho (2010), 57% of students in Africa stated that climate change was not a topic in their taught courses (though the figures were better in other regions—Asia/Oceania 41%, Latin America 39%, Europe 29% and North America 17%), and 90% in Africa stated that it was overlooked in their campus life (in Latin America 79%, Asia/Oceania 68%, Europe 51% and North America 38%).

Furthermore, the task of achieving a deep transformation is less straightforward than is often presented. One crucial debate in the literature on education for sustainable development is the extent to which education institutions should promote criticality towards sustainability—i.e. encourage scrutiny of its core tenets and consideration of alternative viewpoints. Many agencies and educators, faced with the impending environmental cataclysm, prioritise the transmission of clear and unambiguous messages; others, such as Jickling and Wals (2008) and Gough and Scott (2007) see this kind of approach as inimical to education, as it lacks a critical and open dimension. In keeping with the latter view, this book asserts that a university education would necessarily have this critical element, given its founding principle of open-ended inquiry. Even if there were in fact no doubts or ambiguity about sustainable development, the transmissive approach would still be wanting, given the complexity of instilling values in human beings (particularly adults who have by that stage already established a set of core values).

But should educators be neutral in relation to sustainable development? Concerns about indoctrination are certainly less pressing at the

---

[2]https://www.sulitest.org/en/the-sulitest-initiative.html.

level of higher education than at school, given the greater age, maturity and independence of the students of the former. Nevertheless, objections are regularly expressed—particularly from right-wing commentators concerned about influences from left-leaning lecturers. Toby Young (2018), for example, has recently bemoaned what he described in the Daily Mail as 'Madrassas of the left' in the UK, while in 2017 a letter was sent to universities from a Conservative MP enquiring how lecturers were dealing with the topic of Brexit, amidst concerns of indoctrination by Remain supporting lecturers. In the USA, students have been encouraged to monitor their lecturers and report any perceived left-wing indoctrination, and similarly in Brazil in 2018 after the election of Bolsonaro. While much of the above is based on an exaggerated fear of the influence of lecturers, there is a serious question about how those teaching in universities should express their political views. The Crick Report (QCA 1998) on citizenship provision in UK schools put forward a helpful categorisation of 'neutral chairman', 'balanced' and 'stated commitment' approaches to dealing with controversial issues— of which sustainable development is certainly one. All of these three may be appropriate in the university classroom: whether to facilitate a discussion in which students freely put forward their views, to provide alternative viewpoints (not necessarily those held by the lecturer) in order to balance out dominant views in the classroom, or to express one's opinion frankly and allow students to express theirs.

From a Freirean perspective the landscape looks somewhat different. Teaching and learning cannot be neutral even when not dealing with explicitly political material, as the pedagogical encounter serves either to domesticate or liberate, to entrench powerlessness or to enhance agency (Freire 1970; McCowan 2009). Not to present a liberatory posture and pedagogy for Freire is an abdication of responsibility on the part of the educator. This posture does not necessarily involve a uniformity of political view among the students, and it is seen to be crucial that the latter construct their own positionings. Nevertheless, the educator must be committed to ensuring the development of *subjects* rather than *objects* of the educational process: educational empowerment and disempowerment providing a reflection of and a precursor of political agency. Not all readers will endorse Freire's political position, but it is hard to deny his profound insights into the links between education and social transformation: to a large extent, the attainment of sustainable development—even in the compromise form it appears in the SDGs—requires deep processes of *conscientisation* among learners.

Indeed, within environmental education, there are strong arguments put forward by advocates such as David Orr (1992) and Stephen Sterling (1996) that the task facing humanity is so great that nothing short of a fundamental transformation of our conception of education is necessary—an idea that resonates with the arguments put forward in the latter parts of this book. This idea is included within the UN Decade of Education for Sustainable Development (DESD, from 2005 to 2014), and its call for 'a different vision of the world'. In the field of higher education, this kind of root and branch approach is seen in Lotz-Sisitka et al. (2015), who call for an overhaul of pedagogy in favour of transformative, transgressive learning.

Much of the valuable learning occurring in universities, however, takes place outside formal teaching instances. Particularly for those studying on a university campus, there are a range of cultural, political and recreational activities through which wider learning is gained, and even in the absence of organised activities, the simple interaction between students in cafes, bars and corridors is part of their broader formation. Here is an instance in which quality and equity interact, since it is more advantaged students that are most likely to be in these stimulating campus-based learning environments, while poorer students are more likely to be studying part-time in less well-equipped institutions. Yet even for those in less luxurious surroundings, there are significant forms of learning that occur from interaction with the student body—particularly in the context of diversity. Students interviewed as part of a research project in South Africa (McCowan et al. 2016) captured this forcefully:

> In the classroom, especially when we have to do things like group work, there you don't have [the divide between white and black students] … And then it exposes you to a person's life. You [tend to realise], this person is not that bad. Maybe I thought white people are like this, but this guy is different. So we've learned to appreciate other people.

In this encounter with diversity, students develop new forms of being and interacting:

> You meet different people that you would never have met before. And also with that comes adaptability. Like sometimes you're going to realise that, oh well, this person doesn't really think the same way I do, so you must learn to try and figure out how you and that person can be in the same space, but not overpowering each other.

Meaningful learning for social transformation interacts with access, then, since it is only a comprehensive university, one that will accept students from varied backgrounds, that will allow for this learning through diversity to occur.

Finally, there are important sources of learning that are facilitated by the university, but take place outside its boundaries. In many cases these experiences are directly linked to the professional development within students' nominated courses, for example work experience or internships, which in some cases may be credit-bearing for students. These experiences are essential in giving students hands-on experience of their professional areas, as well as exposing them to real-life challenges that are hard to simulate within the classroom. Yet they may be entirely unconnected with students' degrees. Voluntary work is an important source of learning for students—learning about the communities in which they are working, learning about inequalities, about the limits of what they can contribute (for more privileged students it is often about understanding that they cannot 'save the world', at least not alone), and in developing specific skills. These opportunities may also contribute to the well-being of the communities in question—a point that will be discussed below in the section on service delivery. The literature on service learning (e.g. Annette 2000; Butin 2003; Clark 1999)—through which a more coordinated approach is taken to learning through voluntary work—is highly developed, particularly in the USA, and there is significant evidence for its benefits. A prime example of a holistic curriculum of this type is the innovative Ashesi University in Ghana, which aims to create ethical leaders for the African region, combining formal taught curriculum (including liberal arts courses such as African Studies) with an extensive programme of community work and other opportunities for experiential learning.

A research project on employability in African universities (McCowan 2014) expressed these interlocking learning spheres as the three Cs: *classroom* (indicating the formal taught component of courses), *campus* (the broader learning environment within the university) and *community* (learning that takes place beyond the gates of the university). Another commonly used frame for understanding the different dimensions of learning is 'about, for and through', which can be applied to various different areas of environment, citizenship, human rights and so forth: *about* sustainable development relating to the knowledge dimension, as well as familiarity with debates in the field; *for* sustainable development relating to skills, and learning to do, whether direct actions for protecting the environment, mobilising politically or community organisation; and *through* sustainable development, the experiential learning generated through involvement in development and sustainability initiatives and actions. The curricular offering of universities and other educational institutions should provide space for all three of these.

2. Knowledge production

While education is not the only function of universities, it is its most prominent role, and the only one that all higher education institutions engage in. The other four roles—which will be outlined here in somewhat less detail—are more sporadically realised, and depend to a large extent on the mission, resources, size and standing of the institutions in question.

Research has been a vital part of the university since the nineteenth century, and with the exception of private liberal arts colleges in the USA that specialise in high-quality teaching, most institutions of renown and high quality engage extensively in it. In fact, in elite institutions, the value of research (to the institution and to individual researchers) is so great that it often ends up squeezing out time and energy for quality teaching. As discussed in Chapter 5, these dynamics are reinforced by international rankings that disproportionately reward high-level research. There is no guarantee, however, that this research will positively impact the SDGs—although we need to be careful in dismissing scholarship that is not tied to immediate outcomes.

The research functions of universities that are most conducive to contributing to the SDGs will combine two elements: basic and applied research. The former—variously known as curiosity-driven, frontier or blue skies research—involves open-ended research questions which may not have a direct bearing on concrete changes in the world in the here and now, and indeed may yield no positive results. Yet despite its unpredictability, this form of research is essential for making the long-term breakthroughs that can ultimately transform societies in very significant ways. So, for example, Einstein's work on relativity of an entirely theoretical nature now has a range of practical applications, for example in GPS.

Nevertheless, the SDGs require more than basic research. They also require applied work in a range of areas—addressing the needs in the areas of environment, health, food security and so forth. Furthermore, there is a process of adaptation of technologies and ideas to diverse contexts. This adaptation is best achieved through interactions between university researchers and user communities in real contexts.

As is the case with teaching and learning, the achievement of the SDGs is not only dependent on STEM areas, despite the centrality of natural science to many of the goals requiring development of new technologies. As argued by Boni and Walker (2016), the development of a new culture of cooperation, peace, justice, equality and respect requires scholarship and learning in the arts, humanities and social sciences, of both a theoretical and applied nature.

But how about institutions that are not listed in the top 200 of the Shanghai list, or indeed not even in the top 1000? What contribution can institutions make that do not have the resources, time, equipment or culture to carry out significant amounts of what is formally known as research? Is it a luxury these institutions simply cannot afford and should not therefore aspire to? Without neglecting the significant constraints placed on lecturers in most institutions in most countries, it is important to recall that research and scholarship are more fundamental than the existence of research projects, research funding, administrators and publications. Research is the systematic exploration of the universe in order to generate knowledge that can be communicated to others, and as such can and should be part of the lives and work of all university-based staff. And even in poorly resourced universities, and in those in which the primary emphasis is on teaching, there are still many academics actively engaged in research and publishing. The current intensification of concentration of research funding in flagship institutions, therefore, is a cause for concern.

Finally, it is important to mention participatory research, whose value in human development has been amply explored in Boni and Walker (2016). In addition to being in accordance with justice, in avoiding data extraction from and exploitation of participants, and ensuring their meaningful involvement, methods like participatory action research can generate insights into the phenomena under investigation that would not be possible otherwise. A further knock-on benefit is in the possibility of building capacity for research within non-university communities.

3. Public debate

A more diffuse function, and one harder to orchestrate and monitor, is that of the university as a space for and contributor to public debate. In Marginson's (2011) analysis of higher education and the public good, this role corresponds to the third of the conceptualisations, that of the public sphere, drawing on Habermas's ideas of a space for civil society debate and opinion formation. Universities fulfil this function by providing physical spaces for discussion—through public lectures, seminars and conferences, or more generally in their classrooms and campus—but also symbolic spaces through critique and the opening of dialogue, and by defending the principles of enquiry, deliberation and public scrutiny. As such, universities should act as 'critical friends' to society, not afraid to speak out against government or injustices of the time, even being a 'counter-majoritarian' voice in the terms of Ignatieff (2018). Lecturers in this way can hold as their ideal the public intellectual, who emerges from the ivory tower to engage, critique and challenge society and the establishment. This public debate role, of course is severely constrained in many societies in which governments or corporations fear challenges to their illegitimate authority and exploitative actions, forming a spiral dynamic in which societies are either moving in a vicious cycle of constraints on academic freedom leading to a weaker voice of universities, or alternatively to a virtuous cycle of a vibrant university space bolstering academic freedom.

4. Service provision

The service provision role of the university may not be its core business, but it may nevertheless be crucial for local communities. In low-income countries, universities often serve as sources of basic facilities—internet, electricity, recreation, sports, meeting space—on account of the lack of these amenities in their surrounding communities. Universities may actively promote provision of basic services such as healthcare, legal advice, architectural and engineering support to impoverished communities as part of their community engagement work. In some cases, these services will be provided through paid consultancies for lecturers, involving an income stream for universities or individual academics; in others they will be funded by the university as part of their public service work (although on account of encroaching commercialisation, the former type is becoming increasingly common); or the work can be carried out by students as part of voluntary work, service learning and work placements.

In other cases, there is an essential link between service delivery and the core activities of open-ended inquiry of the university. The teaching hospital is perhaps the best-known example of this kind of symbiosis, through which communities receive healthcare (in some cases of the highest quality available), and the universities have an essential space in which to provide clinical training to their prospective health professionals. In Brazil, law students staff legal advice clinics for lower income communities that cannot afford access to paid lawyers. There are many other examples of this kind, located along a continuum from services of a high level of quality and reliability to other instances which are more exploratory and with more unpredictable outcomes.

5. Embodiment

Finally, there is the role of 'embodiment'. What is meant here is that we view the university not as a means of production of impact on the society outside of itself, but as a space of society in its own right. This view of educational institutions as constitutive of in addition to instrumental in producing societal good has been explored in Chapter 2, as well as in previous work in relation to citizenship (McCowan 2009) and human rights (McCowan 2013), and is equally applicable to sustainability. To some extent this role corresponds to the 'through' of the triad of learning about, for and through. This enactment is important for various reasons. First, because universities are significant spheres of society in their own right—involving thousands of people, many of whom pass a number of years within their confines; second, because they act as exemplars for other institutions in society; and third, because a contradiction between the stated commitments and messages promoted to students and the institution's actual workings in practice are not lost on students, and can foster significant resentment and loss of faith. An obvious example here is an institution's responsibility for avoiding environmental damage, whether energy waste, encouraging reuse and recycling, using sustainably sourced foods, avoiding local pollution, collecting rainwater or other measures (Orr 1994; Cortese 2003). It is distressing how rarely these measures are in place, even in universities purportedly promoting the SDGs. There are times of the year when my own institution simultaneously powers radiators to heat classrooms and air conditioning to cool them! In these circumstances, students are unlikely to take seriously institutional encouragement to preserve energy.

The most obvious manifestation of this principle for universities is in becoming environmentally sustainable institutions—often referred to as 'greening the campus' (Leal Filho et al. 2015). But it also involves embodying principles of equality, in terms of addressing gender-based violence, sexual harassment, racial prejudice, exclusion of those with disabilities, and other forms of disrespect and discrimination.

These questions can also be viewed at the level of the higher education system, national and global. As Shields (2019) argues, the current desires for international mobility among students, and global competition among institutions to snap them up, has led to large increases in international travel, with significant impacts on the environment through carbon emissions. Academic staff mobility, international research and international conferences have similar implications. Higher education systems, therefore, in advocating for their positive role in addressing the SDGs, must be fully aware of the negative impacts hey may simultaneously be having.

Evidence of Impact

The swelling wave of interest in sustainable development since the 1990s has brought a range of initiatives in higher education. The Talloires Declaration was signed in 1990 by 22 universities to commit themselves to acting as sustainable institutions, and promoting environmental literacy among their students and broader communities. It has now grown to a community of more than 500 institutions under the Association for University Leaders for a Sustainable Future. The Association for the Advancement of Sustainability in Higher Education brings together nearly 1000 universities in North America, and has established the Sustainability Tracking, Assessment & Rating System (STARS) for institutions to measure their sustainability performance. The Higher Education Sustainability Initiative is a UN backed network of institutions established in 2012, and has made available an 'SDG Accord' that universities and colleges can sign up to. United Nations Academic Impact (UNAI) works with HEIs to support the UN mandate and achieve the SDGs, and has created a series of university hubs around the world for achieving each of the goals. The International Association of Universities has established the Higher Education and Research for Sustainable Development portal, and the Global University Network for Innovation (GUNI) is also active in sustainable development issues. SIDA in partnership with the United Nations Environment Programme (UNEP) runs the International Training Programme in education for sustainable development with a range of universities in Africa and Asia. Periperi U brings together 12 HEIs across the African continent to build capacity for addressing disaster risk. A number of other initiatives are outlined in Gough and Scott (2007), for example the Mainstreaming Environment and Sustainability in African Universities (MESA) initiative promoted by UNEP, the UNESCO teacher education for sustainability initiative as part of the DESD, and the Higher Education Funding Council for England's (HEFCE) work around sustainability in teaching, research and management. Furthermore, specific institutions have been founded to promote sustainable development, such as Earth University in Costa Rica, as will be discussed in Chapter 10.

These local, national and international initiatives are important, and in addition to having direct impact, can also influence broader change across the systems. However, the success of the SDGs depends ultimately on the influence of everyday universities in their everyday work, so it is here that we must turn. In 2013 I was involved in a large-scale literature review together with two of my UCL colleagues—Moses Oketch and Rebecca Schendel—on the impact of tertiary education on development (Oketch et al. 2014). The review was carried out for DFID with a view to justifying and orienting their investment in tertiary education in lower income countries, given the competing demands of primary and secondary education, and of other sectors. The focus was on the impact that tertiary institutions might have on the society outside, and it was here that most of the research initially identified fell by the wayside. Of some 7000 studies that came through our initial database search, only 99 made it through to the final analysis. While there is a huge amount of writing on higher education—even in low-income countries—very little of it shows evidence of impact on society.

Some caveats are needed here. The study focused only on low and lower middle-income countries (according to the World Bank classification), so did not include contexts such as China, South Africa and Brazil where there are much larger numbers of studies, and only covered the period 1990–2013. The review targeted mainly literature in English and used predominantly mainstream online article databases, thereby missing the substantial amount of research carried out in other languages, and published in local print journals. Nevertheless, in spite of these limitations, the review can give us some pointers as to the evidence available for impact, and also on the focus of research attention.

Table 8.1 shows the distribution of studies by development outcome (N.B. the total numbers here exceed 99 as studies were listed more than once if they had multiple foci).

Table 8.1 Breakdown of included studies by development outcome

Development outcome	Number of studies
Economic growth	63
Income equality	42
Gender equality	34
Institutions[a]	26
Health	24
Poverty reduction	22
Governance	17
Improvement of lower levels of education and/or literacy	9
Population growth	7
Environment	6

[a]i.e. studies looking at higher education's role in strengthening societal institutions

Source Oketch et al. (2014)

We can see immediately that there is a significant skew towards economic outcomes of tertiary education. The most extensive body of research relating to the impact of higher education on society is that assessing graduate earnings. In the review, higher earnings for graduates were seen in Sub-Saharan Africa (Al-Samarrai and Bennell 2007; Gyimah-Brempong et al. 2006; Rolleston and Oketch 2008), South Asia (Abbas and Foreman-Peck 2008; Afzal 2011; Azam 2010), South-East Asia (Doan and Stevens 2011; Glewwe et al. 2002; Schady 2003) and the Pacific Islands (Born et al. 2008).

This body of literature is strongly rooted in human capital theory, and generally assumes that there is a causal link between the learning gained in higher education and increases in worker productivity, with the latter reflected in higher salaries.[3] Yet there are many factors

---

[3]With the exception of a few studies that explicitly focus on improvements in productivity—e.g. Larbi-Apau and Sarpong (2010)—higher salaries are used as a proxy for productivity in this body of research.

affecting salary levels, and no guarantee that a higher salary is evidence of greater productivity: universities may simply have a 'screening' role for prospective employers. Furthermore, higher salaries indicate primarily a private return to higher education: while it would be assumed that positive externalities such as higher tax payments would accompany them, we need more information about the actual impacts of the work undertaken—particularly since in some cases graduates will be working for companies whose activities undermine social justice and environmental protection.

The sections below will focus on the evidence identified in the review that relate to the public good benefits of higher education beyond earnings, and specifically to those highlighted in the SDGs. The impact identified related primarily to the education, knowledge production and service delivery modalities identified above, with the embodiment aspect not included in the research, and evidence of the public debate role proving too hard to capture. The studies included show an overwhelmingly positive influence of higher education, although in many areas there is a disheartening lack of evidence.

In addition to impact through earnings, economic growth and productivity, the review covered three areas of relevance to the SDGs: technology transfer, capabilities and institutions. In the first of these, the findings were ambiguous. Conclusive evidence was not provided of a major impact at the macro-level of research and innovation on productivity (relating to SDG 8 'Promote sustained, inclusive and sustainable economic growth, with decent work for all' and SDG9, 'Build resilient infrastructure & promote sustainable industrialisation'). This may be because of poor linkages between the university and industrial sectors—although there were indications that technological uptake and adaptation could be increased with the proportion of workers with higher education. There was some evidence that research outputs had a positive impact at the local level: for example, on agriculture—relating to SDG2 'End hunger, achieve food security & improve nutrition' (e.g. Ca 2006; Collins 2012), and local government (e.g. Magara et al. 2011).

More positive outcomes were found for capabilities (capacities developed at the individual level) and institutions (formal organisations or social norms), both in terms of availability of research and the findings of the studies. In relation to capabilities, there were three main areas of impact identified in the studies. First, citizenship and political participation (not well covered in the SDGs, but acknowledged in SDG 4.7 and with some link to SDG 16 'Promote peaceful & inclusive societies'), with tertiary education seen to be linked with higher levels of political activity and democratic attitudes within Africa (e.g. Luescher-Mamashela et al. 2011; Mattes and Mughogho 2009); second, a range of areas relating to health and well-being (SDG 3), including knowledge of risks of smoking in India (Sansone et al. 2012), lower fertility in Sudan (Ahmed 2010), food security in East Timor (Raghbendra and Dang 2012) and multi-country studies on a range of outcomes (Tilak 2003, 2010 and Gyimah-Brempong 2010). In relation to gender empowerment and equality (SDG 5), there were studies on Pakistan (Malik and Courtney 2011), India (Singh et al. 2006), Eritrea (Müller 2004), and across Africa (Gyimah-Brempong 2010), although in a number of other cases findings were ambiguous in the context of strongly opposing social norms.

Lastly there is the strengthening of institutions. The counterpoint to individual political empowerment is the existence of democratic, responsive and just institutions, and in this area there were studies relating to Africa (Gyimah-Brempong 2010; Mattes and Mozaffar 2011), and on social norms in Pakistan (Shafiq 2010) and Nepal (Truex 2011). While the review could not cover fully the extensive contribution of tertiary education to professional development, there were some studies included on the strengthening of public services, for example in Uganda (Magara et al. 2011) and specifically within refugee camps in Kenya (Wright and Plasterer 2010). There were a number of other studies that relate to specific SDGs, including peace building (SDG 16— Harris and Lewer 2005), disability (referred to in a number of the goals) (Mwaipopo et al. 2011) and countering deforestation (SDG 15— Ehrhardt-Martinez 1998).

Despite the lack of rigorous, publicly available research, therefore, the indications are that tertiary education institutions in many different contexts across the world—and even in countries with significant resource constraints—are having an impact on sustainable development in their societies, relating to the full range of areas from inclusive economic growth, strengthening of governance, improvement in health and well-being, gender equality and environmental protection. The review also identified a range of barriers that were preventing systems from achieving their potential in many cases, ones that relate closely to the quality challenges assessed in the previous chapter.

In spite of the current emphasis on evidence-based policy (mischievously termed by some as 'policy-based evidence'), not every decision made in personal practice, institutional strategy and national policy is realistically going to be based on full and rigorous research findings. Some of the more subtle roles of the university are very hard to research: how to gauge, for example, the impact on society of the Twitter activity of critical academics in an authoritarian state? In these cases we are dealing with subtle movements in individual and collective understandings of society that may not manifest themselves in concrete changes in the short term. Nevertheless, there are many aspects of the work of universities that can and should be researched. Many of the positive benefits of universities are known intuitively by those who work within them, but systematic studies and evidence can provide a more robust basis on which to communicate those benefits to others. It is particularly important to have this evidence, as despite an upsurge of belief in higher education, there are still many who doubt it is a wise investment of funds, particularly public funds.

In high-income countries, a more substantial evidence base on the positive impacts of higher education on society has been built, through studies such as Bynner et al. (2003) and McMahon (e.g. 1999, 2003, 2009). McMahon's work is highly innovative in providing an economic assessment not only of market benefits, but also non-market benefits. While there are certainly concerns about assigning monetary value to some of these goods, it is important that these outcomes are acknowledged within mainstream economics. Nevertheless, while these studies—predominantly in English-speaking countries of the Global North—provide us with significant pointers as to the potential role of higher education and development, there is no substitute for research carried out within the other diverse contexts that make up the globe.

Strengthening Impact

The studies covered in the Oketch et al. (2014) review focus on the impact of universities in lower income countries within their own contexts, but clearly the situation is far more complex. Knowledge to a large extent escapes corralling, and research conducted in high-income countries does end up affecting lower income countries (even if not necessarily in the way we might wish). In many cases the work of international development agencies will draw on skills and knowledge production generated in Northern universities, and there are a range of partnership schemes that specifically focus on facilitating these kinds of knowledge conduits. In the context of globalisation, therefore, it is misleading to suggest that the impact of higher education in Niger will only emanate from universities that are located in Niger.

Nevertheless, there are strong reasons why—in addition to facilitating the flows of knowledge between different parts of the world—we should be concerned with the capacity of universities within lower income countries. First, it is a matter of justice that low-income countries have the capacity for knowledge production and not just importation. In a similar way to the age old industrial dependency of countries in the Global South exporting mineral and agricultural products for production of higher value goods in the Global North, so they are currently locked into relations of, at best, carrying out data collection for high-level theorising and synthesising in Global North institutions, or worse having no relevant participation. It is essential that we avoid a knowledge production apartheid and ensure a vibrant research environment for institutions in all countries.

Furthermore, there is a highly positive contribution that low-income countries can make to global debates and generation of knowledge. Diverse epistemological and language traditions can enrich the global academic community by providing diverse perspectives, encouraging the questioning of assumptions and putting forward new conceptualisations and solutions. Finally, there is a more practical point that—even in the context of universally valid knowledge—local adaptations are needed. Universities, very often through the consultancy work of their academic staff, have a crucial role to play in providing contextual adjustments to ideas and technologies in order to maximise their impact.

Global inequalities in knowledge production are even more severe than in income: G20 countries have 86% of global GDP but produce 94% of scientific publications (UNESCO 2015). Disparities between institutions in countries of different size, wealth and stature follow expected patterns. In the Scimago Country Ranking, the USA, China, UK, Germany and India occupy the top five positions, all with well over 100,000 publications in 2017, while a large majority of the countries in the world have less than 1000 publications in the same year. These indicators focus on internationally recognised publications, mostly in English, and represent just a small fraction of all publications, not accounting for the vast majority of outlets of academic work, nor alternative forms of publication. Nevertheless, it is undeniable that there are large disparities in the quantity and quality of research produced by different HEIs around the world. There are a confluence of factors that hamper the ability of these institutions to carry out research: the lack of external funding available, competing demands on lecturers' time (teaching overload, moonlighting to supplement meagre salaries), emphasis on income-generating consultancy over longer-term research, lack of research training and doctoral programmes, and the absence of a vibrant research environment and culture.

International collaborations provide an important source of funds, exposure and capacity-building for many higher education systems, but most partners are located at flagship institutions, with little impact on the periphery of the system. Furthermore, financial control and gain, as well as publication credit is often monopolised by the institutions in the Global North. There are also the power imbalances alluded to above of Southern partners as data collectors, with the North as theorisers and analysts.

There are a range of initiatives underway to address the imbalances of research output across global regions. The Development Research Uptake in Sub-Saharan Africa (DRUSSA) programme of the Association of Commonwealth Universities, which ran from 2011 to 2016, was significant in promoting the communication and use of research in the interests of poverty reduction: this initiative acknowledges that the challenges are not only with the conducting of research, but also its dissemination and uptake within the academic community, and in policymaker and practitioner communities. INASP is an organisation entirely oriented towards this end: starting life as the International Network for the Availability of Scientific Publications, its remit has evolved from promoting academic publishing in the Global South to fostering developmentally beneficial research, and facilitating its dissemination, uptake and impact in countries in Africa, Asia and Latin America. There are also regional associations like CODESRIA (Council for the Development of Social Science Research in Africa) that fosters knowledge production across the region, with important initiatives in, for example, engaging diaspora African researchers to spend periods of time building capacity in their countries of origin. The World Bank funded African Centres of Excellence initiative has provided welcome investment for research and graduate study in universities across the region, yet has complex ramifications: while the gathering of expertise can be helpful and provide a hub for regional capacity-building, concentration of resources in already developed institutions can simply reproduce internal inequalities and prevent other institutions from developing.

Of course, in looking at the impact on the SDGs, it not solely a question of how much research, but also what kinds of research. Incentives are not always for developmentally beneficial research, although many national research councils (e.g. the Economic and Social Research Council in the UK) do value social and economic impact in addition to scientific values of rigour and originality. As discussed in Chapter 4, the work of Arocena et al. (2014, 2015) in the context of Uruguay provides useful pointers for how research can be transformed to have more developmental impact.

Then there is the (often forgotten) community engagement. Alternatively going by the names of public service, service, extension or third stream activities, it is in almost all institutions the least active of the three pillars, with the smallest proportion of funding, with the least staff time dedicated to it, and the least prestige accorded. Correspondingly, only two of the studies that were identified in the Oketch et al. (2014) review assess impact via community engagement activities. Current trends of status competition, unbundling and commercialisation all act against community engagement in different ways, as explored in Chapter 5.

Nevertheless, these activities are crucial to the achievement of the SDGs. Most countries are a long way from universal access to higher education, so extension activities are the only means of universities engaging with a broader segment of the population. Furthermore, the addressing of development challenges—the 'wicked problems' facing resource-constrained contexts—can only be achieved through an engagement of universities' theoretical knowledge with real contexts, mediated by dialogue with local communities (Akpan et al. 2012; Kitawi 2014; Mtawa et al. 2016). Community engagement, therefore, is not charity, nor a gesture of goodwill on the part of institutions: it is central to the translation of university-based enquiry into positive change in society.

As discussed in Chapter 5, community engagement activities have increased markedly in the era of the entrepreneurial university, but in their transmogrified form as 'third stream' activities, aiming to generate income for the institution. The commercialised forms of engagement have obvious limits in terms of promoting the public good, particularly with impoverished communities who may not be able to pay for university services. The case of the Intercultural University of Veracruz, Mexico, outlined at the start of the chapter, provides an inspiring example of community engagement—involving a two-way exchange of knowledge—and engaged research together with communities. Yet UVI benefits from public funding and freely given time of lecturers and community members: providing meaningful opportunities for public service in the context of reductions of public funding and constraints on time is highly challenging.

While knowledge production, public debate, service provision and embodiment are all crucial—and the achievement of the SDGs depends on all of the modalities—the overwhelming argument for the strengthening of universities in the Global South is that of the educational development of their students. Even if there were justification for sending Global North trained professionals to solve the problems of the Global South, this would simply not be possible by reason of numbers.

There is no escape from the reality that all countries, however poor, need high-quality higher education systems. Insufficient investment in and attention to higher education in the Global South has limited its practical impact on the SDGs to date.

The question of professional development is absolutely crucial for the achievement of the SDGs, as so many of the areas depend on skilled and knowledgeable specialists applying best practice in their particular areas, whether teaching, health care, social work, local government or engineering. In a study of Earth University in Costa Rica, an institution oriented towards sustainable development, Rodriguez-Solera and Silva-Laya (2017) show the positive impact graduates in agricultural engineering have their communities of origin, of a social, economic and environmental nature. Forming professionals for the SDGs is not just about traditional subject knowledge, or even professional competencies. It is also about an ethical stance, and a commitment to social justice. This dimension is best drawn out in the work of Melanie Walker and Monica McLean (2013), who have explored the development of pro-poor and public good professionals. Other examples are seen in the Developmental Leadership Programme (DLP) which assessed the role of secondary and higher education in Ghana in forming ethical leaders committed to the public good (Jones et al. 2014), in Gough and Scott's (2007) discussion of the UK Royal Academy of Engineering initiative to infuse engineering courses with ideas of sustainable development, and in Bourn (2018) who assesses the global dimensions of various professional programmes.

The faith placed on higher education by the architects of the SDGs was not misplaced: the university is ideally placed to contribute to the goals through its education, knowledge production, service delivery, public debate and embodiment roles. In a number of cases across the world it is already fulfilling this function. Nevertheless, there are significant constraints on the institution fulfilling its potential, through the limitations in access and quality outlined in the previous chapters, as well as the undermining trends of status competition and commercialisation. Furthermore, research on higher education itself needs to be significantly strengthened to provide a fuller knowledge base for advocacy, and for understanding the conditions for enhancing the sector.

References

Abbas, Q., & Foreman-Peck, J. (2008). The Mincer human capital model in Pakistan: Implications for education policy. *South Asia Economic Journal, 9*(2), 435–462.

Afzal, M. (2011). Microeconometric analysis of private returns to education and determinants of earnings. *Pakistan Economic and Social Review, 49*(1), 39–68.

Ahmed, H. M. S. (2010). 'Non-market returns to women education in Sudan: Case of fertility.' *Journal of Comparative Family Studies, 41*(5), 783–798.

Akpan, W., Minkley, G., & Thakrar, J. (2012). In search of a developmental university: Community engagement in theory and practice. *South African Review of Sociology, 43*(2), 1–4.

Al-Samarrai, S., & Bennell, P. (2007). Where has all the education gone in Sub-Saharan Africa? Employment and other outcomes among secondary school and university leavers. *The Journal of Development Studies, 43*(7), 1270–1300.

Annette, J. (2000). Education for citizenship, civic participation and experiential learning and service learning in the community. In D. Lawton, J. Cairns, & R. Gardner (Eds.), *Education for citizenship*. London: Continuum.

Arbuthnott, K. D. (2009). Education for sustainable development beyond attitude change. *International Journal of Sustainability in Higher Education, 10*(2), 152–163.

Arocena, R., Göransson, B., & Sutz, J. (2014). Universities and higher education in development. In B. Currie-Alder, S. M. R. Kanbur, D. Malone, & R. Medhora (Eds.), *International development: Ideas, experience, and prospects*. Oxford: Oxford University Press.

Arocena, R., Goransson, B., & Sutz, J. (2015). Knowledge policies and universities in developing countries: Inclusive development and the "developmental university". *Technology in Society, 41,* 10–20.

Azam, M. (2010). India's increasing skill premium: Role of demand and supply. *The B.E. Journal of Economic Analysis & Policy, 10*(1), 1–28.

Barth, M. (2015). *Implementing sustainability in higher education: Learning in an age of transformation*. London: Routledge.

Barth, M., Godemann, J., Rieckmann, M., & Stoltenberg, U. (2007). Developing key competencies for sustainable development in higher education. *International Journal of Sustainability in Higher Education, 8*(4), 416–430.

Boni, A., & Walker, M. (2016). *Universities and global human development: Theoretical and empirical insights for social change*. London: Routledge.

Born, J. A., McMaster, J., & De Jong, A. B. (2008). Return on investment in graduate management education in the South Pacific. *International Journal of Management in Education, 2*(3), 340–355.

Bourn, D. (2018). *Understanding global skills for 21st century professions*. London: Palgrave Macmillan.

Butin, D. W. (2003). Of what use is it? Multiple conceptualisations of service learning within education. *Teacher College Record, 105*(9), 1674–1692.

Bynner, J., Dolton, P., Feinstein, L., Makepiece, G., Malmberg, L., & Woods, L. (2003). *Revisiting the benefits of higher education: A report by the Bedford Group for Lifecourse and Statistical Studies, Institute of Education*. Bristol: Higher Education Funding Council for England.

Ca, T. N. (2006). *Universities as drivers of the urban economies in Asia: The case of Vietnam* (World Bank Policy Research Working Paper 3949). Washington, DC: World Bank.

Clark, T. (1999). Rethinking civic education for the 21st century. In D. Marsh (Ed.), *Preparing our schools for the 21st century (1999 ASCD yearbook)*. Alexandria, VA: ASCD.

Collins, C. S. (2012). Land-grant extension as a global endeavor: Connecting knowledge and international development. *The Review of Higher Education, 36*(1), 91–124.

Commonwealth Secretariat. (2017). *Curriculum framework for the Sustainable Development Goals*. London: Commonwealth Secretariat.

Cortese, A. D. (2003). The critical role of higher education in creating a sustainable future. *Planning for Higher Education, 31*(3), 15–22.

Doan, T., & Stevens, P. (2011). Labor market returns to higher education in Vietnam. *Economics: The Open Access Open-Assessment E-Journal, 5*, 1–21.

Ehrhardt-Martinez, K. (1998). Social determinants of deforestation in developing countries: A cross-national study. *Social Forces, 77*(2), 567–586.

Fensham, P. J. (1978). Stockholm to Tbilisi—The evolution of environmental education. *Prospects, 8*(4), 446–455.

Freire, P. (1970). *Pedagogy of the oppressed*. London: Penguin Books.

Gardner, M. (2017, September 15). Germany has leading position in tertiary STEM subjects. *University World News*. Available at https://www.universityworldnews.com/post.php?story=20170915095958885. Accessed 3 October 2018.

Glewwe, P., Gragnolati, M., & Zaman, H. (2002). Who gained from Vietnam's boom in the 1990s? *Economic Development and Cultural Change, 50*(4), 773–792.

Gough, S., & Scott, W. (2007). *Higher education and sustainable development: Paradox and possibility*. London: Routledge.

Gyimah-Brempong, K. (2010, October 27–29). *Education and economic development in Africa*. Paper presented at the 4th African Economic Conference, Tunis.

Gyimah-Brempong, K., Paddison, O., & Mitiku, W. (2006). Higher education and economic growth in Africa. *Journal of Development Studies, 42*(3), 509–529.

Harris, S., & Lewer, N. (2005). Post-graduate peace education in Sri Lanka. *Journal of Peace Education, 2*(2), 109–124.

Huckle, J., & Sterling, S. (Eds.). (1996). *Education for sustainability*. London: Earthscan.

Ignatieff, M. (2018). *Academic freedom and the future of Europe* (Centre for Global Higher Education Working Paper No. 40). Available at https://www.researchcghe.org/publications/working-paper/academic-freedom-and-the-future-of-europe/. Accessed 5 October 2018.

Jickling, B., & Wals, A. E. J. (2008). Globalisation and environmental education: Looking beyond sustainable development. *Journal of Curriculum Studies, 40*(1), 1–21.

Jones, A., Jones, C., & Ndaruhutse, S. (2014). *Higher education and developmental leadership: The case of Ghana* (Development Leadership Programme, Research Paper No. 26). http://publications.dlprog.org/Higher%20Education%20and%20Developmental%20Leadership%20-%20The%20Case%20of%20Ghana.pdf.

Kitawi, A. (2014). Community capacity development in universities: Empowering communities through education management programmes in Strathmore University (a pilot study). *Contemporary Issues in Education Research, 7*(2), 75–94.

Larbi-Apau, J. A., & Sarpong, D. B. (2010). Performance measurement: Does education impact productivity? *Performance Improvement Quarterly, 22*(4), 81–97.

Leal Filho, W. (2010). Climate change at universities: Results of a world survey. In W. Leal Filho (Ed.), *Universities and climate change: Introducing climate change to university programmes*. Berlin: Springer.

Leal Filho, W., Manolas, E., & Pace, P. (2015). The future we want. *International Journal of Sustainability in Higher Education, 16*(1), 112–129.

Lotz-Sisitka, H., Wals, A., Kronlid, D., & McGarry, D. (2015). Transformative, transgressive social learning: Rethinking higher education pedagogy in times of systemic global dysfunction. *Current Opinion in Environmental Sustainability, 16*, 73–80.

Luescher-Mamashela, T. M., Kiiru, S., Mattes, R., Mwollo-ntallima, A., Ng'ethe, N., & Romo, M. (2011). *The university in Africa and democratic citizenship: Hothouse or training ground?* Wynberg: Centre for Higher Education Transformation.

Magara, E., Bukirwa, J., & Kayiki, R. (2011). Knowledge transfer through internship: The EASLIS experience in strengthening the governance decentralisation programme in Uganda. *African Journal of Library Archives and Information Science, 21*(1), 29–40.

Malik, S., & Courtney, K. (2011). Higher education and women's empowerment in Pakistan. *Gender and Education, 23*(1), 29–45.

Marginson, S. (2011). Higher education and public good. *Higher Education Quarterly, 65*(4), 411–433.

Mateos Cortés, L. S., & Dietz, G. (2016). Universidades interculturales en México: balance crítico de la primera década. *Revista mexicana de investigación educativa, 21*, 683–690.

Mattes, R., & Mozaffar, S. (2011). *Education, legislators and legislatures in Africa.* Wynberg: Centre for Higher Education Transformation.

Mattes, R., & Mughogho, D. (2009). *The limited impacts of formal education on democratic citizenship in Africa* (Centre for Social Science Research Working Paper 255). Cape Town: University of Cape Town.

Maxwell, N. (1984). *From knowledge to wisdom: A Revolution in the Aims and Methods of Science.* Oxford: Basil Blackwell.

McCowan, T. (2009). *Rethinking citizenship education: A curriculum for participatory democracy.* London: Continuum.

McCowan, T. (2013). *Education as a human right: Principles for a universal entitlement to learning.* London: Bloomsbury.

McCowan, T. (2014). *Can higher education solve Africa's job crisis? Understanding graduate employability in Sub-Saharan Africa* (Policy Brief). Manchester: British Council.

McCowan, T., Walker, M., Fongwa, S., Oanda, I., Sifuna, D., Adedeji, S., et al. (2016). *Universities, employability and inclusive development: Repositioning higher education in Ghana, Kenya, Nigeria and South Africa* (Final Research Report). British Council.

McKeown, R., & Hopkins, C. (2003). EE ≠ ESD: Defusing the worry. *Environmental Education Research, 9*(1), 117–128.

McMahon, W. W. (1999). *Education and development: Measuring the social benefits.* Oxford: Oxford University Press.

McMahon, W. W. (2003). Investment criteria and financing education for economic development. In J. B. G. Tilak (Ed.), *Education, society, and development* (pp. 235–256). New Delhi: A.P.H. Publishing.

McMahon, W. W. (2009). *Higher learning, greater good*. Baltimore: John Hopkins Press.

Mogensen, F., & Schnack, K. (2010). The action competence approach and the 'new' discourses of education for sustainable development, competence and quality criteria. *Environmental Education Research, 16*(1), 59–74.

Mtawa, N., Fongwa, S., & Wangenge-Ouma, G. (2016). The scholarship of university-community engagement: Interrogating Boyer's model. *International Journal of Educational Development, 49,* 126–133.

Müller, T. R. (2004). "Now I am free"—Education and human resource development in Eritrea: Contradictions in the lives of Eritrean women in higher education. *Compare: A Journal of Comparative and International Education, 34*(2), 215–229.

Mwaipopo, R. N., Lihamba, A., & Njewele, D. C. (2011). Equity and equality in access to higher education: The experiences of students with disabilities in Tanzania. *Research in Comparative and International Education, 6*(4), 415–429.

Oketch, M. O., McCowan, T., & Schendel, R. (2014). *The impact of tertiary education on development: A rigorous literature review*. London: Department for International Development.

Orr, D. (1992). *Ecological literacy: Education and the transition to a postmodern world*. Albany: State University of New York Press.

Orr, D. (1994). *Earth in mind*. Washington, DC: Island Press.

Qualifications and Curriculum Authority (QCA). (1998). *Education for citizenship and the teaching of democracy in schools: Final report of the Advisory Group on Citizenship*. London: Qualifications and Curriculum Authority.

Raghbendra, J., & Dang, T. (2012). Education and the vulnerability to food inadequacy in Timor-Leste. *Oxford Development Studies, 40*(3), 341–357.

Rodríguez-Solera, C. R., & Silva-Laya, M. (2017). Higher education for sustainable development at EARTH University. *International Journal of Sustainability in Higher Education, 18*(3), 278–293.

Rolleston, C., & Oketch, M. (2008). Educational expansion in Ghana: Economic assumptions and expectations. *International Journal of Educational Development, 28*(3), 320–339.

Sansone, G. C., Raute, L. J., Fong, G. T., Pednekar, M. S., Quah, A. C. K., Bansal-Travers, M., et al. (2012). Knowledge of health effects and intentions to quit among smokers in India: Findings from the Tobacco Control Policy (TCP) India pilot survey. *International Journal of Environmental Research and Public Health, 9*(2), 564–578.

Sauvé, L. (1996). Environmental education and sustainable development: A further appraisal. *Canadian Journal of Environmental Education, 1,* 7–33.

Schady, N. R. (2003). Convexity and sheepskin effects in the human capital earnings function: Recent evidence for Filipino men. *Oxford Bulletin of Economics and Statistics, 65*(2), 171–196.

Schmelkes, S. (2008). Creación y desarrollo inicial de las universidades interculturales en México: problemas, oportunidades, retos. In *Diversidad Cultural e Interculturalidad En Educación Superior: Experiencias En América Latina*. Bogotá: Organización de las Naciones Unidas para la Educación, la Ciencia y la Cultura, Instituto Internacional de la UNESCO para la Educación Superior en América Latina y el Caribe.

Schmelkes, S. (2009). Intercultural universities in Mexico: Progress and difficulties. *Intercultural Education, 20,* 5–17.

Shafiq, M. N. (2010). Do education and income affect support for democracy in Muslim countries? Evidence from the "Pew Global Attitudes Project". *Economics of Education Review, 29*(3), 461–469.

Shields, R. (2019). The sustainability of international higher education: Student mobility and global climate change. *Journal of Cleaner Production, 217,* 594–602.

Singh, R., Thind, S. K., & Jaswal, S. (2006). Assessment of marital adjustment among couples with respect to women's educational level and employment status. *Anthropologist, 8*(4), 259–266.

Stirling, S. (1996). Education in change. In J. Huckle & S. Sterling (Eds.), *Education for sustainability*. London: Earthscan.

Tilak, J. B. G. (2003). Higher education and development in Asia. *Journal of Educational Planning and Administration, 17*(2), 151–173.

Tilak, J. B. G. (2010). Higher education, poverty and development. *Higher Education Review, 42*(2), 23–45.

Truex, R. (2011). Corruption, attitudes, and education: Survey evidence from Nepal. *World Development, 39*(7), 1133–1142.

United Nations. (2015). *Transforming our world: The 2030 agenda for sustainable development*. Available at https://sustainabledevelopment.un.org/post2015/transformingourworld. Accessed 26 May 2016.

UNESCO. (2015). *UNESCO science report—Towards 2030*. Paris: UNESCO.

UNESCO. (2017). *Education for Sustainable Development Goals: Learning objectives*. Paris: UNESCO.
Vare, P., & Scott, W. (2007). Learning for a change: Exploring the relationship between education and sustainable development. *Journal of Education for Sustainable Development, 1*(2), 191–198.
Walker, M., & McLean, M. (2013). *Professional education, capabilities and the public good: The role of universities in promoting human development*. London: Routledge.
Wright, L-A., & Plasterer, R. (2010). Beyond basic education: Exploring opportunities for higher learning in Kenyan refugee camps. *Refuge: Canada's Periodical on Refugees, 27*(2), 42–56.
Young, T. (2018, August 19). It's no wonder degrees are going out of fashion when universities have become the Madrassas of the Left. *Mail on Sunday*.

Part III

9

The Limits of Developmental Impact

Until this point, this book has for the most part assumed that universities should do everything in their power to help achieve the Sustainable Development Goals. While there are notable flaws in the SDG framework—not least of which its rather naïve faith that the inherent contradictions of capitalism can be transcended through new technology, regulation and changes in individual behaviour—it has been considered an improvement, if only a small one, on the current course on which the world is set, lurching steadily towards the precipice.

Yet the difficulties with the role proposed for universities as engines of development do not only concern the vision of development in question. There is also the issue of whether they can be drivers of anything so concrete and so practical. Can an institution oriented towards ideas, thought, theory and debate really fulfil such an immediate and practical role in society as bringing about prosperity, ecological well-being and justice? Might indeed there be dangers in tying the institution to these predefined ends? This chapter will examine these crucial and rarely posed questions, through the contemporary buzzword of 'impact'. As explored in Chapter 4, non-academic impact is one of the primary characteristics of the developmental university, and of the role given to universities in the SDGs. Chapter 8 assessed how these positive benefits of universities around the world on the SDGs might be maximised in practice. This chapter will take an alternative perspective and argue that there are some elements of the Humboldtian (and possibly the mediaeval) universities that should not be abandoned in the quest for greater relevance to society—and indeed that the survival and flourishing of the university in some measure depends on them.

Impact has manifested itself most prominently in the discourse and policy of high-income countries, and it is here that the primary focus of this chapter will rest. Its inclusion within the UK's 2014 Research Excellence Framework (REF), in which it was allocated 20% of the assessment of academic research quality, has brought the question to the fore there. Impact evaluation has also been trialled in the Netherlands and Australia, while the European Research Council evaluates grants in relation to commercial and social innovation, and has also introduced an extra funding stream to turn research into "non-academic impacts" (Gunn and Mintrom 2016: 249). In the USA, the impact gauge Science and Technology for America's Reinvestment: Measuring the effect of Research on Innovation, Competitiveness and Science (STAR METRICS) has been developed since 2010. While there has been significant scepticism and some outright opposition—particularly in less applied disciplinary areas—there is little doubt that the impact agenda for universities is here to stay.

Problematic aspects of research impact have been addressed in some recent works, focusing on issues of restriction of autonomy and academic freedom, of falsification and embellishment ("impact sensationalism"), excessive pressure on academics (particularly early career ones), controversial or negative impacts, and financial costs to universities and government (e.g. Chubb and Watermeyer 2017; Gunn and Mintrom 2017; Smith et al. 2011; Watermeyer 2016). This chapter draws on a number of these critiques, in a systematisation of the limitations of the impact agenda, and puts forward a new categorisation of the stages of impact, so as to gain a fuller perspective on the normative and practical implications for the university. While acknowledging the urgent global challenges in the contemporary age and the significant role of universities in addressing them, the chapter views the current impact agenda, and by extension the developmental model, as one which presents risks for the university. Nevertheless, the argument here is not to remove or retreat from impact altogether, but to transform it to achieve a broader conception of the types of impact that are of value, and a greater attention to the processes through which it is achieved.

The Meaning and Historical Trajectory of Impact

The rise of impact in higher education is not an aberration, but is part of a historical evolution of the university that has tied it ever closer to society's needs. Perhaps there has never been a period in which the university was entirely divorced from society—despite the apparent hostility between town and gown in earlier centuries (Perkin 2007). In its allegiances to Church and/or (city) state, and in the imparting of professional knowledge, even from mediaeval times the university had some practical functions in relation to the outside world. Nevertheless, a significant change took place through the nineteenth century with the linking of universities more closely with the emerging industries, and the development of new practical courses such as engineering, accountancy and agriculture. As discussed in Chapter 4, the emergence of the land grant universities in the USA in the latter part of the nineteenth century is perhaps the most striking example of this new practical bent of the university, explicitly created to support agricultural and industrial development of areas not served by higher education (McDowell 2003), and the developmental university has continued in this vein.

Since the latter parts of the twentieth century, the ties between university and society have taken a more explicitly economic dimension. Universities are now tasked with being hubs for innovation—particularly in technology, at the heart of a vibrant network of entrepreneurs and spin-off companies—the 'third generation' university in Wissema's (2009) terms. The shift in the knowledge production function of universities has been conceptualised in terms of Mode 1 and Mode 2 knowledge (Gibbons et al. 1994), the former—the traditional disciplinary-based open-ended academic research—being replaced by applied, multidisciplinary research with immediate practical ends. The changing role of the university is strongly linked to the emergence of the knowledge economy, and the critical role attributed to technological innovation and high-level skills in the workforce (Gunn and Mintrom 2016). Evaluation of impact can also be linked to broader shifts in public sector management, with the rise of performativity, and the replacement of professional trust with accountability (Fielding 2003; Nixon 2004).

The discussions above have highlighted the political economy influences on the emergence of impact—changing patterns of governance, the increasing pressures to justify the use of dwindling state funding, and the need to generate private funds through selling products of economic value to individuals and corporations. Yet we can also point to cultural and epistemological roots of the move to impact in the context of post-modernity (Barnett 2004), with the questioning of absolute truth and morality—and therefore of the role of the university, as depicted in many accounts of the institution (Readings 1996; Santos 2004), leading to an increasing onus on the institution to justify its existence through demonstrations of worth. From the 1970s, there has also been increasing attention to the obligation of scientists to society and quests for new ways to assess research, leading to debates around relevance, 'research use', 'research utilisation' and 'knowledge utilisation' (Martin 2011; Walter et al. 2003; Weiss 1979).

As stated above, a prominent appearance of impact has been in the 2014 REF in the UK. Examples of projects submitted in the last review include improving public understanding of the Israel-Palestine conflict, introducing a new international standard of loudness for use in industry, reduction in Ford engines' carbon dioxide emissions and influencing government social care support (Jump 2015). As with the developmental university, a key point is that impact in this sense is understood as being *non-academic*: simply producing knowledgeable graduates, or high-quality research is not considered as impact, even when there is a tangible change (for example, the uptake of a new theory within the research community). Impact, therefore, involves not only the movement from the university to the outside society, but also from the academic to the non-academic sphere. Common forms of impact are influences on policy, creation of new products or patents and uptake of ideas or technologies by local communities. As defined by the REF 2014 guidance, impact is "an effect on, change or benefit to the economy, society, culture, public policy or services, health, the environment or quality of life, beyond academia" (REF 2011: 26). The guidance continues:

> Impact includes, but is not limited to, an effect on, change or benefit to:
>
> * the activity, attitude, awareness, behaviour, capacity, opportunity, performance, policy, practice, process or understanding
> * of an audience, beneficiary, community, constituency, organisation or individuals
> * in any geographic location whether locally, regionally, nationally or internationally.

Research Councils UK (2017) define impact similarly as:

> the demonstrable contribution that excellent research makes to society and the economy. This occurs in many ways – through creating and sharing new knowledge and innovation; inventing groundbreaking new products, companies and jobs; developing new and improving existing public services and policy; enhancing quality of life and health; and many more.

It can be seen here that in the way utilised in higher education policy circles the notion of impact has an exclusively positive sense. It is understood as the process by which the beneficial knowledge generated by the university brings desirable change in society (negative impacts—amusingly referred to as 'grimpact'—although certainly possible, are not generally contemplated).

As an initial disambiguation, it is important also to mention a highly prominent use of the term 'impact' in academic publishing, in particular in the Clarivate Analytics[1] journal impact factor. This usage departs from the sense outlined above as it relates to impact within

---

[1] Formerly Thomson Reuters.

the academic community—in this case, the number of citations to an article within a given time period—although it also reflects concern that research and scholarship 'gets out there' and has exposure and influence. A relevant dimension of contemporary academic publishing is the emphasis on open access in order to ensure that the fruits of research are accessed and used by as broad a range of communities as possible: for example, the requirement of the UK research councils that publications resulting from research they have funded be placed in open access repositories. In Walter et al. (2003) these forms of impact through dissemination of research are termed 'conceptual', in contrast to 'direct' or 'instrumental', the latter corresponding to impact on the non-academic community; Research Councils UK (2017) makes a similar distinction between 'academic' and 'economic and societal' impacts. The focus of this chapter, however, will primarily be on the 'direct' or 'economic and societal' forms, since it is this sense that is most relevant to the SDGs.

The above-mentioned statements from the 2014 REF and Research Councils UK provide a satisfactory working definition of the concept, and while explicitly relating to research, are relevant for teaching too. However, they hide the significant complexities of the process, involving questions of both a descriptive and normative nature. The REF guidance quoted above stipulates the kinds of impact envisaged (e.g. attitudes, behaviour), the range of beneficiaries (e.g. individual, community) and the location (locally, regionally etc.). The REF evaluation furthermore has two components, *reach* and *significance*: the former the breadth element (the beneficiaries of the impact) and the latter the depth element (the strength of the impact). In terms of beneficiaries, sometimes called 'user communities', distinctions have been drawn between primary and secondary beneficiaries (Upton et al. 2014); there might also be a possibility of non-human beneficiaries—such as elements in the natural environment—though with a view that there would ultimately be some human benefit. Nevertheless, while a range of important distinctions are made in these documents, the schemes outlined above fall short of providing a satisfactory frame for understanding the dynamics of the process as a whole.

An Analytical Framework for Impact

In order to move beyond the rhetoric of impact, a more comprehensive analytical frame is needed to identify its constituent elements. At its most reductive, impact is seen as an 'either-or': either an activity is having an impact, or it is not. A slightly expanded view will acknowledge the extent of that impact—a quality we can term *intensity*. Yet in order to fully understand impact we also need to know what kind of influence is involved, who is instigating that influence, to whom, with what time frame, and by what means. We can conceptualise the impact of universities, therefore, in terms of six elements:

1. *Source*
2. *Form*
3. *Trajectory*
4. *Intensity*
5. *Timescale*
6. *Destination*

Source
This element relates to the origin of the impact, whether in terms of actors or activities. Does the impact derive from an individual, group, an institution or group of institutions? And does it emerge from a research project, a form of teaching or another activity? This element also draws our attention to the motivation of the impact, whether the activity in question was driven and designed by the actors themselves or commissioned in response to external demand.

Form
The nature of the impact is an aspect that has been discussed fairly extensively in current debates and in the literature. The Economic and Social Research Council (ESRC) (2017) categorises these into instrumental, conceptual or capacity building. We might also think in terms of economic, social, cultural, political, technological, and so forth, or a combination of these. Another way of categorising is according to

"activity, attitude, awareness, behaviour, capacity, opportunity, performance, policy, practice, process or understanding", as seen above in REF (2011: 26). An interesting question is raised here as to the extent to which the form of impact is contemplated within the original activity (e.g. a research project), or only materialises when reaching the destinations (e.g. in its application in industry).

Trajectory
The third element refers to the vehicle, means or process through which the impact takes place. Is it, for example, through dissemination of research findings to policymakers, formation of values in undergraduate students, or establishment of a patent for an innovative product? Trajectories can display different degrees of intentionality: in some cases a project may have built in an impact plan with specified outcomes, in others significant impact may have occurred in entirely serendipitous ways. Given the diversity of activities undertaken by the contemporary university, the pathways through which impact on society can take place are multiple, as indicated by the framework put forward in Oketch et al. (2014), for example. Ashwin (2016) puts forward the idea of a 'translation device' mediating in this way between knowledge production and impact on society.

Intensity
The strength or depth of the influence, corresponding to the element of 'significance' in REF (2011) is here referred to as *intensity*. How we might understand intensity depends on the form of impact in question—whether we are referring to changes in attitudes or to increases in national GDP; or whether we are referring to conflict resolution or fuel efficiency. Impact can be diffuse or it can be concentrated; there can be a large impact on a small area or a minor impact across a large area.

Timescale
The timing of impact—how long it takes from the original conducting of the activity to causing an effect in the destination—is highly variable. Differences may be due to the types of trajectory (as outlined above), or to its form, or simply to the amount of resources available for dissemination. It is important to observe the interactions between this element

and the previous one: in some cases there may be an intense impact to start off with, and but one that dissipates rapidly; in others the impact may be slow to emerge, but prove to be highly significant in the long term.

Destination
Finally there is the question of the recipient or benefactor of the impact. Is it individual or collective? How equitably are the benefits distributed? This element is addressed in the REF 2014 guidance through the notion of 'reach', and distinctions between different kinds of user communities. Notions of public and private returns are also relevant here, with impact either restricted to specific individuals or corporations, or in the case of non-rivalrous and non-excludable goods, potentially for the benefit of all (Marginson 2011).

These elements can be used in empirical analysis, to gauge the process, participants and effects, and therefore to assess what kinds of impact are possible, and under what circumstances. Take the example of a (fictional) research project on natural sweeteners. The *source* of the impact is a multi-institution research project in Paraguay on the composition and uses of the Stevia plant. The research is being carried out in conjunction with Coca-Cola, and the findings of the research are taken up immediately by the company (*timescale*), as well as being subsequently disseminated in the public sphere, minus the commercially sensitive material (*trajectory*). The *destination* and *form* of the impact are multiple, and *intensity* variable: significant economic benefits for the company, some financial gain for Paraguayan farmers, a new variety of low-calorie fizzy drink for consumers, and loss of lands and environmental destruction for indigenous groups in the country.

What the scheme shows us is that it is unhelpful to see 'impact' in a unitary way: in fact it is a multifarious process that operates through diverse channels and involves multiple actors, and cannot be determined to be inherently positive or negative. 'Having impact' is, therefore, a woefully inadequate criterion for universities or for research, both in terms of understanding descriptively what is happening and evaluating it normatively. These are among the complexities that will be outlined in the section that follows.

Perils of Impact in Developmental Universities

It should be clear from the preceding chapters in this book that the argument presented here is not that the university cannot or should not aim to have a positive impact on society—indeed, these benefits are extensive and essential in our contemporary context, and are in fact often underestimated. The problem lies instead with the particular ways in which the impact agenda has been conceptualised and implemented. Some of these points have been broadly acknowledged in public debate and in the moderate number of publications on the topic, particularly the threat to blue skies research, short-termism, economisation and difficulties of evaluation (e.g. Fielding 2003; Gunn and Mintrom 2016; Watermeyer 2016). As Fielding (2003: 289) states about the impact agenda in education more broadly:

> My sense is that it valorises what is short-term, readily visible and easily measurable. My sense is also that it has difficulty comprehending and valuing what is complex and problematic, what is uneven and unpredictable, what requires patience and tenacity.

One of these risks concerns the fact that matters of impact are not entirely technical but involve normative moral and political questions. In keeping with the 'evidence-based policy' and 'what works' agenda—the supposed movement from ideological or convention-based decision-making to one based entirely on objective empirical evidence—impact is presented as a neutral endeavour. Needless to say, 'what works' is predicated on a prior question, namely what we want to achieve, and that in turn is based on fundamental values relating to human life, the nature of being and knowing, and the ideal society.

Views on the kinds of impact that universities should have vary by focus, with some emphasising economic benefits, others cultural and aesthetic, or democratic participation and social cohesion (the dimension of *form* outlined above). Even within a specific area there may be contestation: two people may both have a purely economistic conception of higher education, but one on reducing absolute poverty, and another on maximising aggregate national income through strengthening investment banking systems; political conceptions of the role of higher education can vary from inculcating a rigid national ideology to promoting Freirean conscientisation and grassroots transformation. A micro-finance scheme for women in Bangladesh can from one perspective be seen as beneficial in empowering them relative to men, while from another as locking them into exploitative capitalist relations; the development of publicly accessible scientific information is a laudable aim for some, but from a fundamentalist religious perspective, is simply reinforcing false views of the origin of the universe. Gunn and Mintrom (2017) also discuss 'controversial impacts', citing "fracking, genetically modified crops, nanotechnologies in food, and stem cell research". How, then, can we speak simply of 'positive' impact?

The distribution of the benefits of impact (the *destination* dimension) also involves a range of contested moral and political questions—i.e. whether contribution, need, desert, utilisation or some other criterion should predominate. It is important in this way to distinguish between private or public goods produced, the latter in its triple sense of countable goods, a collective sense of good, and the public sphere (Marginson 2011). The impact may not in fact involve a net gain for society as a whole: it may simply be providing positional advantage for some people in relation to others, along the lines of 'zero-sum game employability' explored in McCowan (2015).

A central problem, therefore, is that the impact agenda assumes not only that impact will be positive, but also popular consensus on the ideal society, or at least the direction in which society should be moving. While from a certain standpoint generation of new knowledge and understanding is always desirable, their application in the 'real' world raises contested issues of society's priorities and the political and moral values underpinning them. In the case of the SDGs, we have in contrast a clear and explicit framework that does not hide its normative orientations, and is in this sense a significant step forward from disingenuous 'what works' approaches. Nevertheless, as explored in later parts of this book, the framework still has its blind spots and hidden assumptions that warrant critique.

Another problematic question is the extent to which the impact can be measured. Much of the academic debate (e.g. Gunn and Mintrom

2017; Penfield et al. 2014; Upton et al. 2014) around impact has in fact focused on this element (indeed, one downside of this has been the lack of attention to other, in some ways more profound, aspects of the question). Even if it were to be shown that impact can be achieved by universities, and it is desirable for them to do so, there are still significant doubts about our ability to identify, assess and evaluate it. The REF in the UK utilises case studies to gauge impact, involving a mainly narrative account of the research and its uptake in different spheres. However, there are those who call for an entirely metric evaluation of impact, one which would allow for greater objectivity and comparability (Jump 2015). There are also difficulties around attribution: it is hard to establish with certainty that a particular change in society is exclusively or even partly attributable to an action taken by a university. Just as problematic perhaps are the destinations of the impact: where we look may be determined a priori by our preferences or prejudices, or simply our inability to track and identify all of the various influences stemming from our work.

A final point concerns commensurability. Quantitative evaluations of impact—and even qualitative ones in some cases—assume that we can compare between different cases, and different forms of impact. However, it is highly dubious whether we can meaningfully rank the impact of a project fostering technological innovation to drive macro-economic growth, against one promoting mutual understanding between diverse ethnic groups in the local community. Can we ever say which has the 'greater' impact?

Ultimately, there is always the danger (seen in all spheres of society) of the tail wagging the dog: that the forms of measurement that are possible (or are seen to be preferable) end up determining what we understand as impact, and conditioning our work in practice. These risks of distorting behaviour, of gaming the system, and even falsification of evidence have been observed at other levels of the education system and in other parts of HE (Chubb and Watermeyer 2017; Martin 2011; Smith et al. 2011). With significant resources attached to these evaluations, the scenario is highly likely—and will also reinforce some of the tendencies outlined below, of a linear, university-owned, predictable and short-term process.

However, while questions of measurement dominate debates on impact in the UK and other high-income countries, in relation to the achievement of the SDGs more broadly there are three more fundamental problems with the framing of universities primarily as engines of development: first, whether in fact universities can reliably fulfil such an instrumental role; second, whether they do so in the linear and predictable way assumed; and third, whether tying the university to societal ends in this way may have unintended negative consequences.

The University as Adaptable Factory

The first issue with developmental impact is that it treats universities as machines for generating desirable outcomes—whether nurturing local businesses, fostering macro-economic growth, ensuring social cohesion, inducting citizens into a national ideology, reducing HIV/AIDS prevalence, writing government policy documents or improving agricultural productivity. This approach is problematic firstly because it assumes that universities have no substantive purposes and nature other than those that are given to them from the outside. Because universities shape human beings it is assumed that they can shape them in any way that they like; because they produce knowledge it is assumed that they can produce any knowledge for any end. For the adaptable factory, if lawnmowers are no longer needed, then the machine tools can be replaced so that quad bikes can be made. Finding the essence of the university may be a forlorn task, but it is not controversial to assert, as Collini (2012) does, that for all of the other things that the institution may do, the pursuit of understanding through open-ended enquiry is a pivotal purpose. This is not to say that universities cannot justifiably engage in other functions, but that to take the institution predominantly or entirely away from this role would be to turn it into a different institution.

One problem with the university as 'adaptable factory' perspective is that it assumes the means are subordinated to the ends, that what the university does is determined purely by an aim to achieve a desired product. There are two counter-positions. In the first place, one can perceive that the process itself has value, that there is intrinsic worth in engaging in enquiry and the pursuit of understanding, independently of its outcomes. There is a long-standing lineage in Western philosophy in support of this position—represented by the Socratic maxim that the unexamined life is not worth living—not to mention Eastern traditions such as Buddhism, and others around the world. Somewhat distinct from this is the argument that there is intrinsic worth to the fruits of teaching and research: that is to say, as argued by Peters (1966) and Hirst (1974)—and by Newman (1947 [1852]) in the field of higher education—that being educated is a good in itself regardless of what one does with that education. In relation to research and scholarship, this position would hold that scientific discoveries and other insights into ourselves and our universe are valuable whether or not we use them to make any tangible impact on the material quality of our lives.

Higher education can be seen to have intrinsic or instrumental value—depending on whether the learning or scholarship in question is seen as being worthwhile in itself or alternatively appealing to external justifications (i.e. whether having a greater understanding of ourselves and the world around us in itself constitutes well-being and a flourishing life, or only in so far as it acts as a conduit for increasing income, etc.). As discussed in relation to 'value' in Chapter 3, universities through history have varied in the emphasis placed on the intrinsic or instrumental benefits, but generally speaking both forms of value coexist, and are not mutually exclusive. Emphasis on impact clearly prioritises the instrumental benefits of higher education. It is not in fact impossible for knowledge seen as intrinsically valuable to have impact: for example, an anthropological research study may have been carried out purely for the intrinsic aim of developing understanding of human origins, but in practice have served to empower a previously misrecognised ethnic group and led to shifts in the political sphere. In practice, the incorporation of impact metrics into research assessments such as that of the UK has occurred alongside traditional gauges of research quality—so is still a far cry from the pure instrumentalism of the university 'without content' (Readings 1996; Lee 2017). Nevertheless, for the most part the impact agenda entails a downgrading of the intrinsic, and its portrayal as a rather precious, self-indulgent or old-fashioned view.

There is nothing inappropriate or harmful in universities promoting instrumental ends—indeed, it would be impossible for them not to do so in practice, and all universities through history have had some instrumental intentions. The point is that the instrumental aims should not take the place of the intrinsic ones, or debilitate them. A number of the early accounts of the developmental university (e.g. Court 1980; Coleman 1986; Lauglo 1982) caution in this way against the potential undermining of the academic core of the university by external engagement activities. In contemporary times, the implication of this point is that universities should not allow applied research with immediate impact to undermine basic, blue skies or curiosity-driven research. Nevertheless, the research conducted can and is likely to still have a significantly positive impact on society. Likewise, in relation to the teaching and learning dimension, students may learn professional skills, but these do not supplant the central aim of university to develop critical, imaginative, aware and knowledgeable individuals.

Impact as Linear and Predictable

A further point is that enquiry, by nature, is not a straightforward linear process that can lead to predefined and predictable outcomes. The assumption that the impact relationship is a linear one has residual echoes from the non-metaphorical meaning of the term impact of one moving object hitting another. From this perspective, knowledge is produced within the university, and is then applied and transferred in some way to beneficiaries outside the university. Oancea (2013: 248) describes this as the 'chain-link' approach, assessing "trajectories of influence from research insights to non-academic changes and benefits". While this may conform to our conventional perception of the events, it hides the more subtle bi- or multi-directional flows that inevitably take place (Smith et al. 2011). Students and staff in universities have lives outside as well as inside the institution, and bring learning, subject matter and values from society into the institution. Furthermore, as indicated in the change of rhetoric in institutions from 'knowledge transfer' to 'knowledge exchange', there is a sense that universities should be taking steps to ensure that they are absorbing ideas and knowledge from other communities, rather than just divulging them. Santos (2004) calls this 'counter-extension', in opposition to the conventional 'extension' role of universities in sharing their knowledge with supposedly less enlightened communities. Whether or not universities succeed in this democratic bi-directional exchange, in a descriptive sense it is problematic to claim a simple linear movement from inside to outside.

There is a further aspect to this question residing in the general complexity of cause and effect. Although it might appear a trite point, all actions inevitably have some impact on the world around—and according to the so-called butterfly effect, apparently small and inconsequential interventions may in the long run bring significant changes. What is at stake then is not some impact versus no impact, but of what kind of impact is desired. Even the rarefied scholarship 'getting dusty on the shelf' brings some kind of change in the life of the academic who wrote it, and in the few people who have read it, so does have an impact on society in some form, and can be unexpectedly powerful in the long term.

A further dimension of this point is that of *ownership*. Once we start to question the linear movement of impact, the *source* of that impact becomes more ambiguous. Evaluations of research impact generally assume that the credit is due to the research team, that academics are the owners of the impact, which is then delivered to others. Yet we might also see the recipients of impact as deserving of credit here, for their openness to the ideas, or their ability to incorporate and contextualise the theory or research into their practice. Ashwin (2016) goes further, by arguing that it is misleading to think of any academic knowledge as attributable to the researchers in question, as it is built on a longer tradition of scholarship stretching back centuries; conventional conceptions of knowledge production being excessively individualised, and ignoring the collective construction of ideas.

Emphasis on impact usually leads to short-termism. Whether through political exigencies, requirements of research methodology or funding streams, the impact that is generally sought-after is one that occurs in a relatively short time span after the university action has taken place. So, for example, community involvement in a water management programme may have immediate effects in terms of allowing the community to store and manage collected rainwater more effectively. However, as widely acknowledged (e.g. Gunn and Mintrom 2017) many impacts from university—including the most valuable ones—are not of this type. Decades would pass before Einstein's theory of relativity would be utilised in GPS navigation. The German tripartite secondary system (imperfectly implemented in the UK in the post-war period) appears a replica of Plato's ideas more than 2000 years before on gold, silver and bronze souls, and the corresponding forms of education needed. Whether or not we consider this to be a positive impact, one can hardly deny its practical significance in changing society. On a smaller scale, much of the learning acquired during higher education may only manifest itself in individuals' lives—and consequently in the work they do and their influence over others—many years after graduating. It is not only a question of impact only being observable after an extended period of time—the *form* and *intensity* of impact can also transform over time, becoming stronger or weaker, or even turning from positive to negative or vice versa. These challenges were seen in complexities around assessing time lag in macro-economic research in the review on the impact of tertiary institutions in lower-income countries discussed in the previous chapter (Oketch et al. 2014).

Consequently, the impact agenda may move universities away from basic research whose immediate relevance may not be apparent, but which in years, decades or even centuries may bring significant benefits to society, towards research with immediate practical relevance, but on a less ambitious scale. Similar concerns are raised by the shift from 'basic', 'blue skies', 'curiosity-driven' or 'frontier' research to Mode 2, applied research.

A further point relates to unpredictability. Are universities machines for impact that can simply be programmed for producing a particular effect? What we know of teaching and learning processes on the one hand, and research and scholarship on the other tells us this is not so. The inherent unpredictability of both of these endeavours means that foreseeing impact will always be a challenge. This characteristic of academic life is apparent to those working within universities, with the serendipitous nature of impact highlighted by respondents in Oancea's (2013) study. In fact, this is not necessarily to be lamented, as we can see the elusiveness and spontaneity of learning and enquiry as part of their richness (McCowan 2009). Upton et al. (2014), argue in this way for "a shift in focus from the outcomes of knowledge exchange to the process of engagement between academics and external audiences" (p. 359) with this process-based approach through intellectual curiosity and "interpretative conversations" allowing for "serendipitous benefits" to emerge. We might also argue that there is a need to fail—in order to encourage deep enquiry, challenge norms and ensure potentially significant breakthroughs, we need to allow a space for failure, with no apparent impact emerging from a given project.

The achievement of concrete objectives is uncertain in an empirical sense—we can provide particular stimuli for students, but we can never be certain what in fact they will take away from the process. Similarly, these objectives falsify the nature of research and scholarship: as Collini (2012: 55) states, "the drive towards understanding can never accept an arbitrary stopping-point, and critique may always in principle reveal that any currently accepted stopping-point *is* ultimately arbitrary". This point reflects a deeper consideration that 'impact' in the sense of an outcome is an illusion, that all is process observed at different stages—as Dewey (1964: 100) notes: "nothing happens which is *final* in the sense that it is not part of an ongoing stream of events". In summary, determining and achieving specific objectives is unviable; yet it can also be seen as having an undesirable effect on the nature of learning and enquiry, closing off the unexpected outcomes that may end up being the most significant and, ironically, impactful.

A Room of Its Own?

Porosity between university and society has become central to discourses of how universities should reframe themselves in the contemporary age. The ivory tower has become an image of exactly what a university should not be, with academics ridiculed if they are seen to be 'out of touch', and research and scholarship seen as worthless if it is not applied to practical ends. Greater integration with society has in part arisen from the commercialisation of the system and the reduction in public funding, on account of the necessity of closer engagement with potential funders. However, there is also a more purposeful side to this integration, promoted by governments and other agencies for bringing benefit to diverse non-academic communities. The notion of 'place' has also become central for some institutions, in developing a local identity and connection to the surrounding community (Ransom 2017).

There is no doubt that closer engagement with external communities is desirable for universities, and can bring benefits to both sides. Nevertheless, in some cases there are risks, particularly when what we might call 'hyper-porosity' has been reached through the process of unbundling, and it becomes difficult to discern a distinctive institutional sphere. There must be some element of differentiation between the space of the university and the other spheres of society: a degree of 'insulation' (Cowen 2012) is needed from the vicissitudes of the outside world, in order to allow for the deeper reflection and study needed to make significant breakthroughs in science and in order for transformative processes of intellectual development to occur. Of course, it is not that learning—indeed transformative learning—cannot occur in the outside society, in the workplace, in everyday life—indeed some forms of valuable learning can only take place in those spaces. However, there is value in a modicum of seclusion and separation from those activities in order to develop different kinds of thought and understanding.

The connected question of university autonomy has had substantial attention from theorists and practitioners over the years, and will not be dealt with in depth here. But clearly it is an issue of relevance for the developmental university—as was raised in the early studies by Coleman (1986) and others. The instrumentalisation outlined above, when tied to specific and externally defined goals, reduces institutional autonomy and academic freedom, as highlighted by Smith et al. (2011) and Watermeyer (2016). Just as a degree of insulation from society is necessary, so independence from control of state and market in institutional organisation is essential. Processes of teaching and research must be allowed to follow the organic course of an enquiry—however opaque the connection with immediate benefits might be, however little demand there might be, or however far from current state interests. While it is natural for the state to want to harness the university for its own ends—particularly if it is supporting it financially—overly heavy control will inevitably dull its capacity and possibly undermine it altogether.

Towards the Generative Intrinsic

The above sections have summarised several risks posed by the impact agenda—some of which have obtained ample attention in public debates and in the literature, others much less so. It is not being argued, however, that the assessment of research impact in its current incipient form is necessarily a pernicious influence—the inclusion in the REF, for example, is relatively moderate, and indeed acknowledges some important aspects of the uptake of research (Francis 2011). Nevertheless, the trend is for these emphases to expand their prominence, and their reach across different aspects of the work of the university, and ultimately for the value of the university as a whole to be solely determined by its impact.

The principal danger highlighted here is that, when it starts to dominate, emphasis on impact can undermine the practice of enquiry that is at the heart of the university. Instead, this chapter argues for a different conceptualisation, one that we might term the *generative intrinsic*. According to this conception, the impact of universities is organic to their intrinsically valuable practice. That is, teaching and research are oriented wholeheartedly to the deepening of understanding—of ourselves, our societies and the universe—the process Collini (2012: 92) terms "extending human understanding through open-ended enquiry". This understanding, along with the practice of enquiry itself, needs no further justification. However, from it emerges a range of instrumentally valuable outcomes, ones that are not entirely predictable or subject to control, but that nevertheless bring significant benefits to society in many spheres. Some of these benefits may be immediate, while others will only manifest themselves after years, decades or even centuries. Instrumental benefits are valued, but do not hollow out the content of the university, and the latter's worth does not stand or fall on predefined goals. As such, the idea of the generative intrinsic acts as a kind of reconciliation of deontological and consequentialist approaches.

Returning to the frame outlined above—of source, form, trajectory, intensity, timescale and destination—the notion of the generative intrinsic has important implications. The first is that the source of the impact will be the quest for human understanding itself—that is, activities that are intrinsically valuable, and not only means for achieving external ends. While those activities may be externally promoted, funded or commissioned, the actors involved will retain autonomy, in accordance with the processes of open-ended enquiry and dialogue in which they are engaged. The element of trajectory becomes highly important in this conception, as also argued by Upton et al. (2014), in their emphasis on process rather than outcome: not only should the initial teaching and research be characterised by open-ended enquiry, but the passage of these ideas to the beneficiaries must also be dialogical, and open to contestation and transformation. As discussed above, the elements of intensity, timescale and sometimes destination will be unpredictable in many instances; moreover, while the form of impact will in many cases correspond closely to the original activity, there may be unforeseen benefits—for example, an archaeological research project that generates unexpected sources of tourist income for a local community, or a business studies degree that instead of producing malleable executives, sparks a campaign against unethical corporate practices.

The primary emphasis on scholarly enquiry argued for here is not, of course, equivalent to stating that universities should not have responsibility to society, or should not be open to it. As argued by Christopher Martin (2011), while it is not justified that (philosophical) scholarship be "valued only in so far as it is seen to have obvious, clear, short-term, social or economic value", there is a requirement for public engagement: "normative claims applicable to the community-at-large must be vetted by the public in some way as a necessary condition of their legitimacy or justifiability" (p. 617). As stated above, given the critical challenges facing the global community and the severe inequalities, universities have an onus to contribute wholeheartedly to enhancing well-being, reducing poverty and promoting social justice. Furthermore, the boundaries between university and society should remain open and porous, in terms of both actors and ideas. Nevertheless, responsibility and openness are not equivalent to the orientation of the work of university towards immediate and direct impact, narrowly conceived, and the latter may indeed work against the former in unexpected ways.

Ultimately, what universities should do is what they do best—to engage in individual and collective exploration of humanity and the universe, so as to enhance and further knowledge and understanding (these processes include both those traditionally understood as teaching and those understood as research). Knowledge and understanding will inevitably have positive impacts, though it is not always possible to predict exactly what, when or how. The change that without doubt needs to take place in universities is an opening towards society—a willingness to share, and importantly also to receive from those communities outside—even without commercial motivations. This form of porosity of boundaries can address the limitations of the aloof, ivory tower model of institution, but does not entail abandoning intellectual enquiry, or curiosity-driven, basic or frontier research. These forms of enquiry, with a *generative intrinsic* role, are paradoxically the greatest chance of universities having a lasting beneficial impact on society—and on the SDGs.

Aesop's fable of the goose that laid the golden eggs comes to mind. Pursuing the impact agenda may indeed be akin to slaughtering the goose in the belief that its innards are solid gold, only to find that, now dead, it is unable to continue laying its golden eggs. The whimsical and unruly nature of knowledge production in universities may be frustrating to policymakers, but there is perhaps no other way of achieving the truly remarkable insights and breakthroughs in knowledge than through open and undirected critical enquiry.

References

Ashwin, P. (2016). 'From a teaching perspective, "impact" looks very different'. *Times Higher Education*, 21 March. [Online]. http://www.timeshighereducation.com/blog/teaching-perspectiveimpact-looks-very-different. Accessed 3 May 2018.

Barnett, R. (2004). The purposes of higher education and the changing face of academia. *London Review of Education, 2*(1), 61–73.

Chubb, J., & Watermeyer, R. (2017). Artifice or integrity in the marketization of research impact? Investigating the moral economy of (pathways to) impact statements within research funding proposals in the UK and Australia. *Studies in Higher Education, 42*(12), 2360–2372.

Coleman, J. S. (1986). The idea of the developmental university. *Minerva: A Review of Science, Learning and Policy, 24*(4), 476–494.

Collini, S. (2012). *What are universities for?* London: Penguin.

Court, D. (1980). The development ideal in higher education: The experience of Kenya and Tanzania. *Higher Education, 9,* 657–680.

Cowen, R. (2012). Robustly researching the relevant: A note on creation myths in comparative education. In L. Wikander, C. Gustaffson, & U. Riis (Eds.), *Enlightenment, creativity and education: Polities, politics, performances* (pp. 3–26). Rotterdam: Sense Publishers and CESE.

Dewey, J. (1964). The continuum of ends-means. In R. Archambault (Ed.), *John Dewey on education: Selected writings.* Chicago: University of Chicago Press.

Economic and Social Research Council. (2017). *What is impact?* Available at http://www.esrc.ac.uk/research/impact-toolkit/what-is-impact/. Accessed 15 July 2018.

Fielding, M. (2003). The impact of impact. *Cambridge Journal of Education, 33*(2), 289–295.

Francis, B. (2011). Increasing impact? An analysis of issues raised by the impact agenda in educational research. *Scottish Educational Review, 43*(2), 4–16.

Gibbons, M., Limoges, C., Nowotny, H., Schwartzman, S., Scott, P., & Trow, M. (1994). *The new production of knowledge: The dynamics of science and research in contemporary societies.* London: Sage.

Gunn, A., & Mintrom, M. (2016). Higher education policy change in Europe: Academic research funding and the impact agenda. *European Education, 48*(4), 241–257.

Gunn, A., & Mintrom, M. (2017, January 12). Five things to consider when designing a policy to measure research impact. *The Conversation.* Available at http://theconversation.com/five-things-to-consider-when-designing-a-policy-to-measure-research-impact-71078.

Hirst, P. H. (1974). *Knowledge and the curriculum.* London: Routledge & Kegan Paul.

Jump, P. (2015, February 19). The impact of impact. *Times Higher Education.*

Lauglo, J. (1982). *The 'utilitarian university', the 'centre of academic learning' and developing countries* (EDC Occasional Papers No. 2).

Lee, S. T. (2017). '*The Structure of a University: A Karatanian interrogation into instrumentalism, idealism and community in postwar British higher education, 1945–2015*' (Unpublished PhD thesis). Birkbeck University.

Marginson, S. (2011). Higher education and public good. *Higher Education Quarterly, 65*(4), 411–433.

Martin, B. (2011). The research excellence framework and the 'impact agenda': Are we creating a Frankenstein monster? *Research Evaluation, 20*(3), 247–254.

McCowan, T. (2009). *Rethinking citizenship education: A curriculum for participatory democracy*. London: Continuum.

McCowan, T. (2015). Should universities promote employability? *Theory and Research in Education, 13*(3), 267–285.

McDowell, G. (2003). Engaged universities: Lessons from the Land-Grant universities and extension. *Annals of the American Academy of Political and Social Science, 585* (Higher Education in the Twenty-First Century), 31–50.

Newman, J. H. (1947 [1852]). *The idea of the university: Defined and illustrated*. London: Longmans, Green.

Nixon, J. (2004). Education for the good society: The integrity of academic practice. *London Review of Education, 2*(3), 245–252.

Oancea, A. (2013). Interpretations of research impact in seven disciplines. *European Educational Research Journal, 12*(2), 242–250.

Oketch, M. O., McCowan, T., & Schendel, R. (2014). *The impact of tertiary education on development: A rigorous literature review*. London: Department for International Development.

Penfield, T., Baker, M. J., Scoble, R., & Wykes, M. C. (2014). Assessment, evaluations, and definitions of research impact: A review. *Research Evaluation, 23*(1), 21–32.

Perkin, H. (2007). History of universities. In J. J. F. Forest & P. G. Altbach (Eds.), *International handbook of higher education* (pp. 159–206). Dordrecht: Springer.

Peters, R. S. (1966). *Ethics and education*. London: George Allen and Unwin.

Ransom, J. (2017). *Mutual influence? Universities, cities and the future of internationalisation*. British Council. https://www.britishcouncil.org/education/ihe/knowledge-centre/internationalisation/mutual-influence-universities-cities. Accessed 3 December 2017.

Readings, B. (1996). *The university in ruins*. Cambridge, MA: Harvard University Press.

REF. (2011, February). *Assessment framework and guidance on submissions*. Research Excellence Framework. Available at http://www.ref.ac.uk/media/ref/content/pub/assessmentframeworkandguidanceonsubmissions/GOS%20including%20addendum.pdf.

Research Councils UK. (2017). *Excellence with impact*. Available at http://www.rcuk.ac.uk/innovation/impact/. Accessed 15 July 2017.

Santos, B. de S. (2004). *A universidade do século XXI: para uma reforma democratica e emancipatória da universidade*. São Paulo: Cortez.

Smith, S., Ward, V., & House, A. (2011). 'Impact' in the proposals for the UK's Research Excellence Framework: Shifting the boundaries of academic autonomy. *Research Policy, 40*(10), 1369–1379 (11).

Upton, S., Vallance, P., & Goddard, J. (2014). From outcome to process, evidence for a new approach to research impact assessment. *Research Evaluation, 23*(4), 352–365.

Walter, I., Nutley, S. M., & Davies, H. T. O. (2003). *Models of research impact: A cross-sector review*. Available from Research Unit for Research Utilisation, University of St Andrews. Available at www.st-and.ac.uk/~ruru/publications.htm. Accessed 11 February 2003.

Watermeyer, R. (2016). Impact in the REF: Issues and obstacles. *Studies in Higher Education, 41*(2), 199–214.

Weiss, C. (1979). The many meanings of research utilization. *Public Administration Review, 39*, 426–431.

Wissema, J. G. (2009). *Towards the third generation university: Managing the university in transition*. Cheltenham: Edward Elgar.

10

The Post-Development University

Towards the end of our visit to the Intercultural University of Veracruz (UVI), we were asked to give a short presentation to students. I explained my interest in visiting Tequila, and in understanding the contributions that the institution was making to the Sustainable Development Goals (SDGs). On asking them how they felt about the SDG framework, I was met with a series of responses, outlining in articulate, forceful but respectful manner how the SDG framework, although well intentioned, was hand in glove with the global capitalist system, and while bringing some palliative changes was ultimately doomed to failure due to its inability to challenge the core of the system. Perhaps I should not have been surprised at receiving a more thoughtful and cogent response on the matter than most academics could give. But it must be remembered that these were students who without UVI may not have been in university at all, whose parents had mostly not completed secondary education, and whose own experience of schooling had provided little in the way of meaningful learning.

What also became clear was that institutions like UVI, while in many ways representing a promising means of achieving the SDGs, also present a strong challenge to them. First, as seen in their politicised undergraduate students, they critique the faith of the SDGs that some regulation and changes in individual behaviour are enough to mitigate the damaging effects of global capitalism. A new paradigm of development is, therefore, necessary—for many at the university, it can be found in *buen vivir*, the philosophy of harmonious social and ecological living originating in the Andes. Second, the work of UVI in its valuing of indigenous languages and traditions lays bare the lack of attention to culture in the SDGs.[1] Third, it highlights the question of epistemology and knowledge traditions—challenging the assumption that there is a single universal knowledge, that of mainstream Western science, and the relegation of all other ways of knowing to the sphere of the quaint, exotic and magical.

While the previous chapter highlighted limitations of the developmental university in terms of impact, and the problems of viewing the institution as a predictable and controllable engine of positive change, this chapter will address an even more fundamental critique: that the whole vision of development on which the developmental university is based is in fact flawed, or at the very least partial. The university, it will be argued, has a duty not only to help achieve the laudable human and ecological ends of the SDGs, but also to critique and reinvent them, while providing a space for alternative forms of thought and practice.

Thus far, this book has not engaged extensively with the question of knowledge. The silence on this issue has allowed the universalist conception to reign by default, assuming that there is only one valid way of gaining, validating and expressing true knowledge about the world. This chapter aims to unsettle those assumptions, and assert that, far from being frivolous and irresponsible on the part of the university, engaging wholeheartedly with alternative knowledge forms is a primary purpose of the institution. The epistemic question is in turn tied to those of ontology (the nature of being) and axiology (what is of value), both questions with unwarrantedly firm positions within the developmental university and in the SDGs.

Furthermore, if we assume that knowledge is universal, the task of social justice is simply to make it accessible to everybody—to

---

[1] Cultural diversity is mentioned in SDG 4.7.

redistribute it. Acknowledging there may be multiple forms of valid knowledge leads us to a different obligation, that of *recognition* rather than *redistribution*. The debate over these two principles of social justice has been vigorous over recent decades (Fraser 1995; Fraser and Honneth 2003; Honneth 2004; Taylor 1994), and has manifested itself in the field of education through the confrontation between, on the one hand, social realists advocating for working-class access to 'powerful knowledge' (mainstream Western scientific knowledge), and on the other, the inclusion of diverse epistemic and cultural traditions within schools and education systems. This chapter opens up the debate on the role of higher education in development by questioning the exclusive *redistribution* emphasis of most perspectives on the issue, and arguing for attention also to *recognition*.

The chapter starts by reviewing challenges to development, and literature around post-development and other alternatives. There is particular engagement with the ideas of Ivan Illich, as he presents a singularly radical and pertinent challenge to educational institutions. Following that, there will be a theoretical discussion about the notion of a post-development university, and consideration of some contemporary examples, along with their significant challenges in practice.

Questioning Development

One positive aspect of the instrumentalism of the developmental university is that it is discerning in terms of which kinds of instrumental influence it considers legitimate. It does not proportion its services willy-nilly in relation to demand or income received, as the entrepreneurial university does, but to a set of aims it considers to be socially just or beneficial for the nation. However, the question is then inevitably raised of whether these conceptions of justice, the ideal society and the good life are in fact justified, of how they are derived and whose vision they represent. For the most part, developmental universities have presented their work simply in relation to the concept of 'development' or benefit for national, or at times local, communities—neither of which takes us much closer to a firm or uncontroversial positioning.

As was discussed in Chapter 2, usage of the term 'development' emerged after the Second World War to describe desirable characteristics of societies focusing mainly on gross domestic product (GDP) levels, but also factors such as solid transport and communications infrastructure, good health and education indicators, reliable institutions and a stable political system, and contrasting these with the features of 'underdeveloped', 'backward' or 'Third World' countries. Needless to say, there is far from consensus as to whether these are the only, the most important, or indeed justifiable goals for a society at all. Clearly, there are a range of aspects of the mainstream conception of development that garner a very high degree of consensus: ensuring clean water supply, preventing hunger, reducing deaths from childbirth and so forth. Yet 'development' goes a long way beyond these consensual issues to involve a range of contestable ones of how we lead our lives and organise collectively. While not possible here to fully cover the extensive and complex debates around the notion of development, it is essential to sketch some of these arguments as they are so bound up with the developmental model of university.

The first problematic element is that the conception of development does not emerge from the views and values of the society in question, but is predefined and assumed to be in its interests. There is only a weak participatory element in the model, and it can be seen as 'assistentialist', delivering development to disadvantaged people, rather than genuinely involving and empowering them. Furthermore, 'development' is taken to be a largely universal trajectory, without strong contextual differentiation. (In practice, some developmental universities have positioned themselves in different ways in relation to this conception, promoting counter-hegemonic views [Almeida Filho and Coutinho 2018] or calling for a process of indigenisation [e.g. Mazrui 1975], representing something of a bridge between the developmental and post-development models.)

From the perspective of dependency theory (e.g. dos Santos 1970), the inevitable implication of adhering to this universalist conception of development—and of the university—is to lock universities and their countries into perpetual relations of subordination. Instead of the vision of free competition on a level playing field presented by the globalists, mimicry of models from the West or North can only place these institutions on the lower rungs of the ladder. It is argued by some that, more than simply entailing that some miss out on the prizes, the periphery is actually essential for the continued super-prosperity of the core, through feeding the latter cheap raw materials which it then converts into high-value products. Higher education systems can be seen to display dependency in this way, through their mimicry and deference to colonial models, as well as through their socialisation of elites with tastes and political views aligned with those of the metropole (Altbach 1977). Developmental universities on the one hand appear to be delinking and reducing economic dependence by fostering local agriculture, industry and empowering their populations; yet at the same time they are buying into the global systems of higher education and capitalism, within which they start off—and probably remain—in a subordinate position.

An alternative perspective on this issue is that the developmental university is flawed not by locking countries into relations of dependency, but in its adherence to notions of modernization that underpin both capitalist and Marxist positions. From this perspective, the developmental university has a significant blind spot in its subservience to Enlightenment conceptions of progress and epistemological underpinnings. Features such as the separation of humankind from the rest of nature, the attitude of domination and exploitation of the natural environment, patriarchy, fragmentation and specialisation of knowledge and individualist and competitive modes of learning are seen to underpin the curriculum and institutional forms of the model. Providing access to higher education for marginalised populations may represent not an equalisation of opportunities, but a form of cultural oppression, if we take a recognition rather than redistribution perspective (Oyarzun et al. 2017).

In response to these critiques, there have been some instances of creation of what we might call 'post-development' universities. These challenge hegemonic Western academic knowledge and conventional disciplines, and in some cases do away with conventional trappings of the university—disciplinary divisions, the professor-student distinction, curricula courses, diplomas and so forth—often influenced by Illich's (1971) ideas of deschooling. A number of these initiatives have been linked to claims for cultural autonomy of indigenous groups in Latin America and elsewhere (Teamey and Mandel 2014), their desire for preservation and furthering of knowledge traditions, and ensuring of an "ecology of knowledges" in the terms of Boaventura de Sousa Santos (2008). It is these forms of institution that will be analysed in this chapter.

Of course, the positions presented above express political and epistemological views that are not shared by all inside or outside universities. Yet there is an aspect of the institution that makes it inimical to any overly rigid conception of social organisation. Given the nature of enquiry discussed in the previous chapter, the unpredictability of science and evolving conceptions of self and society, the developmental university—if it is indeed a thinking and enquiring university—may in fact lead to its own undermining and possibly destruction. It is hard for any university to have a fixed, definite and unitary conception of the way society should be. In fact, one of the most valuable functions of the university is as a space for critique, whether that be of the government, of the market and transnational corporations, or what Ignatieff (2018) terms majoritarian thinking, and its non-conformism should be permitted, and indeed nurtured.

Ideas of Post-development

Like some other instances of the prefix 'post', it is not implied that post-development comes *after* development in a chronological sense—rather it is a response and a critique from within the paradigm. And as such it is predicated on and owes much to it. Indeed, it is not easy to dismiss the claim from critics of poststructuralism more broadly that in its rejection of the Enlightenment, it is affirming and manifesting one of the Enlightenment's central principles—that of critique itself.

Post-development (e.g. Sachs 1992; Escobar 1995; Rahnema and Bawtree 1997) applies to the notion of development the kinds of critiques that were applied by postcolonial theory to the colonial condition. The fundamental characteristic of these critiques is that—unlike Marxist positions that challenge inequalities within the current paradigm and put forward a blueprint for their resolution and transcendence—they question the entire conceptual edifice on which ideas of inequality and society are based. In this way, rather than determining how best to ensure the rapid development of low-income contexts so as to even out the disparities in the world order, post-development questions the very notion of development. It is not that poor contexts need to develop better, they need to step out of the whole logic of development that holds them in a subordinate position.

What, then, are the tenets of development that make it problematic? As outlined above, the notions of development that came to prominence since the Second World War are multifaceted, but are generally characterised by material wealth, extensive physical infrastructure (transport, communications etc.), urbanisation, high levels of consumption and trade, and liberal democratic institutions. In terms of social norms, it is generally assumed that developed countries require, as their means and their end, protection of individual liberties and rights, and competition and hierarchies between individuals. Development is strongly predicated on the notion of progress, that societies can endlessly improve their situation, and most prominently on the notion of economic growth—the primary myth of our times (Gudynas 2016). Finally, the accumulation that is legitimised and encouraged by the above forms of capitalist development necessarily involves exploitation of the non-human animal world and the natural environment—the side-effects of which may be seen as lamentable but ultimately necessary for 'progress' (Rist 2002).

Critiques of development from a post-development perspectives assert instead that progress is an illusion that masks hegemonic domination, and is neither inevitable nor desirable for the world's diverse populations. Development is not only a game in which the Global South and marginalised populations are destined to lose, but one whose prizes themselves are ultimately toxic: accumulation of wealth far beyond that which an individual can enjoy brings us no real benefit and only results in destruction of communities and diverse cultures.

The answer then is to divest oneself of the entire worldview of development, to cease to act within its logic, and if possible to delink from the exploitative economic system, and to live in autonomous cooperative communities. These ideas resonate with philosophies of living from various parts of the world. The notion of *buen vivir* (the Spanish translation of the Quechua term *sumak kawsay,* meaning 'good living'), is rooted in indigenous Andean thought, but has been reinvented through contemporary indigenous counter-hegemonic political movements across Latin America. Its fundamental tenet is that the good life is not one of competition for resources, and exploitation of the natural environment for endless accumulation, but a state of harmony between human beings and between the human community and the non-human environment (Brown and McCowan 2018; Olivera Rodríguez 2017; Vanhulst and Beling 2014; Villalba 2013). Ubuntu is a concept common to the Nguni Bantu peoples of southern Africa, with a literal meaning of humanity, but often explained as "I am because you are", a recognition of the self in the existence of the other. As with *buen vivir,* Ubuntu has enjoyed a contemporary *renaissance*, forming the basis for an alternative philosophy of living and of education, embracing a communal and cooperative spirit that challenges the assumptions of greed and individualism of neoliberalism (Assié-Lumumba 2017; Murove 2014).

These ideas have naturally coalesced with the defence of indigenous peoples' rights, on account of the clear divergence of their belief systems, traditions and practices from mainstream society, and the savage destruction of their ways of life and local environment through commercial interests and state intervention. Some commentators have in fact criticised post-development for being nothing more than neo-traditionalist rejection of modernity (Pieterse 2000). Nevertheless, post-development is not about the preservation of premodern lifestyles, or the romanticisation of a non-industrial state of nature, but a delinking from or transcendence of the destructive accumulation of capitalism—and thus can be a characteristic of groups within urban industrial areas, as much as rainforest dwellers or nomadic pastoralists.

Equally, it is dangerous to see the debate over post-development as pitting Western against non-Western knowledge, belief and practice. It is undeniable that the roots of dominant conceptions of development are in the European Enlightenment, and that free-market capitalism emerged in Western countries—so there is a degree to which these views do represent the West. Yet they represent only one of a range of competing currents of thought in so-called Western countries, and there is contestation within these countries between fixed and dogmatic worldviews and more open ones. Conversely, much of the most entrenched defence of capitalist development today is within non-Western countries. It is more helpful to understand these dynamics as contestation being played out in all contexts, though of course with particular histories that have been coloured by the recent historical period of European colonisation, and contemporary neocolonialism of the Global North.

Yet in this chapter, the task is not to defend the view of post-development or even provide a full account of it, and it is acknowledged that there are valid critiques and reservations about the paradigm. What the book does endorse strongly is the existence of multiple valid ways of understanding and representing the world, the injustice of marginalising and demeaning these views, and the need for education to acknowledge and be informed by those diverse perspectives. Specifically, the chapter explores how these principles might be incorporated into the idea of the university.

Post-Development and Education

Education is central to post-development thought—naturally so, on account of its attribution of the root of the problem not to material conditions and relations, but to our mental constructs, our understandings of the world, our goals and aspirations. Education is a vital cog in the machine of oppression, through its monopolisation of valued learning, through the constraints it places on thought and imagination, and through its instilling of the tastes and behaviours for entry into the appropriate level of the global capitalist system; but education is also the response, the process through which liberation can be achieved and a natural and essential part of autonomous, non-oppressive living (Skinner et al. 2016).

A seminal writer in the post-development tradition is Ivan Illich, the Austrian-born Catholic priest turned social critic, who questioned in a range of works the foundations of Western modernity, analysing in turn health, education, technology, energy and work. Illich's primary critique was that industrial societies had entered into a perverse logic that was undermining the principles on which they were built: health systems were making people ill, prisons were making people into criminals and time-saving devices were using up all our time. The new technologies of modernity were serving to dehumanise, separating people from enriching practice and from each other; in its place he advocated for 'conviviality', a recuperation of non-alienating action and relations (Illich 1973).

His book *Deschooling Society* (Illich 1971) became one of the primary educational critiques of the 20th century, advocating, in idiosyncratic prose, that society should abandon formal education altogether. Illich shared with critical sociologists of education of the time the premise that the hidden curriculum of schools served to reproduce social inequalities; but he went much further to argue that schools were bad for learning per se. All people's education, and the fabric of society itself, would be aided by the eradication of schools and the consequent flowering of learning in all spaces of society. Similar ideas have been expressed through the notion of *unschooling*, whereby children are encouraged to learn through self-directed interactions with the world, though are not necessarily synonymous with *homeschooling*, which in some instances can involve the shielding of the child from free circulation of ideas (for example in fundamentalist religious families), rather than opening her towards them.

Two contemporary writers and activists of note within the deschooling tradition are Gustavo Esteva (2007; Prakash and Esteva 2008) (whose experience with *Unitierra* will be documented in the section that follows), and Manish Jain (2001; Akomolafe and Jain 2016). Both of these writers—from their bases in Mexico and India—share Illich's basic tenets, and are critical of the common deficit view of learners (and particularly of indigenous peoples and rural populations), which leads to their exclusion from higher education institutions. However, they give greater prominence than Illich did to the forms of knowledge and learning that are being steamrollered by the mainstream education system, the local and indigenous knowledge that is being devalued and lost as communities opt *en masse* for conventional schools. This tragic loss is captured in the popular documentary *Schooling the World*, which tells the story of the negative impacts of formal schooling in the Ladakh region of northern India.

Curiously, the most prominent heir of Illich's ideas on deschooling has in fact been the libertarian right. Anarcho-capitalists, techno-entrepreneurs and Silicon Valley libertarians are just as distrustful of mainstream school systems as Marxists and left anarchists, but for quite different reasons: namely, the excessive intervention of the state in the interests of citizenship and equality, and the inability of the school system to foster innovation and creativity for the market. A range of manifestos for non-school education have emerged along those lines (e.g. Leadbetter and Wong 2010), the best-known being Sugata Mitra's 'hole in the wall' experiment, through which slum children in India taught themselves to use computers left unattended on the side of the street. Manifestations in higher education have been discussed in Chapter 5 in the context of unbundling, with the emergence of MOOCs, use of digital technology, micro-credentials and alternatives to university study (such as Uncollege and the Thiel Fellowships) providing potential threats to the continuing dominance of the university as an institution of higher learning.

These forms of deschooling, however, disassociate themselves from the means of traditional schooling, but without providing an alternative vision of the ends. They are either based on an individualist or family based conception of good and eschew collective goals, or buy into the forms of endless progress based on predatory capitalism outlined above. Instead, this chapter will outline ideas and experiences of deschooling at the higher education level adhering to principles of social justice, recognition of diversity and ecological protection.

Towards the Post-Development University

Chapter 4 painted a picture of the developmental university, an institution designed to foster development for the benefit of all in society, reduce poverty and enhance well-being. The developmental university is working for a vision that is a far cry from the rampant and destructive capitalism against which post-development rails. Yet it does share some fundamental assumptions in terms of 'progress', universal (Western) knowledge, the scientific method, the material basis of well-being and the relegation of the cultural and spiritual to the sphere of the decorative. This section will outline a model of a very different kind of university, one that departs in some fundamental ways from mainstream models (although does not depart from all Enlightenment ideals).

Education is generally seen as having value outside of itself, in projecting forward on to a desired future life for an individual, or for a society. So, for example, it is seen to equip children with the basic literacy, factual knowledge, mathematic and scientific skills that they will need in their coming lives; it equips young adults with the vocational skills needed in subsequent work. This is what we might call the *projective* role of education, being primarily instrumental and forward looking. However, there is another way to understand education, though less commonly invoked—what we might call the *expressive* function. Here, we see education not as operating to bring about another state of affairs, but as a sphere of society in its own right, and as a current instantiation of the values or states of being it endorses (discussed in Chapter 8 in relation to embodiment). So, in a projective sense, education might be tasked with creating engaged citizens who will participate constructively in the civic life of their polities, to vote, campaign and engage in public deliberation. Yet we can also see this civic dimension as occurring during the experience of education itself—in the interactions with other students, in the degree of respect and recognition accorded to diverse groups, and so forth.[2]

The developmental university works very much in the projective mode. It is an institution that has a predominantly instrumental vein, aiming to transform the outside society from an under-developed into a developed one. However, the post-development university is as much an expressive as a projective venture. While it might have designs on

---

[2]This distinction has been drawn in previous work between education *through*, as opposed to *about* or *for* democracy etc., and separation and harmony modes, as opposed to the unification mode of proximity [McCowan 2009].

bringing a transformation in the outside society, it is just as interested in embodying its principles, in creating a space in which those ideas and values can manifest themselves, survive and flourish.

So what are those principles? There are two primary characteristics of what I will here call the post-development university: first, *deinstitutionalisation*, the divestiture of the trappings of institutional forms of education; and second, *ecology of knowledges*, the creation of a plural epistemological and ontological space.

Deinstitutionalisation

Illich's primary insight is that the institutions that human communities establish to promote valued goods can with time serve to undermine or even destroy them. In the field of education, he presented a damning critique of school systems, arguing that they served in fact to obstruct learning, and disempower individuals from engaging in meaningful learning in every part of their lives and through the whole length of the life course. He pointed to major impediments: educational professionals (reliance on teachers for learning, and discrediting other sources of learning in society); diploma disease (obsessive thirst for qualifications, with meaningful learning subordinated to teaching to the test); the hidden curriculum (the set of rituals, norms and expectations that are unconsciously absorbed into students while at school—for example competition rather than cooperation); and finally, the self-reproductive cycle (the endless projection of the school system into the future, given its essential status in conferring opportunities for work and further study).

Deinstitutionalisation, therefore, is the resuscitation of learning from the rotting structure of the school and university system. In relation to the four elements above, it aims firstly to free education from dependence on certified professional teachers, allowing people to learn by themselves, and to learn from a range of different people. This position goes beyond that of Freire (1970), who aimed to transform the role of the teacher to one based on horizontal and respectful dialogue, to challenge the very existence of teacher. This is not to say that teaching vanishes, or there is no such thing as knowledge, experience or expertise that people can pass to each other. It is that this role moves beyond the teachers employed by schools to involve a wide range of people in society. Clearly this aim is problematic in the context of a 'university', which would appear by definition to have some distinctive space in relation to society, and therefore a discrete body of staff associated with it. As will be seen more concretely in the following section, experimentation with deschooled universities does often involve a particular set of 'teachers', but not ones with recognised status or teaching qualifications, or alternatively a horizontal community of learners who teach each other. In distance education, such as online learning through MOOCs, the possibilities of teacherless interactions are even greater. Illich's early proposals for peer networks, through directories of expertise, were early precursors of these ideas, though being in the pre-internet age were severely hampered by lack of appropriate technology.

Second, deinstitutionalised universities operate outside qualifications frameworks. The most obvious manifestation—and with the most radical implications in terms of the role of the institution—is in cases in which no certification through a degree or other qualification is provided for the learning acquired. But this move also involves a range of other changes: removal of admissions requirements, meaning that all candidates regardless of their prior performance or characteristics can enter the institution; removal or reformulation of course structure, modules, organisation and sequencing of material; changes to structures of governance, particularly removal of hierarchical management; and exiting from national systems of higher education. This process ultimately leads to autonomous institutions, linking in with the broader movement of autonomy as an aspiration in anarchist thought, and in indigenous and other social movements.

The hidden curriculum of mainstream schooling is also challenged—particularly the emphasis on competition and individual performance, as well as conformity to society's norms of capitalism, patriarchy and state authority. Here we see one of the paradoxes of deinstitutionalisation, in that clearly we cannot move from something to nothing when it comes to the hidden curriculum—one hidden curriculum will inevitably be replaced by another—though the aspiration among proponents is that it will be a more inclusive, egalitarian and emancipatory one.

Finally, there is the cycle of self-perpetuation. With the exchange value of education removed by delinking from national systems and qualifications frameworks, the perverse logic that currently forces parents into sending their children to schools they do not value will no longer hold sway. The forms of education in existence will only be maintained if they can continue to provide a meaningful learning experience for those involved. Cycles of social reproduction through education are also disrupted, since these educational experiences are also free-of-charge, and therefore cannot be rationed on the basis of individual or family wealth.

These ideas have been touched on in the discussion of deinstitutionalisation forms of unbundling in Chapter 5—involving breaking down the boundary between educational institutions and society, the emergence of non-commodified educational interactions through the networking and sharing potential of new technologies. While the post-development university makes the most of these possibilities of digital technologies, it is also wary of their dehumanising and commodifying force in the contemporary world, and encourages face-to-face interaction and engagement with the natural world.

Many readers will display incredulity at these moves, which in many ways signal the end of 'education' as we commonly refer to it. And with good reason: it is exactly this end which is desired by Illich and his followers. Yet it is important to point out that deinstitutionalisation is not a permanent process, but a cycle. When the above transformations take place, a new form of institutionalised learning is likely to be created, one which with time will start to ossify and display the same kinds of failings and contradictions as the previous one, and which in turn will need to be replaced. Furthermore, it might be asked why these ventures call themselves universities at all—rather than adult learning, community learning or some other non-institutional term. Many do not in fact, but those that retain the term university are doing so in a subversive way—aiming to challenge the way we conventionally see educational institutions, and valued learning spaces.

Ecology of Knowledges

Post-development aims to decentre the single narrative of the means and ends of development, and replace it not with another single narrative, but with a multiplicity of perspectives. In the sphere of higher education, this aim translates to the highly radical agenda of questioning the knowledge of the academy. The knowledge that is currently in the mainstream of universities around the world (with surprisingly little diversity throughout all of the global regions) is largely the Western curriculum and knowledge forms—though it must be remembered that is what is conventionally called 'Western' has drawn substantially from other world regions, most directly from North Africa, the Middle East and South Asia. This knowledge tradition is dominated by natural sciences following the empirical scientific method, but also includes arts and humanities with very different orientations. The post-development university does not deny or challenge the validity of Western mainstream academic knowledge, what it questions is its monopoly on valid knowledge. It aims to provide a space for the learning of, and enquiry within diverse knowledge traditions, being respectful to each of them, and enriching all of them (including Western knowledge) through contact with the other.

The term *ecology of knowledges* has been popularised by Portuguese sociologist Boaventura de Sousa Santos (2014), in his critique of 'abyssal thinking' and the dominant epistemology based on scientific thought. Nevertheless, the underpinning ideas are common to a number of critiques and proposals made by social theorists and educationists over the past half century, as well as the actions and initiatives of indigenous and other social movements. Some institutions in Latin America have adopted the name 'pluriversity' instead of 'university', to indicate this epistemic pluralism, for example Amawtay Wasi in Ecuador.

It is not merely a question of the stores of valuable information held in the collective memory of indigenous groups. Often, statements are made about the importance of gathering local knowledge on the properties of plants, of traditional irrigation or procedures for avoiding rising water levels: however, for the most part these are not alternative knowledge systems, but isolated facts and strategies that are then incorporated into the Western knowledge system, while the latter remains basically intact. Instead, what is required here is a place for the fundamentally different world views, and forms of apprehending reality existent across different cultures. There must be room for differences of ontology—about diverse ways of understanding the fundamental nature of the universe, humanity and society—and also epistemology—the ways in which knowledge is generated and acquired.

An ecology of knowledges, and a *dialogue* of knowledges, in practice can occur through an institution containing within itself a range of different knowledge traditions, residing in its students, its teachers and its practices; or it can focus on a single knowledge tradition, for example that of a specific indigenous group. The latter also counts as a form of ecology of knowledges, given the inevitable presence of mainstream Western knowledge in all spheres of our societies, and the consequent movement between the alternative and the mainstream form. Dialogue of knowledges must involve epistemological openness, and not the replacement of one dogma with another. It also aims for intercultural understanding, trying to foster recognition and engagement between cultures, rather than reinforcing boundaries between them.

There are a number of practical implications of the move towards an ecology of knowledges. First is linguistic diversity: it is inevitable that the enabling of diversity of knowledge and cultural traditions is predicated on diversity of language, given the close relationship between the two. It hardly needs to be said that the world is passing through a process of linguistic homogenisation, with increasing usage of English throughout the world, and loss of smaller languages in favour of national and international languages in many countries. Second, this movement involves a challenge to the traditional disciplinary divisions. In fact, these challenges are already evident even within mainstream Western institutions, as interdisciplinary, or even transdisciplinary work has become increasingly valued as a way of solving complex societal issues. In the case of the post-development university, the disciplines are challenged not only for instrumental reasons, but because of their rooting in a specific cultural tradition, and the influence that these divisions have on our modes of thought.

Other challenges to the curriculum correspond to the process that in some places has been termed *decolonisation*—with a long trajectory of debate in Latin America, and a strong recent emergence in South Africa in the context of the #Rhodesmustfall campaign. Despite the significant increase in the numbers and proportion of black students in higher education since the fall of Apartheid in 1994, the staff body has been slow to change, and the curriculum remains rooted in Eurocentrism and a Western epistemology and worldview (Posholi 2017; Mbembe 2016).

The account given thus far—and the cases explored below—focus very much on the teaching aspect of higher education, and it is true that most alternative higher education institutions do not engage with the formal elite forms of funded research and publication. Nevertheless, they are strongly engaged in research in the broader sense of enquiry and scholarship, very often integrated together with the teaching dimension—both for facilitators and students—with a strong dimension of community engagement as well, integrated with the other elements.

This section has treated separately the characteristics of deinstitutionalisation and ecology of knowledges, but to what extent are they really separate, or alternatively interrelated and interdependent? It is certainly possible to have one without the other, or at least a predominance of one. The Open University of Chile, for example, which I visited in 2011, displayed deinstitutionalisation without an ecology of knowledges. Housed in unused space in a downtown office block in Santiago, it aimed to open up higher learning to all, without the barriers of entrance exams and fees, and without reliance on rigid course structures and qualifications frameworks. Yet it was not as concerned with dislodging epistemic hegemonies. On the other hand, many of the initiatives for inclusion of indigenous peoples in higher education globally have provided space for indigenous languages, culture and knowledge traditions, while retaining the fundamental features of traditional institutions (Mato 2018).

Nevertheless, the two dynamics are mutually reinforcing. There is, unsurprisingly, a degree of consonance between the knowledge forms present in the Western university and the institutional forms supporting them: divisions between levels of study, distinctions between students, lecturers, managers and non-academic staff, boundaries between disciplinary areas and between university and society reflect deeper conceptions of learning, enquiry and knowledge. A loosening of institutional structures can facilitate the emergence of different forms of knowing; likewise, the presence of alternative ontologies and epistemologies makes more meaningful the existence of alternative institutional structures.

Finally, it is important to emphasise that in addition to these two primary characteristics of deinstitutionalisation and ecology of knowledges, the post-development university also adheres to the general principles of avoiding exploitation of human populations and of the natural environment. So it shares some elements with the developmental university, though departs from it in its openness to multiple conceptions of development and forms of knowledge.

From Theory to Practice

The above account has said a fair amount about what the post-development university is not, and traced only the broad contours of what it is. To a large degree this is because it can manifest itself in many different forms, and is formed through particular acts of experimentation in practice. This section will give examples of how these ideas have become concrete.

As stated above, there are two main types of expression of the post-development university: those focused on a specific knowledge tradition, and those adhering to none or providing a multiplicity of traditions. Both provide a counterpoint to the conventional university, with particular challenges—in the case of the former of slipping into another orthodoxy, and of the latter of establishing the basis of selection for the curriculum. There are also initiatives that focus more on deinstitutionalisation and others on ecology of knowledges. This section will explore two initiatives that position themselves in distinct ways in relation to these tensions, one located in Mexico, the *Universidad de La*

Tierra (University of the Land, *Unitierra* for short), and one in Brazil, the *Instituto dos Conhecimentos Indígenas e Pesquisa do Rio Negro* (Rio Negro Institute of Indigenous Knowledge and Research).

Unitierra

In 2015 I made the journey to Oaxaca to visit the visionary social commentator and educationist Gustavo Esteva at his anti-institution institution of higher learning. This university, famously, has no lecturers, no courses, no admissions requirements and gives out no diplomas at the end. Unitierra is the archetypal deinstitutionalisation university, in keeping with Esteva's close association with Illich during the latter's lifetime and lengthy stay in Mexico as founder of the Intercultural Documentation Centre (Centro Intercultural de Documentación, CIDOC). The initiative is part of a flowering of autonomous educational ventures in the wake of the Zapatista uprising of indigenous peoples in the 1990s, and although it has no formal link to the Zapatista movement, shares many of its goals in defending an autonomous space for Mexico's indigenous population against the onslaught of dehumanising and exploitative industrial development. The university has no formal recognition from the state, receives no state funding, and charges no fees from students: it relies primarily on voluntary contributions of time, and small amounts of income from international exchange visits and university partnerships. It has inspired similar experiences in Chiapas, Mexico and California.[3]

Unitierra accepts as students all adults who have a desire to learn and engage in a project for community development. They thereby join the community of learners in areas as diverse as philosophy, architecture, video editing and urban gardening. There are two main modes of learning: mentoring, through which students are paired up with an experienced practitioner, and collective discussions, held in the house used by the university in the city of Oaxaca. For example, during my visit, a discussion was held on the alternative currency known as *tumin*,

---

[3] http://enlivenedlearning.com/2013/01/16/visiting-another-unitierra-in-san-cristobal-chiapas/.

with the university hosting a number of political activists and representatives of indigenous communities who were experimenting with the currency. Learning also takes place seamlessly within life in the community:

> Our challenge thus became to find ways to regenerate community in the city, to create a social fabric in which we all, at any age, would be able to learn and in which every kind of apprenticeship might flourish. (Esteva 2007)

Unitierra makes a point of not issuing diplomas or degrees (except for those it emits satirically to community elders with no formal education in recognition of their wisdom and expertise): learning is its own reward, and requires no formal emblem.

Unitierra is expertly documented in the short film made by educators and activists Kelly Teamey and Udi Mandel,[4] along with similar examples of autonomous higher education experiences Red Crow Community College and Swaraj University. The latter initiative, founded by Manish Jain and colleagues, shares many features of Unitierra, having no admissions requirements and emitting no diplomas, and promoting self-directed learning, the recuperation of linguistic and cultural traditions, ecological awareness and green entrepreneurship.

The Rio Negro Institute of Indigenous Knowledge and Research

The challenges of being within or outside the mainstream have been addressed in a rather different way by the indigenous peoples of a remote region of the Brazilian Amazon near the Colombian border.[5] A partnership between the Federation of Indigenous Organisations of

---

[4] http://enlivenedlearning.com.

[5] This section draws on research carried out by the author in 2014 as part of the research project "Indigenous education: innovation, teacher participation and assessment".

the Rio Negro[6] and the NGO Socio-Environmental Institute[7] led to the development of a project for an institute of higher learning in the region (FOIRN/ISA 2013). This project grew out of the successes of indigenous schools in the region and the increasing number of young people completing the secondary level, accompanied by concerns about their being forced to move to the state capital Manaus, and being drawn permanently away from their communities, their culture and language.

> So what was thought of was a form of advanced study that would be in sync with the philosophy of the indigenous people.... Often, when their children go to study, sometimes they don't manage to finish, other times they finish but when they come back they end up dislocated – it seems they've lost their direction: they don't feel from the community any more, but neither do they feel part of the society outside. So this is a concern of many of the community leaders, the parents. (Interview with local NGO worker)

This institution is still in the process of being established—drawing on a series of collaborative meetings dating back to 2009—and at time of writing is struggling for survival on account of the political crisis caused by the impeachment of President Roussef, and the 2018 election of Bolsonaro. Nevertheless, it merits attention as it provides a distinct model of how to reconcile autonomy with mainstream support. The institution aims to break with the conventional disciplinary categories of mainstream institutions by orienting work in four axes: "Stewardship of the world" (broadly covering environmental and natural sciences), "Narratives of origin, routes of transformation" (broadly covering arts and humanities), "Indigenous economy" and "Development, and territorial and project management". These wide-ranging subject areas are delivered partly in Portuguese and partly in one of three indigenous languages: Baniwa, Tukano and Nheengatú. The lecturers of the institution are a combination of community elders with little in the way of formal qualifications, and academics with conventional postgraduate

---

[6]Federação das Organizações Indígenas do Rio Negro.
[7]Instituto Socioambiental.

degrees—thus beginning to challenge conventional notions of academic 'expert', critiqued by Illich (1971). It is also based in multiple locations: partly in the town that serves as a regional capital—São Gabriel da Cachoeira—and partly at a distance in the small communities dotted along the Rio Negro and tributaries. This blended mode aids in avoiding brain drain from the communities to the cities. The alternative curriculum also serves to equip young people to work in the communities, rather than exclusively in the urban space, but also enables them to interact effectively in the environment of mainstream society. Beyond its teaching function, it also aims to provide a distinctive contribution to knowledge:

> [T]his university starts with a fantastic approach of deconstruction that is 'other knowledges', beyond Western, scientific knowledge – it already comes with this other richness. So in my opinion it's also a scientific experience of great quality. An inclusive science, of other points of view....
> (Interview with local NGO worker)

In order to realise this vision, the Institute has adopted an institutional form termed "social organisation": with this status it can receive state funding, but is not a federal or state level higher education institution, and therefore does not need to comply with all forms of legislation and regulation around curriculum structure, accreditation and management, features that threatened the 'thematic' universities discussed in Chapter 4. Nevertheless, it has chosen not to opt entirely out of the qualification frameworks: initially, the courses will lead to the qualification of *tecnólogo*, broadly equivalent to an *associate* or *foundation* degree rather than a full bachelors.

These are two of many alternative institutions around the world, with different emphases, whether environmental (Barefoot College in India, Earth University in Costa Rica, Schumacher College in the UK), indigenous (UNIBOL in Bolivia, URACCAN in Nicaragua), health (University of Global Health Equity in Rwanda), peace-building (University for Peace in Costa Rica), social movements, co-operativism and new forms of political organisation (Popular University of Social Movements [international], the Lincoln Social Science Centre in the UK), as well as various popular universities and folk high schools (Stromquist and da Costa 2017). The 'Ecoversities Network'[8] has now been set up to foster stronger links and mutual support between many of these institutions. Each of these have different relationships to national systems of higher education, and challenge to different degrees what Vandana Shiva (1993) calls the "monoculture of the mind".

Challenges of Delinking

The fundamental challenges facing these initiatives are resources and recognition. While they are relatively cheap compared to fully fledged higher education institutions, buildings and staff time are required even for the most basic activities. Gaining a steady source of income normally requires state funding or a wealthy benefactor—either of which would undermine the institutions' autonomy—or alternatively charging fees directly to students, which would restrict access and alter the nature of the relationship between learners and the learning environment. Beyond resources, the initiatives also need recognition: here used not in the sense of cultural justice, as a counterpoint to redistribution (Taylor 1994), but in a more general sense of public acknowledgement of its validity. Recognition is needed from prospective students, to ensure that they will be motivated to come to the institution to learn in the first place, and of the students' learning at the end of the day so as to provide them with opportunities in employment and other spheres of life. As seen above, many of these institutions function entirely outside the qualifications system and provide no certification for their graduates. This means that their students are effectively opting out of most forms of valued salaried employment—a significant sacrifice for all other than those who are already financially secure, or who are without any employment prospects at all.

The challenges provide an inevitable incentive for alternative initiatives to seek resources and recognition as a way of protecting the

---

[8] http://ecoversities.org/.

viability of the venture. The problem is that resources and recognition if pursued too vigorously can end up undermining the initial project; the embodiment of the values of epistemological pluralism, autonomy and egalitarianism can be threatened by encroaching influence from external funders and the modifications and compromises needed to fit in with national systems and qualifications frameworks.

Post-development has been criticised for its romanticism (Pieterse 2000). While there may be some influence from the Romantic movement of the eighteenth and nineteenth centuries, it is not romantic in the sense of being naïvely idealistic. What is being proposed here is not a return to a Garden of Eden existence of innocence at one with nature: there is no winding back the clock to before modernity. But recognition of the realities of the contemporary world and its historical conditioning does not imply resignation to its current *modus operandi*. These initiatives also show us that, despite the significant barriers to operating within a hostile environment, alternatives are possible.

The paradox facing these initiatives is that facing all social experimentation and innovation: how is it possible to create a democratic, inclusive and egalitarian space within an anti-democratic, exclusive and unequal society? And yet, how is the anti-democratic, exclusive and unequal society to change if we do not create alternatives? The viability of this kind of university in the contemporary world is indeed highly questionable. The hegemony of the mainstream system and its apparatus of legitimisation and self-perpetuation is strong enough to marginalise all other attempts to near irrelevance. Even those strongly critical of the mainstream system generally find the thought of a university without degrees to be little more than a humorous thought experiment.

But given the obvious shortcomings of our models of development and higher education's contributions to them, action is needed, both within the mainstream and outside. While autonomous institutions like the ones outlined in this chapter may to date have had little effect on the core higher education systems, their very existence is crucial for showing that alternatives are possible and for understanding how they work in practice. Ultimately, all institutions need to take these ideas on board and look beyond the SDGs. For those doubtful of the possibility of reconciling the 3 Ps—people, planet and profit—given capitalism's underlying logic of accumulation through exploitation of nature and workers, a fundamentally different paradigm is needed for sustainable development to be achieved. Higher education institutions cannot bring about this new paradigm and new society on their own, but through their prefigurative function, do play a crucial role in carving out a space for alternative vision and practice.

References

Akomolafe, B., & Jain, M. (2016). Practitioner perspective: This revolution will not be schooled—How we are collectively improvising a 'new story' about learning. In A. Skinner, M. Baillie Smith, E. J. Brown, & T. Troll (Eds.), *Education, learning and the transformation of development*. Oxford: Routledge.

Almeida Filho, N., & Coutinho, D. (2018). Counter hegemonic higher education in a remote coastal region of Brazil: The Federal University of Southern Bahia as a case-study. In R. Aman & T. Ireland (Eds.), *Educational alternatives in Latin America: New modes of counter hegemonic learning*. London: Palgrave Macillan.

Altbach, P. G. (1977). Servitude of the mind? Education, dependency and neo-colonialism. *Teachers College Record, 79*(2), 187–204.

Assié-Lumumba, N. D. T. (2017). The Ubuntu paradigm and comparative and international education: Epistemological challenges and opportunities in our field. *Comparative Education Review, 61*(1), 1–21.

Brown, E., & McCowan, T. (2018). Buen vivir: Reimagining education and shifting paradigms (Forum). *Compare, 48*(2), 317–323.

dos Santos, T. (1970). The structure of dependency. *American Economic Review, 60*(2), 231.

Escobar, A. (1995). *Encountering development: The making and unmaking of the Third World*. Princeton: Princeton University Press.

Esteva, G. (2007, November 7). Reclaiming our freedom to learn. *Yes Magazine*.

FOIRN/ISA. (2013). *Instituto dos Conhecimentos Indígenas e Pesquisa do Rio Negro: Formação e Pesquisa Avançada*. São Gabriel da Cachoeira: FOIRN/ISA.

Fraser, N. (1995). Recognition or redistribution? A critical reading of Iris Young's Justice and the Politics of Difference. *Journal of Political Philosophy, 3*(2), 166–180.

Fraser, N., & Honneth, A. (2003). *Redistribution or recognition? A political-philosophical exchange.* London: Verso.

Freire, P. (1970). *Pedagogy of the Oppressed.* London: Penguin Books.

Gudynas, E. (2016). Beyond varieties of development: Disputes and alternatives. *Third World Quarterly, 37*(4), 721–732.

Honneth, A. (2004). Recognition and justice outline of a plural theory of justice. *Acta Sociologica, 47*(4), 351–364.

Ignatieff, M. (2018). *Academic freedom and the future of Europe* (Centre for Global Higher Education Working Paper No. 40). Available at https://www.researchcghe.org/publications/working-paper/academic-freedom-and-the-future-of-europe/. Accessed 5 October 2018.

Illich, I. (1971). *Deschooling society.* New York: Harper & Row.

Illich, I. (1973). *Tools for conviviality.* New York: Harper & Row.

Jain, M. (Ed.). (2001). *Unfolding learning societies: Deepening the dialogues.* Vimukt Shiksha Series. Shikshantar: The Peoples' Institute for Rethinking Education and Development. Available at http://shikshantar.org/sites/default/files/PDF/learningsocieties2.pdf.

Leadbetter, C., & Wong, A. (2010). *Learning from the extremes.* San Jose: Cisco.

Mato, D. (2018). Educación superior y pueblos indígenas: experiencias, estudios y debates en América Latina y otras regiones del mundo. *Revista del Cisen Tramas/Maepova, 6*(2), 41–65.

Mazrui, A. A. (1975). The African university as a multinational corporation: Problems of penetration and dependency. *Harvard Educational Review, 45,* 198.

Mbembe, A. J. (2016). Decolonizing the university: New directions. *Arts & Humanities in Higher Education, 15*(1), 29–45.

McCowan, T. (2009). *Rethinking citizenship education: A curriculum for participatory democracy.* London: Continuum.

Murove, M. F. (2014). Ubuntu. *Diogenes, 59*(3–4), 36–47.

Olivera Rodríguez, I. (2017). Las potencialidades del proyecto educativo de la Universidad Veracruzana Intercultural: una crítica al desarrollo desde la noción del Buen vivir. *Revista de la Educación Superior, 46*(181), 19–35.

Oyarzun, J. M., Perales Franco, C., & McCowan, T. (2017). Indigenous higher education in Mexico and Brazil: Between redistribution and recognition. *Compare, 47*(6), 852–871.

Pieterse, J. N. (2000). After post-development. *Third World Quarterly, 21*(2), 175–191.

Posholi, L. (2017, September 5). *Decolonising the curriculum in South African universities*. Presentation at the UKFIET conference, Oxford.

Prakash, M. S., & Esteva, G. (2008). *Escaping education: Living as learning in grassroots cultures* (2nd ed.). New York: Peter Lang.

Rahnema, M., & Bawtree, V. (Eds.). (1997). *The post-development reader*. London: Zed.

Rist, G. (2002). *The history of development: From western origins to global faith*. London: Zed Books.

Sachs, W. (1992). *The development dictionary: A guide to knowledge as power*. London: Zed.

Santos, B. de S. (Ed.). (2008). *Another knowledge is possible: Beyond northern epistemologies*. London: Verso.

Santos, B. de S. (2014). *Epistemologies of the South: justice against epistemicide*. New York: Routledge.

Shiva, V. (1993). *Monocultures of the mind*. London: Zed Books.

Skinner, A., Baillie Smith, M., Brown, E. J., & Troll, T. (Eds.). (2016). *Education, learning and the transformation of development*. Oxford: Routledge.

Stromquist, N. P., & da Costa, R. B. (2017). Popular universities: An alternative vision for lifelong learning in Europe. *International Review of Education, 63*, 725–744.

Taylor, C. (1994). *Multiculturalism: Examining the politics of recognition*. Princeton, NJ: Princeton University Press.

Teamey, K., & Mandel, U. (2014, October 24). *Challenging the modern university, perspectives and practices from indigenous communities, social and ecological movements*. Paper presented at the Forum on Higher Education and International Development, London.

Vanhulst, J., & Beling, A. E. (2014). Buen vivir: Emergent discourse within or beyond sustainable development? *Ecological Economics, 101*, 54–63.

Villalba, U. (2013). Buen vivir vs development: A paradigm shift in the Andes? *Third World Quarterly, 34*(8), 1427–1442.

11

Back from the Brink

It is no longer overly dramatic to state that as a species we are on the brink of cataclysm. According to the report of the Intergovernmental Panel on Climate Change (IPCC 2018), we have already caused 1 °C of global warming since pre-industrial levels, with the figure likely to rise to 1.5 °C between 2030 and 2052. To avoid a temperature rise of 2 °C, with even more devastating effects (falling disproportionately on the poorest across the world), we will need to reduce fossil fuel use by 45% from 2010 levels by 2030 and move entirely to renewables by 2050. Despite the growth of green energies, this target is very unlikely to be met, in large part due to the active blocking of progressive policies by fossil fuel industry lobby groups (Klein 2015). The likelihood is that the temperature rise will be considerably greater than 2 °C. Even for those sceptical that the temperature increases have human causes, there is plenty of other evidence of the disastrous nature of our impact on the natural environment: the flooding of the oceans with plastics that are entering into the food chain, air pollution in major cities that has now been shown to be causing cognitive damage, poisoning of waterways through fertilizer use, continuing destruction of ancient forests, and rapid extinctions of plant and animal species. David Orr opened

Chapter 1 of *Earth in Mind* (originally published in 1994) with the following passage:

> If today is a typical day on planet Earth, we will lose 116 square miles of rain forest, or about an acre a second. We will lose another 72 square miles to encroaching deserts, the results of human mismanagement and overpopulation. We will lose 40 to 250 species, and no one knows if the number is 40 or 250. Today the human population will increase by 250,000. And today we will add 2,700 tons of chlorofluorocarbons and 15 million tonnes of carbon dioxide to the atmosphere. Tonight the earth will be a little hotter, its waters more acidic and the fabric of life more threadbare. (p. 7)

A quarter of a century later, these problems are no less acute, and new ones have appeared. Even if we can postpone environmental cataclysm in the short term, there will undoubtedly be intensified conflicts over resources over the coming decades, leading to unimaginable human suffering and destruction. Cormac McCarthy's apocalyptic vision in *The Road* is now a real possibility.

As George Monbiot (2018) has recently argued in relation to a campaign for major UK coffee chains to use recyclable cups, this is not a matter that can be solved only through more responsible consumer choices. For it is born of the entire paradigm of consumerism, a world view, a way of life—bolstered by corporate interests. In a global order that is progressively incorporating all countries and all cultural groups within itself, we are caught in what is no less than an addiction to acquisition of products and experiences at a level that—even for the restricted percentage of the global population that can currently enjoy them to the full—is entirely unviable. The world needs new technology for sure, in order to be more efficient in production and use of food, generation of energy, transport and so forth. Yet it needs much more than that, a veritable shift of perspective in life.

The Sustainable Development Goals (SDGs) are not a complete or final answer to the challenges facing humanity. In many ways they are not demanding enough, and display the kinds of compromises that must be made in order to ensure universal agreement among United

Nations member countries. They are far too shy in challenging the accumulative capitalist paradigm that has contributed to our woes. They also have a range of blind spots in relation to culture, language, identity and alternative forms of knowledge. Nevertheless, it would be obstinacy to claim that nothing is better than something. For all their flaws, the SDGs do represent a step in the right direction, given the suicidal path we are currently on. The intermediate goals in relation to protection of the natural environment, upholding of basic rights and attention to equality, peace and cooperation are moving us in the right direction.

The university has a key role to play in this enterprise. It is often viewed as a kind of workshop for solutions to these technological challenges, busily bringing into being the next form of wind turbine or more efficient jet engine that can alleviate negative human impacts. Without doubt this is a critical function. Yet the role of universities goes far beyond this. It is not only a calculating machine for generating answers to problems that are facing us, but a creator of new ideas, of new forms of thinking that have not yet been experienced. Our problem is not just that we do not have the right answers, but that we do not have the right questions.

The Argument in a Nutshell

The inclusion of higher education in the SDGs marks a significant turning point in the views of higher education in the international development community—supranational agencies, national governments and international NGOs. The sector is no longer viewed as a fossilised and wasteful entrench of the elites, siphoning money away from primary schooling for the poor, but as a dynamic force for spurring development in the interests of all. The guarantees of access included in the goals are weak, but do at least represent an acknowledgement of the importance of this level of education. Higher education also has an important instrumental role in the conceptualisation of the SDGs.

The basis of this proposed new role is the 'developmental university', a model of institution that—in contrast to medieval, Humboldtian and entrepreneurial versions—is oriented towards service to society, and particularly the most disadvantaged populations, bringing tangible impact on their lives through the application of knowledge. It is an institution that can extend quality education beyond the elites, and engage in research and community engagement for the public good.

Yet tragically, higher education internationally is not currently able to deliver on these promises. In the first place, admission is still restricted, despite rapid expansion of systems in recent decades, and those lower income students who do manage to gain access are usually confined to lower prestige institutions. Higher education does not yet represent an equalising factor in terms of social and economic opportunities, and is not providing opportunities for all to develop their interests, talents and wisdom. The poor quality of many higher education institutions prevents them from carrying out their functions adequately and having a substantial impact on outside communities: these problems are caused primarily by lack of resources, but also by issues of governance and pedagogical culture. Furthermore, the incentives of commercialisation of the sector encourage rapid increases in enrolments without corresponding investments—market failure being caused by demand for credentials even in the absence of high quality learning. Status competition on the other hand encourages institutions to be more exclusive in their intake and to focus their energies on high level academic research and publications, rather than engagement with local communities and developmental impact.

While international development agencies are aware of these issues, the policies they have adopted to date have done little to address them. Investments have been insufficient, as in all levels of education. Historically, higher education has had a large proportion of educational aid, but most has gone towards funding scholarships in the donor countries: this trend would appear to be reinforced by SDG 4.b, which advocates for "substantially expand[ing] globally the number of scholarships available to developing countries". While in some cases this has led to much-needed capacity building, it has also weakened the lower income countries' higher education systems, with many of the talented students obtaining scholarships never returning to their countries of origin. Little has been invested in strengthening low- and middle-income country higher education systems, and certainly not enough to make up for the ravages of the structural adjustment programmes in the 1980 and 1990s. Those investments that are made often run counter to the principles of the developmental university, for example concentrating research activity in a few elite institutions, advocating narrow forms of skills-based employability without attention to broader human development, or encouraging online education in the absence of adequate connectivity and learner autonomy. The emphasis on international partnerships by various agencies such as Department for International Development (DFID), the British Council and the US philanthropic foundations is well directed: North-South and South-South partnerships if non-hierarchical and based on mutual benefit can be fruitful, and draw on the positive histories of internationalisation in HE (Sehoole and Knight 2013; Stephens 2009), linking in with the third of Marginson's (2011) 'imaginaries', the globally networked higher education space. Yet, other more commercial forms of internationalisation, such as the establishment of branch campuses of Northern universities in the Global South, and elite student mobility to established centres, can serve to undermine domestic systems, and lead to cultural homogenisation.

Attempts to find solutions that are 'affordable' and efficient are of course laudable, but there is little point in enabling access to higher education for students—and safeguarding the viability of the higher education sector as a whole—if the overarching purpose and potential for impact of the institution are whittled away. The implications, therefore, are that—if international agencies and national governments are indeed serious about ensuring the prosperity of their populations and achieving sustainable development—then a new form of university and a new form of higher education policy are needed, ones which will guarantee access for all groups in society, will provide them with a broad curriculum with adequate conditions for learning, will engage strongly with external communities and share the fruits of their knowledge for the benefit of all.

Yet the above vision assumes that the model of development embodied in the SDGs (liberal democratic institutions, capitalist economy with regulation to ensure some redistribution and upholding of basic human rights) is right and is necessary. In fact, it is highly likely that the contradictions in such a model make it unviable in the future, and that even a regulated form of capitalism will make environmental disaster and human conflict on a global scale inevitable. For the viable long-term prospering of humanity, a new model is needed, one that is not based on accumulation and consumption, but instead on frugality and sharing. The university, therefore, cannot act as a blind workhorse for this vision of development, but needs to provide constant scrutiny and critique of the model, and imagine alternatives.

Towards the Developmental University

In developing these ideas, this book has utilised the frame of value, function and interaction. We can understand the nature of the university, in this way, by identifying the set of values on which it is based (e.g. nation building, employability, the quest for truth, social justice etc.), the functions it carries out (teaching undergraduates, public communication of science, curating historical archives) and the interactions it has with society (inward and outward movement of ideas and actors). The combination of these factors determines the kind of institution it is and the way it impacts on society.

The frame has been used primarily in an analytical, rather than a normative, way, yet there are normative implications. Universities should recognise and promote both the intrinsic and instrumental value of knowledge, and guard against the excessive instrumentalisation (particularly economic instrumentalisation) currently dominant. In Chapter 9, the notion of the *generative intrinsic* was proposed to capture this dual role, rooted in the value of enquiry. In relation to function, there can and should be wide variation in the kinds of orientation an institution has, but it is important to maintain awareness of the relationship between functions and the core purpose of the institution, as well as synergies between different kinds of activities. As discussed in Chapter 4, unbundling presents a threat to some of the potentialities in the university, given the 'interrelated' (rather than 'tie-in' or 'convenience') relationships of components in the bundle, for example teaching and research. Finally, in relation to interaction, opening to society is undoubtedly a positive trend, although a degree of insulation is necessary in order to maintain a space for autonomous, critical thought.

One of the most pernicious and sadly prevalent vices of higher education in the contemporary world is its tendency to see itself at the will and whim of global forces. Universities routinely frame what they do as 'responding' to the forces of globalisation, 'adapting' to the contemporary world, or 'delivering' on the demands placed on them by various stakeholders. It is a view that in part reflects the reality of shrinking financial autonomy, and the consequent need to please its various paymasters. But it also reflects a deeper change of self-view: from an institution that can shape society and individuals, to one that is shaped by them.

The developmental model of university is admirable in resisting this tendency (its dependence on the state notwithstanding), and in instead asserting its protagonism in society. It is a maker, a forger; it creates public goods and the public good, rather than running errands for whatever stakeholders happen to call on it. Furthermore, its protagonism is strongly oriented towards social justice: the opening up of the university, a focus in particular on the most marginalised communities in society, and the most marginalised countries and regions of the world. It overcomes the university's reluctance over the centuries to incorporate new priorities and practices, to diversify its spheres of interest, and move away from self-indulgent esoterism.

In the post-2015 development era, this role for the university has swung dramatically back into the spotlight, given the critical need for high-level professional skills, locally relevant research and innovation, and coordinated action between knowledge producers, the state, industry and civil society organisations. Indeed, the university contemplated by the SDGs is nothing other than the developmental university (despite the contradictions in practice between this role and the higher education policy advocated at the international level by the same supranational organisations). Given the severe challenges facing the world in present times, of protracted conflict, refugee crises, enduring absolute poverty in various parts of the world, rising global temperatures, pollution, water shortage and persistent socioeconomic inequalities, a committed and resourceful higher education sector concerned with the welfare of the whole of humanity is nothing short of essential.

Nevertheless, the university cannot solve every one of society's problems, any more than the judiciary, police force or health system can. While it does have a degree of adaptability, it is an institution with its own specific characteristics, and those characteristics bring opportunities but also peculiarities and limitations. As an institution focused on developing human understanding through open ended inquiry, it is highly adept at forming critical and methodical scholars who can turn their minds towards solving intractable problems of science and society. It can also—and has on a number of times through history—generated ideas or discoveries that have profoundly changed human life. Yet it is not a dependable machine for creating all the kinds of value that are desired in the contemporary world. It is unpredictable what the impact of pedagogical engagements or research and scholarship might be, in terms of their outcomes and timeline. The forms of enquiry engaged in by universities need to follow their own (sometimes whimsical) course, rather than being regulated by outside interests. Finally, the critical enquiry engaged in by universities will inevitably question the very conceptions of development that underpin this instrumental role.

These points force us not to downgrade our expectations of or value given to the university, but to revise our understanding of the role that it can play. As frustrating as it might be for policymakers looking for quick and certain fixes to the immediate problems facing them, universities to a certain extent need to be left to follow their own course, which at times will bring substantial material benefits to society, and at others not. It may indeed mean that states and other stakeholders are less willing to provide funding for the institution: that may be a sacrifice that needs to be made in order to retain the core of the university.

The argument put forward here is relevant not just for the university in the most impoverished parts of the globe that are invoked when we think of the targets of minimum human wellbeing of the Millennium Development Goals (MDGs)—but of every part of it, as entailed by the demands for equality and environmental protection in the SDGs. As discussed above, the contemporary research university in high income countries has a developmental element, alongside others. Indeed, this is the real nature of the models discussed in this book: instead of historically existent discrete forms, they are ideal types that exists in our imaginary and also in the practice of institutions, though not in pure forms. The developmental model, alongside the Humboldtian, medieval, entrepreneurial and other forms, jostle for space within the real universities of today.

In the penultimate chapter, this book has put forward ideas of the 'post-development' university, one which breaks from the paradigm of development as modernization, dissolves and recreates institutional structures and practices, and engages with multiple forms of knowledge. In addition to the *projective* role commonly assigned to education in attending to the future ends of forming the individual and society, this model also has an *expressive* role, in instantiating and representing the space for emancipated learning and enquiry.

The university that can address current development challenges may have some of these revolutionary elements—epistemological pluralism for example—but also features of the traditional university—deep enquiry, critical debate and a community of scholars. In nurturing the developmental model in our contemporary institutions, with its commitment to society, its protagonism and its willingness to get its hands dirty, we must not lose sight of the more quixotic, atemporal and ethereal aspects that are just as much a part of its being, and that ironically may bring as much practical benefit to society as explicit efforts at development.

Principle and Action

It would not be in keeping with the arguments laid out in the previous chapters of this book to recommend a specific form of university. The pursuit of human understanding through enquiry—understood here as the core purpose of the university—can take place in a variety of different ways, as indeed it has historically in places like Nalanda, and is enriched by being approached from different perspectives and within different cultural contexts. The argument for a dialogue of knowledges is not only a question of justice therefore, in defending different cultural and linguistic groups around the world from forced assimilation, misrepresentation or lack of recognition. It is a question of positive benefit for all, avoiding the 'monoculture of the mind' (Shiva 1993), and the closure of the possibility of illumination through other perspectives.

Of course, this position takes us back to the tensions between redistribution and recognition, the social realist critique of epistemic relativism and assertion of the need for disadvantaged groups to have access to powerful knowledge. It is certainly the case that powerful knowledge (and crucially the credentials associated with it) is vital to social mobility within our current unjust systems. The problem is that, while extending access to dominant forms of thought, value, knowledge, culture and language within education may give the less well off a chance at social mobility (though certainly not a guarantee), it is at best a short-term strategy, and one that leaves the unjust and undesirable situation almost entirely intact. What needs to be done longer term is to disassociate university prestige from the conferment of opportunities subsequently in society. A hierarchy of recognised value (which exists nationally and globally, and is reinforced by the various rankings systems) inevitably leads to homogenisation of mission and a vicious struggle for position. The problem with rankings is not that they measure Nobel prizewinners, publications in high quality journals and research income: all of those things can be indicators of valuable work in the institutions in question, and the world would be a worse place without them. It is that those things are taken to be the only scale on which universities measure themselves, setting in motion a desperate squeeze into a mould not appropriate for most institutions, joining a race in which all but a few are destined to be losers.

We should avoid homogeneity, but heterogeneity of higher education systems is a good only if it can prevent the systematic reproduction of socioeconomic inequalities. In this way we can attempt a reconciliation of the demands for redistribution and recognition, understanding that with time universities would no longer wield the kinds of regressive influence they have wielded historically. We move therefore from a system focused primarily on certification, exchange value of degrees and homogenisation of form and knowledge tradition, to one focused on learning, heterogeneity and on the use value and the intrinsic value of that learning.

This book therefore advocates for a flowering of diverse forms of higher education institution. Nevertheless, that diversity is connected by a unifying set of principles; it is not a relativistic approach in which any view or act is as good as any other. Ten such principles are listed below:

Principles:

1. *The promotion of human understanding*
   The fundamental purpose of the university is to foster ever deeper understanding of humanity and the universe, in all their many facets and dimensions. This purpose is addressed in a direct way through taught courses, and in indirect ways through the conducting and communication of research and scholarship.
2. *Engagement in open-ended enquiry*
   The fundamental activity carried out by the university is enquiry, understood in its broadest sense, and incorporating pedagogical interactions and exploration through research and scholarship. This enquiry needs to be open-ended in the sense that it is determined only by the search for understanding, and not by external constraints or goals.
3. *University as protagonist*
   In the context of squeezes on public funding and undermining of academic expertise, universities have been increasingly desperate to ingratiate themselves with external funders, and to prove themselves adaptable to external changes wrought by globalization and new technologies. Instead the university needs to see itself as protagonist, forging a better, more just and more enlightened society.
4. *University as an autonomous space*
   The university has responsibilities to society, and should act to maximize its positive impact. Nevertheless, it is not a factory that can be adapted to any kind of social purpose. It has its own specific characteristics and intrinsic value that limit what it can do, and its generative capacity may be undermined by excessive instrumentalisation.

5. *Fair access, open to all*
   All people have a right to access higher education at some point during their life, once they have achieved the requisite academic preparation. Systems need to expand to accommodate all learners, and take measures to prevent stratification of the system. A fair system depends on availability, accessibility and horizontality.
6. *Education as human development*
   University education has personal, civic and professional ends, and all sides of an individual's development need to be addressed, rather than narrow forms of employability. Teaching and learning should be oriented towards the enhancement of capabilities and human development, and involve diverse areas of study including the artistic, philosophical, technical and scientific.
7. *Dialogue of knowledges*
   Higher education, science and knowledge production are on a path of increasing homogenisation. It is important to acknowledge and provide space for the diverse ontological and epistemological perspectives in existence across the world. This is a matter of justice for those groups in question, but also a means of enriching the processes of enquiry for all.
8. *Non-commodification*
   The commodification of education—its packaging into products for buying and selling, with a view towards profit-making—is harmful to education as it distorts the pedagogical relationship, the framing of knowledge and in many cases can drive down quality. Resources are of course needed for education, but funding solutions must not undermine the core purpose of the institution.
9. *Technology as a humanising force*
   Developments in information and communications technology have had contradictory effects, serving on the one hand to reduce the space for human interaction and agency, and open higher education up to commercialisation, and on the other hand to enable connections, networks and movements to emerge, and to challenge capitalism by allowing for non-commercial sharing. Technology in higher education should be adopted not for its own sake, but to enhance these latter, humanising trends.

10. *Public good benefit*
    All universities produce public and private goods, but the former have been undermined in recent years through increasing marketisation. Higher education should prioritise the production of public goods through their diverse activities and function as a public sphere, creating a space for deliberation.

The purpose of this book is not to provide simple, concrete recommendations to policy makers and university managers. Part of the problem in fact is that the international development community and those struggling with the challenges of contemporary higher education systems are dedicating most of their energy and ingenuity to finding solutions to problems in the short term. Ultimately action is needed of course, but action requires thought, and there is a flagrant lack of reflection, questioning of assumptions and imagination. What we need is to stop and engage in deep consideration of the fundamental question: which university for which development? That question cannot be answered once and for all but is an ongoing quest, and a debate to be engaged in by successive communities and societies.

Nevertheless, there are some clear practical implications from the analysis in this book. Some of these relate to macro-level policy at the international and national levels, and some to the sphere of particular universities and classrooms. Many of these are already focal points for academics, students, reformers, social movements, lecturers' unions and civil society organisations around the world. They will be highlighted in very brief form here, as a summary of the more detailed discussions earlier in the book:

Spheres of action:

1. *Reorienting international policy towards strengthening of domestic higher education systems*
    In the current international development landscape, donor agencies look set to continue their support for education systems in lower income countries. This support should be reoriented so as to foster the strengthening of domestic higher education systems, including teaching and research of quality, rather than enhancing access

through low-cost private provision, cross-border providers in the form of online or branch campuses, and taking steps to avoid brain drain and encourage the return of scholars based overseas.
2. *Introduction of affirmative action policies*
Higher education systems in all parts of the world are highly unjust, and serve in some instances not just to reproduce but to exacerbate socio-economic inequalities. Affirmative action policies are needed to promote access for disadvantaged students on the basis of their potential, particularly in high prestige institutions.
3. *Alternative models of higher education should be nurtured*
As a means of working *beyond*, there needs to be a space for innovative, radical and counter-hegemonic forms of higher education institution, in order to fuel our imagination, and plant the seeds for a new form of society. These initiatives are likely to be frugal and autonomous, but they do need resources and recognition.
4. *For-profit entities should have no place in higher education*
Profit-making should not be an incentive for provision of educational services, and will be detrimental to quality when there is a trade-off between profits and level of provision. Companies are currently exploiting the desperation of less advantaged students to obtain higher education credentials.
5. *Creation of alternative rankings*
The current international university rankings show little divergence from a valuing of high level research and publications, with scant attention to teaching quality, community engagement and commitment to social justice. Universities should resist these gauges, and either step outside of the rankings, or create different forms, placing emphasis on other aspects of the work of the university, and fostering their development as a result.
6. *Strengthening community engagement*
Commercialisation of higher education has weakened the already fragile third pillar of the university: community engagement or service. Steps should be taken to reinstate forms of activity not oriented towards income generation, involving public communication of research, opening the university doors to community groups, and other forms of partnership, dialogue and exchange.

7. *Frugality*
    Many of the current policy drives revolve around the 'cost disease'—the spiralling expenses associated with higher education provision, particularly with ever increasing numbers of students. While societies can certainly allocate more resources towards higher education, we must accept that frugality will also be essential—less extravagant but nonetheless intellectually rigorous forms of higher education—if we are genuine about expanding access to all.

The achievement of the SDGs depends on higher education, but not just *more* of it: instead, it requires the emergence of a new form of institution, with a new set of practices and commitments. To bring changes in higher education we do not need to wait for a change of government, the arrival of a new society, or the eradication of inequalities at primary and secondary level. There are changes that can be brought in the daily lives of universities, through the actions of academics, students, professional staff, those in management positions, and in outside communities. In addition to actions in the mainstream system, at its margins there needs to be a flowering of alternative, experimental and innovative initiatives. These changes can happen in the here and now.

Yet we must also acknowledge that there are constraints on our actions, and even our imaginations, within the current global landscape, brought by dominant political, economic and cultural structures and modes of thought. We can only hope that a virtuous cycle is set in motion in which educational and societal transformation can enable and reinforce one another. Furthermore, it is obvious that processes of learning do not start in higher education, and many of the dispositions, values, skills and knowledge forms will already be in place. Orr (1994) argues that *biophilia*, which must underpin any societal transformation towards sustainability, can only be developed in the early years of life. Clearly, higher education transformation must take place in a context of transformation of the entire education system, and of conceptions and practices of learning through society.

This book argues, ultimately, that we need higher education to work *for* and *beyond* sustainable development, and to do so simultaneously. The university in the developmental vein must generate material benefits for those living in poverty around the world, and create technologies that will help ameliorate our current environmentally destructive practices. But it also needs to forge the conditions for a new kind of world. It must keep its eye constantly on the ultimately flawed nature of the dominant model of development, and the complicity of its own structures and practices, in order to pave the way to its own destruction and rebirth.

References

IPCC. (2018). *Global warming of 1.5°C.* An IPCC Special Report on the impacts of global warming of 1.5°C above pre-industrial levels and related global greenhouse gas emission pathways, in the context of strengthening the global response to the threat of climate change, sustainable development, and efforts to eradicate poverty. Available at https://www.ipcc.ch/sr15/. Accessed 1 November 2018.

Klein, N. (2015). *This changes everything: Capitalism vs. the climate.* London: Simon and Schuster.

Marginson, S. (2011). Higher education and public good. *Higher Education Quarterly, 65*(4), 411–433.

Monbiot, G. (2018, September 6). We won't save the Earth with a better kind of disposable coffee cup. *The Guardian.*

Orr, D. (1994). *Earth in mind.* Washington, DC: Island Press.

Sehoole, C., & Knight, J. (2013). *Internationalisation of African higher education: Towards achieving the MDGs.* Rotterdam: Sense Publishers.

Shiva, V. (1993). *Monocultures of the mind.* London: Zed Books.

Stephens, D. (Ed.). (2009). *Higher education and international capacity building: 25 years of the higher education links programme.* Oxford: Symposium.

References

Abbas, Q., & Foreman-Peck, J. (2008). The Mincer human capital model in Pakistan: Implications for education policy. *South Asia Economic Journal, 9*(2), 435–462.

Abukari, A. (2010). The dynamics of service of higher education: A comparative study. *Compare, 40*(1), 43–57.

Afzal, M. (2011). Microeconometric analysis of private returns to education and determinants of earnings. *Pakistan Economic and Social Review, 49*(1), 39–68.

Ahmed, H. M. S. (2010). 'Non-market returns to women education in Sudan: Case of fertility.' *Journal of Comparative Family Studies, 41*(5), 783–798.

Ajayi, J. F. A., Goma, L. K. H., Johnson, G. A., & Association of African Universities. (1996). *The African experience with higher education.* Accra: Association of African Universities in association with James Currey and Ohio University Press.

Akomolafe, B., & Jain, M. (2016). Practitioner perspective: This revolution will not be schooled—How we are collectively improvising a 'new story' about learning. In A. Skinner, M. Baillie Smith, E. J. Brown, & T. Troll (Eds.), *Education, learning and the transformation of development.* Oxford: Routledge.

Akpan, W., Minkley, G., & Thakrar, J. (2012). In search of a developmental university: Community engagement in theory and practice. *South African Review of Sociology, 43*(2), 1–4.

Al-Samarrai, S., & Bennell, P. (2007). Where has all the education gone in Sub-Saharan Africa? Employment and other outcomes among secondary school and university leavers. *The Journal of Development Studies, 43*(7), 1270–1300.

Allais, S. (2014). A critical perspective on large class teaching: The political economy of massification and the sociology of knowledge. *Higher Education, 67*(6), 721–734.

Almeida Filho, N., & Coutinho, D. (2018). Counter hegemonic higher education in a remote coastal region of Brazil: The Federal University of Southern Bahia as a case-study. In R. Aman & T. Ireland (Eds.), *Educational alternatives in Latin America: New modes of counter hegemonic learning*. London: Palgrave Macillan.

Almond, G., & Verba, S. (1963). *The civic culture: Political attitudes and democracy five nations*. London: Sage.

Altbach, P. G. (1977). Servitude of the mind? Education, dependency and neo-colonialism. *Teachers College Record, 79*(2), 187–204.

Altbach, P. G., & Hazelkorn, E. (2018, August 14). Can we measure education quality in global rankings? *University World News*. Available at https://www.universityworldnews.com/post.php?story=20180814184535721. Accessed 5 September 2018.

Altbach, P. G., Reisberg, L., & Rumbley, L. E. (2009). *Trends in global higher education: Tracking an academic revolution*. A report prepared for the UNESCO 2009 World Conference on Higher Education. Paris: UNESCO.

Amutabi, M. N. (2002). Crisis and student protest in universities in Kenya: Examining the role of students in national leadership and the democratisation process. *African Studies Review, 45*(2), 157–178.

Anderson, R. D. (2004). *European universities from the enlightenment to 1914*. Oxford: Oxford University Press.

Anderson, R. D. (2006). *British universities past and present*. London: Continuum.

Annette, J. (2000). Education for citizenship, civic participation and experiential learning and service learning in the community. In D. Lawton, J. Cairns, & R. Gardner (Eds.), *Education for citizenship*. London: Continuum.

Arasa, J., & Calvert, M. (2013). Negotiating professional identities in higher education in Kenya: Dilemmas and priorities of faculty. *Journal of Post-Compulsory Education, 18*(4), 402–414.

Arbuthnott, K. D. (2009). Education for sustainable development beyond attitude change. *International Journal of Sustainability in Higher Education, 10*(2), 152–163.

Arocena, R., Göransson, B., & Sutz, J. (2014). Universities and higher education in development. In B. Currie-Alder, S. M. R. Kanbur, D. Malone, & R. Medhora (Eds.), *International development: Ideas, experience, and prospects*. Oxford: Oxford University Press.

Arocena, R., Goransson, B., & Sutz, J. (2015). Knowledge policies and universities in developing countries: Inclusive development and the "developmental university". *Technology in Society, 41,* 10–20.

Arocena, R., & Sutz, J. (2005). Latin American universities: From an original revolution to an uncertain transition. *Higher Education, 50*(4), 573–592.

Ashwin, P. (2016). 'From a teaching perspective, "impact" looks very different'. *Times Higher Education*, 21 March. [Online]. http://www.timeshighereducation.com/blog/teaching-perspectiveimpact-looks-very-different. Accessed 3 May 2018.

Assié-Lumumba, N. D. T. (2017). The Ubuntu paradigm and comparative and international education: Epistemological challenges and opportunities in our field. *Comparative Education Review, 61*(1), 1–21.

Azam, M. (2010). India's increasing skill premium: Role of demand and supply. *The B.E. Journal of Economic Analysis & Policy, 10*(1), 1–28.

Bacevic, J. (2018). With or without U? Assemblage theory and (de)territorialising the university. *Globalisation, Societies and Education*. https://doi.org/10.1080/14767724.2018.1498323.

Ball, S. J. (2012). Performativity, commodification and commitment: An I-spy guide to the neoliberal university. *British Journal of Educational Studies, 60*(1), 17–28.

Barber, M., Donnelly, K., & Rizvi, S. (2013*). An avalanche is coming*. London, UK: Institute for Public Policy Research. Available at http://www.ippr.org/files/images/media/files/publication/2013/04/avalanche-is-coming_Mar2013_10432.pdf?noredirect=1. Accessed 9 February 2017.

Barnett, R. (1990). *The idea of higher education*. Buckingham: Society for Research into Higher Education and Open University Press.

Barnett, R. (1992). *Improving higher education: Total quality care*. Bristol: SRHE and Open University Press.

Barnett, R. (2004). The purposes of higher education and the changing face of academia. *London Review of Education, 2*(1), 61–73.

Barnett, R. (2017). *The ecological university: A feasible utopia*. Abingdon: Routledge.

Barth, M. (2015). *Implementing sustainability in higher education: Learning in an age of transformation*. London: Routledge.

Barth, M., Godemann, J., Rieckmann, M., & Stoltenberg, U. (2007). Developing key competencies for sustainable development in higher education. *International Journal of Sustainability in Higher Education, 8*(4), 416–430.

Becker, G. S. (1962, October). Investment in human capital: A theoretical analysis. *Journal of Political Economy, 70*(Suppl.), 9–49.

Beckett, K. (2011). R. S. Peters and the concept of education. *Educational Theory, 61*(3), 239–255.

Bengtsson, S., Barakat, B., & Muttarak, R. (2018). *The role of education in enabling the sustainable development agenda*. London: Routledge.

Benneworth, P. (Ed.). (2013). *University engagement with socially excluded communities*. Berlin: Springer.

Bernasconi, A. (2007). Is there a Latin American model of the university? *Comparative Education Review, 52*(1), 27–52.

Bernstein, B. (1970). Education cannot compensate for society. *New Society, 15*(387), 344–347.

Biggs, J. (1999). What the student does: Teaching for enhanced learning. *Higher Education Research & Development, 18*(1), 57–75.

Birch, E., Perry, D. C., & Taylor, H. L., Jr. (2013). Universities as anchor institutions. *Journal of Higher Education Outreach and Engagement, 17*(3), 7–16.

Bloom, D., Canning, D., & Chan, K. (2006). *Higher education and economic development in Africa*. Washington, DC: World Bank.

Boit, J. M., & Kipkoech, L. C. (2014). Effects of democratizations of university education on quality of higher education in Kenya: A case of Moi University. *International Journal of Educational Administration and Policy Studies, 6*(1), 5–8.

Bok, D. (2003). *Universities in the marketplace: The commercialization of higher education*. Princeton: Princeton University Press.

Boni, A., Lopez-Fogues, A., & Walker, M. (2016). Higher education and the post 2015 agenda: A contribution from the human development approach. *Journal of Global Ethics, 12*(1), 17–28.

Boni, A., & Walker, M. (2013). *Human development and capabilities: Re-imagining the university of the twenty-first century*. London: Routledge.

Boni, A., & Walker, M. (2016). *Universities and global human development: Theoretical and empirical insights for social change*. London: Routledge.

Born, J. A., McMaster, J., & De Jong, A. B. (2008). Return on investment in graduate management education in the South Pacific. *International Journal of Management in Education, 2*(3), 340–355.

Bothwell, E. (2018, September 6). THE developing ranking based on Sustainable Development Goals. *Times Higher Education*.

Bourn, D. (2018). *Understanding global skills for 21st century professions*. London: Palgrave Macmillan.

Bowen, W. G. (2013). *Higher education in the digital age*. Princeton: Princeton University Press.

Bowen, W. G., & Bok, D. (1998). *The shape of the river: Long-term consequences of considering race in college and university admissions*. Princeton, NJ: Princeton University Press.

Bowles, S., & Gintis, H. (1976). *Schooling in capitalist America: Educational reform and the contradictions of economic life*. New York: Basic Books.

Boyer, E. L. (1990). *Scholarship reconsidered: Priorities of the professoriate*. Princeton, NJ: The Carnegie Foundation for the Advancement of Teaching.

Brennan, J., & Naidoo, R. (2008). Higher education and the achievement (and/or prevention) of equity and social justice. *Higher Education, 56*(3), 287–302.

Brewis, E., & McCowan, T. (2016). *Enhancing teaching in African higher education: Perspectives of quality assurance and academic development practitioners in Ghana, Nigeria, Kenya and South Africa*. British Council.

Brighouse, H., & Swift, A. (2006). Equality, priority, and positional goods. *Ethics, 116*, 471–497.

Brinkmann, S. (2015). Learner-centred education reforms in India: The missing piece of teachers' beliefs. *Policy Futures in Education, 13*, 342–359.

Brown, E., & McCowan, T. (2018). Buen vivir: Reimagining education and shifting paradigms (Forum). *Compare, 48*(2), 317–323.

Brundtland Commission. (1987). *Our common future* (Report of the World Commission on Environment and Development). Oxford: Oxford University Press.

Bush, K., & Saltarelli, D. (2000). *The two faces of education in ethnic conflict*. Paris: UNICEF Innocenti Research Centre.

Butin, D. W. (2003). Of what use is it? Multiple conceptualisations of service learning within education. *Teacher College Record, 105*(9), 1674–1692.

Bynner, J., Dolton, P., Feinstein, L., Makepiece, G., Malmberg, L., & Woods, L. (2003). *Revisiting the benefits of higher education: A report by the Bedford Group for Lifecourse and Statistical Studies, Institute of Education*. Bristol: Higher Education Funding Council for England.

Ca, T. N. (2006). *Universities as drivers of the urban economies in Asia: The case of Vietnam* (World Bank Policy Research Working Paper 3949). Washington, DC: World Bank.

Calhoun, C. (2006). The university and the public good. *Thesis Eleven, 84*(1), 7–43.

Calvert, M., & Muchira-Tirima, K. (2013). Making sense of professionalism and being a professional in a Kenyan higher education context. *Journal of Education for Teaching, 39*(4), 370–382.

Carayannis, E. G., & Campbell, D. F. J. (2012). *Mode 3 knowledge production in quadruple helix innovation systems: 21st-century democracy, innovation, and entrepreneurship for development.* New York and London: Springer.

Carpentier, V. (2012). Public-private substitution in higher education: Has cost-sharing gone too far? *Higher Education Quarterly, 66,* 363–390.

Carpentier, V. (2019). The historical expansion of higher education in Europe: Spaces, shapes and rationales. In J. L. Rury & E. H. Tamura (Eds.), *The Oxford handbook of the history of education.* Oxford: Oxford University Press.

Carvalho, C. A. (2006). O PROUNI no governo Lula e o jogo político em torno do acesso ao ensino superior. *Educação & Sociedade, 27*(96), 979–1000.

Case, J. M., McKenna, S., Marshall, D., & Mogashana, D. (2018). *Going to university: The influence of higher education on the lives of young South Africans.* Cape Town: African Minds.

Castells, M. (1994). The university system: Engine of development in the new world economy. In J. Salmi & A. Verspoor (Eds.), *Revitalizing higher education* (pp. 14–40). Oxford: Pergamon.

Castells, M. (2001). Universities as dynamic systems of contradictory functions. In J. Muller, N. Cloete, & S. Badat (Eds.), *Challenges of globalisation: South African debates with Manuel Castells.* Pinelands: Maskew Miller Longman.

Chaves, V. L. J. (2017). Política de expansão da educação superior no Brasil – o Prouni e o Fies como financiadores do setor privado. *Educação em Revista, 32*(4), 49–72.

Chaves, V. L. J., & Amaral, N. C. (2016). Política de expansão da educação superior no Brasil – o Prouni e o Fies como financiadores do setor privado. *Educação em Revista, 32*(4), 49–72.

Chaves, V. L. J., Reis, L. F., & Guimarães, A. R. (2018). Dívida pública e financiamento da educação superior no Brasil. *Acta Scientiarum. Education, 40*(1). https://doi.org/10.4025/actascieduc.v40i1.37668

Chege, M. (2015). Re-inventing Kenya's university: From a "Graduate-mill" to a development-oriented paradigm. *International Journal of Educational Development, 44,* 21–27.

Cheng, Y. C., & Tam, W. M. (1997). Multi-models of quality in education. *Quality Assurance in Education, 5*(1), 22–31.

Childs, A. (2015). Why does so little foreign aid go to support universities? *The Conversation*. Available at http://theconversation.com/why-does-so-little-foreign-aid-go-to-support-universities-43160. Accessed 13 October 2015.

Childs, P., & Stromquist, N. (2015). Academic and diversity consequences of affirmative action in Brazil. *Compare, 45*(5), 792–813.

Chubb, J., & Watermeyer, R. (2017). Artifice or integrity in the marketization of research impact? Investigating the moral economy of (pathways to) impact statements within research funding proposals in the UK and Australia. *Studies in Higher Education, 42*(12), 2360–2372.

Clancy, P., & Goastellec, G. (2007). Exploring access and equity in higher education: Policy and performance in a comparative perspective. *Higher Education Quarterly, 61*(2), 136–154.

Clark, B. R. (1998). *Creating entrepreneurial universities: Organisational pathways of transformation*. New York: Elsevier.

Clark, T. (1999). Rethinking civic education for the 21st century. In D. Marsh (Ed.), *Preparing our schools for the 21st century (1999 ASCD yearbook)*. Alexandria, VA: ASCD.

Clark, W. C., & Dickson, N. M. (2003). Sustainability science: The emerging research program. *Proceedings of the National Academy of Sciences in the United States of America, 100*(14), 8059–8061.

Clegg, S. (2011). Cultural capital and agency: Connecting critique and curriculum in higher education. *British Journal of Sociology of Education, 32*(1), 93–108.

Cloete, N., Bailey, T., Pillay, P., Bunting, Ian, & Maassen, P. (2011). *Universities and economic development in Africa*. Cape Town: Centre for Higher Education Transformation.

Coleman, J. S. (1986). The idea of the developmental university. *Minerva: A Review of Science, Learning and Policy, 24*(4), 476–494.

Coleman, J. S., Campbell, E. Q., Hobson, C. F., McPartland, J., Mood, A. M., Weinfeld, F. D., et al. (1966). *Equality of educational opportunity*. Washington, DC: U. S. Office of Education.

Collini, S. (2012). *What are universities for?* London: Penguin.

Collins, C. S. (2012). Land-grant extension as a global endeavor: Connecting knowledge and international development. *The Review of Higher Education, 36*(1), 91–124.

Comissão de Implantação da UNILA. (2009a). *A UNILA em construção: Um projeto universitário para a América Latina*. Foz do Iguaçu: IMEA.

Comissão de Implantação da UNILA. (2009b). *UNILA: Consulta internacional. Contribuições à concepção, organização e proposta político-pedagógica da Unila.* Foz do Iguaçu: IMEA.

Commission for University Education. (2014). *Universities standards and guidelines, 2014.* Available at http://www.cue.or.ke/images/phocadownload/UNIVERSITIES_STANDARDS_AND_GUIDELINES_June_2014.pdf. Accessed 24 May 2016.

Commission for University Education. (2016). *State of university education in Kenya.* Nairobi: Commission for University Education.

Commission for University Education. (2017). *Accredited universities in Kenya—March 2017.* Available at http://www.cue.or.ke/images/phocadownload/Accreditted_Universities_March_2017.pdf. Accessed 17 October 2017.

Commonwealth Secretariat. (2017). *Curriculum framework for the Sustainable Development Goals.* London: Commonwealth Secretariat.

Cortese, A. D. (2003). The critical role of higher education in creating a sustainable future. *Planning for Higher Education, 31*(3), 15–22.

Court, D. (1980). The development ideal in higher education: The experience of Kenya and Tanzania. *Higher Education, 9,* 657–680.

Court, D. (1999). *Financing higher education in Africa, Makerere: The quiet revolution.* New York and Washington: Rockefeller Foundation and The World Bank.

Cowen, R. (1971). The utilitarian university. In B. Scanlon (Ed.), *The world yearbook of education 1971/72: Higher education in a changing world.* London: Evans Brothers Limited.

Cowen, R. (2012). Robustly researching the relevant: A note on creation myths in comparative education. In L. Wikander, C. Gustaffson, & U. Riis (Eds.), *Enlightenment, creativity and education: Polities, politics, performances* (pp. 3–26). Rotterdam: Sense Publishers and CESE.

Craig, R. (2015). *College disrupted: The great unbundling of higher education.* New York, NY: Palgrave Macmillan.

CTB. (2018). *Mesmo com mais estudantes negros na educação superior o racismo avança.* Available at http://portalctb.org.br/site/secretarias-da-ctb-nacional/igualdade-racial/mesmo-com-mais-estudantes-negros-na-educacao-superior-o-racismo-avanca. Accessed 1 October 2018.

Cummings, W. (1998). The service university in comparative perspective. *Higher Education, 35*(1), 69–90.

Dabalen, A., Oni, B., & Adekola, O. A. (2000). *Labour market prospects for university graduates in Nigeria.* The Nigeria University System Innovation Project Study.

de Carvalho, C. H. (2017). Capital concentration and financialization in Brazilian private higher education. *Academia*. Available at http://academia.lis.upatras.gr/index.php/academia/article/view/2835 Accessed 9 November 18.

de Gayardon, A. (2018). There is no such thing as free higher education: A global perspective on the (many) realities of free systems. *Higher Education Policy*. https://doi.org/10.1057/s41307-018-0095-7.

de Gayardon, A., Callender, C., Deane, K. C., & DesJardins, S. (2018). *Graduate indebtedness: Its perceived effects on behaviour and life choices—A literature review* (Centre for Global Higher Education Working Paper no. 38). Available at https://www.researchcghe.org/perch/resources/publications/wp38.pdf. Accessed 5 September 18.

de Jonghe, A. (2005). Reorganising the teaching-research tension. *Higher Education Management and Policy, 17*(2), 61–76.

de Ridder-Symoens, H. (Ed.). (1996). *A history of the university in Europe: Volume 2, Universities in early modern Europe (1500–1800)*. Cambridge: Cambridge University Press.

DeMillo, R. A. (2015). *Revolution in higher education: How a small band of innovators will make college accessible and affordable*. Cambridge: MIT Press.

Deneulin, S., & Townsend, N. (2007). Public goods, global public goods and the common good. *International Journal of Social Economics, 34*(1/2), 19–36.

Department for Education (DfE). (2018). *Widening participation in higher education, England, 2016/17 age cohort—Official Statistics*. Available at https://www.gov.uk/government/statistics/widening-participation-in-higher-education-2018. Accessed 28 November 2018.

Dewey, J. (1964). The continuum of ends-means. In R. Archambault (Ed.), *John Dewey on education: Selected writings*. Chicago: University of Chicago Press.

Dewey, J. (1966 [1916]). *Democracy and education*. New York: MacMillan.

Diamond, J. M. (1997). *Guns germs and steel: The fate of human societies*. New York: W. W. Norton.

Dianati, S. (2016). *What do Massive Open Online Courses (MOOCs) have to do with 'good' education? An ideology critique of MOOCs* (Unpublished PhD thesis). Flinders University.

Doan, T., & Stevens, P. (2011). Labor market returns to higher education in Vietnam. *Economics: The Open Access Open-Assessment E-Journal, 5*, 1–21.

dos Santos, T. (1970). The structure of dependency. *American Economic Review, 60*(2), 231.

Duru-Bellat, M. (2012). Access to higher education: What counts as fairness in both an individual and systemic perspective? (Methodological Discussion Paper No. 1).

Eco, U. (2013). *Perché le università?* Universitas 131. Available at http://disf.org/files/eco-perche-universita.pdf. Accessed 1 December 2018.

Economic and Social Research Council. (2017). *What is impact?* Available at http://www.esrc.ac.uk/research/impact-toolkit/what-is-impact/. Accessed 15 July 2018.

Ehrhardt-Martinez, K. (1998). Social determinants of deforestation in developing countries: A cross-national study. *Social Forces, 77*(2), 567–586.

Esteva, G. (2007, November 7). Reclaiming our freedom to learn. *Yes Magazine*.

Escobar, A. (1995). *Encountering development: The making and unmaking of the Third World*. Princeton: Princeton University Press.

Etzkowitz, H., Webster, A., Gebhardt, C., & Cantisano Terra, B. R. (2000). The future of the university and the university of the future: Evolution of ivory tower to entrepreneurial paradigm. *Research Policy, 29,* 313–330.

Fensham, P. J. (1978). Stockholm to Tbilisi—The evolution of environmental education. *Prospects, 8*(4), 446–455.

Fielding, M. (2003). The impact of impact. *Cambridge Journal of Education, 33*(2), 289–295.

Fioreze, C., & McCowan, T. (2018). Community universities in the South of Brazil: Prospects and challenges of a model of non-state public higher education. *Comparative Education, 54*(3), 370–389.

FOIRN/ISA. (2013). *Instituto dos Conhecimentos Indígenas e Pesquisa do Rio Negro: Formação e Pesquisa Avançada*. São Gabriel da Cachoeira: FOIRN/ISA.

Foley, A. R., & Masingila, J. O. (2014). Building capacity: Challenges and opportunities in large class pedagogy (LCP) in Sub-Saharan Africa. *Higher Education, 67*(6), 797–808.

Francis, B. (2011). Increasing impact? An analysis of issues raised by the impact agenda in educational research. *Scottish Educational Review, 43*(2), 4–16.

Fraser, N. (1995). Recognition or redistribution? A critical reading of Iris Young's Justice and the Politics of Difference. *Journal of Political Philosophy, 3*(2), 166–180.

Fraser, N. (1998). From redistribution to recognition? Dilemmas of justice in a 'post-socialist' age. In A. Philipps (Ed.), *Feminism and politics*. New York: Oxford University Press.

Fraser, N., & Honneth, A. (2003). *Redistribution or recognition? A political-philosophical exchange*. London: Verso.

Freire, P. (1970). *Pedagogy of the oppressed*. London: Penguin Books.

Gardner, M. (2017, September 15). Germany has leading position in tertiary STEM subjects. *University World News*. Available at https://www.universityworldnews.com/post.php?story=20170915095958885. Accessed 3 October 2018.

Garrod, N., & Macfarlane, B. (2009). *Challenging boundaries: Managing the integration of post-secondary education*. Abingdon: Routledge.

Gehrke, S., & Kezar, A. (2015). Unbundling the faculty role in higher education: Utilizing historical, theoretical, and empirical frameworks to inform future research. In *Higher education: Handbook of theory and research* (pp. 93–150). Cham: Springer International Publishing.

Geiger, R. (1986). *Private sectors in higher education: Structure, function and change in eight countries*. Ann Arbor: University of Michigan.

Gibbons, M., Limoges, C., Nowotny, H., Schwartzman, S., Scott, P., & Trow, M. (1994). *The new production of knowledge: The dynamics of science and research in contemporary societies*. London: Sage.

Giroux, H., & McLaren, P. (1986). Teacher education and the politics of engagement: The case for democratic schooling. *Harvard Educational Review, 56*(3), 213–240.

Glewwe, P., Gragnolati, M., & Zaman, H. (2002). Who gained from Vietnam's boom in the 1990s? *Economic Development and Cultural Change, 50*(4), 773–792.

Global Initiative to End all Corporal Punishment of Children. (2018). *Progress*. Available at https://endcorporalpunishment.org/countdown/. Accessed 1 September 2018.

Globo. (2017, August 28). *Estudo mostra que mensalidade média de medicina é 10 vezes maior que a de pedagogia no Brasil*. Available at https://g1.globo.com/educacao/noticia/estudo-mostra-que-mensalidade-media-de-medicina-e-10-vezes-maior-que-a-de-pedagogia-no-brasil.ghtml. Accessed 1 June 2018.

Goddard, J., Hazelkorn, E., Kempton, L., & Vallance, P. (Eds.). (2016). *The civic university: The policy and leadership challenges*. Cheltenham: Edward Elgar.

Goldmeier, G. (2018). *Social justice and citizenship education: Reflective equilibrium between ideal theories and the Brazilian context*. The thesis submitted at the Institute of Education, University College London.

Goodfellow, R., & Lea, M. (Eds.). (2013). *Literacy in the digital university: Critical perspectives on learning, scholarship and technology (research into higher education)*. London and New York: Routledge and Taylor & Francis.

Gorard, S. (2010). Education can compensate for society—A bit. *British Journal of Educational Studies, 58*(1), 47–65.

Gough, S., & Scott, W. (2007). *Higher education and sustainable development: Paradox and possibility.* London: Routledge.

Graeber, D. (2018). *Bullshit jobs: a theory.* London: Penguin.

Green, A. (1990). *Education and state formation: The rise of education systems in England, France and the USA.* London: Macmillan.

Grobbelaar, S., & de Wet, G. (2016). Exploring pathways towards an integrated development role: The University of Fort Hare. *South African Journal of Higher Education, 30*(1), 162–187.

Grove, J. (2013, January 3). Troubling FX as Falmouth forces staff to go private. *Times Higher Education.*

Gudo, C. O., Olel, M. A., & Oanda, I. O. (2011). University expansion in Kenya and issues of quality education: Challenges and opportunities. *International Journal of Business & Social Science, 2*(20), 203–214.

Gudynas, E. (2016). Beyond varieties of development: Disputes and alternatives. *Third World Quarterly, 37*(4), 721–732.

Gunn, A., & Mintrom, M. (2016). Higher education policy change in Europe: Academic research funding and the impact agenda. *European Education, 48*(4), 241–257.

Gunn, A., & Mintrom, M. (2017, January 12). Five things to consider when designing a policy to measure research impact. *The Conversation.* Available at http://theconversation.com/five-things-to-consider-when-designing-a-policy-to-measure-research-impact-71078.

Gupta, V. K. (2018). Burning libraries: A review through the lens of history. *Journal of Indian Library Association, 54*(1), 17–26.

Gurin, P., Dey, E. L., Hurtado, S., & Gurin, G. (2002). Diversity and higher education: Theory and impact on educational outcomes. *Harvard Educational Review, 71*(3), 332–366.

Gyimah-Brempong, K. (2010, October 27–29). *Education and economic development in Africa.* Paper presented at the 4th African Economic Conference, Tunis.

Gyimah-Brempong, K., Paddison, O., & Mitiku, W. (2006). Higher education and economic growth in Africa. *Journal of Development Studies, 42*(3), 509–529.

Hanushek, E. (2013). Economic growth in developing countries: The role of human capital. *Economics of Education Review, 73,* 204–212.

Hanushek, E., & Woessmann, L. (2008). The role of cognitive skills in economic development. *Journal of Economic Literature, 46*(3), 607–668.

Harris, S., & Lewer, N. (2005). Post-graduate peace education in Sri Lanka. *Journal of Peace Education, 2*(2), 109–124.

Harvey, L., & Green, D. (1993). Defining quality. *Assessment and Evaluation in Higher Education, 18*, 8–35.

Hattie, J., & Marsh, H. W. (1996). The relationship between research and teaching—A meta-analysis. *Review of Educational Research, 66*, 507–542.

Hazelkorn, E. (2015). *Rankings and the reshaping of higher education: The battle for world class excellence* (2nd ed.). Basingstoke, UK: Palgrave Macmillan.

Hirst, P. H. (1974). *Knowledge and the curriculum*. London: Routledge & Kegan Paul.

Hoare, A., & Johnston, R. (2011). Widening participation through admissions policy—A British case study of school and university performance. *Studies in Higher Education, 36*(1), 21–41.

Honneth, A. (2004). Recognition and justice outline of a plural theory of justice. *Acta Sociologica, 47*(4), 351–364.

hooks, b. (1994). *Teaching to transgress: Education as the practice of freedom*. London: Routledge.

Huckle, J., & Sterling, S. (Eds.). (1996). *Education for sustainability*. London: Earthscan.

Huisman, J. (2000). Higher education institutions: As different as chalk and cheese? *Higher Education Policy, 13*, 41–53.

Huntington, S., & Nelson, J. (1976). *No easy choice: Political participation in developing countries*. Cambridge, MA: Harvard University Press.

Ignatieff, M. (2018). *Academic freedom and the future of Europe* (Centre for Global Higher Education Working Paper No. 40). Available at https://www.researchcghe.org/publications/working-paper/academic-freedom-and-the-future-of-europe/. Accessed 5 October 2018.

Illich, I. (1971). *Deschooling society*. New York: Harper & Row.

Illich, I. (1973). *Tools for conviviality*. New York: Harper & Row.

INEP (Instituto Nacional de Estudos e Pesquisas Educacionais Anísio Teixeira). (2013). *Censo da Educação Superior 2013*. Brasília: INEP.

INEP. (2017). *Censo da Educação Superior. Notas Estatísticas 2017*. Brasília: INEP.

Inter-University Council for East Africa, IUCEA. (2014). *Regional higher education qualifications gaps* (Vol II).

IPCC. (2018). *Global warming of 1.5°C*. An IPCC Special Report on the impacts of global warming of 1.5°C above pre-industrial levels and related global greenhouse gas emission pathways, in the context of strengthening the global response to the threat of climate change, sustainable development, and efforts to eradicate poverty. Available at https://www.ipcc.ch/sr15/. Accessed 1 November 2018.

Jacobs, L. (2013). A vision of equal opportunity in postsecondary education. In H.-D. Meyer, E. P. St. John, M. Chankseliani, & L. Uribe (Eds.), *Fairness in access to higher education in a global perspective: Reconciling excellence, efficiency, and justice*. Rotterdam: Sense Publishers.

Jain, M. (Ed.). (2001). *Unfolding learning societies: Deepening the dialogues*. Vimukt Shiksha Series. Shikshantar: The Peoples' Institute for Rethinking Education and Development. Available at http://shikshantar.org/sites/default/files/PDF/learningsocieties2.pdf.

Jaspers, K. (1960). *The idea of the university*. London: Peter Owen.

Jickling, B., & Wals, A. E. J. (2008). Globalisation and environmental education: Looking beyond sustainable development. *Journal of Curriculum Studies, 40*(1), 1–21.

Jones, A., Jones, C., & Ndaruhutse, S. (2014). *Higher education and developmental leadership: The case of Ghana* (Development Leadership Programme, Research Paper No. 26). http://publications.dlprog.org/Higher%20Education%20and%20Developmental%20Leadership%20-%20The%20Case%20of%20Ghana.pdf.

Jump, P. (2015, February 19). The impact of impact. *Times Higher Education*.

Kant, I. (1979). *The conflict of the faculties*. Lincoln: University of Nebraska Press.

Kenya National Bureau of Statistics. (2018). *University enrolments*. Available at https://www.knbs.or.ke/download/university-enrolment/. Accessed 15 September 2018.

Kerr, C. (1963). *The uses of the university*. New York: Harper Torchbooks.

King, K. (2017). Lost in translation? The challenge of translating the global education goal and targets into global indicators. *Compare: A Journal of Comparative and International Education, 47*(6), 801–817.

King, K., & Palmer, R. (2013). Post-2015 agendas: Northern tsunami, southern ripple? The case of education and skills. *International Journal of Educational Development, 33*, 409–425.

Kinser, K. (2002). Working at for-profit universities: The University of Phoenix as a new model. *International Higher Education, 28*, 13–14.

References

Kinser, K., Levy, D., Casillas, J. C. S., Bernasconi, A., Slantcheva Durst, S., Otieno, W., et al. (2010). *The global growth of private higher education*. ASHE Higher Education Report Series. Wiley: San Francisco.

Kitawi, A. (2014). Community capacity development in universities: Empowering communities through education management programmes in Strathmore University (a pilot study). *Contemporary Issues in Education Research, 7*(2), 75–94.

Klees, S. J. (2016). Human capital and rates of return: Brilliant ideas or ideological dead ends? *Comparative Education Review, 60*(4), 644–672.

Klein, N. (2015). *This changes everything: Capitalism vs. the climate*. London: Simon and Schuster.

Larbi-Apau, J. A., & Sarpong, D. B. (2010). Performance measurement: Does education impact productivity? *Performance Improvement Quarterly, 22*(4), 81–97.

Lauglo, J. (1982). *The 'utilitarian university', the 'centre of academic learning' and developing countries* (EDC Occasional Papers No. 2).

Laurillard, D., & Kennedy, E. (2017). *The potential of MOOCs for learning at scale in the Global South* (Working Paper No. 31). London: Centre for Global Higher Education.

Le Blanc, D. (2015). Towards integration at last: The Sustainable Development Goals as a network of targets. *Sustainable Development, 23,* 176–187.

Leadbetter, C., & Wong, A. (2010). *Learning from the extremes*. San Jose: Cisco.

Leal Filho, W. (Ed.). (2010a). *Universities and climate change: Introducing climate change to university programmes*. Berlin: Springer.

Leal Filho, W. (2010b). Climate change at universities: Results of a world survey. In W. Leal Filho (Ed.), *Universities and climate change: Introducing climate change to university programmes*. Berlin: Springer.

Leal Filho, W., Manolas, E., & Pace, P. (2015). The future we want. *International Journal of Sustainability in Higher Education, 16*(1), 112–129.

Leal Filho, W., Morgan, E., Godoy, E., Azeiteiro, U., Bacelar-Nicolau, P., Veiga Ávila, L., et al. (2018). Implementing climate change research at universities: Barriers, potential and actions. *Journal of Cleaner Production, 170,* 269–277.

Lee, S. T. (2017). '*The Structure of a University: A Karatanian interrogation into instrumentalism, idealism and community in postwar British higher education, 1945–2015*' (Unpublished PhD thesis). Birkbeck University.

Leher, R. (2010). Educação no governo de Lula da Silva: a ruptura que não aconteceu. In J. P. de A. Magalhães (Ed.), *Os anos Lula: contribuições para um balanço crítico 2003–2010* (pp. 369–412). Rio de Janeiro: Garamond.

Levy, D. C. (1986). *Higher education and the state in Latin America: Private challenges to public dominance.* Chicago: University of Chicago Press.

Locatelli, R. (2017). *Education as a public and common good: Revisiting the role of the state in a context of growing marketization* (Unpublished PhD thesis). University of Bergamo.

Lotz-Sisitka, H., Wals, A., Kronlid, D., & McGarry, D. (2015). Transformative, transgressive social learning: Rethinking higher education pedagogy in times of systemic global dysfunction. *Current Opinion in Environmental Sustainability, 16,* 73–80.

Lucas, R. E. (1988). On the mechanics of development. *Journal of Monetary Economics, 22*(1), 3–42.

Luescher-Mamashela, T. M., Kiiru, S., Mattes, R., Mwollo-ntallima, A., Ng'ethe, N., & Romo, M. (2011). *The university in Africa and democratic citizenship: Hothouse or training ground?* Wynberg: Centre for Higher Education Transformation.

Macfarlane, B. (2011). The morphing of academic practice: Unbundling and the rise of the para-academic. *Higher Education Quarterly, 65*(1), 59–73.

MacGregor, K. (2015, April 10). Higher education is key to development—World Bank. *University World News.*

Magara, E., Bukirwa, J., & Kayiki, R. (2011). Knowledge transfer through internship: The EASLIS experience in strengthening the governance decentralisation programme in Uganda. *African Journal of Library Archives and Information Science, 21*(1), 29–40.

Malik, S., & Courtney, K. (2011). Higher education and women's empowerment in Pakistan. *Gender and Education, 23*(1), 29–45.

Mamdani, M. (2018). The African university. *London Review of Books, 40*(14), 29–32.

Marginson, S. (2007). The public/private divide in higher education: A global revision. *Higher Education, 53*(3), 307–333.

Marginson, S. (2011). Higher education and public good. *Higher Education Quarterly, 65*(4), 411–433.

Marginson, S. (2014). Emerging higher education in the post-confucian heritage zone. In D. Araya & P. Marber (Eds.), *Higher education in the global age* (pp. 89–112). New York: Routledge.

Marginson, S. (2016a). The worldwide trend to high participation higher education: Dynamics of social stratification in inclusive systems. *Higher Education, 72,* 413–434.

Marginson, S. (2016b). *Higher education and the common good*. Melbourne: Melbourne University Press.

Marginson, S. (2017). Limitations of human capital theory. *Studies in Higher Education, 44*(2), 287–301.

Marginson, S. (2018). Public/private in higher education: A synthesis of economic and political approaches. *Studies in Higher Education, 43*(2), 322–337.

Marginson, S., & Considine, M. (2000). *The enterprise university: Power, governance, and reinvention in Australia*. Cambridge, UK: Cambridge University Press.

Martin, B. (2011). The research excellence framework and the 'impact agenda': Are we creating a Frankenstein monster? *Research Evaluation, 20*(3), 247–254.

Martin, C. (2018). Political authority, personal autonomy and higher education. *Philosophical Inquiry in Education, 25*(2), 154–170.

Martinez, R. (2016). *Creating freedom: Power, control and the fight for our future*. London: Canongate.

Masehela, L. (2018). The rising challenge of university access for students from low-income families. In P. Ashwin & J. Case (Eds.), *Higher education pathways: South African undergraduate education and the public good*. Cape Town: African Minds.

Mason, P. (2015). *Post-capitalism: A guide to our future*. London: Penguin.

Mateos Cortés, L. S., & Dietz, G. (2016). Universidades interculturales en México: balance crítico de la primera década. *Revista mexicana de investigación educativa, 21*, 683–690.

Mathebula, M., & Calitz, T. (2018). #FeesMustFall: A media analysis of students' voices on access to universities in South Africa. In P. Ashwin & J. Case (Eds.), *Higher education pathways: South African undergraduate education and the public good*. Cape Town: African Minds.

Mato, D. (2018). Educación superior y pueblos indígenas: experiencias, estudios y debates en América Latina y otras regiones del mundo. *Revista del Cisen Tramas/Maepova, 6*(2), 41–65.

Mattes, R., & Mozaffar, S. (2011). *Education, legislators and legislatures in Africa*. Wynberg: Centre for Higher Education Transformation.

Mattes, R., & Mughogho, D. (2009). *The limited impacts of formal education on democratic citizenship in Africa* (Centre for Social Science Research Working Paper 255). Cape Town: University of Cape Town.

Maxwell, N. (1984). *From knowledge to wisdom: A revolution in the aims and methods of science*. Oxford: Basil Blackwell.

Mazrui, A. A. (1975). The African university as a multinational corporation: Problems of penetration and dependency. *Harvard Educational Review, 45,* 198.

Mbembe, A. J. (2016). Decolonizing the university: New directions. *Arts & Humanities in Higher Education, 15*(1), 29–45.

McCowan, T. (2004). The growth of private higher education in Brazil: Implications for equity and quality. *Journal of Education Policy, 19*(4), 453–472.

McCowan, T. (2009). *Rethinking citizenship education: A curriculum for participatory democracy*. London: Continuum.

McCowan, T. (2012). Is there a universal right to higher education? *British Journal of Educational Studies, 60*(2), 111–128.

McCowan, T. (2013). *Education as a human right: Principles for a universal entitlement to learning*. London: Bloomsbury.

McCowan, T. (2014). *Can higher education solve Africa's job crisis? Understanding graduate employability in Sub-Saharan Africa* (Policy Brief). Manchester: British Council.

McCowan, T. (2015a). Theories of development. In T. McCowan & E. Unterhalter (Eds.), *Education and international development: An introduction*. London: Bloomsbury.

McCowan, T. (2015b). Should universities promote employability? *Theory and Research in Education, 13*(3), 267–285.

McCowan, T. (2016). Three dimensions of equity of access in higher education. *Compare, 46*(4), 645–665.

McCowan, T., Ananga, E., Oanda, I., Sifuna, D., Ongwenyi, Z., Adedeji, S., et al. (2015). *Students in the driving seat: Young people's views on higher education in Africa* (Research Report). Manchester: British Council.

McCowan, T., Walker, M., Fongwa, S., Oanda, I., Sifuna, D., Adedeji, S., et al. (2016). *Universities, employability and inclusive development: Repositioning higher education in Ghana, Kenya, Nigeria and South Africa* (Final Research Report). British Council.

McDowell, G. (2003). Engaged universities: Lessons from the Land-Grant universities and extension. *Annals of the American Academy of Political and Social Science, 585* (Higher Education in the Twenty-First Century), 31–50.

McGrath, S. (2010). The role of education in development: An educationalist's response to some recent work in development economics. *Comparative Education, 46,* 237–253.

McGrath, S. (2014). The post-2015 debate and the place of education in development thinking. *International Journal of Educational Development, 39,* 4–11.

McKenzie, L. (2018, December 18). EdX's struggle for sustainability. *Inside Higher Education.* Available at https://www.insidehighered.com/digital-learning/article/2018/12/18/quest-long-term-sustainability-edx-tries-monetize-moocs#.XBjaIfy8UTo.twitter. Accessed 20 December 18.

McKeown, R., & Hopkins, C. (2003). EE ≠ ESD: Defusing the worry. *Environmental Education Research, 9*(1), 117–128.

McMahon, W. W. (1999). *Education and development: Measuring the social benefits.* Oxford: Oxford University Press.

McMahon, W. W. (2003). Investment criteria and financing education for economic development. In J. B. G. Tilak (Ed.), *Education, society, and development* (pp. 235–256). New Delhi: A.P.H. Publishing.

McMahon, W. W. (2009). *Higher learning, greater good.* Baltimore: John Hopkins Press.

MEC. (2018). *Prouni – Programa Universidade para Todos.* Available at http://prouniportal.mec.gov.br/dados-e-estatisticas/10-representacoes-graficas. Accessed 15 October 2018.

Meyer, H.-D., St. John, E. P., Chankseliani, M., & Uribe, L. (Eds.). (2013). *Fairness in access to higher education in a global perspective: Reconciling excellence, efficiency, and justice.* Rotterdam: Sense Publishers.

Milbrath, L., & Goel, M. (1977). *Political participation: How and why do people get involved in politics?* (2nd ed.). Chicago: Rand McNally College.

Milton, S. (2019). Syrian higher education during conflict: Survival, protection, and regime security. *International Journal of Educational Development, 64,* 38–47.

Milton, S., & Barakat, S. (2016). Higher education as the catalyst of recovery in conflict-affected societies. *Globalisation, Societies and Education, 14*(3), 403–421.

Mincer, J. (1981). Human capital and economic growth (Working Paper 80). Cambridge, MA: National Bureau of Economic Research. http://www.nber.org/papers/w0803.pdf.

Mogensen, F., & Schnack, K. (2010). The action competence approach and the 'new' discourses of education for sustainable development, competence and quality criteria. *Environmental Education Research, 16*(1), 59–74.

Mokua, E. (2018, December). Massive student failure in 2018 KCSE exam signals system crisis. *Daily Nation.*

Molebatsi, P. (2018, June 19). *How can the notion of the 'public good' contribute to conceptions of the 'developmental university'?* Paper presented at the

CEID Annual Conference 2018—Higher Education and International Development, University College London.

Monbiot, G. (2018, September 6). We won't save the Earth with a better kind of disposable coffee cup. *The Guardian*.

Montgomery, L., & Neylon, C. (2018). *In a globalised and networked world, what is the unique value a university can bring?* Introducing Open Knowledge Institutions. Available at http://blogs.lse.ac.uk/impactofsocialsciences/2018/09/17/in-a-globalised-and-networked-world-what-is-the-unique-value-a-university-can-bring-introducing-open-knowledge-institutions/. Accessed 5 October 2018.

Morley, L., & Lugg, R. (2009). Mapping meritocracy: Intersecting gender, poverty and higher educational opportunity structures. *Higher Education Policy, 22*(1), 37–60.

Morrow, W. (2009). *Bounds of democracy: Epistemological access in higher education*. Pretoria: HSRC Press.

Motter, P., & Gandin, L. A. (2016). Higher education and new regionalism in Latin America: The UNILA project. In S. Robertson, K. Olds, R. Dale, & Q. A. Dang (Eds.), *Global regionalisms and higher education: Projects, processes, politics*. Cheltenham: Edward Elgar.

Mountford-Zimdars, A., & Sabbagh, D. (2013). Fair access to higher education: A comparative perspective. *Comparative Education Review, 57*(3), 359–368.

Mtawa, N., Fongwa, S., & Wangenge-Ouma, G. (2016). The scholarship of university-community engagement: Interrogating Boyer's model. *International Journal of Educational Development, 49*, 126–133.

Müller, T. R. (2004). "Now I am free"—Education and human resource development in Eritrea: Contradictions in the lives of Eritrean women in higher education. *Compare: A Journal of Comparative and International Education, 34*(2), 215–229.

Murove, M. F. (2014). Ubuntu. *Diogenes, 59*(3–4), 36–47.

Mwaipopo, R. N., Lihamba, A., & Njewele, D. C. (2011). Equity and equality in access to higher education: The experiences of students with disabilities in Tanzania. *Research in Comparative and International Education, 6*(4), 415–429.

Neubauer, C., & Calame, M. (2017). Global pressing problems and the Sustainable Development Goals. *Higher education in the world 6—Towards a socially responsible university: Balancing the global with the local*. Global University Network for Innovation.

Neves, C. E. B. (2009). Using social inclusion policies to enhance access and equity in Brazil's higher education. In J. Knight (Ed.), *Financing access and equity in higher education*. Rotterdam: Sense Publishers.

Newman, J. H. (1947 [1852]). *The idea of the university: Defined and illustrated*. London: Longmans, Green.

Newton, P. M. (2018). How common is commercial contract cheating in higher education and is it increasing? A systematic review. *Frontiers in Education, 3*, 67.

Nixon, J. (2004). Education for the good society: The integrity of academic practice. *London Review of Education, 2*(3), 245–252.

Nixon, J. (2011). *Higher education and the public good: Imagining the university*. New York and London: Continuum.

Norões, K., & Costa, B. (2012). Affirmative policies in Brazil: Black movements and public higher education. *Educational Thought, 9*(1), 24–31.

Norões, K., & McCowan, T. (2015). The challenge of widening participation to higher education in Brazil: Injustices, innovations and outcomes. In M. Shah, A. Bennett, & E. Southgate (Eds.), *Widening higher education participation: A Global perspective*. Amsterdam: Elsevier.

Novelli, M., & Lopez Cardozo, M. (2008). Conflict, education and the global south: New critical directions. *International Journal of Educational Development, 28*(4), 473–488.

Nussbaum, M. (2000). *Women and human development: The capabilities approach*. Cambridge, MA: Cambridge University Press.

Nybom, T. (2003). The humboldt legacy: Reflections on the past, present, and future of the European university. *Higher Education Policy, 16*, 141–159.

Nybom, T. (2007). A rule-governed community of scholars: The humboldt-vision in the history of the European university. In P. Maassen & J. P. Olsen (Eds.), *University dynamics and European integration* (pp. 55–79). Dordrecht: Spinger.

Oakeshott, M. (1989). The idea of a university. In T. Fuller (Ed.), *The voice of liberal learning: Michael Oakeshott on education* (pp. 95–104). New Haven and London: Yale University Press.

Oancea, A. (2013). Interpretations of research impact in seven disciplines. *European Educational Research Journal, 12*(2), 242–250.

Oanda, I. (2013). Implications of alternative higher education financing policies on equity and quality: The Kenyan experience. In D. Teferra (Ed.), *Funding higher education in Sub-Saharan Africa*. Basingstoke: Palgrave Macmillan.

Oanda, I. (2018). Admission policies and practices and the reshaping of access patterns to higher education in Africa. In M. E. Oliveri, C. Wendler, & R. Lawles (Eds.), *Higher education admissions and placement practices: An international perspective*. Cambridge: Cambridge University Press.

Oanda, I. O., Chege, F., & Wesonga, D. (2008). *Privatisation and private higher education in Kenya: Implications for access, equity and knowledge production*. Dakar: CODESRIA.

Oanda, I. O., & Jowi, J. (2012). University expansion and the challenges to social development in Kenya: Dilemmas and pitfalls. *Journal of Higher Education in Africa, 10*(1), 49–71.

Odhiambo, G. O. (2011). Higher education quality in Kenya: A critical reflection on key challenges. *Quality in Higher Education, 17*, 299–315.

Odhiambo, G. O. (2013). Academic brain drain: Impact and implications for public higher education quality in Kenya. *Research in Comparative and International Education, 8*, 510–523.

Odhiambo, G. O. (2014). Quality assurance for public higher education: Context, strategies and challenges in Kenya. *Higher Education Research & Development, 33*(5), 978–991.

OECD. (2008). *Tertiary education for the knowledge society*. Paris: OECD.

OECD. (2015). *Development aid at a glance. Statistics by region. 1. Developing countries*. 2015 ed. Available at http://www.oecd.org/dac/stats/documentupload/1%20World%20-%20Development%20Aid%20at%20a%20Glance%202015.pdf. Accessed 13 October 2015.

OECD. (2018). *Education at a glance 2018*. Paris: OECD.

Okari, D. (2015, February 1). How universities and colleges sell diplomas and clean up degrees. *Daily Nation*.

Oketch, M. O. (2016). Financing higher education in Sub-Saharan Africa: Some reflections and implications for sustainable development. *Higher Education, 72*(4), 525–539.

Oketch, M. O. (2003). Market model for financing higher education in Sub-Saharan Africa: Examples from Kenya. *Higher Education, 16*(3), 313–332.

Oketch, M. O., McCowan, T., & Schendel, R. (2014). *The impact of tertiary education on development: A rigorous literature review*. London: Department for International Development.

Olivera Rodríguez, I. (2017). Las potencialidades del proyecto educativo de la Universidad Veracruzana Intercultural: una crítica al desarrollo desde la noción del Buen vivir. *Revista de la Educación Superior, 46*(181), 19–35.

Opembe, N. (2018, January 28). State-sponsored students in the private universities got raw deal. *Daily Nation*.

OPNE. (2018). *12—Educação Superior*. Available at http://www.observatoriodopne.org.br/indicadores/metas/12-ensino-superior/indicadores. Accessed 1 August 2018.

Orr, D. (1992). *Ecological literacy: Education and the transition to a postmodern world*. Albany: State University of New York Press.

Orr, D. (1994). *Earth in mind*. Washington, DC: Island Press.

Otieno, W. (2010). Growth in Kenyan private higher education In K. Kinser, D. Levy, J. C. S. Casillas, A. Bernasconi, S. Slantcheva Durst, W. Otieno, et al. (Eds.), *The global growth of private higher education* (pp. 51–62). ASHE Higher Education Report Series. San Francisco: Wiley.

Owuor, N. A. (2012). Higher education in Kenya: The rising tension between quantity and quality in the post-massification period. *Higher Education Studies, 2*(4), 126–136.

Oyarzun, J. M., Perales Franco, C., & McCowan, T. (2017). Indigenous higher education in Mexico and Brazil: Between redistribution and recognition. *Compare, 47*(6), 852–871.

Parsons, S., & Bynner, J. (2002). *Basic skills and political and community participation: Findings from a study of adults born in 1958 and 1970*. London: Basic Skills Agency.

Paulson, K. (2002). Reconfiguring faculty roles for virtual settings. *Journal of Higher Education, 73*(1), 123–140.

Pedrosa, R., Simões, T., Carneiro, A., Andrade, C., Sampaio, H., & Knobel, M. (2014). Access to higher education in Brazil. *Widening Participation and Lifelong Learning, 16*(1), 5–33.

Penfield, T., Baker, M. J., Scoble, R., & Wykes, M. C. (2014). Assessment, evaluations, and definitions of research impact: A review. *Research Evaluation, 23*(1), 21–32.

Perkin, H. (2007). History of universities. In J. J. F. Forest & P. G. Altbach (Eds.), *International handbook of higher education* (pp. 159–206). Dordrecht: Springer.

Peters, R. S. (1966). *Ethics and education*. London: George Allen and Unwin.

Pherali, T., & Lewis, A. (2019). Developing global partnerships in higher education for peacebuilding: A strategy for pathways to impact. *Higher Education*. https://doi.org/10.1007/s10734-019-00367-7.

Pieterse, J. N. (2000). After post-development. *Third World Quarterly, 21*(2), 175–191.

Pitan, O. S., & Adedeji, S. O. (2012). Skills mismatch among university graduates in the Nigerian labour market. *Journal of US-China Education Review, 2*, 90–98.

Posholi, L. (2017, September 5). *Decolonising the curriculum in South African universities*. Presentation at the UKFIET conference, Oxford.

Prakash, M. S., & Esteva, G. (2008). *Escaping education: Living as learning in grassroots cultures* (2nd ed.). New York: Peter Lang.

Psacharopoulos, G. (1994). Returns to investment in education: A global update. *World Development, 22*(9), 1325–1343.

Psacharopoulos, G., Tan, J.-P., Jimenez, E., & World Bank Education and Training Department. (1986). *Financing education in developing countries: An exploration of policy options*. Washington, DC: World Bank.

Qualifications and Curriculum Authority (QCA). (1998). *Education for citizenship and the teaching of democracy in schools: Final report of the Advisory Group on Citizenship*. London: Qualifications and Curriculum Authority.

Raghbendra, J., & Dang, T. (2012). Education and the vulnerability to food inadequacy in Timor-Leste. *Oxford Development Studies, 40*(3), 341–357.

Rahnema, M., & Bawtree, V. (Eds.). (1997). *The post-development reader*. London: Zed.

Ransom, J. (2017). *Mutual influence? Universities, cities and the future of internationalisation*. British Council. https://www.britishcouncil.org/education/ihe/knowledge-centre/internationalisation/mutual-influence-universities-cities. Accessed 3 December 2017.

Rawls, J. (1971). *A theory of justice*. Cambridge: Harvard University Press.

Readings, B. (1996). *The university in ruins*. Cambridge, MA: Harvard University Press.

Reay, D., Ball, S. J., David, M., & Davies, J. (2001). Choices of degree or degrees of choice? Social class, race and the higher education choice process. *Sociology, 35*(4), 855–874.

REF. (2011, February). *Assessment framework and guidance on submissions*. Research Excellence Framework. Available at http://www.ref.ac.uk/media/ref/content/pub/assessmentframeworkandguidanceonsubmissions/GOS%20including%20addendum.pdf.

Republic of Kenya. (2007). *Kenya Vision 2030—A globally competitive and prosperous Kenya*. Nairobi: Office of the Prime Minister, Ministry of State for Planning, National Development and Vision 2030.

Republic of Kenya. (2013). *National manpower survey basic report*. Nairobi: Ministry of Labour.

Republic of Kenya. (2015). *Economic survey*. Nairobi: Kenya National Bureau of Statistics.

Republic of Kenya. (2017). *Economic survey*. Nairobi: Kenya National Bureau of Statistics.

Research Councils UK. (2017). *Excellence with impact*. Available at http://www.rcuk.ac.uk/innovation/impact/. Accessed 15 July 2017.

Rhoads, R. A., Saenz, V., & Carducci, R. (2005). Higher education reform as a social movement: The case of affirmative action. *The Review of Higher Education, 28*(2), 191–220.

Rist, G. (2002). *The history of development: From western origins to global faith*. London: Zed Books.

Robertson, S. L. (2016). Piketty, capital and education: A solution to, or problem in, rising social inequalities? *British Journal of Sociology of Education, 37*(6), 823–835.

Robertson, S. L., & Komljenovic, J. (2016a). Non-state actors, and the advance of frontier higher education markets in the global south. *Oxford Review of Education, 42*(5), 594–611.

Robertson, S. L., & Komljenovic, J. (2016b). Unbundling the university and making higher education markets. In A. Verger, C. Lubienski, & G. Steiner-Kamsi (Eds.), *World yearbook in education: The global education industry*. London: Routledge.

Rodríguez-Solera, C. R., & Silva-Laya, M. (2017). Higher education for sustainable development at EARTH University. *International Journal of Sustainability in Higher Education, 18*(3), 278–293.

Rolleston, C., & Oketch, M. (2008). Educational expansion in Ghana: Economic assumptions and expectations. *International Journal of Educational Development, 28*(3), 320–339.

Romer, P. M. (1986). Increasing returns and long-run growth. *The Journal of Political Economy, 94*(5), 1002–1037.

Rüeg, W. (Ed.). (1992). *A history of the university in Europe*. Cambridge: Cambridge University Press.

Ryle, G. (1949). *The concept of mind*. London: Penguin Books.

Sachs, J. D. (2008). *Common wealth: Economics*. New York: Penguin Press.

Sachs, J. D. (2012). From millennium development goals to Sustainable Development Goals. *Lancet, 379*, 2206–2211.

Sachs, W. (1992). *The development dictionary: A guide to knowledge as power*. London: Zed.

Sall, E., Lebeau, Y., & Kassimir, R. (2003). The public dimensions of the University in Africa. *Journal of Higher Education in Africa, 1*(1), 126–148.

Sampaio, Helena. (2011, Outubro). O setor privado de ensino superior no Brasil: continuidades e transformações. *Revista de Ensino Superior da UNICAMP* (Edição nº 4). https://www.revistaensinosuperior.gr.unicamp.br/edicoes/ed04_outubro2011/05_ARTIGO_PRINCIPAL.pdf.

Sankalia, H. (1934). *The University of Nalanda*. Madras: Paul.
Sansone, G. C., Raute, L. J., Fong, G. T., Pednekar, M. S., Quah, A. C. K., Bansal-Travers, M., et al. (2012). Knowledge of health effects and intentions to quit among smokers in India: Findings from the Tobacco Control Policy (TCP) India pilot survey. *International Journal of Environmental Research and Public Health, 9*(2), 564–578.
Santos, B. de S. (2004). *A universidade do século XXI: para uma reforma democratica e emancipatória da universidade*. São Paulo: Cortez.
Santos, B. de S. (Ed.). (2008). *Another knowledge is possible: Beyond northern epistemologies*. London: Verso.
Santos, B. de S. (2014). *Epistemologies of the South: justice against epistemicide*. New York: Routledge.
Santos, B. de S. (2015). *Epistemologies of the south: Justice against epistemicide*. New York: Routledge.
Santos, B. de S., & Almeida Filho, N. (2008). *A universidade no século XXI: Para uma universidade nova*. Coimbra: Almedina.
Sauvé, L. (1996). Environmental education and sustainable development: A further appraisal. *Canadian Journal of Environmental Education, 1*, 7–33.
Sawyerr, A. (2004). Challenges facing African universities: Selected issues. *African Studies Review, 47*(1), 1–59.
Schady, N. R. (2003). Convexity and sheepskin effects in the human capital earnings function: Recent evidence for Filipino men. *Oxford Bulletin of Economics and Statistics, 65*(2), 171–196.
Schendel, R. (2016). Constructing departmental culture to support student development: Evidence from a case study in Rwanda. *Higher Education, 72*(4), 487–504.
Schmelkes, S. (2008). Creación y desarrollo inicial de las universidades interculturales en México: problemas, oportunidades, retos. In *Diversidad Cultural e Interculturalidad En Educación Superior: Experiencias En América Latina*. Bogotá: Organización de las Naciones Unidas para la Educación, la Ciencia y la Cultura, Instituto Internacional de la UNESCO para la Educación Superior en América Latina y el Caribe.
Schmelkes, S. (2009). Intercultural universities in Mexico: Progress and difficulties. *Intercultural Education, 20*, 5–17.
Schön, D. (1983). *The reflective practitioner: How professionals think in action*. London: Temple Smith.
Schultz, T. W. (1961). Investment in human capital. *American Economic Review, 51*, 1–17.
Schweisfurth, M. (2013). *Learner-centred education in international perspective: Whose pedagogy for whose development?* Oxford: Routledge.

Sehoole, C., & Knight, J. (2013). *Internationalisation of African higher education: Towards achieving the MDGs*. Rotterdam: Sense Publishers.

Selingo, J. J. (2013). *College unbound: The future of higher education and what it means for students*. Boston: New Harvest.

Selingo, J. J. (2017). *The networked university: Building alliances for innovation in higher education*. London: Pearson.

Sen, A. (1992). *Inequality re-examined*. Oxford: Clarendon Press.

Sen, A. (1999a). *Development as freedom*. New York: Oxford University Press.

Sen, A. (1999b). Democracy as a universal value. *Journal of Democracy, 10*(3), 3–17.

Sen, A. (2009). *The idea of justice*. London: Allen Lane Penguin.

Shafiq, M. N. (2010). Do education and income affect support for democracy in Muslim countries? Evidence from the "Pew Global Attitudes Project". *Economics of Education Review, 29*(3), 461–469.

Shattock, M. (2009). *Entrepreneurialism in universities and the knowledge economy: Diversification and organisational change in European higher education*. Bletchley, UK: Open University Press.

Shields, R. (2019). The sustainability of international higher education: Student mobility and global climate change. *Journal of Cleaner Production, 217*, 594–602.

Shields, R., & Watermeyer, R. (2018). Competing institutional logics in universities in the United Kingdom: Schism in the church of reason. *Studies in Higher Education*. https://doi.org/10.1080/03075079.2018.1504910.

Shiva, V. (1993). *Monocultures of the mind*. London: Zed Books.

Shore, C. (2010). Beyond the multiversity: Neoliberalism and the rise of the schizophrenic university. *Social Anthropology/Anthropologie Sociale, 18*(1), 15–29.

Siegfried, J., Sanderson, A., & McHenry, P. (2007). The economic impact of colleges and universities. *Economics of Education Review, 26*, 546–558.

Sifuna, D. N. (1998). The governance of Kenyan public universities. *Research in Post-Compulsory Education, 3*(2), 175–212.

Sifuna, D. N. (2010). Some reflections on the expansion and quality of higher education in public universities in Kenya. *Research in Post-Compulsory Education, 15*(4), 415–425.

Singh, M. (2012). Re-inserting the 'public good' into higher education transformation. In B. Leibowitz (Ed.), *Higher education for the public good—Views from the south* (pp. 1–16). Stoke on Trent, UK: Trentham Books and Stellenbosch: Sun Media.

Singh, R., Thind, S. K., & Jaswal, S. (2006). Assessment of marital adjustment among couples with respect to women's educational level and employment status. *Anthropologist, 8*(4), 259–266.

Skinner, A., Baillie Smith, M., Brown, E. J., & Troll, T. (Eds.). (2016). *Education, learning and the transformation of development*. Oxford: Routledge.

Slaughter, S., & Leslie, L. L. (1997). *Academic capitalism: Politics, policies, and the entrepreneurial university*. Baltimore, MD: Johns Hopkins Press.

Smith, A., & Vaux, T. (2003). *Education, conflict and international development*. London: DFID.

Smith, A., & Webster, F. (Eds.). (1997). *The postmodern university? Contested visions of higher education in society*. Buckingham, UK: Open University Press.

Smith, S., Ward, V., & House, A. (2011). 'Impact' in the proposals for the UK's Research Excellence Framework: Shifting the boundaries of academic autonomy. *Research Policy, 40*(10), 1369–1379 (11).

Stephens, D. (Ed.). (2009). *Higher education and international capacity building: 25 years of the higher education links programme*. Oxford: Symposium.

Stewart, F. (1985). *Planning to meet basic needs*. London: Macmillan.

Stiglitz, J. E. (1999). Knowledge as a global public good. *Global Public Goods, 1*(9), 308–326.

Stiglitz, J. E. (2007). *Making globalization work*. London: Allen Lane.

Stirling, S. (1996). Education in change. In J. Huckle & S. Sterling (Eds.), *Education for sustainability*. London: Earthscan.

Streeten, P. (1977). The basic features of a basic needs approach to development. *International Development Review, 3,* 8–16.

Streitwieser, B., Brueck, L., Moody, R., & Taylor, M. (2017). The potential and reality of new refugees entering German higher education: The case of Berlin institutions. *European Education, 49*(4), 231–252.

Stromquist, N. P., & da Costa, R. B. (2017). Popular universities: An alternative vision for lifelong learning in Europe. *International Review of Education, 63,* 725–744.

Stevenson, J., Burke, P.-J., & Whelan, P. (2014). *Pedagogic stratification and the shifting landscape of higher education*. York: HEA.

Stevenson, J., & Willott, J. (2007). The aspiration and access to higher education of teenage refugees in the UK. *Compare, 37*(5), 671–687.

Tabulawa, R. T. (2013). *Teaching and learning in context: Why pedagogical reforms fail in Sub-Saharan Africa*. Dakar, Senegal: Council for the Development of Social Science Research in Africa.

Tabulawa, R., Polelo, M., & Silas, O. (2013). The state, markets and higher education reform in Botswana. *Globalisation, Societies and Education, 11*(1), 108–135.

Takayama, K., Sriprakash, A., & Connell, R. (2015). Rethinking Knowledge production and circulation in comparative and international education: Southern theory, postcolonial perspectives, and alternative epistemologies. *Comparative Education Review, 59*(1), v–viii.

Tam, M. (2001). Measuring quality and performance in higher education. *Quality in Higher Education, 7*(1), 47–54.

Task Force on Higher Education and Society, World Bank and UNESCO. (2000). *Higher education in developing countries: Peril and promise.* Washington, DC: World Bank.

Tavares, M., & Romão, T. (2015). Emerging counterhegemonic models in higher education: The Federal University of Southern Bahia (UFSB) and its contribution to a renewed geopolitics of knowledge (interview with Naomar de Almeida Filho). *Encounters in Theory and History of Education, 16,* 101–110.

Taylor, C. (1994). *Multiculturalism: Examining the politics of recognition.* Princeton, NJ: Princeton University Press.

Teamey, K., & Mandel, U. (2014, October 24). *Challenging the modern university, perspectives and practices from indigenous communities, social and ecological movements.* Paper presented at the Forum on Higher Education and International Development, London.

Teichler, U. (2008). Diversification? Trends and explanations of the shape and size of higher education. *Higher Education, 56*(3), 349–379.

Tian, L., & Liu, N. C. (2018a). Rethinking higher education in China as a common good. *Higher Education.* https://doi.org/10.1007/s10734-018-0295-5.

Tian, L., & Liu, N. C. (2018b). *Local and global public good contributions of higher education in China* (Working Paper 37). Centre for Global Higher Education. Available at https://www.researchcghe.org/perch/resources/publications/wp37.pdf. Accessed 1 December 2018.

Tilak, J. B. G. (2003). Higher education and development in Asia. *Journal of Educational Planning and Administration, 17*(2), 151–173.

Tilak, J. B. G. (2008). Higher education: A public good or a commodity for trade? Commitment to higher education or commitment of higher education to trade. *Prospects, 38,* 449–466.

Tilak, J. B. G. (2010). Higher education, poverty and development. *Higher Education Review, 42*(2), 23–45.

Tjeldvoll, A. (1998). The idea of the service university. *International Higher Education, 13*(Fall), 9–10.

Tomaševski, K. (2001). *Human rights obligations: Making education available, accessible, acceptable and adaptable.* Right to Education Primers No. 3. Gothenburg: Novum Grafiska.

Tomaševski, K. (2006). *Human rights obligations in education: The 4-A scheme.* Nijmegen: Wolf Legal Publishers.

Trindade, H. H. C. (2009). UNILA: Universidade para a integração Latino-Americana. *Educación Superior y Sociedad, 14*(1), 147–153.

Trow, M. (1974). Problems in the transition from elite to mass higher education. In OECD (Ed.), *Policies for higher education* (pp. 51–101). Paris: OECD.

Truex, R. (2011). Corruption, attitudes, and education: Survey evidence from Nepal. *World Development, 39*(7), 1133–1142.

Turner Johnson, A., & Hirt, J. (2014). Universities, dependency and the market: Innovative lessons from Kenya. *Compare, 44*(2), 230–251.

UNESCO (United Nations Educational, Scientific and Cultural Organization). (1998, October). *World declaration on higher education for the twenty-first century: Vision and Action.* Adopted at the World Conference on Higher Education, Paris.

UNESCO. (2004). *Education for all: The quality imperative* (EFA Global Monitoring Report 2005). Paris: UNESCO.

UNESCO. (2015). *UNESCO science report—Towards 2030.* Paris: UNESCO.

UNESCO. (2016). *Education for people and planet: Creating sustainable futures for all* (Global Education Monitoring Report). Paris: UNESCO.

UNESCO. (2017). *Education for Sustainable Development Goals: Learning objectives.* Paris: UNESCO.

UNESCO Institute for Statistics (UIS). (2018). *Education: Enrolment by level of education.* Available at http://data.uis.unesco.org/. Accessed 1 September 2018.

UNESCO Institute for Statistics (UIS). (2019). *Initial government funding per student, US$.* Available at http://data.uis.unesco.org/. Accessed 9 January 19.

UNESCO/IIEP. (2017). *Six ways to ensure higher education leaves no one behind* (Policy Paper 30). Paris: UNESCO.

UNICEF. (2000). *Defining quality in education.* New York: UNICEF. Available at http://www.unicef.org/education/files/QualityEducation.PDF. Accessed 25 May 2016.

United Nations (UN). (2015a, August 2). *Transforming our world: The 2030 agenda for sustainable development.* New York: United Nations.

United Nations. (2015b). *Transforming our world: The 2030 agenda for sustainable development.* Available at https://sustainabledevelopment.un.org/post2015/transformingourworld. Accessed 26 May 2016.

United Nations High-Level Panel of Eminent Persons on the Post-2015 Development Agenda. (2013). *A new global partnership: Eradicate poverty and transform economies through sustainable development.* New York: United Nations.

Universities UK. (2013). *Patterns and trends in UK higher education 2013: Section B—Patterns of institutional diversity.* London: Universities UK.

UniversityNow. (2017). *Why we're different: Making higher education affordable.* Available at http://unow.com/making-education-affordable/. Accessed 9 February 2017.

Unterhalter, E. (2003). The capabilities approach and gendered education: An examination of South African complexities. *Theory and Research in Education, 1*(1), 7–22.

Unterhalter, E., Allais, S., Howell, C., McCowan, T., Morley, L., Oanda, I., & Oketch, M. (2017). *Higher education and the public good: Concepts, challenges and complexities in Africa.* Working paper for the research project, Higher education and the public good in four African countries.

Unterhalter, E., & Brighouse, H. (2007). Distribution of what for social justice in education? The case of education for all by 2015. In M. Walker & E. Unterhalter (Eds.), *Amartya Sen's capability approach and social justice in education.* New York: Palgrave Macmillan.

Unterhalter, E., Vaughan, R., & Smail, A. (2013). *Secondary, post secondary and higher education in the Post-2015 discussions.* London: British Council.

Upton, S., Vallance, P., & Goddard, J. (2014). From outcome to process, evidence for a new approach to research impact assessment. *Research Evaluation, 23*(4), 352–365.

USAID. (2015). *Education.* Available at https://www.usaid.gov/education. Accessed 13 October 2015.

Välimaa, J. (2018). The Nordic idea of university. In R. Barnett & M. Peters (Eds.), *The idea of the university: Contemporary perspectives.* New York: Peter Lang.

Vanhulst, J., & Beling, A. E. (2014). Buen vivir: Emergent discourse within or beyond sustainable development? *Ecological Economics, 101,* 54–63.

Vare, P., & Scott, W. (2007). Learning for a change: Exploring the relationship between education and sustainable development. *Journal of Education for Sustainable Development, 1*(2), 191–198.

Vasagar, J. (2011, October 11). No frills university college offers half price degrees. *The Guardian*. Available at https://www.theguardian.com/education/2011/oct/17/coventry-university-college-half-price-degree. Accessed 9 February 2017.

Villalba, U. (2013). Buen vivir vs development: A paradigm shift in the Andes? *Third World Quarterly, 34*(8), 1427–1442.

Waas, T., Verbruggen, A., & Wright, T. (2010). University research for sustainable development: Definition and characteristics explored. *Journal of Cleaner Production, 18*(7), 629–636.

Walker, M. (2018). Dimensions of higher education and the public good in South Africa. *Higher Education, 76*(3), 555–569.

Walker, M., & Fongwa, S. (2017). *Universities, employability and human development*. New York: Springer.

Walker, M., & McLean, M. (2013). *Professional education, capabilities and the public good: The role of universities in promoting human development*. London: Routledge.

Walker, M., McLean, M., Dison, A., & Peppin-Vaughan, R. (2009). South African universities and human development: Towards a theorisation and operationalisation of professional capabilities for poverty reduction. *International Journal of Educational Development, 29*(6), 565–572.

Walter, I., Nutley, S. M., & Davies, H. T. O. (2003). *Models of research impact: A cross-sector review*. Available from Research Unit for Research Utilisation, University of St Andrews. Available at www.st-and.ac.uk/~ruru/publications.htm. Accessed 11 February 2003.

Wangenge-Ouma, G. (2007). Higher education marketisation and its discontents: The case of quality in Kenya. *Higher Education, 56*(4), 457–471.

Wanzala, O. (2015, October 3). Suspension of courses puts varsity regulator on the spot. *Daily Nation*.

Watermeyer, R. (2016). Impact in the REF: Issues and obstacles. *Studies in Higher Education, 41*(2), 199–214.

Watters, A. (2013, April). MOOC Mania: Debunking the Hype around Massive Open Online Courses. *School Library Journal*. Available at http://www.thedigitalshift.com/2013/04/featured/got-mooc-massive-open-online-courses-are-poised-to-change-the-face-of-education/. Accessed 12 September 2018.

Weiss, C. (1979). The many meanings of research utilization. *Public Administration Review, 39*, 426–431.

Wheelahan, L. (2007). How competency-based training locks the working class out of powerful knowledge: A modified Bernsteinian analysis. *British Journal of Sociology of Education, 28*(5), 637–651.

Wildavsky, B. (2014, May/June). Evolving toward significance or MOOC ado about nothing. *International Educator,* 74–79.
Williamson, B. (2018). The hidden architecture of higher education: Building a big data infrastructure for the 'smarter university'. *International Journal of Educational Technology in Higher Education, 15*(1), 1–26.
Willis, P. (1978). *Learning to Labour: How working class kids get working class jobs*. Aldershot Gower: Saxon House/Teakfield.
Winch, C. (2006). Graduate attributes and changing conceptions of learning. In P. Hager & S. Holland (Eds.), *Graduate attributes, learning and employability* (pp. 67–89). Dordrecht: Springer.
Wissema, J. G. (2009). *Towards the third generation university: Managing the university in transition*. Cheltenham: Edward Elgar.
Wolff, J., & de-Shalit, A. (2013). On fertile functionings: A response to Martha Nussbaum. *Journal of Human Development and Capabilities, 14*(1), 161–165.
World Bank. (1999). *Knowledge for development*. World Development Report. New York: Oxford University Press.
World Bank. (2002). *Constructing knowledge societies: New challenges for tertiary education*. Washington, DC: World Bank.
World Bank. (2010). *Financing higher education in Africa*. Washington, DC: World Bank.
World Bank. (2018). *Data. Unemployment with advanced education (% of total labor force with advanced education)*. Available at https://data.worldbank.org/indicator/SL.UEM.ADVN.ZS. Accessed 5 November 2019.
Wright, L-A., & Plasterer, R. (2010). Beyond basic education: Exploring opportunities for higher learning in Kenyan refugee camps. *Refuge: Canada's Periodical on Refugees, 27*(2), 42–56.
Yang, L. (2017). *The public role of higher learning in Imperial China* (Working Paper No. 28). Centre for Global Higher Education. Available at https://www.researchcghe.org/perch/resources/publications/wp28.pdf. Accessed 1 December 2018.
Yesufu, T. M., & Association of African Universities. (1973). *Creating the African university: Emerging issues in the 1970's*. Ibadan, Nigeria: Oxford University Press for the Association of African Universities.
Young, M. F. D. (2008). *Bringing knowledge back in: From social constructivism to social realism in the sociology of education*. London: Routledge.
Young, T. (2018, August 19). It's no wonder degrees are going out of fashion when universities have become the Madrassas of the Left. *Mail on Sunday*.

Zgaga, P. (2009). Higher education and citizenship: 'The full range of purposes'. *European Educational Research Journal, 8*(2), 175–188.

Žižek, S. (2018). *Like a thief in broad daylight: Power in the era of post-humanity.* London: Penguin.

Index

A

Academic journals 19, 76, 121
Access 5, 6, 10, 11, 13, 14, 16, 20, 21, 35, 52, 71, 79, 92, 94, 95, 100, 104, 105, 111, 127, 130, 132, 134, 135, 137, 139–142, 149–163, 165–169, 188, 195, 201, 211, 212, 214–216, 225, 229, 240, 241, 256, 279, 281, 300, 307–309, 314, 316–319
Affirmative action 107, 133, 139, 140, 152–154, 158, 163, 165, 168, 318
Aid 9, 17, 62, 98, 141, 308
Alternative universities 278
Applied knowledge 101

B

Basic needs 32, 35, 49

Brazil 14, 19, 20, 30, 45, 74, 93, 95, 102, 104–107, 109, 110, 122, 124, 137, 152, 157, 159, 161, 163–165, 168, 204, 205, 223, 229, 232, 296

C

Capabilities 18, 32, 39, 40, 42, 48, 69, 205, 234, 235, 316
Capitalism 43, 65, 116, 140, 251, 278, 281, 284, 287, 288, 290, 301, 310, 316
Certification 30, 290, 300, 314
Citizenship 11, 35, 36, 49, 50, 75, 219, 223, 226, 230, 235, 287
Climate change 216, 217, 222, 305
Commercialisation 21, 45, 80, 81, 108, 111, 123, 189, 229, 240, 241, 269, 308, 316, 318

Commodification 18, 69, 116, 117, 123, 125, 135–137, 139, 142, 316
Community engagement 7, 21, 45, 49, 70, 74–76, 95–98, 105–107, 111, 119, 121–123, 135, 137, 140, 142, 149, 178, 180, 203, 212, 219, 229, 239, 240, 294, 308, 318
Conflict 4, 22, 43, 48, 62, 92, 110, 254, 258, 306, 310, 311
Conscientization 18, 35
Consumerism 306
Curriculum 31, 34, 44, 48, 49, 93, 94, 105, 109, 120, 129, 130, 134, 141, 154, 158, 169, 193–195, 212, 221, 225, 281, 286, 289, 290, 292, 294, 295, 299, 309

Democracy 8, 33, 36, 41, 47, 50, 52, 83, 288
Department for International Development (DFID) 8, 195, 232, 309
Dependency theory 18, 280
Developmental university 19, 64, 80, 84, 92, 93, 96–103, 106, 108, 176, 180, 219, 251, 253, 254, 265, 269, 278, 279, 281, 282, 287, 288, 295, 307, 309, 311
Disciplines 64, 154, 221, 281, 293
Diversity 11, 19, 28, 40, 62, 94, 105, 126, 127, 154, 157, 158, 166, 180, 216, 218, 224, 225, 258, 287, 292, 293, 315

Economic growth 12, 32–34, 40, 47, 50, 52, 80, 121, 136, 215, 233, 234, 236, 263, 283
Employability 118, 132, 133, 194, 195, 204, 226, 309, 310, 316
Enquiry 54, 63, 64, 74, 82, 84, 99, 203, 228, 240, 263–265, 268–271
Enrolment ratios 7, 159
Entrepreneurial university 61, 65, 67, 80, 98, 99, 116, 240, 279
Environmental education 219, 224
Equality 9–11, 35, 71, 72, 139, 140, 152, 155, 158, 179, 212, 215–217, 220, 227, 230, 233, 235, 236, 287, 307, 312
Equity 5, 13, 20, 140, 151, 152, 158, 164, 167, 169, 182, 200, 201, 224

For-profit higher education 124
Freire, Paulo 17, 22, 36, 115, 223, 289
Frugality 310, 319
Funding 4, 5, 40, 42, 49, 50, 52, 53, 64, 65, 71, 79, 92, 102, 108–111, 123, 135, 137, 141, 159, 161, 167, 181, 182, 192, 199, 202, 228, 232, 238–240,

Index 357

252, 254, 267, 269, 296, 299, 300, 308, 312, 315, 316

G

Gender 10, 11, 14, 35, 38, 47, 152, 153, 158, 160, 179, 212, 215, 217, 218, 220, 230, 233, 235, 236
Ghana 20, 47, 93, 100, 103, 104, 109, 179, 221, 225, 241
Globalisation 22, 43, 237
Governance 18, 32, 94, 95, 107, 130, 177, 189, 196, 198–200, 219, 233, 236, 254, 290, 308
Graduate destinations 20

H

Health 6–8, 32, 35, 40, 49, 98, 103, 106, 109, 117, 121, 135, 180, 212, 219, 227, 229, 233, 235, 236, 241, 255, 280, 286, 299, 312
Horizontality 152, 155, 157, 165–169, 316
Human capital theory 7, 18, 28, 33–35, 51, 69, 205, 233
Human development 28, 31, 38–40, 48, 228, 309, 316
Human rights 8, 11, 39, 40, 226, 230, 310
Humboldtian university 61, 64, 80, 99

I

Illich, Ivan 134, 279, 281, 285–287, 289–291, 296, 299

Impact 5, 7, 16–18, 21, 35, 38, 49–52, 62, 70, 72, 73, 80, 84, 93, 94, 99, 100, 102, 106, 111, 115, 119, 120, 122, 125, 134, 137, 142, 150, 159, 160, 163, 177, 178, 180, 182, 183, 187, 193, 200, 205, 206, 214–216, 218–220, 227, 230–239, 241, 251–268, 270–272, 278, 287, 305, 307–310, 312, 315
Indigenous peoples 11, 158, 212, 284, 286, 294, 296, 297
Information and communications technology (ICT) 128, 129, 178, 188
Innovation 4, 7, 8, 34, 47, 49, 53, 82, 92–94, 101, 107, 131, 183, 197, 201, 215, 220, 234, 252–255, 262, 287, 301, 311
Instrumental value 40, 69, 72, 140, 215, 264, 310
Internationalisation 18, 79, 105, 121, 309
Intrinsic value 38, 68, 73, 80, 81, 84, 117, 150, 155, 180, 315

K

Kenya 20, 42, 137, 152, 159, 163, 164, 177, 181–184, 186, 190–192, 203, 235

L

Labour market 30, 34, 43, 73, 124, 132
Land grant university 94, 253
Language 14, 15, 31, 34, 43, 69, 81, 104, 127, 158, 166, 211, 212,

232, 237, 278, 293, 294, 298, 307, 314
Learning outcomes 14, 42, 43, 51, 205

M
Marketisation 126, 137, 140, 169, 189, 200, 317
Massification 4, 109, 152
Massive open online courses (MOOCs) 129, 131, 132, 139, 141, 287, 290
Medieval university 63, 215
Mexico 20, 47, 118, 202, 211, 240, 286, 295, 296
Millennium Development Goals (MDGs) 9, 10, 16, 35, 312
Multiversity 7, 60, 66, 76, 94, 126, 133

N
Non-formal education 10, 29, 221
Non-Governmental Organisations (NGOs) 51, 307

O
Organisation of Economic Cooperation and Development (OECD) 7, 9, 51, 141, 202, 205, 221

P
Pedagogy 47, 124, 134, 168, 191, 195–199, 201, 223, 224

Political participation 8, 35, 41, 235
Post-development 180, 279–285, 287–289, 291–293, 295, 301, 313
Post-modernism 5
Poverty 5, 12, 35, 53, 92, 96, 104, 110, 136, 180, 206, 211, 215, 216, 218, 220, 233, 238, 260, 271, 287, 311, 320
Primary education 5, 7, 8, 10, 16, 18, 35, 38
Professional development 151, 176, 191, 193, 199, 225, 235, 241
Programme for International Student Assessment (PISA) 14, 38, 51, 205
Public debate 51, 219, 220, 228, 234, 240, 241, 260, 270
Public good 6, 18–20, 69–71, 93, 100, 102, 110, 111, 116, 117, 133, 139, 228, 234, 240, 241, 261, 308, 311, 317
Publishing 19, 43, 79, 141, 215, 228, 239, 255, 256

Q
Quality assurance 30, 179, 184, 190, 200, 201
Quality of higher education 176, 181, 183, 184, 188, 191

R
Race/ethnicity 160
Rankings 4, 15, 38, 47, 111, 116–122, 125, 141, 175, 205, 226, 314, 318

Regulation 137, 184, 200, 218, 251, 278, 299, 309
Religion 14, 116, 152, 158
Research 4, 6, 7, 11, 12, 15, 17–21, 31, 36, 44, 45, 48, 49, 60, 63–67, 69–72, 74–76, 78–82, 93–95, 97–101, 103, 104, 106–108, 111, 116, 117, 119, 121–123, 127–129, 133–135, 137, 138, 140–142, 149, 153, 166, 176–180, 183, 184, 189, 192, 193, 195, 203–205, 212, 214, 215, 218, 219, 224, 226–228, 231–241, 252, 254–260, 262, 264–272, 294, 296, 297, 308, 309, 311, 312, 314, 315, 317, 318
Research Excellence Framework (REF) 252, 258, 262, 270
Returns to education 6, 7

Scholarships 9, 11, 107, 153, 162, 165, 182, 308
Science, Technology, Engineering and Mathematics (STEM) 221, 227
Secondary education 44, 49, 51, 160, 182, 199, 232, 277
Sen, Amartya 39, 205
Social class 43, 160, 179
Social media 47
Social reproduction 42, 48, 291
Status competition 21, 38, 116, 117, 121, 135, 142, 240, 241, 308
Student mobility 309

Sustainable development 10–12, 17, 19, 32, 49, 50, 136, 216–219, 221–224, 226, 231, 232, 235, 241, 302, 309, 319

Teaching and learning 44, 45, 69, 131, 134, 177, 184, 185, 190–192, 194, 196–202, 223, 227, 265, 267, 316
Technical and vocational education (TVET) 20
Technology 34, 49, 53, 65, 67, 94, 127, 128, 139, 140, 202, 220, 221, 234, 251, 253, 286, 287, 290, 306, 315, 316

Unbundling 18, 21, 76, 111, 116, 117, 127–136, 138–142, 240, 269, 287, 291, 310
United Nations Educational, Scientific and Cultural Organisation (UNESCO) 6, 9, 12, 14, 15, 19, 75, 150, 158, 178, 221, 232, 238
University autonomy 269

World Bank 5–7, 9, 34, 49, 141, 158, 159, 202, 204, 232, 239

Printed in the United States
By Bookmasters